五菱之光
一部造车史

Wuling

A Trailblazer in
the Automobile Manufacturing

Lin Xueping（林雪萍） 著

电子工业出版社
Publishing House of Electronics Industry
北京·BEIJING

Introduction

This compelling book explores the rise of China's manufacturing prowess, providing a captivating narrative of a regional automotive enterprise's remarkable journey. From its humble beginnings, the enterprise confronts harrowing challenges, ultimately establishing itself as a global powerhouse. This story is set against the glorious backdrop of China's industrial evolution spanning over six decades, offering a window into the thrilling saga of the country's automotive sector.

It is a tale of resilience and growth, illustrating the intricate interplay between local and international dynamics. Woven seamlessly into the narrative are three compelling strands: the unwavering determination of entrepreneurs, the transformative journey of the manufacturing system, and the dynamic trends defining the age of Chinese manufacturing. Together, these elements create a majestic and dynamic portrait of industry.

图书在版编目（CIP）数据

五菱之光 ： 一部造车史 = Wuling: A Trailblazer
in the Automobile Manufacturing ： 英文 / 林雪萍著.
北京 ： 电子工业出版社, 2025. 4. -- ISBN 978-7-121
-50001-5

Ⅰ. F426.471

中国国家版本馆 CIP 数据核字第 2025VH7033 号

责任编辑：马文哲
印　　刷：北京捷迅佳彩印刷有限公司
装　　订：北京捷迅佳彩印刷有限公司
出版发行：电子工业出版社
　　　　　北京市海淀区万寿路 173 信箱　邮编：100036
开　　本：720×1000　1/16　印张：18.75　字数：492 千字
版　　次：2025 年 4 月第 1 版
印　　次：2025 年 4 月第 1 次印刷
定　　价：168.00 元

凡所购买电子工业出版社图书有缺损问题，请向购买书店调换。若书店售缺，请与本社发行部联系，联系及邮购电话：（010）88254888，88258888。

质量投诉请发邮件至 zlts@phei.com.cn，盗版侵权举报请发邮件至 dbqq@phei.com.cn。

本书咨询联系方式：qincong@phei.com.cn。

Preface

The automotive industry stands out as the most enchanting sector of the manufacturing industry. Beyond its immense social value, significant workforce contribution, and embodiment of diverse innovative technologies, it is the cultural influence it exerts, that elevates it beyond the status of a mere industry. An example of this cultural influence can be observed in Ford Motor Company's establishment of mass production methods, with the assembly line becoming a cultural export promoted by the U.S. government during World War II. Another, more widely recognized, manifestation is found in classic Hollywood movies. Japan's industrial accomplishments and essence seem intricately tied to the automotive realm, specifically to Toyota. Toyota's lean production has elevated its manufacturing paradigm to a radiant "beacon" with a global impact, and every Japanese manufacturer contributes to this gentle radiance. In Germany, where the automotive industry accounts for 5% of the national GDP and employs 4% of the workforce, the sheer quality of German-made cars speaks volumes about German manufacturing as a whole.

Cars wield a potent public wealth effect, intricately connecting individual wealth, collective prosperity, and societal welfare. They decisively shape the fate of industries in a country or region, warranting all the praise one can offer for such an influential sector.

Without the automotive culture, the epic of industrial culture would be so impoverished, much like recounting ancient Chinese culture without including Tang poetry. No industry can, like the automotive sector, consistently spark captivating cultural trends that transcend eras. The well-known auto magnates, humming melodic tunes, stroll past rows of cars, leaving in their wake a succession of gleaming car Logos. This spectacle elicits excitement and cheers from onlookers, intertwined with inevitable sentiments of both regret and disdain.

These dynamic individuals and their cars arouse our anticipation for more stories, each narrative crafted to elicit emotional responses that resonate with the sentiments within our hearts.

The Chinese automotive industry is still in its infancy. During the two decades leading up to the turn of the century, its position resembled a tug-of-war, marked by constant debates accompanying with every advance and retreat. In its earlier stages, tractors played the leading role, and it was only at the start of the 21st century that

China truly joined the race and engaged the accelerator. Once the entrepreneurs took their positions, they burst forth like racers, unleashing immense speed and passion. The most thrilling stories in the global automotive industry are unfolding right here, on China's fervent land.

This book endeavors to reconstruct a tumultuous history through the developmental journey of an automobile manufacturing enterprise. Undoubtedly, entrepreneurs take center stage in this narrative, and the era itself emerges as an undeniable force. The times present a formidable reality, offering entrepreneurs a taste that is half bitter, half sweet, with intertwined flavors of hardship and success. For those enterprises that decline, all that remains in the end is bitterness. However, for those that endure, the taste of success sweetens the experience.

The question arises: How should the developmental history of an enterprise be documented? Chronicling history should avoid the pitfalls of hindsight bias. Lessons learned from success or the insights gained from failure often resemble a rearview mirror—adept at reflecting the past, yet incapable of guiding us toward the future.

Living in the present confines us to one side of time's ever-shifting wall. When we look back, the past is clear, but as we peer forward, the wall obstructs our view, shrouding the future in mystery. Decision-makers always find themselves bound to this side of time's barrier. This limitation presents the most significant challenge in chronicling the developmental history of an enterprise.

The most organic method for recounting the developmental history of an enterprise is to follow the timeline, much like rowing a boat downstream with the current—a continuous forward progression, never backward. However, if we simply unfurl the scroll of history along this linear path, it becomes challenging to clearly explain the causes and effects of significant events. Embracing Ray Huang's macro-history perspective, a revolutionary historical event is not that important. Rather, it is the culmination of 50 or even 100 years of historical buildup. In other words, if an event is not triggered one way, it is likely to be triggered in another. Yet, these seemingly inconsequential fragments of everyday life, often dismissed as trivial and worthless, in fact, offer the most meticulous and orderly reflection of the universe's order. An exemplar of this is found in the book *1587, A Year of No Significance: The Ming Dynasty in Decline*, which begins with a farce resulting from a mistakenly summoned court meeting in the year 1587. A seemingly insignificant interaction between the emperor and officials during an inconspicuous year conceals the code for the rise and fall of the Ming Dynasty. To understand the profound significance of each event, one must look far back into the past.

Therefore, an alternate narrative approach for the developmental history of an enterprise is to organize the content into thematic sections. Throughout a business's lifespan, certain landmark events always stand out, and can be comprehensively explored from its inception to its conclusion. This thematic approach offers the flexibility to freely traverse within the realm of time, clearly delineating the causality of each event. However, this narrative style does compromise the authority of time. If time were an invisible wall that can be freely traversable, the inherent tragic nature of life's hardships would be greatly discounted, rendering each entrepreneur an all-knowing superhuman navigating through history repeatedly. Unfortunately, such an approach risks diminishing the reader's curiosity and engagement.

Fortunately, this book has found an approach that called the "time slider". Much like watching a video on a smartphone, readers can slide their fingers along the timeline, moving backward and forward. If the clarity is lacking, one can rewind to an earlier point for a better understanding before progressing forward. In certain instances, it is also possible to scroll ahead to gain insights into future developments. Nevertheless, the overarching chronological order of time is generally maintained.

This narrative technique is artfully exemplified in George Packer's work, *The Unwinding: An Inner History of the New America*, which describes the gradual disintegration of the American manufacturing industry and how it eroded the lives of the lower class. Examining the table of contents reveals in that book, strictly organized as a period history, dissects the years from 1978 to 2012 into more than a dozen distinct time segments. Across these sections, a diverse cast of characters, both minor and major, takes turns to appear, with some recurring throughout the narrative. Packer integrates two grand historical themes, that is, the disintegration of American manufacturing and the innovative resurgence led by information technology, into the fabric of everyday life—a water bill, a Pontiac car, the recurring crises of PayPal's founders, or politicians' promises. In the blink of an eye, the steel mill in Youngstown disappeared, and Delphi Automotive Systems, spun off from the parts division of General Motors (GM), went bankrupt, leaving behind nothing but drifting rust and fields of despair. Time appears to stand still after this industrial dissolution, and the era seems frozen in place. As one social class declines, another ascends, heralding the emergence of new colossal fortunes. At every pivotal moment in each character's story, the "time slider" switches back and forth, enabling protagonists to traverse from the south of the city to the north and then to the east in just a few sentences, defying the conventional constraints of time. Amidst these shifts, a decade passes, yet the Pontiac car remains unchanged.

This approach, in my opinion, is an excellent method for portraying the developmental history of an enterprise. The temporal dizziness induced by this narrative technique is just a subtle shift in the perspective of the camera lens. Stepping back to observe individuals within the broader currents of an era, these locally fluctuating time snippets still follow the grand order of the historical timeline. Therefore, this book meticulously unfolds its narrative along the timeline, like the gradual unfurling of a scroll. The unrevealed scenes signify events remain undisclosed, leaving witnesses, as well as you and me, to rely on speculation. For the unfolded scenes, when necessary, the time machine is activated to rewind and revisit past events before returning to the present moment. By combining a one-way timeline with the "time slider" narrative approach, it not only upholds the dignity of time, preventing complete anticipation of what lies beyond the wall of time, but also elucidates historical clues once overlooked, making our present footing more realistic.

With the narrative challenges resolved, the spotlight now falls on the protagonists of the story: the entrepreneurs.

Arguably, entrepreneurs are the group most engaged in a high-stakes game with the times, facing the most brutal competition. The era deals the cards, and entrepreneurs must make guesses. A correct guess allows entry into the next round, while an incorrect one incurs penalties and necessitates continued guessing, albeit with diminishing opportunities. No hero possesses the foresight to predict every card. Due to the substantial investment, each new model in the automotive industry represents a high-stakes "gamble", heightening the intensity of the competition. The remarkable achievements in the Chinese automotive industry today do not solely hinge on an unbroken streak of good luck. Every entrepreneur has traversed a maze of setbacks and triumphs, penalties, and toasts. Only the enduring flame of faith sustains them to this day. Alan Greenspan, former chairman of the Federal Reserve, who served for 19 years, highly praised the innovative spirit of entrepreneurs in his book *Capitalism in America: A History*, stating, "Great entrepreneurs are never at rest; they must keep building and innovating in order to survive." "To be or not to be" remains the eternal theme for entrepreneurs.

The main protagonist in this narrative, SAIC-GM-Wuling (SGMW), is a local state-owned enterprise, through mixed ownership reform, ultimately emerged as a trailblazer on the international stage. The storyline is clear and straightforward.

However, the legendary aspect of the story lies in the fact that in a southern city grappling with talent shortages, outdated logistics, and the absence of a supply chain, the enterprise managed to rise from the status of a "novice" in car manufacturing, remarkably propelling Liuzhou to a prominent position among China's automotive cities. Notably, it created numerous stunning and widely acclaimed "legendary cars", around which many lively citizen stories have unfolded. Subsequent discussions have revolved around these vehicles, highlighting the cultural significance of automobiles and the dynamic spirit of the local populace. Surprisingly, Liuzhou, a tranquil and habitable city, has given rise to an enterprise that has made noteworthy contributions. The interplay between the government and the enterprise, coupled with the response from both the city and the cars, collectively staged a grand drama of regional industrial upgrading. These distinctive attributes set SGMW apart from any other car company, even as they all contend with life-threatening challenges.

This book does not overly emphasize the heroic demeanor of entrepreneurs, instead seeking to reveal the managers' hesitance, underscoring that everyone has weakness, and true heroes are those who pull their hair and forge ahead, when faced with marshy terrain. In SGMW's developmental journey, notable successes were achieved after the joint venture, with models like Wuling Sunshine, Wuling Hongguang, Baojun 730, and Wuling Hongguang Mini EV marking two decades of remarkable progress. However, the managers have always walked a fine line. As Ford significantly reduced automobile costs, GM rose to prominence by catering to the diverse needs of consumers. Volkswagen won hearts with armor-like durability, and Toyota revolutionized machinery rhythm with lean production. The disruptive emergence of Tesla wiped century-old formulas off the blackboard, redesigning the framework of automobiles. In China, the car creator of Liuzhou saw through the drastic changes in social psychology during the rapid expansion of Chinese society, and presented a fitting gift to enthusiastic strivers. This marked a significant triumph for the Chinese automotive industry in the field of social psychology. However, social trends and consumer preferences are fluid, making entrepreneurs akin to participant in a cliff-edge marathon. In the automotive industry, even with one or two successful models and a span of three to five years of glory, a company is far from being worry-free. Therefore, it likely takes at least a decade to see whether a car company has truly achieved a phase of victory in the automotive industry. Entrepreneurs face difficulties, and those who navigate the cycles successfully are even rarer. This book aims to chronicle the journey of this group of determined individuals, and the narrative adopts the perspective of the headlights of a night-driving car, piercing through darkness, the unknown conditions, and insecurity.

At the same time, part of the narrative delves into the major trends of the era. Only by reconstructing the zeitgeist can one gain a better understanding of the entrepreneurs' predicament. This inspiration is encapsulated in this book's subtitle, "A Trailblazer in the Automobile Manufacturing". A car company is a microcosm of its time. This book pays tribute to Li Anding's work, *A Tale of Cars in China: 30 Years, from Start to Fast Lane*, which through vivid material and the perspective of a witness, preserves valuable memories for the development of the Chinese automotive industry—An approach deserving of commendation. Another facet of the narrative is dedicated to China's manufacturing system. I believe that Chinese manufacturing requires an appropriate narrative framework to spotlight the subtle yet profound contributions made within factories. There exists a dearth of scriptwriters exploring Chinese factories, and many extraordinary stories remain unnoticed on the workshop's floor. The improvements in manufacturing and quality that occur in the workshop, seemingly inconspicuous, are fundamental elements in Chinese manufacturing in reality. To unveil the hidden beauty of manufacturing, there is a need for more visual language and innovative approaches. The site of Chinese manufacturing inherently possesses value. SGMW's factory is home to many outstanding manufacturing engineers who starting from scratch to learn the intricacies of car manufacturing, have reached the pinnacle of manufacturing capabilities—A prowess gradually lost by the American automotive industry. Even Rick Wagner, former CEO of GM, expressed admiration for the accomplishments in Liuzhou. Behind every business legend stands, there is an unmentioned manufacturing engineer, and this book endeavors to shine a spotlight on a few of these inconspicuous figures.

The trends of the era, the art of management, and the beauty of manufacturing form the three main threads that the book aspires to present to readers, which will serve as the key themes for my future writings on the history of business development. Of course, let's do not forget the "time slider"!

I hope that this book can serve as a meaningful beginning for documenting the history of Chinese business development. Chinese entrepreneurs, a highly respectable group, have brewed a fine vintage of Chinese manufacturing. Now, as its aroma permeates, it invites everyone to savor it.

Lin Xueping

Taoranting Park, Beijing

Contents

Chapter 1 Prologue: One City, One Legacy

Liuzhou is a city that exudes beauty and often deceives the senses. Its allure lies in its karst topography, imparting a unique charm. Verdant mountains, steadfast in their rise, command expansive spaces with an air of leisure, reminiscent of drifting clouds and wild cranes. The peaks encircle the city nestled against the mountains, and both exist in joyful harmony. When casually lifting your gaze through the well-aligned seams of the city's towering buildings, a solitary peak's graceful contour leaps into view. Further in the distance, a forest of peaks underpins the vast, luminous sky. The city's layout, a blend of complex geometries, paints a scene of intriguing depth and allure.

The Rivers here possess a character of their own and a pristine quality. The Liujiang River, Liuzhou's lifeblood, flows steadily from the upstream reaches of Guizhou Province. After entering the city at the Three Rivers Converge (Sangjiangkou) from the Northwest, it abruptly turns North, then gracefully curves back Southeast, resembling an immortal taking three swaying steps in a drunken dance, outlining the shape of a teapot. This teapot-like course of the Liujiang has earned Liuzhou the moniker "City of Teapot." The quality of the water here is exceptional, like water waiting to be poured from a teapot. Navigating through this city sometimes requires crossing the river three times, evoking a surreal sensation of traveling back in time.

Upon entering Liuzhou City, one is immediately enveloped in a futuristic ambiance, as if spatial norms are being disrupted, compelling one to reevaluate their understanding of cars, the cityscape, and space itself. On the bustling roads, small cars abound, their lengths often more than half shorter than regular vehicles, creating a stark contrast as they weave through traffic. For newcomers, this induces a sense of disproportion, akin to entering a cinematic sci-fi realm where one's own body seems enlarged and the surrounding space more expansive, causing a sudden acceleration of the heartbeat. The geometric equilibrium of space, established over the years, is now thoroughly disrupted, demanding a recalibration of perspectives. The perpetual procession of vehicles flashes by, conjuring familiar yet perplexing illusions. At times, one might even feel as if these cars are robots, ushering them into a sci-fi realm where humans and machines coexist in harmonious synchrony.

Green hills sprawl leisurely like people lounging, the clear river meanders forward with lively energy, and the streets are dotted with moving objects, each in pure, harmonious colors. Together, these elements craft an enchanting cityscape. This charm is attributed to the unique macaron shades of small cars—soft and serene, offering a gentle caress to the eyes even in the brightest sunlight. Beyond their delectable tastes, macarons, the delightful French confections, have colors revered in the world of fashion. This distinctive color palette blends pure tones like pink, yellow, and green with a hint of gray, which creates a subtle saturation that ultimately presents a visual feast, radiating warmth and an irresistible temptation. The confections and their colors harmonize, captivating many and evoking images of joy and delight.

Liuzhou, cradled in serenity, resonates with the gentle rhythms of the Liujiang River caressing its banks. The endless flow of cars, painted in macaron hues ranging from sweet to pure to dreamy, dazzles the eye, bestowing upon Liuzhou the most unique color signature.

Standing as a steadfast evergreen in Liuzhou's industrial landscape, this factory proudly survives amid the relics of its industrial past. The karst terrain, shaped by millions of years of natural forces, narrates a tale of endurance and time; in contrast, a mere few decades have sufficed to solidify the legacy of this remarkable enterprise. Its small electric cars have achieved a miraculous feat, become the global sales champion among electric vehicle models. Even Japan, renowned as the "King of Mini-cars", has meticulously analyzed these cars, seeking to decode the secret behind their widespread popularity.

A vibrant palette of colors and boundary-pushing dimensions, intermingling with traditional vehicles, transforms the entirety of Liuzhou City into a stage for behavioral drama, pulsating with fresh vitality. In collaboration with the Liuzhou Municipal Government of the Guangxi Zhuang Autonomous Region, an innovative project dubbed "Human, Machine, Society" has been unveiled.

The city's vitality is thus sparked to life. These cars, like beating notes, orchestrate the melodies of life across Liuzhou's avenues. Between a city and a car, myriad tales unfold, resonating with the profound connection shared between Aichi Prefecture in Japan and Toyota.

Liuzhou distinguishes itself in China by serving as the production base for four major automotive giants: FAW Group, Dongfeng Motor Corporation, SAIC Motor, and China National Heavy Duty Truck Group (CNHTC). Alongside the Guangxi Automobile Group, these entities collectively form the leading automotive powerhouses of the region. As an emblematic industrial city, Liuzhou mirrors China's modern industrial evolution. Despite facing challenges in transportation, infrastructure, and higher education, especially when compared to cities like Shanghai, Changchun, Wuhan, and Hefei, Liuzhou much like the relentless Liujiang River, perseveres in its industrial march forward.

The Liuzhou Industrial Museum, repurposed from an old cotton textile factory, stands as a grand testament to the city's industrial legacy. Upon entry, visitors are greeted by a towering presence reminiscent of Optimus Prime from the Transformers series—A colossal 10-meter-tall automotive parts stamping press. This 150-tonne press, as quiet as an elder on a rocking chair during a summer afternoon, harbors untold stories of its battles from yesteryear. Initially a celebrated piece of equipment at the Renault factory in France during the 1950s, this press was treasured and imported from France in the 1980s, an era when steel embodied strength and symbolized the gateway to the future.

Inquisitive museum-goers are certain to encounter a myriad of awe-inspiring exhibits. From lathes and generators of televisions and refrigerators, these weathered relics overflow with tales from Liuzhou's industrial heyday. Surprisingly, all these were manufactured in Liuzhou. Though they no longer "speak", their faded luster silently conveys the narrative of their glorious past.

On the second floor of the museum, a faded photograph reveals the former master of the stamping press at the entrance. The stamping press's steel that once formed its mighty frame now courses through the veins of the new protagonist in this story—An entity that holds a distinctive position in Liuzhou. It introduced the fiercely competitive automobile industry to one of Southern China's quietest cities. The unquenched flames of battle continue to burn over this city, home to approximately 4 million inhabitants. Alfred P. Sloan, who led General Motors (GM) for 23 years and reshaped the automobile industry, firmly believed in "competition as an article of faith, a means of progress, and a way of life"[1]. From this perspective, the essence of competition is deeply ingrained in the DNA of this enterprise, standing in stark

---

[1] Alfred P. Sloan. *My Years with General Motors*[M]. Liu Xin. Huaxia Publishing House, 2017, 6.

contrast to Liuzhou's peaceful and unhurried lifestyle. The company always seemed ready for a decisive battle. Looking westward along the Liujiang River, the mountains and rivers have remain unchanged for eons. However, the communication towers perched atop the mountains consistently disrupt the silence, resembling wind chimes that remind us of the industrial civilization deeply rooted amidst the natural landscape.

Following the trail of the press's photograph leads to the company's Hexi base in Liunan District, Liuzhou. The red brick wall next to the gate, engraved with the bold words "Perseverance with Self-Strengthening", shows the marks of time, exuding historical depth. Within the factory grounds, coconut trees sway gently, with people intentionally walking under their shades. Nearby, a four-story red brick building, unembellished in its design, stands with a structure that follows a low-high-low pattern, featuring the shape of the Chinese character "凸". Behind it, a white-painted cooling tower stands sentinel-like, gazing into the distance. The open square in front reveals a small pond where koi fish swim leisurely. At first glance, it may seem like a place devoid of stories or thrilling sights.

In its silent eloquence, the red building stands as the enigma of this tale, its essence woven not in words but in its very presence. The words "Perseverance with Self-Strengthening" etched at the gate, are the sole clue it offers and the entirety of its intended conveyance.

Chapter 2 Bygone Tales Along the Liujiang River 1958–1998

2.1 Nationwide Dreams of Automobiles

Liuzhou's manufacturing identity is deeply intertwined with its strategic position in transportation. The beauty of Liuzhou is poetically captured by the ancient Chinese poet Liu Zongyuan, stating, "Layers of hills enshroud far-reaching views; the Liujiang winds like thoughts in intricate cues." The city's very nature is defined by these meandering bends, and its strength lies in connectivity. Historically a crucial waterway from Guangxi to Guangdong, Liuzhou has perennially stood as the bustling "Central Port of Guangxi", a nexus of craftsmanship and commerce. Its manufacturing ambitions trace back to the early 20th century, particularly during the warlord era in the 1920s, marked by the establishment of munitions factories. Its early industrial ventures included the production of wood-fired automobiles and aircraft.

At the dawn of the People's Republic of China, regions nationwide yearned for support from the central government. Among these, the eminent 156 Key Projects, a suite of large-scale industrial initiatives assisted by the Soviet Union, commanded national attention. These projects laid the foundation for China's industrial landscape, profoundly influencing its industrial geography and the status of various cities. During this period, possessing industry was synonymous with possessing wealth. However, as China's frontier region supporting Vietnam[1], Guangxi received none of the boon of the 156 Key Projects. Undeterred, the people of Liuzhou leveraged their existing resources, advancing the development of lead-zinc and brick factories. The tide shifted during the Second Five-Year Plan[2] when Guangxi, previously lacking in

---

① Liuzhou Industrial Museum. *From a Trading Port in Central Guangxi to a Renowned Industrial City: A History of Liuzhou's Industrial Development*[M]. Guangxi Normal University Press, 2013, 64.

② China's Second Five-Year Plan refers to the national economic development plan covering the years 1958 to 1962.

steel and fertilizer resources, received substantial central backing for the development of heavy industry. Three strategic industrial zones were established in Guangxi: Nanning, Guilin, and Liuzhou. This period saw a surge in industrial support flowing into these areas from major industrial centers like Shanghai and Shenyang. The former, as an industrial metropolis, contributed six factories to Liuzhou, spanning sectors like knitting, enamelware, and towel manufacturing. In a reciprocal gesture, Guangxi granted privileges to workers relocating from Shanghai, preserving their higher wage levels and converting their rural household registrations to urban ones. Amidst a landscape marked by hardship and scarcity, the people of Liuzhou, driven by dedication and sincerity, planted the early seeds of industrial development.

In March 1958, following the establishment of the Guangxi Zhuang Autonomous Region, Liuzhou witnessed a significant surge in industry activity. This period was marked by the commencement of several key projects in fields such as metallurgy, fertilizer production, and manufacturing, resulting in the establishment of pivotal enterprises like the Liuzhou Steel Factory, Liuzhou Power Machinery Factory, and Liuzhou Construction Machinery Factory. Notably, Liuzhou Construction Machinery Factory originated from the Shanghai Huadong Steel Factory and later evolved into Guangxi LiuGong Machinery Co., Ltd. These developments laid the foundational pillars for Liuzhou's burgeoning industrial landscape, particularly in the realms of steel, automotive, and engineering machinery.

The year 1958 heralded the dawn of Liuzhou's industrial era, coinciding with the beginning of the Great Leap Forward and China's first surge in the wave of automobiles. Across the country, there was a fervent push for rapid development in the automotive industry, accompanied by the establishment of hundreds of auto parts factories. Despite the enthusiasm and vigor, the conditions were rudimentary, resulting in manufacturing processes akin to crude blacksmithing or carpentry. Some factories, lacking proper testing means, resorted to directly replicating parts from FAW's Jiefang trucks, using the actual components as measuring standards. The nationwide endeavor to produce automobiles resembled toy manufacturing, and unsurprisingly, the resulting vehicles struggled to function effectively. Notable examples included brands such as Shanghai and Nanjing Yuejin, both light trucks, which, plagued by issues such as short lifespans, oil leaks, noises, and missing parts, soon faced production cuts and reorganization. In the fervor that prioritized enthusiasm over scientific rigor, numerous auto repair and assembly shops sprang up, only succumb to the impracticalities of their approach[1].

The automotive industry is a gemstone of industrialization—captivating in its allure yet formidable at its core. It epitomizes a bastion of complexity and stringent standards, accessible only to those equipped with specialized technical know-how. This domain is not for the inexperienced or the faint-hearted; its doors remain closed to those driven solely by ambition. China's automotive industry, still in its infancy, was yet to master the art of navigating this intricate and demanding landscape.

2.2 A Quest for Direction

The Liuzhou Machinery Factory, originally engaged in military product manufacturing, served as the cradle of Guangxi's mechanical industry. Much like the nurturing waters of the Liujiang River, it fostered the city's path toward industrialization. In 1958, responding to the burgeoning demands of the shipbuilding industry, the factory expanded its production base and established the Liuzhou Power Machinery Factory, initiating research and production of marine diesel engines. Given Guangxi's historical reliance on waterways for transportation, the autonomous region looked to its rivers, particularly the Xijiang and Liujiang, as crucial conduits leading to the Guangzhou port. The Liujiang River, flowing directly into the Guangzhou port, solidified Liuzhou's strategic significance as a key junction. Specializing in the production of 500-horsepower marine diesel engines (1 metric horsepower ≈ 0.735 kilowatts), the Liuzhou Power Machinery Factory primarily catered to vessels operating in and out of Guangxi's aquatic and maritime gateways.

However, the factory's inception coincided with the looming threat of obsolescence. Much like the children of impoverished families born into hunger, it faced immediate challenges. In 1959, China grappled with severe economic difficulties, leading to virtually no demand for shipbuilding. This stark reality disrupted the factory's initial plans, compelling the nascent enterprise to expand its facilities while desperately seeking any opportunity to sustain its workforce.

It was an era of great leaps forward, brimming with fervent industrialization ambitions.

---

[1] Editorial Department of China's Automotive Industry History. *History of China Automotive Industry: Special Subjects, 1901–1990*[M]. China Communications Press, 1996, 127+431.

Agricultural production is the most pressing need of China, and the national dream of mechanizing agriculture took center stage. In June 1960, the Ministry of Agricultural Machinery proposed establishing a factory in Guangxi to manufacturing paddy field tractors. The People's Government of Guangxi Zhuang Autonomous Region approved the Liuzhou Machinery Factory's project to build a tractor factory, including the production of engines and gears—A development met with widespread approval and anticipation. The factory pivoted from diesel engine production to tractor manufacturing, and the diesel engine research team transforming into a tractor research group.

Between 1961 and 1962, China faced the most challenging period of adjustment. Caught in the whirlwind rapid changes, the members of the research team barely had time to revel in the success of their prototype tractors before the tractor factory was designated for delayed construction. The ongoing diesel engine and tractor projects were abruptly halted, with nearly half of the equipment mothballed and almost half of the workforce laid off.

During these turbulent times, following directives from the People's Government of Guangxi Zhuang Autonomous Region, the Liuzhou Power Machinery Factory, having branched off from the Liuzhou Machinery Factory, became an independent entity with separate financial accounting, embarking on its journey as a standalone operation.

While the structures of the factory had been built, it lacked enclosing walls due to budget constraints, leaving four workshops and an office building standing isolated in a wasteland, often frequented by neighboring farmers' cattle grazing at the doorsteps. This was creatively resolved by the workers who planted dense bamboo groves around the perimeter. Within a year, the bamboo had grown tall and thick into a "bamboo fence", naturally enclosing the factory and effectively keeping the cattle out. Yet, the Liuzhou Power Machinery Factory, much like a lost child, looked around in confusion, uncertain of the path ahead and without anyone to provide guidance during those directionless time.

The rumble of tractors in the fields captured people's attention. During that era, tractors symbolized the pinnacle of productivity, and were considered a luxury. Determined to forge its path to sustenance, the Liuzhou Power Machinery Factory set out to manufacture a tractor. After five years of prototype development, in December 1965, the factory finally received approval: The Honghe Fengshou-37 tractor was designated as a national standard product, then the State Planning Commission approving its annual production plan of 5,000 units.

The factory's survival hinged on technical prowess—The key to securing sustenance and ensuring the enterprise's vitality. This fundamental principle of survival began to resonate deeply with everyone involved.

However, during that period, the factory's capacity to produce tractors was limited, far from the mass production needed to sustain its workforce. In 1965, the factory director, adhering to the philosophy of "nurturing specialization through diversification", turned to machining work to support the tractor factory. The Liuzhou Power Machinery Factory began producing components for gasoline-powered chainsaws for the Liuzhou Machinery Factory, with 90% of the output intended for forestry operations in Northeast China. To manage this new production line, the Liuzhou Power Machinery Factory even established a dedicated assembly plant in Beijing.

In January 1966, the Liuzhou Tractor Factory was officially established, replacing the former Liuzhou Power Machinery Factory. After eight years of relentless effort, the enterprise finally found its direction of development. This year is also the beginning of China's Third Five-Year Plan.

However, the emergence of tractors was ill-timed, coinciding with the Cultural Revolution, a period when people's focus shifted away from production. In the subsequent five years, the annual output of the Liuzhou Tractor Factory is significantly short of its projected capacity.

During this period, the Liuzhou Agricultural Machinery Factory produced the first automobile in Liuzhou, and the Liuzhou Special Automobile Factory was also established [1]. Various manufacturing endeavors were explored as a means of subsistence and survival. Years later, these two enterprises, in collaboration with Dongfeng Motor Corporation and FAW Group, evolved into Dongfeng Liuzhou Motor Co., Ltd. and FAW Jiefang Liuzhou Special Automobile Co., Ltd., respectively, both playing significant roles in Liuzhou's automotive industry.

In 1972, the central government directed considerable attention to Guangxi's development, investing RMB 25 million (equivalent to about RMB 2 billion in 2021 terms), with agricultural machinery identified as a key area of development. This

---

[1] Committee for the Study of Cultural and Historical Data of the Liuzhou Municipal Committee of the Chinese People's Political Consultative Conference. *The Historic Moments of Liuzhou's Automobile Industry*[M]. Jieli Publishing House, 2011, 66.

substantial investment reinvigorated the struggling tractor industry. The Liuzhou Tractor Factory launched a continuation project to produce 5,000 tractors annually, establishing new engine workshops, oil pump workshops, precision casting workshops, and a central laboratory. By the end of 1975, the factory had nearly achieved its production target set by the State Planning Commission, manufacturing over 4,500 tractors annually.

In 1978, the Liuzhou Tractor Factory reached its full production capacity of 5,000 units, generating nearly RMB 50 million in revenue and turning losses into profits. Despite standing among the top eight tractor factories nationwide during its heyday, the Liuzhou Tractor Factory distinguished itself through its unique trajectory. While the other seven major tractor factories were managed by the Ministry of Agricultural Machinery (also known as the Eighth Ministry of Machine Building), the Liuzhou Tractor Factory is under the jurisdiction of the local government. At the same time, unlike these factories, which generally adopted specialized divisions of labor, the Liuzhou Tractor Factory, lacking support for unified resource allocation, had to establish a complete manufacturing process in-house, ranging from casting and forging to machining, essentially covering the manufacture of all components. Without the direct oversight of the central government or the support of allied enterprises, the Liuzhou Tractor Factory evolved into a versatile facility capable of producing chassis, transmissions, suspension systems, and engines—A miniature "tractor kingdom" with its own right.

Proudly, among the eight major tractor factories in 1978, the Liuzhou Tractor Factory stood out as the only one without incurring losses. At that time, Liuzhou's industry was flourishing, with industrial sparks igniting across the city. Key enterprises like the Liuzhou Tractor Factory drove the development of supporting component manufacturers, embodying the "hen laying eggs" strategy[1], where the primary industry (the "hen") fostered the growth of ancillary businesses (the "eggs"), creating an integrated and self-sustaining industrial ecosystem. This approach not only bridged gaps in the supply chain, but also ensured a more robust and interconnected industrial foundation for Liuzhou.

---

① Liuzhou Industrial Museum. *From a Trading Port in Central Guangxi to a Renowned Industrial City: A History of Liuzhou's Industrial Development*[M]. Guangxi Normal University Press, 2013, 116.

2.3 The Ephemeral Arc of Joy

In 1979, the spring breeze of economic reform ushered in a new epoch in China, catalyzing the dissolution of the planned procurement and distribution system. This transformation was propelled by rural reform and the steadfast implementation of the household contract responsibility system with remuneration linked to output (household responsibility system), signifying a pivotal shift toward a market-regulated economy. The Liuzhou Tractor Factory faced severe stagnation in sales of its main products, with production plummeting into a deep trough. What had been an upward trajectory suddenly took a downturn, resembling the descending arc of a parabola.

During this time, private ownership remained a profoundly sensitive social topic, approached with caution and a degree of reservation. Automobiles were indisputable symbols of luxury. Prior to 1984, county-level officials and regiment-level officers were restricted to using BJ212 jeeps, prohibited from using regular cars. Given the absence of private car purchases, only governments and institutional bodies could buy cars using public funds, thereby rendering all cars de facto state assets. The role of a driver, as portrayed in Lu Yao's *Ordinary World*, where a county official's son assumes such a position, was a source of envy during this era. The idea of owning a car or a tractor was beyond most people's imagination. Following the implementation of the reform and opening-up policy, the introduction of the household responsibility system in rural areas triggered a sudden decline in tractor demand. Under the collective system, tractors were allocated to communes at the county level, representing collective purchasing power; once produced and stored, they were sold without specific considerations for the end-user. However, with the implementation of the new household responsibility system, a tractor priced at about RMB 8,000 was financially unattainable and often unnecessary for individual farming households. Discourses regarding whether farmers could possess their own walking tractors persisted into the early 1980s, as evidenced in *China Comment*, a publication affiliated with Xinhua News Agency[1].

The precipitous decline of the tractor market allowed little time for enterprises to

---

[1] Li Anding. *A Tale of Cars in China: 30 Years, from Start to Fast Lane*[M]. SDX Joint Publishing Company, 2017, 71.

acclimate. It was as if someone had abruptly turned the radio dial, transitioning directly from a planned economy to a market economy, transforming the melodic strains of a gentle folk song into the bold notes of rock music. While society embraced the future with renewed optimism, enterprises grappled with the challenges of adapting to market changes. Tractors, just like before, continued to roll out of factory gates, their robust engine hums filling the air, but now, they were met with silence, no longer echoed by the demands of the bygone era.

Liuzhou Tractor Factory faced financial discrepancies as sales were recorded but payments remained unrecovered. Buyers, even in affluent regions like Yulin City in Guangxi, typically remitted no more than 20% upfront. The burden of unrecoverable payments weighed heavily on the enterprise. During that period, tractors manufactured by factories were distributed to communes through local agricultural machinery bureaus. However, it was shockingly discovered during factory inspections that many tractors remained unused. The sales data reported to the enterprise was misleading. Faced with cash-strapped communes and an accumulating surplus of products, the only viable solution appeared to be allowing communes to take the tractors first, with the hope that they would settle payment upon receiving government subsidies. Amidst the country's transition from a planned to a market economy, the factory found itself falling behind. Tractors were dispatched, but the anticipated financial returns did not materialize. Eventually, the factory mobilized its middle management to retrieve the tractors from the communes. Unfortunately, some machines had already been damaged, and their tires had aged. Soon, the returned tractors, many of which were now inoperable, overwhelmed the once spacious factory grounds, turning it into a storage space for what was essentially unusable scrap.

By the end of 1980, the Liuzhou Tractor Factory found itself burdened by an accumulation of nearly two thousand tractors, bringing production to a standstill. The once flourishing era of a planned economy, marked by assured purchases and sales, had dissipated, leaving behind only echoes of a bygone time. The factory, previously a source of pride for its 3,000 employees, now loomed as a heavy burden.

The sustainability of tractor production became untenable, with each unit manufactured only contributing to mounting losses. The enterprise had no choice but to cease tractor manufacturing and pivot to other industries, initiating a desperate battle for survival. The new strategy was to produce anything viable—from agricultural essentials to looms, sewing machines, and even children's bicycles— anything to keep the business afloat. In quick succession, the employees successfully developed the 1515-56" automatic shuttle weaving machine. The Liuzhou Municipal Government granted authorization for the Liuzhou Tractor Factory to produce this urgently needed machine for various textile factories. This was followed by the successful development of an even more advanced model, the 1,515K wide-width weaving machine. Throughout this transformative period, the enterprise adhered to a guiding principle: "Self-Reliant, Factory Thrives; Break-Even Goals, Diversify Drives."

This approach rekindled the spirit and determination of the workforce, despite the unfamiliar territory of textile machinery. Nonetheless, establishing effective sales channels remained a challenge. At that time, a weaving machine factory in Zhejiang Province operated at peak capacity but confronted a severe shortage of cast iron components. Given that 90% of weaving machine parts are castings, with few machining components, the Liuzhou Tractor Factory, with its underutilized foundry and skilled workforce in part production, found an opportunity to address this gap and satisfy the Zhejiang-based factory's needs. Through personal connections, the two factories established a mutually beneficial collaboration: the Liuzhou Tractor Factory produced the necessary components, which were then shipped to the weaving machine factory for final assembly.

During this period, Liuzhou Tractor Factory swiftly adapted its production to align with market demands, leading to the development of the Wanjia sewing machine. This versatile machine, capable of sewing, edging, embroidering, and making buttonholes, gained widespread popularity upon its launch in 1981.

These diverse endeavors culminated in the factory's return to profitability in 1981, saving the teetering business. In that year, the leadership of Guangxi Zhuang Autonomous Region, upon a review of the factory's situation, advised to prioritize market demands, produced what people need, and didn't solely rely on state plans. With this directive imposed pressure, it granted the freedom to adapt[1], a crucial pivot for the factory's survival and future trajectory.

History often repeats itself in dramatic ways. The 1981 directive to "produce based on market needs and produce what people need", forty years later, echo powerfully as a more iconic and widely embraced expression.

---

[1] Jia Ke. Finding Oneself in Crisis[J]. *Auto Business Review*, 2020, 12.

2.4 The Rise of Mini Vehicles

In the 1980s, Liuzhou's industry was on a quest for breakthroughs. Termed "The Eight Titans"[1], eight major state-owned industrial enterprises in the city dedicated themselves to the production of everyday necessities.

An exhibit in the Liuzhou Industrial Museum portrays a newlywed home furnished with Liuzhou-made products, vividly reflecting the light industrial production level of that era. Back then, the epitome of a "well-off life" was succinctly encapsulated with "three turns and a ring", a phrase denoting the four coveted household items within the country's production capabilities: bicycles, sewing machines, watches, and radios. The first three items are named for their rotating mechanisms, whereas the radio is named for its ability to emit sound. Local factories in Liuzhou manufactured these items, with brands such as 555 being famous for its clocks, Bee sewing machines, Forever bicycles, and Mountain Flower radios. Slightly more luxurious items like Shuangma electric fans and Dule refrigerators were also once the second-best-selling products nationally[2].

Of particular note is that the 555 clocks, Forever bicycles, and Bee sewing machines were the fruits of horizontal collaboration between local enterprises in Liuzhou City and the Shanghai China Clock Factory, Shanghai Forever Bicycle Co., Ltd., and Shanghai No.3 Sewing Machine Factory. This inter-city collaboration facilitated knowledge exchange and bolstered regional economic development. Liuzhou's distinct role as a trading center and transportation hub further contributed to the open and outward-looking nature of its people.

Among these products, the one that endured well into the 21st century was the "Golden Throat Lozenge". Originating from Liuzhou No.2 Sweet Factory, one of "The Eight Titans", this popular throat lozenge brand is a testament to enduring success. Unfortunately, not all these iconic brands could maintain their glory over the years. Often, the entrepreneur's vision and legacy play a crucial role in steering a

---

① "The Eight Titans" of Liuzhou City represented a diverse range of state-owned enterprises, including businesses specializing in the manufacturing of electric fans, toothpaste, switches, alloy materials, machine tools, and instruments, along with those engaged in the production of candy and refrigerators.

② Liuzhou Industrial Museum. *From a Trading Port in Central Guangxi to a Renowned Industrial City: A History of Liuzhou's Industrial Development*[M]. Guangxi Normal University Press, 2013, 167.

brand through historical currents to remain relevant in the present day.

At the beginning of 1980, a Mitsubishi Minicab from Japan was introduced into China by relevant authorities. The initial plan was, Liuzhou Machinery Factory and Shenyang Tractor Plant individually developed the engine and chassis. Learning about this, Liuzhou Tractor Factory treated Japanese mini-vehicles as ideal for developing China's low-cost passenger and freight transportation, presenting a golden opportunity to shift its production focus. The factory director, Ding Shu, proactively pursued and ultimately secured permission to collaborate on the prototype with Liuzhou Machinery Factory.

To kick-start the process, Liuzhou Tractor Factory imported two Japanese prototype vehicles, one van and one passenger car. Next, the Mitsubishi Minicab (L100) prototype was meticulously disassembled and examined. It was found that the minivan consisted of over 2,500 different types of parts, totaling more than 5,500 pieces, many of which had to be painstakingly sketched bit by bit. Without proper measuring tools, the team resorted to direct comparisons of physical parts, aligning them as closely as possible to the original dimensions. Initially, drafting was done using manual T-squares, later upgraded to semi-automatic drawing boards. Working through sweltering and humid summer days, the surveyors often labored bare-chested, with towels draped over their necks to wipe away sweat as they conducted measurements on-site. Whether crafting molds, prototyping steering gears and driving shafts, or completing dynamic balance tests, the hammer was indispensable. It was the go-to solution for various issues, swiftly resolving any unevenness with a few strikes.

By January 1982, Liuzhou Tractor Factory had successfully prototyped the first LZ110 mini-truck—A vehicle crafted through manual hammering and mold techniques, signifying a major breakthrough in the field of mini-vehicle manufacturing. In the summer of 1982, the first LZ110K minivan was also successfully prototyped.

"Exhausted yet unaware of the heat, lamenting only the fleeting summer days." These skilled craftsmen, the creators, were unknowingly participating in a race of speed and passion. A brand-new track was emerging in China's mini-vehicle industry.

2.5 The Year of Administrative Intervention

1982 is a significant milestone for China's automotive industry, a year of groundbreaking developments. For the first time, the government sanctioned joint ventures between Chinese and foreign companies, heralding the advent of a momentous era in automobile manufacturing. A new management system was initiated, with the establishment of the China National Automotive Industry Corporation (CNAIC) in May, reflecting the state's ambition to centrally plan and coordinate the country's automotive sector through administrative clout.

These administrative directives endowed the CNAIC with a unique status, entrusting it with the management of seven major joint venture companies, including Dongfeng, Nanjing, Jiefang, and the Shanghai Automobile and Tractor Industry Corporation, among others. As the automotive sector unfolded its ambitious blueprint, a new era loomed on the horizon. In contrast to the prioritized development of the sedan industry, China's nascent mini-vehicle sector vividly reflected local initiatives in automobile manufacturing and regional economic vitality. Even military industrial enterprises under the Ministry of Aviation Industry and the Ministry of Ordnance Industry, which later became designated mini-vehicle manufacturers, had histories of independent attempts at prototyping mini-vehicles. Everywhere, there was a surge of vitality, reminiscent of the phrase, "The east wind serves as the harbinger of spring, signaling life in every blade of grass and bloom."

For the regulatory bodies, their primary objective was to rectify the imbalance in the cargo vehicle product structure, characterized by a scarcity of heavy and light trucks, and to enhance the role of road transport. As a result, despite the overarching planning of national automotive products, mini-vehicles were not yet integrated into the expansion strategy of mainstream automobile manufacturers. For instance, the Shanghai Automobile and Tractor Industry Corporation, founded in 1983, comprised enterprises from various sectors, including machinery, agriculture, handicrafts, and farming. These enterprises were modest in scale and production output, with highly decentralized affiliations. Although mini-vehicles were once identified as one of the eight key products of the Shanghai Automobile and Tractor Industry Corporation, they essentially played a backup role. Within the Beijing–Tianjin–Hebei Auto Industry Joint Venture, Beijing focused on light vehicles, Tianjin on mini-vehicles, and Hebei on modified vehicles, with each region specializing in its own sector without overlapping. Among the initial product plans of major automotive associations, only the Beijing-Tianjin-Hebei venture prioritized mini-vehicles in Tianjin. However, Tianjin's automotive manufacturing capabilities were then on the periphery of China's automobile industry.

The mini-vehicle market saw an influx of "outsiders". Apart from Tianjin's established automotive enterprises, many participants were military factories, agricultural machinery plants, and machine tool factories. These newcomers ventured into vehicle manufacturing driven by survival pressures. During this period, as the country's external situation eased and economic activities shifted from preparation for war and famine to the development of national welfare and livelihood, military enterprises faced a decline in military orders, forcing them to pivot to civilian production for sustenance. In the wake of policy shifts from a planned to a market economy, state-owned enterprises, with decades-old product lines, found it challenging to adapt, making survival a pressing concern. This prompted numerous established machinery companies to diversify into manufacturing products in demand by society. A notable example of this military-to-civilian transition is Changhong TV, emerging from the state-owned Changhong Machinery Factory, which produced airborne fire-control radars and was one of the initial 156 Key Projects. Changhong TV came into prominence under the leadership of a young visionary in 1985. He was among the youngest plant directors within the enterprises under the Ministry of Electronics Industry, and an early adopter of the new management system introduced during the beginning of the state-owned enterprise reform, where the factory director assumes full responsibility[1]. The bold and proactive style of the leading figure at Changhong propelled the company becoming the "King of Color TV" in China. The times silently nurtured and called upon Chinese entrepreneurs.

Another factor driving numerous "outsiders" from military and agricultural machinery sectors into the automotive domain was the burgeoning market prospects of mini-vehicles. Mini-vehicles, at the time, represented uncharted territory in China, with definite market demand, low entry thresholds, and minimal competition with established automobile companies. For many state-owned enterprises in transition, mini-vehicles were a lifeline to escape difficulties. Similar to modified and agricultural vehicles, mini-vehicles became a preferred choice for non-traditional automotive enterprises venturing into vehicle manufacturing.

The establishment of the CNAIC was an endeavor to integrate automobile manufacturing into unified planning and management, primarily aimed to reform, then fragmented, disorganized, and suboptimal state of the automotive industry[2]. Many believed in the effectiveness of top-down, holistic planning. However, the

---

① Xu Daijun. Changhong: An Epitome of State-Owned Enterprise Reform and Development[R] *State-Owned Assets Report*, 2019, 11.

② Li Gang. An Oral History of an Automobile Professional[R] Tsinghua Alumni Association, May 2009.

corporation's vice-ministerial level cast a shadow over its efficacy, especially when compared to the ministerial-level China State Shipbuilding Corporation (CSSC), established in the same month. This disparity somewhat reflected the automotive industry's lower status compared to shipbuilding, undermining the corporation's ability to drive the vast industry forward. By 1984, FAW in Jilin and Dongfeng Motor Corporation in Hubei were the first to request autonomy from the corporation, sparking a direct challenge from local governments. This round ended in a swift victory for the local authorities, leading to a further dilution of CNAIC's power and severe questioning of its administrative legitimacy. Soon, the corporation was advised to focus on more abstract responsibilities and was, ultimately, dissolved. The history of automobile manufacturing in China is marked by untamed vigor and unconventional methods, resembling a form of primal industrialization. The unleashed energy at the grassroots level rapidly challenged the automotive industry, Was traditionally regarded as a pinnacle of industrial civilization.

When CNAIC was established, a plethora of mini-vehicle manufacturers had already emerged across the country. To the competent authorities, the proliferation of these manufacturers posed a risk of fragmentation, disorganization, and inferior quality. To address this, on August 12, 1982, CNAIC convened a significant meeting in Tianjin to deliberate on the mini-vehicle sector. Key figures, including the company chairman and chief engineer, attended the gathering, which drew a total of 130 participants from 63 different units, including notable entities like the Ministry of Ordnance Industry and the Ministry of Aviation Industry. The meeting aimed to unify thoughts, draw lessons from the historical pitfalls of fragmented, redundant, and small-scale automobile production, and collectively explored product direction, planning objectives, and site selection principles for joint mini-vehicle construction[①]. Notably, Liuzhou Tractor Factory was not initially invited to this crucial meeting. In response, the factory's determined director, Ding Shu, arranged for an LZ110 mini-truck to be driven all the way to Tianjin, forcefully making their presence known at the conference. This bold move left a lasting impression on the leadership attending the conference.

Following the meeting, CNAIC conducted an extensive market survey to address the demand for mini-vehicles. The survey, divided into two routes covering both the northern and southern regions, spanned over a duration of two months. In October

---

① As recorded in the *China Automotive Industry Yearbook.*

1982, the State Planning Commission granted approval to CNAIC's report on the mini-vehicle construction forum. It recommended establishing one production base, two assembly points, and one modification point for mini-vehicles, following the principles of utilizing existing enterprise foundations, securing reliable fundings, and ensuring developmental capabilities.

Upon receiving the survey report from CNAIC and the mini-vehicle market forecast report from the Beijing–Tianjin–Hebei venture, the State Planning Commission and the State Economic Commission issued a notification in April 1983, designating Tianjin as the national mass production base for mini-vehicles. Fortunately, Liuzhou Tractor Factory was selected as a designated production enterprise, along with the Harbin Weijian Machinery Factory (later Hafei Motor) under the Ministry of Aviation Industry, while Jilin Light-Truck Factory was designated as a modification point.

This notification served as a clarion call, officially recognizing the mini-vehicle industry in China and paving the way for its robust development. It also instructed non-designated enterprises to cease further trial production and arrange for conversion after completing the current trial production volume. This directive led some non-designated factories to withdraw, such as Nanjing Motor Vehicle Plant pivoting to motorcycle production. However, other manufacturers, recognizing the market potential of mini-vehicles, continued their pilot production efforts, striving to quickly achieve mass production capabilities and earn national recognition.

2.6 The Strategic Reorientation of Two Cities

In the 1980s, the majority of joint automotive companies in China sought ways to circumvent the CNAIC's product planning, "staking claims" in product development to foster large-scale enterprise growth. Among them, Jiefang and Dongfeng were notably aggressive. However, the Shanghai Automobile and Tractor Industry Corporation, embarking on a challenging joint venture with Volkswagen, adopted a more conservative strategy—"Shanghai vehicles made way for Volkswagen Santana sedans"—demonstrating an unique strategic vision. Since the late 1960s, Shanghai City had been producing light-duty trucks, establishing a significant market presence over a decade. However, in 1982, an agreement with Volkswagen to assemble and purchase 100 Santana sedans was signed, paving the way for the sedan joint venture. The production of Shanghai light-duty trucks ceased that year to facilitate the sedan project. However, the trucks did not immediately vacate the shared factory space, and some covert assembly activities led to dissatisfaction from Volkswagen's German representatives. The successful execution of the Santana venture also marked the end of Shanghai City's mini-vehicle dream. In 1986, preparations for mini-vehicle production in the city were halted, and all completed tooling and related technology were transferred to the Liuzhou Tractor Factory.

To exclusively focus on the Santana sedan joint venture, Shanghai City not only halted the production of its well-established light-duty trucks, but also discontinued the ready-to-launch mini-vehicle project. Strategically, this decision was astute and decisive. On another level, the city's ability to concentrate on the Santana sedan strategy, thoroughly implementing the product planning, was attributed to its efficient single administrative division and vertical management. This efficiency was unattainable by other inter-provincial conglomerates entangled in sectional interests.

Similarly, with a focus on specialization, Liuzhou redirected its efforts toward mini-vehicle production. Having become a designated mini-vehicle manufacturer, Liuzhou Tractor Factory decided to cease producing sewing machines and looms, transferring these technologies to sister units. This single-minded dedication marked a significant shift in the company's strategy. To better serve customers, Liuzhou Tractor Factory established a mini-vehicle quality feedback system for users, pioneering a systematic approach for a mini-vehicle manufacturer to incorporate customer feedback into its operations.

In 1984, the Wanjia LZ110 mini-truck was officially launched, achieving sales of over 2,300 units. Following the success of sewing machines, another Wanjia product made its mark. *Wanjia*, meaning "ten thousand families" in Chinese, is a trademark bearing a sense of communal warmth, akin to the simple yet meaningful names like *jianguo* (build the country) or *aimin* (love the people) given to children in that era. For ambitious manufacturers of the time, the dream was to have their brand welcomed into thousands of households.

In the same year, the State Council officially allowed farmers to own motor vehicles, including tractors, as production tools[①]. At this juncture, Liuzhou Tractor Factory made the surprising decision to exit the tractor market and fully enter the mini-vehicle market, renaming itself Liuzhou Mini-Vehicle Factory the following

① "State Council Regulations on Individual or Joint Household Purchase of Motor Vehicles, Boats, and Tractors for Transportation Business", *State Council Gazette* no. 4 (1984).

years, which was a significant choice. While tractor manufacturing seemed to be entering a golden age, Liuzhou Mini-Vehicle Factory resolutely abandoned tractor production to embark on an entirely different developmental path, metaphorically kicking off the "cloth shoes" and putting on the new "running shoes."

At the bustling starting line of the automotive race, many companies were undergoing pivotal transitions as well. The Shenyang Small Tractor Factory, a key manufacturer since 1956, ventured into mini-truck production in 1984 following successful technical evaluations. However, the factory continued its production of the original walking tractors concurrently with the newly introduced mini-cars. Both the names "Shenyang Light Vehicle Factory" and "Shenyang Small Tractor Factory" featured prominently in their advertising, indicating their dual focus. This strategy of "straddling two boats" initially led to a dispersion of strategic resources; while seemingly shrewd, it proved risky. Shenyang Light Vehicle Factory quickly receded from the national mini-vehicle market competition, in stark contrast to Liuzhou Mini Vehicle Factory, which retained the "Mini-Vehicle" title the longest among mainstream mini-vehicle manufacturers. In an era of fierce competition with limited resources, it was the focused and determined entities that fought their ways out, as the market battle tested the strategic resolve of businesses.

The profound historical significance of the decision-makers' choices at this crossroads only became evident years later. Two categories of motor vehicles for farmers emerged: Tractors exclusively for farming and those designed for both agricultural and commercial using, representing distinct paths. The surge in China's economic vitality began with unleashing the energy of the farmers, with the rapid transition of Chinese society into a wealth acceleration phase mainly propelled by urban and rural residents seeking prosperity. The transformation of Liuzhou Tractor Factory into Liuzhou Mini Vehicle Factory transcended a mere name change; it signified an alignment with an emerging trend, attuned to the times. This strategic shift, subtly conceived in the spirit of the era, marked a significant adaptation to the evolving industrial landscape.

In November 1984, leveraging a five-year collaboration with Japan's Suzuki, Chang'an Automobile in Chongqing launched its first minitrucks and minivans. This marked a transformative shift from its military precursor, the Chongqing Chang'an Arsenal, into a civilian automotive enterprise. Formerly a large military factory producing items such as oil drill bits and shotguns with limited success, Chang'an Automobile found a turning point when its market research team specializing in civilian products, stumbled upon a Suzuki mini-car on the streets of Guangzhou, inspiring their venture into the mini-vehicle market. Concurrently, personnel from Jilin Light-Truck Factory, during their time in Beijing, encountered an imported mini-car used by the Ministry of Posts and Telecommunications, culminating in an agreement to manufacture specialized mini-cars tailored to their needs.

The resonant call of history, echoing from a distance, reaches only a select few who discern its subtle melody and respond with a dance. At the heart of seizing opportune moments lies the essence of swift action, recognizing that the right moment, once missed, may never grace us again.

By the end of 1982, China's industrial landscape had undergone a remarkable transformation. A total of 21 factories had ventured into mini-vehicle production or prototype development, with five of them transitioning from engine manufacturing to complete vehicles producing[1]. Among the remaining 16 mini-vehicle manufacturing facilities, there was a diverse mix. Established automobile manufacturers such as Tianjin Automobile Industry Group, Wuhan Automobile Industry Group, and Guangzhou Automobile Group were present. There were also newcomers to the automotive industry, like Jilin Light-Truck Factory, which had emerged from enterprises like Jilin Fuel Injection Equipment Factory. In addition, several factories were in the process of transitioning from military to civilian production, exemplified by Harbin Weijian Machinery Factory, Jiangxi Changhe Machinery Factory, and Anhui Huaihai Machinery Factory, while several other factories were initially focused on agricultural machinery, such as Liuzhou Tractor Factory and Shenyang Small Tractor Factory. Interestingly, there were facilities that appeared unrelated to the automotive realm, such as Guizhou Communication Machinery Factory and Nanjing No.4 Machine Tool Plant.

Throughout the 1980s, China's mini-vehicle industry was in its infancy, while heavy, medium, and light trucks, along with sedans, had already established a solid foundation as key products of major automotive companies. With the initiation of economic reform, mini-vehicle production in China was virtually non-existent. Among the four primary enterprises designated in the national mini-vehicle plan, only Tianjin Automotive Industry Group was a core member of the Beijing–Tianjin–Hebei venture, while the other three were not specialized car manufacturers.

---

① Editorial Review Board of China's Automotive Industry History. *History of China Automotive Industry, 1901–1990*[M]. China Communications Press, 1986, 214.

The palpable impact of lacking knowledge and the true difficulty of a task are only revealed through hands-on experience. Without a formal design concept, imitation served as the stepping-stone for Liuzhou Mini-Vehicle Factory from 1984 to 1986. The factory began its journey by replicating models from Japan's Mitsubishi, subsequently developing its first generation of mini-vehicles and a series of variant models.

The discovery of the replicas by Mitsubishi created a turning point, leading to a collaborative approach that presented a golden opportunity. The ensuing negotiations between Liuzhou Mini-Vehicle Factory and Mitsubishi spanned two years, culminating in a full-scale technology transfer agreement encompassing every aspect, from engines to car bodies.

At the time, the People's Government of Guangxi Zhuang Autonomous Region and Mitsubishi had reached an agreement on contract terms, setting the stage for a signing ceremony in Beijing. However, due to policy issues and industry competition, the deal was not finalized. This turn of events left the leaders of the Guangxi Zhuang Autonomous Region and Liuzhou City deeply disheartened. Jin Zhenhua, the then-director of Liuzhou Mini-Vehicle Factory, shed tears at the unexpected outcome, exemplifying the saying, "A man does not easily shed tears, only at the point of utmost grief". In reflective silence, the management team made their way back to their office in Beijing. The abrupt halt in cooperation bewildered the Japanese personnel, resulting in harsh criticism of Mitsubishi's senior director and the eventual dismissal of their head of the China Office.

The failed signing ceremony did not entirely crush the spirit of the people of Liuzhou. Tapping into the region's inexhaustible vitality and determination, they quickly conceived an ingenious solution: The signing of a "partial agreement". This approach involved finalizing a deal exclusively for the car body with Mitsubishi, excluding the engine and complete car assembly, which allowed the project to endure under revised terms.

While not ideal, this partial agreement played a pivotal role in preserving the enterprise's manufacturing, underscoring the tenacity and ingenuity of the people in Liuzhou. Nestled by the Liujiang River and at the convergence of three waterways, the residents of Liuzhou have consistently exhibited an open-minded and resourceful spirit, enabling them to adapt and flourish in the face of challenges.

Due to the unavailability of Mitsubishi's engines, Liuzhou Mini-Vehicle Factory encountered a significant developmental hurdle, resulting in a chronic problem for the vehicles, akin to a heart disease for humans. Initially relying on engines from Liuzhou Machinery Factory, the factory found itself insufficient to meet demand. Subsequently, the factory sought engines from Tianjin Daihatsu, which unfortunately proved disappointing due to subpar quality. In the end, the factory sought assistance from Harbin Dongan Auto Engine. This unfortunate prologue of inadequacies presented significant challenges to their journey.

During this period, the mini-vehicle segment, transitioning from military to civilian production, began bypassing the CNAIC to directly import Japanese mini-vehicles. In July 1984, China National Aero-Technology Import & Export Corporation (CATIC) signed a technology transfer contract with Japan's Suzuki, covering the complete manufacturing technology of minivans, mini tourist cars, and 18 types of variant vehicles. The Ministry of Aviation Industry then disseminated this technology to its subsidiaries, Harbin Aircraft Industry Group, Changhe Aircraft Industry Corporation, Xi'an Aircraft Industry Croup, and Harbin Dong'an Auto Engine. They were guided to mass-produce mini-vehicles and engines using Suzuki's technology, following a development and production strategy of high starting points, large volumes, specialization, and joint development. Contrary to the Ministry of Aviation Industry's decentralized approach, the Ministry of Ordnance Industry adopted an integrated method for its mini-vehicle projects involving Suzuki's technology. The manufacturing of complete mini-vehicles using this technology was centralized at Chongqing Chang'an Arsenal, while Suzuki engines were designated for production at Jiangling Machinery Manufacturing Plant. The intent was to establish Chongqing Chang'an Arsenal as the leader of a mini-vehicle production consortium. Suzuki, renowned as the "King of Mini-cars" in Japan, replicated its advanced technology across six Chinese entities. This left Liuzhou Mini-Vehicle Factory trailing, facing the challenge of catching up with these well-equipped competitors.

2.7 The Essence of the Enterprise

In 1985, Liuzhou introduced an innovative talent recruitment policy known as the "three noes": no need for a personal dossier, no transfer of salary relations, and no concern for seniority. This policy, considered revolutionary at the time, advertised in the newspaper *Reference News*, attracted a flood of young people, including graduates from agriculture, military, and even tank engineering backgrounds. The policy's deviation from traditional practices where graduates were typically assigned jobs, and possessing a dossier was essential for job mobility, marked a bold departure in talent acquisition.

Amidst a great surge of talent recruitment, individuals charted their paths in this dawning era of new opportunities. Shen Yang, having graduated from university and worked in the railway department, was drawn to Liuzhou in 1985 by the unique recruitment advertisement. Initially rejected by Liuzhou Machinery Factory due to a mismatch in specialization, he found a place at Liuzhou Mini-Vehicle Factory, leaving his dossier in Yunnan Province. Years later, as a delegate at the 18th National Congress of the Communist Party of China (CPC), Shen Yang returned to Yunnan to reclaim his dossier, which had been misplaced for 27 years. This once "unregistered" talent eventually restored his historical record.

During this period, Liuzhou Mini-Vehicle Factory welcomed about 30 new talents, with a select few being university graduates specifically assigned to the factory. Yao Zuoping, a graduate from the last agricultural machinery class at Wuhan Automotive Polytechnic University under the Ministry of Machinery Industry, was among those allocated to Liuzhou Mini-Vehicle Factory. At that time, allocations by the Ministry of Machinery Industry were still part of the national official system. However, the majority of talent was recruited independently, focusing on merit and skill without consideration of one's background.

This initiative marked a significant influx of talent, infusing new vitality into the workforce. As these employees ascended to managerial positions in subsequent years, it highlighted the enduring importance of the ongoing quest for skilled personnel in this industrial city in Southern China.

The talent recruitment advertisement in the newspaper, while successful in attracting job hunters, also presented challenges for Liuzhou City. In 1986, the city faced criticism from the central media for deviating from the widespread practice of restricting job mobility for those without a dossier. Consequently, the "small window" that Liuzhou had opened for talent was quickly shut. Starting in 1987, university graduates were ushered into a system of dual-choice employment, encompassing both planned assignments and free job selection.

This widespread talent migration laid a solid foundation for the younger, better-educated professionals at Liuzhou Mini-Vehicle Factory.

During this era, Liuzhou Mini-Vehicle Factory embarked on a quest for the perfect automotive brand emblem. A company-wide contest was launched to design the car Logo. While the consideration of the "W" symbol from the defunct Wanjia sewing machines was contemplated, trademark registration issues prevented its use. Concurrently, the LZ100 minivan received official approval at a prestigious event[1], marking a notable milestone celebrated in the presence of CNAIC officials. Intriguingly, this acclaimed product still lacked a name, even amid the congratulatory atmosphere.

Confronted with the urgency of selecting a brand name, then-director Jin Zhenhua made a prompt decision. Then-chief engineer Tong Yuzhuo revisited the trademark office to register a trademark for their mini-car, but initial name suggestions such as "Siling," "Zuanshi," and "Baoshi" were already taken. At the trademark office, Tong encountered an engineer who spontaneously offered to design a logo. On the spot, he conceived "Wuling," accompanied by a symbol featuring five diamonds. The approval was swift, with the decision and payment finalized right there and then.

In a cost-effective move, a new trademark was born.

The original design featured five vertical diamonds forming a "W," reminiscent of the logo for Wanjia sewing machines. However, it faced criticism for its resemblance to a dog's tooth. At this point, new employees began to make their mark. Wei Hongwen, a fresh university graduate who had recently joined the company, re-envisioned the Wuling logo. He refined the design by removing superfluous elements, aiming to better reflect the "W" in Wuling and creating an image akin to a soaring bird. This redesigned emblem not only highlighted the company's core products but also symbolized its burgeoning strength and growth potential.

The unanimously approved trademark heralded the official inception of the Wuling Logo, encapsulating a new epoch brimming with hope and a readiness to ascend. In 1987, as the Liuzhou Mini-Vehicle Factory unveiled its van model, this vibrant and fresh Logo was prominently featured, signifying not only a new chapter, but also the brand's aspirational leap forward[2].

From 1984 to 1987, the Liuzhou Mini-Vehicle Factory ventured into sedan production, establishing partnerships with Japanese and French firms. A notable collaboration was with France's Citroën to manufacture the discontinued VIZAR

---

[1] On October 30, 1984, the LZ100 minivan's performance indicators successfully met the criteria in the national testing and evaluation.

[2] The Glorious Years Editing Group. *The Glorious Years: The Development of Guangxi Automobile Group Over Sixty Years (1958–2018)*[M]. Guangxi People's Publishing House, 2018, 43.

model. The introduction of cost-effective designs and second-hand equipment brought notable changes, including a "Transformer-like" stamping press that turned into a workshop highlight. However, due to the lack of support from higher authorities and licensing issues, the factory could only produce and sell a few hundred units locally in Guangxi, leading to the project's termination.

The growth of the sedan industry necessitates significant investment and output, depending on support either from the central government or local authorities. For a state-owned enterprise at the local level lacking backing from the central government and financial assistance from the autonomous regional government, significant breakthroughs proved elusive. Additionally, an alternative route pursued by private enterprises was not feasible at the time, hindered by restricted market access.

During that period, national policy was geared toward supporting only the "Big Three and Small Three"[1] automotive enterprises. Therefore, it was premature for the Liuzhou Mini-Vehicle Factory to venture into sedan production. The factory's aspiration to produce sedans was quashed before it could take off, prompting a redirection of focus toward mini-vehicle production.

In the competitive market landscape, Liuzhou Mini-Vehicle Factory found itself somewhat marginalized, overshadowed by prominent mini-vehicle manufacturers such as Chang'an, Hafei, and Changhe, along with Tianjin Daihatsu, all of which received considerable support. In this context, Liuzhou Mini-Vehicle Factory seemed to be a more dispensable player.

The Liuzhou Mini-Vehicle Factory resembled a lonely hunter in the wilderness, depending solely on its own skills and relentless determination to survive. The factory was under unending pressure to sustain itself. Each leader was compelled to engage in arduous and persistent entrepreneurial endeavors, embodying a spirit of tireless pursuit and resilience in the face of daunting challenges.

In 1989, the employees of Liuzhou Mini-Vehicle Factory acutely felt the challenges of survival as vehicle sales plummeted, leading to a factory-wide discussion about the enterprise spirit, spearheaded by the factory's party committee. The consensus from these discussions was the spirit of "Perseverance with Self-Strengthening", encapsulating the factory's core ethos. Faced with constraints in talent, funding, and location, the factory relied on its resilience and cohesion to

---

[1] "Big Three" refers to SAIC Volkswagen, FAW-Volkswagen, and Dongfeng Peugeot-Citroën, whereas "Small Three" refers to Beijing Jeep Corporation, Tianjin Daihatsu, and Guangzhou Peugeot.

overcome adversity. The graduates of the 1960s, as the first generation of entrepreneurs, left a legacy of perseverance and relentless self-improvement.

Galvanized by the discussion on enterprise spirit, the factory leadership formed an elite team with 108 members, mostly university graduates, to reinvigorate their efforts. Embracing the newly affirmed corporate spirit, this team ventured across the country to boost vehicle sales, signifying a renewed driving and dedication to the company's mission.

Simple but powerful slogans often serve as a rallying force for local enterprises, with the spirit and energy of the employees constituting the very essence of an enterprise. Absent this spirit, an enterprise can become soulless, akin to a team devoid of combativeness. It is crucial to preserve this spirit, ensuring it never wanes or weakens.

The ethos of embracing adversity and persistent entrepreneurship is deeply woven into Liuzhou's identity. Although interpreted differently by each generation, these values collectively define the city's character. Over the years, "The Spirit of Liuzhou" has crystallized as the city's emblem, encapsulating traits of openness, innovation, and relentless self-improvement. The city and its principal enterprise are intertwined in both geography and culture, often reflecting each other's responses to historical challenges. Their united endeavors toward progress weave a tightly interconnected story, mutually influencing and echoing throughout history.

2.8 Steadfast in the Tide: The Unswerving Path to Rewards

The introduction of Japanese mini-vehicles into China during the 1980s was a product of intense market competition. As a newcomer, China's mini-vehicle industry did not evolve through a gradual process; rather, it experienced a leapfrog development, propelled by strategies such as imitation, completely knocked down (CKD) assembly, and the introduction of technology.

Starting from scratch in the 1980s, China's mini-vehicle industry saw rapid expansion, reaching an annual production capacity of approximately 200,000 units by the end of the decade. Eight enterprises produced over 10,000 mini-vehicles annually, accounting for about 10% of China's total car production at the time. While production capacity could be quickly ramped up, market development required more time. The nascent industry, despiting its rapid growth and advanced products, grappled with an immature market.

The disparity, where production capacity significantly exceeded actual output, was not unique to the mini-vehicle industry. Statistics from the Seventh Five-Year Plan period show that, the automotive industry added over 600 large-scale stamping machines capable of producing 250 tonnes or more, cumulatively amounting to a production capacity for 2 million vehicles. However, this capacity did not achieve its expected impact[①]. From the perspective of national regulatory authorities, even with the support provided during the Seventh Five-Year Plan, the key manufacturers had not yet reached a significant production scale. Moreover, new projects were continuously being launched across various regions. If the trend of dispersed investment, irrational allocation, redundant construction, and repeated introduction of technology continued, China's automotive industry would find it is difficult to embark on a path of large-scale development.

As the 20th century neared its final decade, following the developments of the Sixth and Seventh Five-Year Plans, China's mini-vehicle industry, predominantly led by new automotive forces, had notably taken shape. By then, the national plan's framework of "Big Three, Small Three, Mini Two" was already in place, with the "Mini Two" referring to mini-vehicle projects transitioned by military enterprises in Chongqing and Guizhou. The industry's "cake" had been portioned out, and within this division, there was no place for Liuzhou Mini-Vehicle Factory.

Tianjin Automobile emerged as a "fortunate one" amidst China's automotive reform. In 1982, at the onset of the restrictive auto market development, only six enterprises were given the green light for foreign joint ventures, and Tianjin Daihatsu was among them. Capitalizing on its early-mover status and collaboration with Japan's Daihatsu, Tianjin Daihatsu flourished in the mini-vehicle sector and later established a distinct presence in the taxi market. For many, their first taxi made experience was in a vehicle from this company. Gazing out of the windows of these Xiali, passengers could take in the vibrant scenes of the city, and these vehicles become symbols of aspirations for a better life.

According to Lianding, a veteran in the automotive industry, Xiali was originally introduced as a two-box hatchback, colloquially dubbed "a shoe" due to its shape. To address this, Xiali was transformed by extending its rear into a three-box sedan. In the

---

① China Automobile Industry Corporation. *China Automotive Industry Yearbook 1991*[M]. Jilin Science and Technology Press, 1991, 12.

1990s, the public's taste in automobiles began to take shape, heavily influenced by Japanese models like the Toyota Crown and Nissan Cedric. During this period, Tianjin Daihatsu successfully held its ground against competitors like Yungque-Subaru and Chang'an-Suzuki Alto. In the intense rivalry among these iconic Japanese mini-vehicles, Tianjin Daihatsu ultimately emerged as the victor.

In the ever-evolving automotive market, competition is relentless. Despite reaching its pinnacle of success, Tianjin Daihatsu failed to adequately prepare for future market shifts. As the demand for sedans surged in China, the company found it challenging to keep pace. In 1997, it transformed from Tianjin Mini-Vehicle Factory to Tianjin Xiali Automobile Co., Ltd., and later went public in 1999. However, a lack of investment in technology and R&D gradually eroded its competitive edge. The year 2001 was pivotal, marking the widespread adoption of sedans in China, and Xiali found itself lagging behind its competitors. This struggle reached a climax in 2002 with the significant industry development of Tianjin Auto Industry merging and reorganizing with FAW Group.

In contrast to its counterparts, Liuzhou Mini-Vehicle Factory stayed committed to its niche in the mini-vehicle market, competing with key players like Changhe, Chang'an, and Hafei. The competition in this sector was intense, with each manufacturer vying for supremacy. While military enterprises like Chang'an and Hafei had the advantage in parts importation, Liuzhou Mini-Vehicle Factory identified and pursued untapped market opportunities by enhancing its distribution channels. Embracing mini-vehicle production, the factory adopted a strategy that included a strong focus on marketing and product quality, ongoing technological improvements, consistent development of new products, and steady management enhancements. This pragmatic, stepwise approach allowed them to adapt and evolve according to their strengths[1].

From 1990 to 1993, Liuzhou Mini-Vehicle Factory consistently ranked in the top three in sales, trailing only behind Chang'an[2]. In the period from 1996 to 1998, it even led the market for three consecutive years. Identifying an unmet need in the rural market, the factory innovated by introducing dual-row seating in its small trucks, a feature absent in other models, including those Japanese models, which typically

---

① "40th Anniversary of the Establishment of Guangxi Zhuang Autonomous Region: A Commemorative Visit to Liuzhou Mini Vehicle Factory," *Bulletin of the People's Government of Guangxi Zhuang Autonomous Region* no. 12 (1998), 34.

② "Survey of Top 100 Large and Medium-Sized Enterprises in China," *Liuzhou Mini Vehicle Factory Report* (1994), 122.

offered single-row seating. This design, accommodating both passengers and cargo needs while providing more space, enabled Liuzhou Mini-Vehicle Factory to secure about 75% of the market share. Based on this innovation, they developed the Wuling Dragon, which featured a flattened interior floor to increase cargo space, significantly boosting user convenience. This straightforward yet customer-centric strategy highlighted the advantages of specializing in the mini-vehicle market. In the 1990s, it clearly demonstrated that enterprises dedicated to carefully nurturing the mini-vehicle market with firm strategic objectives were the most successful.

In February 1996, Liuzhou Wuling Automobile Enterprise Group was established, operating alongside Liuzhou Mini-Vehicle Factory as one entity with two brands. The company, which incorporated the long-standing Liuzhou Machinery Factory established in 1928, carried forward its legendary industrial heritage. This merger signified the continuation and evolution of a significant industrial lineage in Liuzhou's automotive sector.

In 1998, the 40th anniversary of Liuzhou Wuling's founding marked a milestone celebrated with enthusiasm in the market. That year, both the production and sales of Liuzhou Wuling Automobile exceeded 100,000 units, ranking first in China's mini-vehicle market. The figure of 100,000, viewed as an auspicious number, laid the foundation for the next ambitious target: One million units. In the narrative of China's automotive history, achieving one million units represented a coveted milestone, signifying a major accomplishment for any enterprise in the industry.

Is not this a miracle? In a mid-sized city in central-northern Guangxi, without the support of the central government, substantial government funding, accompanying facilities, or joint venture partnerships, an enterprise that initially produced only a few thousand tractors annually astonishingly evolved into a modern automobile factory boasting an annual output of 100,000 vehicles.

However, prosperity is often transient. Life, like the morning dew under the early sun, is ephemeral; world affairs, always in flux, can rapidly shift from stability to chaos. In 1998, a tumultuous year marked by the Asian financial crisis, every sector, including the burgeoning automotive industry, felt the full force of the storm. Skyscrapers that once stood tall could crumble in mere moments, and once-familiar faces might suddenly turn into strangers. Amidst this turmoil, only the Liujiang River continued to flow undisturbed, quietly embracing the vicissitudes into its depths, bending in a majestic U-turn, a testament to the perpetual cycle of growth and decline.

Chapter 3 The Maelstrom of Transformation 1999–2000

3.1 Crisis in State-Owned Enterprises

During the mid to late 1990s, China's dynamic and rapidly growing private sector stood in stark contrast to some of its less efficient state-owned enterprises.

The year 1998 was a particularly tumultuous period for state-owned enterprises, marking a critical nadir in their journey[1]. During this year, Chinese government responded decisively to these adversities, launching ambitious reforms with a goal to revitalize these enterprises within three years. The State Council initiated three fundamental institutional reforms focusing on labor, personnel, and distribution systems, setting them into motion. In May 1998, the Guangxi Zhuang Autonomous Region made a pivotal decision to reform and restructure enterprises, with Liuzhou City at the forefront of these initiatives. Within these systemic reforms, it was identified that the overhaul of the personnel system was the decisive starting point, while the transformation of the distribution system took center stage. As a prominent entity in Guangxi's automotive sector and a quintessential state-owned enterprise, Liuzhou Wuling stood at the threshold of a profound transformation, akin to a fortress primed for a sensational detonation.

In 1998, Liuzhou Wuling proudly maintained its leading status in China's mini-vehicle rankings for the third consecutive year. While this accomplishment, outwardly dazzling, was often hailed as the most illustrious era throughout the factory's history, beneath these remarkable figures lurked turbulent undercurrents roiling within the mini-vehicle industry, unmasking a treacherous market landscape.

Liuzhou Wuling's spectacular achievements resembled a precarious balancing

---

[1] Gao Yuan, "Interview with Shao Ning: Reflecting on the Days During the 'Three-Year Reform and Difficulty Relief for SOEs'", August 2016.

act on stilts—towering yet vulnerable. The company's seemingly jubilant facade masked the perils lurking beneath. Outwardly, Liuzhou Wuling was celebrated as one of China's four major designated mini-vehicle manufacturers. However, it found itself competing with more formidable rivals—Changhe, Hafei, and Chang'an—each boasting legacies inherited from military enterprises: Changhe and Hafei inherited from the Ministry of Aviation Industry and Chang'an inherited from the Ministry of Ordnance Industry. Despite its accolade as "China's mini-vehicle leader", Liuzhou Wuling grappled with poor cost management, burdened by an unwieldy organizational structure function like a black hole, surreptitiously siphoning the fruits of its hard work. Several departments within Liuzhou Wuling struggled to turn a profit, some with evident inefficiencies. For instance, the production cost of a single wheel hub blank in the casting workshop reached as high as RMB 197—excluding additional expenses incurred due to quality issues and rework—while the market price stood at a mere RMB 79. This discrepancy led to Liuzhou Wuling's cars being priced approximately RMB 3,000 higher than those of its rivals.

Contrary to expectations, high production volume of Liuzhou Wuling did not necessary to translate low costs. Rooted in the ethos of diligence and resilience, the company was not inherently equipped with a low-cost manufacturing edge. The people of Liuzhou harbored a distinctive "creative spirit"—a natural propensity for grassroots mechanical innovation and hands-on problem-solving. This spirit awaited ignition, a fresh beginning, to transform low-cost manufacturing into a true stronghold for Liuzhou Wuling. The broader Chinese industrial landscape also requires time to understand that low cost involves more than scientific management or the craftsman spirit among engineers. Rather, it is a hard-earned potion, achieved through consistent, and long-term effort. Skimping on quality is not a hallmark of industrial low-cost; instead, genuine value-driven low-cost is a sophisticated phase of industrial maturation.

A more critical, yet less visible, threat was emerging in the end-user market. The mini-truck segment, pioneering market competition in the automotive industry, had evolved into an intensely competitive battlefield. This stood in stark contrast to the sedan market of the time, which benefited significantly from policy support. Following the establishment of the "Big Three and Small Three" joint-venture sedan framework in 1987, policy focus shifted toward the production volumes and localization rates of joint-venture brands. In 1994, China transitioned to a buyer's market, intensifying competition in the sedan sector. By the year 1999, more than half of the 11 sedan manufacturers were facing financial losses[①], making bolstering joint-venture automobiles essentially synonymous with supporting the backbone of China's sedan industry.

Consequently, private companies aspiring to enter the sedan production arena were confronted with daunting obstacles, akin to an impenetrable wall created by stringent policies that effectively barred their entry into the automotive industry. The "Hammer Sedan" Geely HQ, masterfully crafted by Li Shufu, a distinguished figure in Chinese car manufacturing, was yet to acquire a commercial sales license, identifiable by a license plate starting with the number 7. In stark contrast, joint venture brands, predominantly foreign car marques, were smoothly and substantially shaping the sedan preferences of Chinese consumers, buoyed by national policy support. This protracted process of nurturing foreign brands, with endeavors protecting these joint ventures, was akin to conducting an unprecedented artificial beauty contest experiment on the highways of a country that would later emerge as the world's leading automotive powerhouse.

Meanwhile, the mini-vehicle market was experiencing rapid expansion at the grassroots level, engulfed in the tumult of relentless price wars and fierce service competition. During this era, the practice of credit sales became a major malignancy, undermining the market's health. The sales figures of mini-vehicle manufacturers resembled enigmatic symbols on a lottery ticket—mere fluctuating numbers with no tangible cash flow.

During this period, many automotive factories, including Liuzhou Wuling, established joint ventures with local dealers, forming a closely-knit family-like network. However, the inflexible and mechanical operational system of Liuzhou Wuling had a cascading effect on the downstream industry. For these joint ventures, the immediate goal was product dispatch, but when it came to the crucial question of payment collection, the typical response was a nonchalant "Sure, next time." The widespread practice of credit sales, especially pronounced in enterprises with poor management, further exacerbated the problem, a situation aptly described by the Chinese proverb "In the abyss, no one knows the depth". In 1998, Liuzhou Wuling's sales revenue fell short of RMB 3 billion, while its operations were deeply mired in losses, with bad debts nearing RMB 1.3 billion—a stark reality revealed by detailed

---

① China Automotive Technology and Research Center and China Association of Automobile Manufacturers. *China Automotive Industry Yearbook 2000*[M]. China Commercial Publishing House, 2000, 365.

internal scrutiny.

The financial lifeline had essentially snapped. To survive, a rebirth was imperative.

3.2 The Surge of Youthful Vigor

In Liuzhou, winter unfolds as a brief and mild affair. The city's branches remain animated with verdant leaves, and each gentle breeze carries with it a soft, almost laughter-like rustling through the trees. The arrival of winter is distinct, yet the people of Liuzhou greet it with understated ease, making little ado about the seasonal shift.

In January 1999, with the gentle onset of winter, a pivotal leadership transition unfolded at Liuzhou Wuling, symbolizing the culmination of a decade's worth of nurturing and the harvesting of seeds sown 15 years earlier. The long-standing factory director, Jin Zhenhua, officially stepped down, passing the reins to 38-year-old Shen Yang, who assumed the role of the new factory director.

The economy, like seasons, ebbs and flows in cycles, oscillating between periods of growth and recession, prosperity and downturn, and depression and recovery. These cycles often commence subtly, unnoticed at first. Similarly, the journey of an enterprise—from decision-making to execution and witnessing outcomes—mimics this cyclical pattern. The harmony between these two cycles can dictate an enterprise's fate, and shape narratives of success or failure. When a business's rhythm aligns with the market's, opportunities abound; however, discord can lead to dire consequences. The decision-making heartbeat of a business is intrinsically linked to its leadership, and shifts in leadership can starkly illuminate the unforgiving nature of these business cycles.

While this leadership change at Liuzhou Wuling may have seemed routine, it inadvertently hinted at the company's imminent restructuring. The need for corporate transformation had been quietly simmering, akin to the subtle sounds of bamboo shoots growing in a dense forest—perceptible even from afar. This transition sparked a cascade of transformations within the industry, unfolding in ways that transcended the expectations and initial decisions of the new leadership.

The young man who had just taken up the baton of leadership had little time to savor his new appointment, as the pressing demands of survival and the imperative to, as the Chinese proverb puts it, ignite "three fires"—a tradition for new officials to make far-reaching changes—took immediate precedence.

The "great fire" was kindled through personnel adjustments. This seemingly innocuous term, "personnel adjustment" stirred an unprecedented whirlwind within the workforce. The trio of reform measures—streamlining organizational structures, appointing competent individuals, and instituting competitive positions—acted like three sharp axes, systematically felling the old structure of Liuzhou Wuling from top to bottom.

The directive for downsizing was issued just before the advent of the Spring Festival.

The company's streamlining efforts were swiftly underway, consolidating the existing 37 administrative departments into just 11 through a decisive merger and reorganization. Accompanying this "surgical" overhaul, business units impeding the company's efficiency, such as casting, heat treatment, and logistics, were divested. Furthermore, employees from company-managed social service departments, including schools, hospitals, kindergartens, and hotels, were systematically redistributed and reassigned.

For the remaining workforce in the factory, a new mandate was established: rigorous implementation of a full workload for all active staffs. Every minute was now accounted for, catching those who once leisurely knitted sweaters during work hours completely by surprise. The most tangible change was evident in the warehouse, which was being emptied out.

Once a cozy haven within the factory, the warehouse was a delightful compound of an array of items, ranging from benches, gloves, and thermos flasks to bearings, springs, and castings. Its shelves, deep and extensive, seemed to stretch into infinity, housing a more diverse stock than any department store. This warehouse embodied a grand collective, resembling a well-filled granary, symbolizing peace and stability. Welcoming those collecting supplies at its entrance, a table surrounded by helpful and cheerful warehouse staff added to the atmosphere of the place. Items were arranged meticulously on the sunlit shelves, where tiny dust particles floated in the beams of sunlight, a testament to the reign of natural light. The entire space was suffused with a sentiment called good times and contentment.

The scene changed abruptly. It was as if the sun had eclipsed and a fierce storm had descended, drastically altering the landscape. A powerful whirlwind seemed to challenge the very integrity of the warehouse's roof. The company's tumultuous reform had been set in motion: inventory underwent extensive audits and was quickly liquidated, rows of shelves were dismantled, and the stock was significantly reduced. In the now sparse warehouse, aimless beams of light scattered haphazardly, illuminating an unrecognizable emptiness.

A pervasive sense of disquiet, tinged with anger, spread among both the office staff and workshop workers. The days of a simple stroll to the warm were gone, welcoming spot for immediate item collection. Now, acquiring any item necessitated a new procedure: filling out request forms, submitting reports for approval, and waiting for centralized procurement. This anxiety of waiting transformed into a "scorching impatience", unfamiliar yet intense.

However, what proved even more agonizing was the extensive layoff of warehouse staff. The "iron rice bowl"—a metaphor for stable, lifelong employment—was irrevocably shattered.

Within just a few weeks, the atmosphere within the Liuzhou Wuling factory transformed into a seething cauldron of tension, bubbling over with unrest. Each new directive stirred the air like a brisk wind, each regulation struck with the precision of an arrow, leaving the factory awash with wounded souls. Conversations among employees were dominated by themes of restructuring and recruitment, job reassignments, and layoffs. While some watched the unfolding events with apprehensive uncertainty, others sought opportunities elsewhere, and a few voiced their frustrations openly. Questions like "How long will this leadership endure?" and "Is Wuling's future in jeopardy?" rippled through the corridors, fueling a whirlwind of rumors and speculation.

At that year's Spring Festival Gala, a poignant skit titled "Yesterday, Today, Tomorrow", featuring Zhao Benshan, Song Dandan, and Cui Yongyuan, captivated the nation's attention. The narrative unfolded as two rural elders, Heitu and Baiyun, recounted the sweeping changes in their lives on a CCTV program. Standing at life's crossroads, with diverging paths ahead, often evokes profound emotions. The skit's symbolic title struck a chord with every Wuling employees, touching their raw emotions. The dumplings on that Spring Festival's Eve seemed to lose their flavor amidst these reflections. For Liuzhou Wuling, it was a moment of critical crossroads. At the skit's conclusion, Heitu's contemplative words, "We used to live by the day; now we should live by the second"[1] resonated deeply, mirroring the sentiments of many at that pivotal time.

---

[1] Zhao Benshan et al. "Yesterday, Today, Tomorrow", CCTV Spring Festival Gala, February 15, 1999.

The leadership team was eager to avoid undue delays. In March 1999, following unexpected heavy rain, a thought-provoking editorial in the company's internal newsletter titled "Achieve Unity in Thinking and Resolutely Pursue New Triumphs in Our Reform Efforts" ignited a vigorous wave of contemplation and debate. As the new year progressed, the factory continued to be swept up in the relentless tide of reform and restructuring.

To effectively implement the three systemic reforms, Shen Yang entrusted three young individuals—Yao Zuoping, Wei Hongwen, and Liu Dexiang—with pivotal roles. Each was assigned specific responsibilities, working in tandem to advance a range of initiatives. One focused on overhauling the procurement department, addressing external vested interests. Another was charged with reconfiguring departmental structures and streamlining hierarchies. The third concentrated on workforce reallocation, spearheading the layoff and relocation office. They quickly became the center of employee discontent, colloquially referred to as the "Three Deformers", The layoff and relocation office, in a twist of sardonic humor, was derisively nicknamed the "Dislocation Office".

The leadership team's resolve was steadfast. To fundamentally transform the organization, rejuvenating its spirit was imperative. Fostering a forward-looking vision demanded vibrant and dynamic leadership. Hence, a sweeping reshuffle unfolded among the middle management, dismantling the entrenched "iron seats" of long-held positions, and the conventional appointment system gave way to a competitive hiring approach. In a transparent recruitment process, 11 young talents stood out from a pool of 150 aspirants, securing their places in middle management. The competitive landscape at Liuzhou Wuling evolved; it was no longer just about management positions. Even workers were subjected to rigorous evaluations, each earnestly competing to secure their roles.

Quick-witted young individuals swiftly acclimated to this new reality. In the past, choosing a job was often about comfort or convenience—a matter of lighthearted boasting. Now, being busy became a badge of significance, a symbol of one's indispensable role in the organization. Amidst the sweeping reforms, a renewed sense of competition and ambition began to stir, reshaping the workplace ethos.

The three systemic reforms eradicated the "big pot" mentality, characterized by uniform distribution without regarding to individual performance. Propelled by this "east wind" of change, a wave of new faces entered the scene. A fierce battle ensued between progressive ideologies and entrenched mindsets. The colossal resistance to reform was almost beyond description, even for those deeply involved. Through persistent communication, coordination, and discussions, the new leadership stood firm against the backlash, methodically rolling out the reform initiatives.

The youthful management team faced the daunting task of proving their capabilities through tangible results, not only to the skeptical veterans but also to the conjecturing staff. The Qing dynasty poem *The First Thunder* by Zhang Weiping aptly captures the essence of this period: "Mute nature has a feeling heart; spring comes to see cold winter part. All flowers are ready to burst, but wait for thunder to roar first."

Despite the initial skepticism and dampened morale, the tangible outcomes of the "three fires" began to manifest. The workforce of Liuzhou Wuling shrank from 5,903 employees pre-reform to 4,497, with a reduction of roughly a quarter. This downsizing instilled urgency in every remaining employees, sharpening their focus and reinvigorating their perspectives. A new seed of change was sown in each person's heart, taking root and beginning to flourish. This transformation is reminiscent of the latent truth in the character Joker's coconut-like heart in Stephen Chow's movie *A Chinese Odyssey*. Just as Joker's hidden wish revealed itself over time, the underlying truth of these reforms became evident in retrospect, though not requiring the 500-year wait that Zixia Fairy endured for her answer from the Monkey King. The employees of Wuling were set to witness the fruits of their transformation much sooner.

3.3 Historical Echoes of Flaming Torches

In 1923, amidst a challenging market downturn for GM, Alfred P. Sloan emerged as the unlikely savior. His appointment as GM's president, marked more by quiet determination than fanfare, came at a time when the company was in disarray, often described as "a total mess". GM's diverse array of car models, instead of presenting strength, were inadvertently competing against each other. This internal rivalry, compounded by Ford's market dominance with its iconic Ford Model T, cast a shadow over GM's future prospects.

In 1978, Lee Iacocca, freshly ousted from Ford Motor Company, assumed leadership of Chrysler Corporation, a company teetering on the brink of bankruptcy. Founded by Walter P. Chrysler, an engineer who had parted ways with GM, Chrysler had navigated a rollercoaster of fortunes over fifty years, and found itself on the precipice, confronting the grim reality of potential bankruptcy and dissolution.

Over the span of six decades, history appeared to echo a familiar tune. Alfred P. Sloan, initially inexperienced, and Lee Iacocca, grappling with cash flow issues, both exhibited exceptional logical acumen and vitality. Remarkably, they each triumphed in quelling the turbulence within their respective companies. A key aspect of their strategy was the radical overhaul of inventory management. In this endeavor, both wielded "two axes" with similar finesse, symbolizing their decisive and transformative actions.

The first was organizational management. GM, despite being an early adopter of decentralized management, struggled with a lack of clear guidelines and a tendency for positions to be allocated based on personal biases, resulting in capricious decision-making. Alfred P. Sloan, the then-president of GM, pioneered the transformation of management into a scientific discipline, a concept later expanded upon and popularized by Peter F. Drucker. His introduction of divisional organization management revolutionized the structural blueprint of modern corporations. In contrast, Lee Iacocca, still stung by his harsh dismissal from Henry Ford II, embodied a more ruthless managerial style. At Chrysler, he decisively addressed the company's inefficient and bloated management system, relieving 33 of the 35 vice presidents from their roles within three years.

The second was the product-line strategy. During this time, GM's product-line up in the United States was muddled by the absence of a coherent policy, constituting a significant operational challenge. GM's seven product-lines, boasting ten different models[1], suffered from a lack of logical segmentation, leading to internal price conflicts. In stark contrast, Ford, with its unwavering belief in the mass production of its singular Model T, had a clear market strategy. GM, on the other hand, offered six distinct vehicle brands, including among others, Buick, Cadillac, and Chevrolet, each vying in overlapping price ranges and market segments.

Alfred P. Sloan ingeniously redefined the "territories" and pricing structures for each GM's brand, strategically positioning Chevrolet as the key contender against Ford's Model T. Chevrolet morphed into a dynamic challenger, offering a diverse array of models that surrounded the Model T—some slightly pricier but with superior performance, others more affordable yet comparably functional. This tactic of relentless pursuit and strategic encirclement swiftly dismantled Ford's single-model

---

[1] Alfred P. Sloan. *My Years with General Motors*[M]. trans. Liu Xin. Huaxia Publishing House, 2017, 55.

production myth. By 1927, merely four years later, Ford's dominance was substantially weakened, leading to a temporary shutdown of its River Rouge plant in America for restructuring, thereby ceding the market dominance to GM. The company's victory in capturing the market crown was a testament to its astute multi-brand strategy and intricate product pricing maneuvers. Although Ford later staged a comeback and led the market briefly, the triumph of the multi-brand strategy in the automotive sector was irrefutably cemented, and the era of Ford's single-model production philosophy was inevitably waning.

In stark contrast, Lee Iacocca's approach to product strategy at Chrysler was radically different. At the time, Chrysler's vehicles were struggling with popularity issues, prompting Lee Iacocca to introduce a "national car" as his game-changing strategy to rejuvenate the brand. Drawing inspiration from Japan's kei car, also referred to as mini-car, celebrated for its compact size, Chrysler's version of the kei car was designed with ample space to comfortably accommodate six Americans, challenging the small dimensions of its Japanese counterpart. Concurrently, the development of large-size mini-vans carved out a new niche in the market for boxy passenger vehicles. These strategic moves significantly boosted Chrysler's popularity, with the mini-van emerging as a sustained profit driver. Astonishingly, from the verge of bankruptcy, Chrysler recorded a profit of USD 2.4 billion six years later, surpassing its cumulative profits from the preceding 60 years. Lee Iacocca's success catapulted him to national fame, solidifying his status as an American hero and a legendary figure in Detroit's automotive industry.

At their core, the "three fires" ignited by new leaders share striking similarities.

3.4 The Second Salvo of Reforms

Despite Wuling Automobile's impressive three-year dominance in mini-vehicle industry sales, its product prices remained higher than its competitors', causing concern for Shen Yang and Yao Zuoping, who recognized the unsustainability of such fierce competition, and with a decisive leadership team now in place, turned their attention—the second "fire"—to tackling Liuzhou Wuling's high operational costs. They perceived the factory as an oversized sponge, saturated with cost inefficiencies waiting to be wrung out. "Tighten management and reduce costs" became the rallying sloyan for this new phase in their strategic battle.

In March 1999, during a key meeting, Shen Yang proposed a strategy to "intensify marketing efforts to exert pressure on the two types of capital", [①] specifically targeting the capital tied up in accounts receivable and inventory. This focused effort aimed to address the substantial RMB 350 million immobilized in these two areas. In response, Liuzhou Wuling established a dedicated office for debt collection, focusing on reclaiming long-standing accounts receivable.

The mini-vehicle industry had long been locked in a relentless price war while simultaneously grappling with escalating consumer demands for higher quality. Within Liuzhou Wuling, implementing cost control was akin to a monumental "battle", comparable to moving a mountain.

Tackling procurement was the first forbidding challenge in this uphill battle.

Similar to practices of many traditional factories, Liuzhou Wuling's procurement process was predominantly governed by informal relationships and social engagements, existing within a gray area where moral self-restraint served as the primary check, given the absence of legal or formal oversight. Compounding the complexity, the company's procurement was fragmented across various departments, each functioning autonomously without cohesive coordination, leading to significant gaps and inefficiencies within the procurement system.

With the gentle breezes of February signaling the arrival of spring, the management stratey of Liuzhou Wuling shifted to the procurement department. The previously scattered purchasing power, divided among six major sections, was unified under a single procurement department. Yao Zuoping was appointed to lead this consolidated entity, centralizing all procurement responsibilities. In tandem with this action, the Procurement Management Committee was established as the supreme authority overseeing Liuzhou Wuling's procurement operations. Comprising department heads, this committee aimed to infuse a new level of clarity and transparency in administrative management of procurement activities.

Drawing insights from the procurement management practices of the Yasing Group and Baosteel Group, and inspired by GM's procurement strategies, Liuzhou Wuling formulated its own "three comparisons" procurement model, which emphasized the critical evaluation of "quality, price, and creditworthiness" in making procurement decisions.

---

① "Two types of capital" refer to the capital tied up in accounts receivable and inventory in a business.

In July 1999, a seminal procurement meeting was held by Liuzhou Wuling at the Mingyuan Hotel in Nanning, Guangxi, marking the official launch of the "Three Comparisons" procurement method. The atmosphere was charged, teetering on the edge of confrontation. Arguments raced forward like swift steeds, and debates echoed with the force of thunder. Suppliers, in an unprecedented move, submitted their bids and publicly disclosed their prices, conclusively putting an end to any under-the-table dealings. The bid announcer's voice, reciting for over two hours, became a harbinger of dramatic cost reductions. Unit prices for components nosedived, some from RMB 10 to RMB 6, others from RMB 100 to just over RMB 70. With each bid announcement, suppliers in the room palpably felt the stakes rise, trembling with anxiety. One supplier, caught in the moment's gravity, quipped with a wry humor, "Every line you read costs my family a BMW."

Conversely, this shift was embraced by some suppliers. With the implementation of the "Three Comparisons" procurement method, businesses that had not previously supplied to Liuzhou Wuling now had a fair opportunity to enter the supply chain. The director of Jiangxi Auto Engineering Plastics Factory, upon securing a successful bid at the meeting, hurried outside the venue. Overwhelmed with excitement, he immediately called the factory to relay the triumphant news.

The introduction of the "Three Comparisons" procurement method effectively addressed Liuzhou Wuling's weakness in cost control. Previously, pricing decisions, often arbitrary and dictated by the finance department, underwent a transformative shift, evolving dynamically through the heat of competition.

While the "Three Comparisons" procurement method successfully resolved the "entry", the challenge of the "exit" problem persisted.

During that period, delayed payments from original equipment manufacturers (OEMs) was an industry-wide problem. Around the time for settlement collection, company financial departments often saw long queues of suppliers awaiting payment. In pursuit of their dues, suppliers frequently resorted to public relations efforts with OEM personnel. Those with strong connections might secure payment within a month, while others, with weaker ties, faced waiting of six months or more to receive their payments.

In the quest to cultivate robust growth within the supply chain, Yao Zuoping, the leader of the procurement department at Liuzhou Wuling, championed the concept of mutual growth with suppliers. He introduced the innovative "overflow payment method", which gave priority to suppliers with strong credit, employing an automated, electronic direct settlement system that eliminated the need for manual intervention. Following the adoption of this method, creditworthy suppliers enjoyed the convenience of receiving payments directly in their accounts without the usual nudges and reminders, resulted in many of them reducing their sales commissions, as expenses typically allocated for public relations efforts were no longer necessary. This payment method marked a significant evolution in payment management, resolving deep-rooted procurement issues related to public relations, and transforming complex procedures into simple, transparent processes. By the end of 2000, this method had been comprehensively integrated into Liuzhou Wuling's operations.

The adoption of integrated management allowed suppliers to be directly involved in the manufacturing process management. In a significant shift, the painting workshop transitioned from traditional per-kilogram pricing of paint to a per-vehicle pricing model, requiring paint suppliers to extend their responsibilities into the product-line. Previously, workshop management practices exhibited certain laxities, such as the casual disposal of half-used buckets of paint. The risk of settling and the resulting coarse, orange-peel-like texture on the car's painted surface often prompted wastage if not used within a two-day window. Under the new integrated management, suppliers became accountable for the cost of painting materials, including waste management. If the paint job was subpar, the supplier would not receive payment for the products. This shift to transparent accountability motivated suppliers to be more meticulous in their resource management. They quickly realized that efficient usage directly impacted their profits, led to a marked decrease of wastage in the workshops, and lead an immediate, visible improvement.

The "Three Comparisons" procurement method stood out for its clear objectives and straightforward execution. It injected fresh impetus into the sales division, created new momentum for a market counteroffensive.

3.5 The Commanding Presence of the ISO 9000 Office

The concept of "quality" in Chinese manufacturing, originally adopted from Soviet practices, was deeply ingrained in the operational mechanisms of enterprises. Traditionally, quality control was viewed as an inspection process, a perspective well exemplified by the Inspection and Metrology Department at Liuzhou Wuling. This prevalent approach, however, often resulted in defects going unnoticed at various production stages, only to be identified in the final phase. By this point, defective products already been manufactured in large quantities, representing a major drawback in the quality inspection approach.

Shen Yang, who had initially worked in the quality inspection department at Liuzhou Wuling, understood that the traditional quality inspection method was a cost-incurring black hole and a critical vulnerability impeding the company's progress. In tandem with personnel reforms, the Inspection and Metrology Department underwent a significant transformation, officially rebranded as the Quality Control Department. Starting with a team over 200 members, this shift reinforced the principle that "quality builds the factory", marking a pivotal change in the company's approach to quality.

Since 1992, China embarked on the "China Quality Promotion" campaign, a widespread initiative that, coupled with the annual CCTV "3·15" gala from 1991 onwards, significantly influenced the public's perception of quality. The CCTV "3·15" gala became China's most impactful program for raising quality awareness at the time, resonating with the growing demand for quality among the people. The synergy of these two movements sparked deeply-held sentiments about quality, akin to a volcanic eruption. The public enthusiastically reached out to various news outlets and authorities, expressing support and even sending letters directly to the State Council. The official agency overseeing the "China Quality Promotion" summarized these letters as emblematic of "heartening events, a long march for quality" and "a beneficial and pragmatic action by the Party and the government for the people". Quality, intrinsically linked with high moral values, once unleashed, became an unstoppable force, surging ahead and leaving an indelible mark akin to flowing lava. Subsequently, China enacted a series of laws and regulations focused on quality, and no enterprise aspiring to rejuvenate its market presence could afford to ignore this tidal wave of enthusiasm for quality. The adoption of the ISO 9000 quality management system certification in the early 1990s turned into the most sought-after accolade for factories. While deemed a fundamental requirement in developed industrial countries, this certificate attained esteemed and honored status within the Chinese manufacturing sector.

Eager to overcome past challenges and make their mark, the young team in the newly formed Quality Control Department at Liuzhou Wuling was determined in their commitment to excellence. Their resolve stemmed from a defining moment in 1998, when the company initiated its push for quality system certification. During this period, the factory's internal production and operations were chaotic and lacked standardization. Automobile parts lay strewn across the premises, and workers' bicycles were haphazardly parked at workshop entrances, sometimes obstructing delivery trucks. Factory tours for leaders and guests required advance notice to the workshops for a hurried cleanup, as navigating the space otherwise would be impossible. Tension was palpable toward the end of 1998 during a preliminary inspection by the CAQC Certification Inc. (CAQC). As the ISO 9000 audit team leader stepped into the stamping workshop and witnessed the disarray, casual chatter among workers, and their water breaks, he abruptly halted the inspection and left swiftly without delving deeper. The audit team's looks and abrupt departure felt like daggers to the hearts of the management team present. At that moment, achieving "quality" seemed like an elusive goal, a towering challenge yet to be conquered.

A new challenge was set in motion. To prepare for the 1999 quality system certification, Liuzhou Wuling established a Quality Certification Promotion Team and set up an office for ISO 9000 implementation, informally dubbed the "9000 Office", empowered to halt production if quality standards were compromised. In a humorous nod to ancient Chinese imperial terminology, where the emperor was usually addressed by the title "His Majesty of Ten Thousand Years", the 9000 Office was quickly nicknamed "His Majesty of Nine Thousand Years", a title reserved for highly influential courtiers just one step below the emperor.

At Liuzhou Wuling, fostering a culture of quality began with a fundamental shift in mindset. The company appointed 72 internal auditors and crafted a comprehensive quality certification implementation plan. To ensure widespread understanding, the plan was made engaging and distributed to every employee, and an extensive information campaign was launched through factory newspapers, the factory television station, and workshop bulletin boards. Immediate changes were implemented, such as prohibiting employees from riding bicycles up to workshop entrances; instead, they were required to park outside the factory. This new rule led to debates, particularly from workers in remote areas like the stamping workshop, who now faced over 10 minutes of walking. Discussions with the 9000 Office ensured about practicality and humane considerations, but the reforms were implemented with determination. With the development of the factory's tier III and tier IV documents, Liuzhou Wuling compiled an ISO version of the quality manual, 34 procedure documents, and 383 departmental support management documents. The introduction of the ISO 9000 quality management system marked a major transformation in the company's approach to quality management, akin to opening a window in a sealed room, allowing the light of quality to pour in. Quality became tangible, structured, and directive. Many young workers, keen to learn, eagerly joined the intensive, enclosed training for internal auditors. This seven-day, all-day intensive training acted like a pressure cooker, swiftly instilling the core principles of quality into them.

Effective management of measuring tools is paramount for any enterprise, not only align with national legal measurement standards, but also adhere to the strict calibration cycles of experimental equipment. Previously, Liuzhou Wuling lacked a formal system in this regard. However, through dedicated training, the company systematically organized a comprehensive set of procedures, including standardization practices, standard measures of length measurement, and the process of submitting tools to higher-level national verification institutions. Over a grueling three-week period, with 12-hour workdays, the young staff meticulously inventoried all measuring tools and created detailed ledgers, laying the groundwork for a measurement system. This endeavor transformed quality into an engaging and proactive pursuit, establishing a robust foundation for Liuzhou Wuling's future quality management practices.

The transformation at Liuzhou Wuling was aptly captured by the saying, "If the gentle breeze warms the heart, even the frozen soil will bloom and bear fruit." In September 1999, a milestone was achieved as the company proudly earned ISO 9001 certification, a "silver medal" of achievement for the management team's inaugural year. However, they knew in their hearts that a grander prize awaited—the coveted "gold medal" of ultimate recognition and triumph.

3.6 The Lament of the Weeping Cars

During the late 1990s, OEMs grappled with challenges in effectively managing their sales channels, especially as they transitioned toward a dealership-based sales model. However, their choices in selecting dealers were constrained, as car dealerships were predominantly state-owned entities, such as local material or mechanical and electrical companies. OEMs found themselves in a position where they had to consign cars to these dealers, subsequently facing the arduous task of pursuing payment collection.

Given the scarcity of qualified car dealership candidates, a single dealer often represented multiple automotive brands. To secure robust sales, OEMs were dependent on these dealers to prioritize their products, forcing them to cater to the whims and preferences of the dealers. This reliance substantially diminished OEMs' leverage when it came to recovering payments, leaving them in a weaker position.

To gain greater control, the joint venture company model began to gain traction. In this model, OEMs and dealerships jointly invested capital to establish joint venture companies, operating locally and separating from the direct control of OEMs and dealerships, focusing exclusively on the represented brand. An example of this is Liuzhou Wuling, which established eight major joint venture companies in various regions, offering advantageous policies, competitive prices, and prioritized vehicle supply. While this model seemed promising, it frequently resulted in inefficiencies due to management struggles to stay abreast and limited market awareness prevailing at the time.

One prevalent practice in the automotive industry was the consignment sales model, marked by pervasive informal credit agreements and triangular debts. Joint venture companies, intrinsically embedded with a "one of us" ethos, tended to operate with excessive leniency, creating an imbalanced situation where the joint ventures reaped benefits while OEMs shouldered the risks. Despite this advantageous setup, most of Liuzhou Wuling's joint ventures incurred substantial losses, with only a minority turning a profit. This imbalance significantly strained the enterprise's cash flow, illustrating the challenges inherent in such joint venture arrangements.

The market landscape at the time was far from favorable for the mini-vehicle sector, which found itself swept up in an intense promotional wave as key players flexed their competitive muscles. Chang'an Automobile embraced an aggressive pricing strategy with the slogan—"Price Slash, Slash Again, Keep Slashing!" Meanwhile, Changhe Automobile not only significantly reduced prices, but also pursued a strategy of penetrating rural areas and small towns with the slogan "Up to the Mountains and Down to the Countryside, Capturing the Vast Market!" These unyielding competitors were not just undercutting prices; they were also making inroads into Guangdong and Guangxi, the bastions of Liuzhou Wuling. By June 1999, Liuzhou Wuling's market share had dwindled from 20% to 15%, a concerning drop for Wuling and a cause for celebration among its rivals. Capitalizing on this shift, Changhe even ventured into Liuzhou City, displaying banners proclaiming "Pick Changhe, Make the Deal in Liuzhou", strategically pricing their vehicles two to three thousand Chinese Yuan cheaper than Wuling's.

The rivalry had quite literally arrived at the doorstep of Liuzhou Wuling.

This challenging scenario pushed the boundaries of endurance to their limits.

Was surrender the only option? At the staff representative conference in July 1999, the factory leadership made a surprising announcement to revise the annual car production target down from the initial goal of 100,000 units to 83,000. This action was met with astonishment, perceived as a timid and almost defeatist approach lacking the determination to boldly confront the challenge. Doubts surfaced regarding the new leadership's tenacity compared to their predecessors, especially as production figures were declining. The pervasive belief that "more quantity equals more success" still heavily influenced the staff's mindset. This, compounded with unresolved issues like high accounts receivable and urgent meetings convened by the local government out of concern for the enterprise, put the new leadership under severe strain. Despite the patience shown by the main leaders of the CPC Liuzhou Municipal Committee and the People's Government of Liuzhou toward the young executives, the enterprise faced pressure to quickly deliver tangible results.

Weighed down by serious deliberations, Shen Yang stood at a crossroads of challenging choices. The cost war had just commenced, signs of progress in quality management were emerging, the sales system was in the midst of an overhaul, and the turmoil of ongoing personnel shifts persisted—all against the backdrop of relentless competition. A strategic withdrawal, a decision to stabilize the current tumult, appeared as the most prudent course of action. A conscious decision to relinquish the ostentatious title of mini-vehicle market leader could afford the company the breathing room it desperately needed. This calculated endurance, often initially misconstrued as timidity, would become a hallmark of the leader's tenure in the years that followed. Perhaps only time would unveil the true bravery hidden beneath the I of perceived reticence.

Amidst the reduction in production, Shen Yang courageously steered toward revamping the sales system. He initiated the establishment of independent sales companies, breaking away from the entrenched joint venture sales framework. Consignment sales, a practice in place for years, had resulted in a convoluted network of overdue, bad, and incomplete accounts, obscuring the financial landscape and choking Liuzhou Wuling's cash flow. The accumulating inventories acted like voracious furnaces, rapidly depleting the company's cash reserves. To quell this financial inferno, Shen Yang's initial front was to conduct thorough inventory audits within the joint venture companies, as a clear understanding of the actual inventory levels was crucial for Liuzhou Wuling to ascertain the receivables from these entities. However, this information was a missing piece in the puzzle—records were not documented, leaving everyone in the dark about the exact number of vehicles stockpiled or sold by the joint venture companies.

The inventory audit process unveiled shocking realities. During the inventory check at a dealership in Wuhan, the sales company's team was met with scenes that left them astounded. Numerous vehicles, once a source of pride for workshop workers and beloved products of R&D staff, were haphazardly discarded in corners, resembling abandoned orphans. These cars were now "weeping cars"—neglected, weather-worn, and with their distress unheeded. Several vehicles had deteriorated to such an extent that, with rust and faded paint, scrapping was the only option, yet ironically, they remained classified as new vehicles and assets in the company's ledger.

The inventory clearing operation was executed with meticulous rigor, mandating that every vehicle be precisely accounted for. The team diligently counted and evaluated the condition of each car right where it stood, and at every location they visited, the findings were disheartening. In the end, numerous joint ventures faced the harsh reality of liquidation and shutdown, and even those performing relatively managed to return only a fraction of the vehicles.

The results were deeply disheartening. Each vehicle recorded in the ledger was methodically written off, their values diminished to nothing. For the new leadership team, this was an alarming revelation and a severe setback, as the actual situation proved to be grimmer than expected. With the decisive action underway, there was no room for second thoughts. Dealers adhering to outdated management practices were promptly phased out. Concurrently, the sales team was rejuvenated with fresh, skilled talent. The inventory audit transcended a mere physical tally of stock; it represented a profound transformation in sales strategy. The emphasis shifted from merely tracking vehicle recovery and financial recoupment to a broader objective—redefining the sales mindset, readying for the future, and forging a stronger, more resilient automobile sales network. This journey was about inspiring and reshaping convictions, where unwavering faith served as the cornerstone of success. Dealers who chose to remain with Liuzhou Wuling found renewed optimism in the resolve displayed by the management team. Their commitment to the company, amidst these challenging times, was fortified by witnessing the leaders' firm determination, signaling a promising path forward.

"Plant a seed in spring, harvest a myriad in fall." The efforts made today will yield significant results in the future. For Liuzhou Wuling, that moment of abundant harvest, a testament to their perseverance and foresight, was a near certainty on the horizon.

3.7 Striking with a Masterstroke

September 1, 1999, marked a night of restlessness.

At that midnight, Wuling dealers across the region awaited a "confidential telegram" from Liuzhou headquarters, standing poised by their fax machines. This enigmatic directive, almost ritualistic in its nature, stirred a mix of unease and eager anticipation among the dealers.

When the "confidential telegram" finally arrived, dealers were met with astonishing news that left many in disbelief. Effective immediately, all models under the Wuling brand were subject to a significant price cut, with reductions soaring up to RMB 8,000.

The launch of the Golden Autumn Campaign struck like a blitzkrieg, catching the dealers off guard with its sudden intensity.

To gear up for this impending price war, Liuzhou Wuling had discreetly executed a pricing sensitivity test in Henan during the preceding three months, a period typically considered the sales off-season. The encouraging response garnered from this test laid the groundwork for initiating such an extensive, nationwide campaign.

Endurance is not synonymous with surrender. It may have appeared as a retreat, but it was merely the precursor to a forceful countermove. Behind the factory walls, reforms and reorganization were unfolding with precision and purpose. By August 1999, Liuzhou Wuling had reached a milestone: the production of 500,000 vehicles, a historic achievement that instilled immense pride in every employee. It was at this pivotal moment that the company's strategic counteroffensive in sales was primed and ready to be deployed, marking the beginning of a new chapter in its journey.

On the eve of launching the Golden Autumn Campaign, an impassioned rally convened in an annex of the Wuling Hotel, dedicated to the newly established sales company. The sales team, donning red headbands, symbolically drank courage-boosting wine, their voices resonating with powerful slogans. The atmosphere was electric, touching everyone's heart. Embracing a do-or-die resolve, these valiant individuals set off to oversee more than 20 offices in various regions, supporting the frontline dealers. This was more than just a campaign; it was a crusade for the company's very existence, a defense of the gains made through painstaking reforms. Rituals, in such contexts, are far from superficial. They are crucibles where a company's spirit is tempered and solidified. Astute corporate leaders understand the power of these rituals to ignite joy and enthusiasm amidst the gloom of challenges. The imagery of these warriors embarking on their mission is deeply moving, laden with the weight of both uncertainty and hope. Such moments, fraught with the suspense of outcomes unknown and aspirations deeply held, etch themselves indelibly in memory, stirring profound emotions long after they have passed.

The new sales company was launching a barrage of sales initiatives, each rolling out in successive waves. Key personnel from the logistics department were sent directly to the front lines, tasked with elucidating and championing these new strategies. Promotional materials, hot off the press, were swiftly dispatched to various locations via air freight, ensuring timely delivery. As the decisive moment approached, on the eve of this decisive juncture, these dedicated envoys of Liuzhou Wuling, following their evening meal, began briefing dealers on the importance of awaiting an imminent, critical fax from the headquarters.

The night the fax arrived was a moment of shock and awe!

Suddenly, the country was inundated with advertisements like "Wuling Automobile: Slash Prices, Give Back to Society!" and "Buy a Wuling, Win Big— Grab Your Chance at Tens of Thousands in Prizes!" It was as if the market had been jolted awake overnight. This surge of momentum was relentless, swiftly sweeping across the country and yielding significant results. In September alone, the company witnessed a staggering revenue of RMB 260 million, mitigating the long-standing capital crunch at Liuzhou Wuling to a notable degree. The market share, which had previously seen a decline, made a remarkable rebound to 20% in that very month, and by the end of November, it had escalated to nearly 30%.

The triumph in sales stood as a resounding validation of strategic acumen. The three-month Golden Autumn Campaign unfolded like a masterful orchestration of hammers, spears, and a surge of audacious courage on the battlefield, demonstrating the front-line's formidable strength and valor. Concurrently, in the more subdued backdrop of the command center, intricate and well-thought-out commercial policies for Wuling's automobile marketing were meticulously crafted. Poised for implementation, this calm and precise strategy resembled a surgical approach, ready to be executed with precision and efficiency.

In December, Liuzhou Wuling's sales company orchestrated a significant meeting in Jinan, Shandong Province, extending invitations to core dealers. This gathering marked the introduction of a comprehensive commercial policy for Wuling automobiles. To the dealers' astonishment, they were handed a thick booklet—a compilation spanning hundreds of pages, meticulously outlining detailed guidelines, which was a stark departure from the past when Wuling's sales policies were typically encapsulated in just two pages.

Even more groundbreaking was the audacious initiative proposed by Liuzhou Wuling—a transition to a payment-before-delivery model. This marked a significant departure from the status quo, as dealers were now required to pay upfront, eliminating the previous practice of purchasing cars on credit. Challenging and reshaping industry norms, this pioneering policy positioned Liuzhou Wuling as the first mini-vehicle manufacturer in the country to cease extending credit to dealers, underscoring the company's commitment to innovating and leading in the competitive automotive market.

This new policy, akin to a stone cast into a pond, created far-reaching ripples. It was not merely a directive to Wuling's own dealers; it posed a formidable challenge to the entire mini-vehicle industry's distribution model. Its introduction at the meeting sparked an uproar among the attendees, instigating dramatically varied reactions. Some dealers were rendered speechless by the surprise, standing dumbfounded; others, their faces drained of color, resorted to nervously smoking, while a few were seen frantically making phone calls, perhaps seeking advice or sharing their astonishment.

Amid the dealers' turmoil at the meeting, a broader narrative unfolded—a significant transformation within the Chinese automotive industry's sales channels. This change had been set in motion back in 1997, with the establishment of the FAW-Volkswagen sales company, marking the onset of manufacturers creating their own marketing systems, a significant transition toward manufacturers assuming control over their sales rights[1]. The year 1999 emerged as a watershed moment for China's automobile sales network. It was then that the Japanese automaker Honda, stepping in to take over the ailing French brand Peugeot, established a joint venture with

---

① Li An'ding. *A Tale of Cars in China: 30 Years, from Start to Fast Lane*[M]. SDX Joint Publishing Company, 2017, 224.

Guangzhou Automobile Group. Honda implemented an aggressive new product marketing strategy in China, decisively assuming the substantial debts of Guangzhou Peugeot, a strategic trade-off for recouping the time lost due to its initial underestimation of the Chinese market. Despite being a late entrant, Honda acted with remarkable agility and innovation. Guangzhou Honda promptly launched the Accord, the first model synchronized with its Japanese release—a groundbreaking move that marked the first simultaneous global market launch in China since the 1984 Volkswagen joint venture. In tandem with this launch, Guangzhou Honda introduced the 4S store model to the Chinese market, an integrated approach encompassing vehicle sales, spare parts, after-sales service, and customer feedback surveys. This model revolutionized the car-buying experience in China, offering an unprecedented level of service and engagement. The notion that "Cars can actually be sold like this!" resonated profoundly, and the Chinese automotive industry was quick to acknowledge the potential of this approach. The 4S store model became a blueprint for the industry, gaining rapid adoption and emulation across the market.

The stark contrast highlighted the decline of the traditional and cumbersome sales model employed by automotive joint ventures. This conventional approach typically involved mechanical and electrical companies, equipment companies, and subsidiaries of transportation departments, all operating under a centralized purchasing and sales system. However, the efficacy of this model in invigorating the sales force proved lacking, and this inflexibility of the traditional sales system and the operational challenges it presented had not gone unnoticed. Astute industry observers had increasingly recognized the inherent limitations and inefficiencies of this approach.

Liuzhou Wuling's audacious decision to disrupt the entrenched consignment sales model to "sell first, pay later" mirrored the evolving landscape of the automotive industry. This leap into uncharted territory was not met with unanimous resistance. After all, the industry was in the midst of a significant overhaul, fueled by an influx of foreign capital and a continuous stream of innovative ideas. These transformative waves frequently jolted industry insiders, igniting a fiery mix of adventure, passion, and exploration in the realm of automotive sales. Dealership network investors found themselves navigating a landscape shrouded in uncertainty, searching for viable new distribution models amid this evolution. In the face of initial skepticism within the dealer community, some leading dealers, such as Guangdong Materials Group Corporation, proactively responded, taking the initiative to embrace the outright purchase marketing model, setting a precedent for others to follow.

In anticipation of this fundamental shift, Wuling had already been proactively engaging with several key dealers, initiating discussions to facilitate a seamless transition. To incentivize and support this significant change, Wuling introduced policy incentives, enhancing the appeal of the proposition for dealers. This strategic move represented a bold experiment for both Wuling and its dealers.

"The first crab might be daunting to try, but the rest prove to be a treat." The pioneering role adopted by major dealers set a precedent, triggering a domino effect within the industry. Once these leading dealers demonstrated success and confidence in the new model, many others, after careful consideration, decided to follow in their footsteps.

In this dynamic of change, it was the brave who led the charge, taking the first bold steps. Those more cautious in nature soon followed suit, while the timid either remained static or fell behind. It was during this pivotal meeting in Jinan that Liuzhou Wuling successfully solidified its payment-before-delivery sales settlement model.

The meeting in Jinan, where the payment-before-delivery model was established, became a seminal moment in the annals of mini-vehicle industry's marketing. In industries like automobile manufacturing, the daily determination of production quantities is often enmeshed in complex logic. Within the traditional dealership model, manufacturers, even if seeing through a telescope, metaphorically speaking, struggled to discern the precise moment when production would translate into revenue. Therefore, this pivotal meeting marked a paradigm shift, allowing manufacturers to step to the other side of this metaphorical lens. Instead of adhering to the conventional approach, production decisions could now be more closely aligned with dealers' actual sales volumes. This transformative change ushered in a departure from years spent pursuing quantity expansion, often clouded by sales confusion, toward a more clear-sighted approach. OEMs could now plan their production schedules with greater certainty and precision, a significant leap forward in aligning production with market demand.

Like hidden mountain peaks emerging from deep clouds and the growing sound of a river as its waters swell, the 1999 Jinan Meeting quietly marked a watershed moment in China's mini-vehicle sales market. This pivotal gathering set a precedent, sparking a swift and widespread shift across the entire mini-vehicle industry. The Jinan Meeting became an exemplar, mirroring the influential impact of Guangzhou Honda's introduction of the 4S store model, infusing new dynamism into the already rapidly evolving automotive sector. The dawn of an era where dealership networks, predominantly run by private enterprises and embracing outright purchase models, was now within sight. Sales channels, rejuvenated and empowered, began to exude newfound vigor, poised to cater to the burgeoning demands of an eager consumer base.

3.8 Forging Wuling's Manufacturing DNA

The Golden Autumn Campaign served as a pivotal counteroffensive, fortified by the groundwork laid by earlier reform initiatives under the banner of "Reshaping the Mindset First". In this strategic drive to sell products at reduced prices, it became imperative for the company to avoid incurring substantial losses. This scenario transformed into a test for manufacturing prowess, with Liuzhou Wuling's keen understanding of the value of low-cost manufacturing as a critical advantage in the competition.

Amidst this crucial phase, despite exploring various external financing measures, Wuling's primary goal remained centered on enhancing its manufacturing system. Emphasizing "financial wisdom before capital", the company recognized that creating a competitive manufacturing system necessitated a fundamental shift in mindset.

Wuling took a decisive step by establishing a dedicated management group, termed "Lean Production Wuling-ization", spearheaded by Yao Zuoping, who served as the head of the procurement department at the time. The choice of this adapted terminology unmistakably signaled Liuzhou Wuling's determination to assimilate and internalize external manufacturing concepts, tailoring them to fit their unique operations.

Following its establishment, the primary mission of the management team was a meticulous analysis of over 360 components comprising GM's global manufacturing system (GMS). Their efforts were concentrated on 5 core principles of lean manufacturing: continuous improvement, standardization, built in quality, short lead time, and people involvement. To facilitate this, the team undertook the substantial task of translating the GMS manual from English to Chinese, and compiled approximately one million words over the course of a month, culminating in a comprehensive educational resource for the Lean Production Wuling-ization.

In their quest to master lean production, Liuzhou Wuling embraced a guiding principle of "read with focus, apply with precision, and learn and generalize", catalyzing a top-down, inclusive learning wave among all employees. It began with a deep, focused engagement with literature, where the aim was not just to read but to unearth transformative insights, followed by application of these insights with precision in the real world, transforming them into tangible Wuling initiatives. This process transcended mere theoretical critique or commentary; it was about real-time, continuous enhancement during practical application. The final stage, "learn and generalize", involved extrapolating broader lessons from specific examples and critically evaluating the learning material to sidestep potential pitfalls. This iterative cycle of reading, applying, and generalizing steadily honed Liuzhou Wuling's prowess in execution, translating theory into effective practice.

The implementation of lean production at Liuzhou Wuling began as a pilot on select production lines. Previously, worker assessments relied on piece-rate systems, lacking collaboration between upstream and downstream processes, and workers were only responsible for completing their individual tasks, resulting in a chaotic workshop environment with scattered parts. This disorganization made delivery and collection akin to navigating a maze, often leading to significant delays. However, the introduction of lean production methods ushered in a transformative era. Assembly lines were implemented in stages, aligning upstream and downstream piece-rate systems, and, miraculously, the once cluttered corridors began to clear. However, this transformation faced resistance. Some veteran workers, accustomed to setting their own pace, found the uniform rhythm of the assembly line constraining. In response, management took decisive action, offering seniority buy-outs to some long-standing employees, particularly those most resistant, who eventually departed from their roles. Through these challenging yet necessary changes, the lean production method cemented its place in Liuzhou Wuling, albeit not without its costs.

Embracing the lean production model, Liuzhou Wuling committed unwaveringly to this course. In a decisive move, they democratized the learning process, allowing every employee to understand the overarching strategy. Starting in May 2000, the company embarked on a substantial educational initiative, organizing a series of training sessions for over 70 middle and senior managers and key business personnel at SAIC-GM and Delphi Automotive Systems. The first cohort, comprising almost the entire middle management team, participated in an intensive two-week training program at SAIC-GM, focusing on GMS as a model of lean production excellence. In his parting address, Shen Yang underscored the significance of this educational endeavor, emphasizing its unprecedented scale for middle-level managers. He stated, "Never before has our company sent such a multitude of middle managers for training. Why this unprecedented move? It is because transformation demands learning. By juxtaposing others' strengths against our own, we pave our way toward change."

The successful execution of any crucial strategic initiative starts with what can be termed "mindset permeation" among middle and senior management.

Following the completion of training for middle-level managers, Liuzhou Wuling advanced to the next phase: educating grassroots leaders, including section chiefs and instructors. These individuals were organized into three separate groups and sent to Shanghai for training. Unlike their counterparts in middle management, these grassroots leaders were tasked with the mission of absorbing and then transferring the principles and methodologies of lean production back to Wuling. Over the course of a month, they immersed themselves deeply in various workshops and sections at SAIC-GM, actively engaging in questioning and exploration with a keen focus on grasping the true essence of lean practices.

For the employees sent for training, the experience was akin to unexpectedly beholding a radiant starlit sky upon opening a skylight in the dead of the night. Brimming with excitement and newfound insights, many of them, upon returning, headed straight to the office with their luggage, bypassing even a brief stop at home. Their eagerness to share their acquired knowledge and experiences and to discuss their renewed motivation for a "re-venture" within the company was evident.

Armed with an abundance of theoretical resources and the fervent commitment of the lean production core team, Liuzhou Wuling launched an extensive training program for its entire staff. Following thorough internal reviews and trial lectures, a comprehensive company-wide training focusing on lean production concepts commenced in June 2001. The training center buzzed with activity, concurrently hosting ten classes, each spanning a duration of ten days. Central to the training curriculum were pivotal elements, including the company's culture, the fundamental principles of lean production, and the development of standardized operation sheets.

Amidst this dynamic wave of learning, the boundary between life and work blurred, as both were united by a shared thirst for knowledge. This fervor led Liuzhou Wuling to progressively implement a "5+1" model, where employees worked for five days and dedicated one day each week exclusively to training. Nestled within the factory's confines, the training center buzzed with constant activity, and in this environment, everyone took on dual roles—both as a learner and an instructor. From this pool of engaged participants, exceptional individuals were identified and honored as the "Top Eight Trainers".

As the entire workforce of Liuzhou Wuling immersed themselves in training, a parallel process unfolded: the absorption and integration of new concepts to devise a production and manufacturing model tailored specifically for the company. The management team of the Lean Production Wuling-ization launched a pilot program, carefully selecting a particular team and section within the final assembly workshop. The approach was methodical, starting from the most fundamental unit—the operator workstation. Here, the focus was on implementing effective on-site 5S management practices and identifying the seven wastes of lean production[①].

In the pilot section, a new initiative was launched to create their own "balance wall", entailing a thorough analysis of critical operational aspects such as safety, personnel, quality, efficiency, and cost, leading to the inception of Wuling's first section-level business plan deployment (BPD) management. Section leaders adopted a hands-on, meticulous approach, using stopwatches to time the production process at each workstation and meticulously recording the duration of every movement and assembly task. These measures were crucial for understanding and quantifying the workflow. Furthermore, leaders replicated these tasks beyond the production line to master the assembly line's rhythm, repeating them 20 times for proficiency. Upon achieving mastery, they established an average time for each task, setting it as the standard operation time.

During this critical phase, the formulation of the *Workstation Operation Standardization Manual* marked a significant milestone, primarily attributed to the unwavering commitment and extended efforts of dedicated workshop section chiefs and engineers, who not only established but continually refined operational standards and manuals for their colleagues. Faced with limited technological resources and the absence of computers in the workshops, they conscientiously drafted the manuals by hand, detailing each step and sketching every procedure. While these initial versions were rudimentary, they encapsulated a wealth of knowledge ready to be learned, absorbed, and integrated into daily operations. To sustain the momentum of the Lean

---

① The 5S management model, a cornerstone of modern enterprise management, encompasses five key principles: sort, set in order, shine, standardize, and sustain. Whereas the seven wastes of lean production include overproduction, waiting, transportation, motion, inventory, overprocessing, and defects.

Production Wuling-ization and monitor its progress, regular updates were solicited from each operational area.

In an environment charged with mutual benchmarking and competition, the workshop, initially a single section, thrived on the drive to keep up and avoid falling behind. This atmosphere, fueled by lean production methods seen at SAIC-GM, spurred a significant transformation. The assembly line expanded into multiple sections, each incorporating the Andon system, a key tool in lean manufacturing. Teams in the pilot section's workshop adopted a proactive and cooperative stance, forming groups to independently handle tasks like developing, wiring, crafting light boxes, routing cables, and installing speakers, aiming to build a basic yet functional Andon system from scratch. While this system might not have matched the intricacy of more advanced versions at every workstation, it operated effectively. Concurrently, the concept of section parks and a formal pre-shift meeting system were developed and integrated, becoming indispensable elements of the Lean Production Wuling-ization process.

Across the factory, a dynamic and organic trend emerged as frontline team members naturally coalesced into various teams, each concentrating on different aspects of lean manufacturing, such as value streams, 5S principles, and pull systems. This self-organization not only signaled an empowering shift within the workforce but also unleashed formidable potential as teams applied their newly acquired knowledge. Given their momentum and enthusiasm for lean principles, it seemed challenging to halt this advancing torrent of learning.

During a pivotal period when Liuzhou Wuling's fragmented production process management no longer aligned with the company's evolving needs, a digital transformation became imperative, leading to the creation of the Wuling Automobile Manufacturing Information Management System. This significant project involved active participation and oversight from top management, including Shen Yang, Yao Zuoping, and Wei Hongwen. Their commitment to innovation extended to external collaboration, notably with Wuhan University of Technology, and consultations with retired former plant manager Ding Shu. After thorough discussions, Yao Zuoping proposed a nuanced informatization strategy, integrating electronic key nodes with excellent employee management to blend human experience with critical operational points, creating a synergistic knowledge system. This approach, inspired by the Toyota Production System's *Jidoka*, which combines automation with human input, aimed to embed human expertise into the information management system at crucial production control points.

As Liuzhou Wuling navigated the early stages of its fragmented manufacturing system, adopting a "semi-informatization" strategy became crucial. This approach enabled staff to effectively integrate with both the information and manufacturing systems, fostering a more cohesive and interconnected working environment.

At this juncture in their journey, Liuzhou Wuling's adaptation of lean production was still in its nascent stages, characterized more by the application of various lean management tools than a cohesive system. The philosophy of lean production had indeed ignited a spark within the company, propelling them into a phase of exploration and discovery. Wuling was actively engaged in the process of identifying its unique DNA and establishing a solid framework for its emerging manufacturing system, soon to be distinguished by its commitment to low-cost, minimalism, and differentiation.

As changes unfolded beyond the factory walls, the automotive industry's landscape underwent unpredictable shifts. Positioned at the lower end of the value chain, the mini-vehicle market was closely connected to consumer purchasing power, yet forecasting the direction of these elements proved challenging. At the onset of the Ninth Five-Year Plan in 1996, authorities set a target of 1.2 million sedans and 150,000 minivans by 2000. However, by the end of this period, sedan production fell short of 600,000 units, significantly lower than projected, while minivan production unexpectedly soared to over 400,000 units. This stark contrast in outcomes revealed a miscalculation by policymakers who had overestimated consumer purchasing power and failed to accurately gauge the importance of minivans in the rural and urban fringe economies.

The real dynamism resided in the heart of the populace, and minivans emerged as the ideal conduits for this vibrant energy. In regions momentarily neglected by strategic planning, it was the grassroots level that throbbed with a robust and lively spirit.

3.9 The Stone of Burden and the Sword of Peril

In 1999, Liuzhou Wuling witnessed a remarkable financial turnaround. Despite a 20% drop in production and sales volumes compared to 1998, the company's profitability soared by 30%, and accounts receivable plummeted to RMB 400 million, marking the beginning of a significant upturn in the company's financial health.

During a dinner hosted by Shen Yang for local dealers in Wuhan, an unexpected call disrupted the ambiance. A finance staff member's voice, tinged with urgency, came through the phone, "We've got cash now, Mr. Shen, our account's finally in the green!" This news struck Shen Yang with overwhelming joy, tears streaming down his face. The room lapsed into stunned silence, the attendees unaware of the reason behind his emotional response. Reinvigorated by the news, Shen Yang, who had been drinking conservatively, filled his glass and jubilantly announced to everyone, "Let's have three more toasts!" The tables erupted in cheers, yet none could grasp the depth of emotion stirring in their leader—a sentiment born from the realization that after so many years, their company was finally seeing positive cash flow on the books.

The year was coming to a close, a period marked by prosperity and contentment. The company found itself in a stable financial position, with no need to borrow funds for payroll, and employees were seeing a notable rise in their earnings. This financial upswing significantly bolstered everyone's confidence in the company. The favorable outcomes of the Golden Autumn Campaign had firmly established the new leadership team's standing. Among Wuling's employees, there was an air of celebration, reminiscent of the vigorous vitality seen in a child's new teeth emerging through the gums—a symbol of growth and new beginnings.

Between 1999 and 2000, Liuzhou Wuling, adopting a dynamic and proactive approach in the highly competitive mini-vehicle market, witnessed a transformative period characterized by a series of strategic shifts and innovations. The company initiated organizational reforms and process reengineering, embraced the principles of Lean Production Wuling-ization and dedicated itself to eliminating all forms of waste. In procurement, innovative methods such as the "Three Comparisons" method, complemented by integrated management and the "overflow payment method", were introduced. The Golden Autumn Campaign represented another strategic milestone. On the quality front, achieving ISO9001 quality management system certification marked a significant step, as did being recognized as a national enterprise technology center. These initiatives were a tangible embodiment of the state-owned enterprise reform strategy of "Excel, Empower, then Enlarge".

The emergence of innovative ideas has the potential to dismantle entrenched structures of the past. This unprecedented self-reinvention at Liuzhou Wuling brought relief to many, yet a persistent sense of crisis continued to overshadow the management team. Despite Wuling's considerable scale, inefficiencies remained glaringly apparent throughout its operations. For Shen Yang, leading the only major automotive company without a joint venture and with an annual production exceeding 100,000 vehicles felt like precariously balancing atop a fragile mountain of eggs. The impressive edifice they had constructed always seemed on the brink of collapse. Shen Yang keenly felt the burden of this responsibility. He lived under the constant shadow of a metaphorical sword, a perpetual threat to the stability and future of the company. Implementing internal management reforms merely removed the stone pressing upon his heart, but the sword hanging overhead cast a far greater shadow over the company's future.

What, then, is this looming sword?

Chapter 4 The Whirlwind of Joint Ventures
2001–2002

4.1 Joint Ventures: A Race Against Time

The year 1998 marked a pivotal juncture for the rise of China's manufacturing sector, spurred by the eruption of the Asian financial crisis that served as a catalyst for a substantial realignment within the global automotive industry. Consequently, the prevailing global manufacturing landscape began to reorient itself, seeking new avenues for value creation. In the aftermath of the crisis, the global manufacturing sector found itself grappling not with a fear for capital, but rather a surfeit for it. Capital, in conjunction with established manufacturers, swiftly reasserted dominance over the global industrial order. This shift also prompted a reassessment of the effectiveness of Korean automotive development model, which had previously enjoyed considerable success. Since 1962, Republic of Korea had systematically nurtured its automotive prowess[1], resulting in the establishment of the widely acknowledged Korean Model. Underpinned by the unique mantra of "National Cars for National Pride" and bolstered by extensive government backing, Republic of Korea had ascended to the position of the world's fifth-largest automobile producer by 1997. However, the Asian financial crisis necessitated a recalibration of strategies within the Korean automotive sector. Consequently, Daewoo was acquired by GM, Samsung Motors became part of Renault-Nissan, and Kia joined the Hyundai Motor Group. These mergers and acquisitions orchestrated by major global automobile manufacturers effectively eradicated some of the industry's relatively smaller competitors. Amidst this shifting landscape, attention turned to the newly accessible Chinese market, which emerged as a fertile ground for global automotive players to pursue value creation and market expansion.

---

① Meng Sizong. *Innovating the Soul of China's Automotive Industry*[M]. Beijing Institute of Technology Press, 2007, 27.

In 1998, Liuzhou Wuling found itself besieged by a cascade of challenges. The rise in steel costs, coupled with price reductions to maintain market share, was eroding the profits of this four-decade-old state-owned enterprise. Dwindling cash flows further impeded the upgrade of equipment, entrenching the company in a vicious cycle. Among China's top four mini-vehicle manufacturers, Changhe, Hafei, and Chang'an—all backed by military industrial groups—stood robust, having already undergone shareholding reforms and embraced foreign investments, thereby gradually solidifying their competitive edge. Notably, Jiangxi Changhe pioneered this approach by forming a joint venture with Japan's Suzuki in 1995, resulting in Changhe Suzuki. With robust support from the Ministry of Aviation Industry, it vigorously expanded its mini-vehicle division. In stark contrast, Liuzhou Wuling, lacking substantial investment for nearly a decade, found itself trailing with antiquated car models and inflated costs. The imperative to secure capital and break free from this dire strait had never been more pressing.

Liuzhou Wuling stood at a pivotal juncture with two strategic choices: either pursue a public listing to facilitate fundraising and transformation, or attract foreign capital for joint ventures. During this period, opportunities for A-share listings were limited, rendering B-shares the more viable option. The trail had been blazed by the JMC model, where Jiangling Motors Corporation (JMC) had issued B-shares, welcoming Ford Motor Company as a strategic ally. This alliance did more than just inject vital capital; it also introduced essential technology, culminating in the debut of the JMC Ford Transit, a notable commercial vehicle model.

Liuzhou Wuling also strategized to float 120 million shares in the B-share market, with an eye on drawing foreign investors. In February 1998, the China Securities Regulatory Commission unveiled a roster of 18 pre-selected B-share companies, a list that included Liuzhou Wuling. Furthering its efforts, the company hosted a roadshow in Hong Kong. However, securing capital in the B-share market, particularly for the automotive sector at that time, proved to be a daunting challenge. Notably, automotive giants from Japan, the United States, and Europe displayed a marked reluctance to engage in collaboration.

While Liuzhou Wuling navigated these challenges, a fresh tempest shook the market, further complicating the timing. The escalating Asian financial crisis swayed securities brokers to conclude that it was not the ideal moment for Liuzhou Wuling to go public. Additionally, the limited volume of Liuzhou Wuling's floating shares in the proposed listing made it less appealing as an investment option, even if it had proceeded with the public offering.

Ultimately, Liuzhou Wuling's endeavors to list on the B-share market ended in disappointment, culminating in a failure.

The Golden Autumn Campaign, launched during the inaugural year of the new leadership, offered a brief respite for Liuzhou Wuling, rapidly enhancing the reputation of its management team. However, the company faced challenges extending beyond mere financial constraints. Government directives also presented obstacles, as the growth cycle of a business often did not align with the tenure of local officials. Local governments' regional industrial planning meant that leaders of local state-owned enterprises had to adeptly navigate both market dynamics and governmental policies. In 1997, with the agricultural vehicle market booming and an acute demand for transportation in rural areas, some voices within the People's Government of Guangxi Zhuang Autonomous Region suggested that Liuzhou Wuling should pivot toward agriculture, proposing the development of vehicles capable of generating electricity and milling rice at night, deeming it the appropriate direction. Meanwhile, the Liuzhou Municipal Government proposed that Liuzhou Wuling should venture into diesel engines to cater to the extensive rural market. However, pursuing the agricultural tractor route would have represented a regressive step for Liuzhou Wuling, akin to turning back the clock and retracing steps from over a decade ago. Decisions driven solely by the whims of these officials and prevailing uncertainties could have plunged the enterprise into a quagmire. In this context, the embrace of a modern enterprise system became crucial. For local state-owned enterprises, the concept of forming joint ventures assumed a newfound, profound significance.

The trio of internal institutional reforms spearheaded by Liuzhou Wuling, alongside the reformation of the supplier value chain, appeared remarkably successful, fostering a sense of accomplishment among some employees. However, Shen Yang, Liuzhou Wuling's general manager, was acutely aware of the company's deficiencies in technology, capital, and a modern enterprise framework—factors that cast a shadow over its future. Recognizing the urgency of a transformative approach, Shen Yang saw joint ventures as the most promising avenue at the time. Having risen through the ranks alongside Liuzhou Wuling, he harbored no grand illusions about the extent of capital support joint ventures could offer. Instead, he was driven by two fundamental objectives: instituting a modern enterprise system and keeping the original brand. Confident in Liuzhou Wuling's state-owned heritage and the competence of its team, Shen Yang was convinced that the team had the potential to be unbeatable under a modern enterprise structure.

Such opportunities, in reality, were readily available.

The year 1999 was pivotal in the evolution of China's automotive industry, marking a period of significant interaction and collaboration between domestic and international auto players. There was a notable transition in China's policy management concerning foreign capital, resulting in heightened international interest in the Chinese automotive sector, unprecedented in its scale. The strategies of global automotive giants in China were experiencing a crucial transformation. Previously, these strategies often hinged on technology transfers and importing components, primarily to support the production of older car models. The underlying logic was straightforward: why introduce newer models when the existing ones could still be exploited?[①] This approach, essentially capitalizing on past successes, resulted in outdated models such as the Santana, Jetta, and Citroën Fukang—long since phased out in their home markets—dominating the Chinese market for over a decade. However, as the dawn of the 21st century approached, the stage was set for an imminent and radical transformation, much like a spark ready to ignite a tinderbox. Concurrently, this period marked the ascent of domestic brands, heralding a new era in China's automotive saga.

The commencement of the largest global division of labor benefits marked a pivotal moment, effectively initiating a transformative phase in automotive history. As the portals to the racing tracks of the new century slowly unfurled, it became evident that not all contenders were equipped to partake. Automotive joint ventures, akin to the first spring rain bringing a refreshing breeze, offered solutions that went beyond just addressing locational disadvantages; they provided an opportunity to develop a more flexible decision-making system. These challenges, which only joint ventures could resolve, had long loomed over Liuzhou Wuling's head like the sword of Damocles, representing both a constant threat and a potential path to transformation.

For Liuzhou Wuling, embroiled in crisis, failing to seize this window of opportunity for joint ventures might equate to forever forfeiting the chance to integrate into the global market. Often, capitalizing on historical opportunities boils

---

① China Association of Automobile Manufacturers. *30 Years of Reform and Opening-up in China's Automobile Industry (1978–2008): A Retrospective and Outlook*[M]. China Logistics Publishing House, 2009, 151.

down to a single, pivotal decision—one that depends heavily on the foresight and determination of key individuals.

4.2 A Half-Torn Business Card and Three "In-Laws"

Entering the purview of Liuzhou Wuling was GM, the United States' largest automobile company, and at that time, Liuzhou Wuling's most coveted prospective joint venture partner. During the early months of 1999, at the Guangxi–Shanghai Investment Conference, Shen Yang, recently appointed as Liuzhou Wuling's general manager, encountered representatives from GM China. Their interaction was both harmonious and engaging, revealing substantial common ground between the two entities.

During that period, GM, leading the global automotive industry, placed considerable emphasis on securing market share. In China, only a select few automotive manufacturers boasted an annual production exceeding 100,000 units. The aviation system, inclusive of the Aviation Industry Corporation of China (AVIC)[①], which owned the Changhe and Songhuajiang brands, was a formidable entity with an output of around 230,000 vehicles, positioning it as a major player closely trailing SAIC Motor, FAW Group, and Dongfeng Motor Corporation. Chang'an, another frontrunner in mini-vehicle sales, had already established a joint venture with Japan's Suzuki. Given GM's stake in Suzuki, this presented an advantageous position for partnering with Chang'an. However, Ford, GM's long-standing rival, was also eager to form a joint venture in China and had set its sights on Chang'an. Meanwhile, the Tianjin Daihatsu minivan was flourishing, and Ford was collaborating with Jiangling Motors, intensifying GM's sense of urgency. At this juncture, multinational sedan companies not yet present in China were stepping up their entry efforts. Key partnerships had been forged: Ford with Chang'an, Hyundai with BAIC Group, Dongfeng with Nissan, BMW with Brilliance Auto Group, and DaimlerChrysler with BAIC Group. The Chinese automotive landscape was a hive of activity and negotiations, with joint venture strategies rapidly taking shape. Global car brands, invigorated by the market's potential, were as active as bees in spring, each seeking

---

① China Association of Automobile Manufacturers. China Automotive Industry Advisory Committee, *History of China Automotive Industry, 1991–2010*[M]. China Machine Press, 2014, 106.

new opportunities. Simultaneously, GM was in discussions with GAC Group to initiate the Opel project. However, due to GAC Group's past unsuccessful partnership with Peugeot, the Opel project faced an abrupt end. Considering multiple factors, GM found Liuzhou Wuling, with its annual sales exceeding 100,000 units, an enticing option for expanding its foothold in the Chinese market, potentially increasing its market share by a swift 3 percentage points.

Within the echelons of GM, a schism of opinions emerged. Some executives held the view that venturing into mini-vehicle models deviated from the company's overarching strategy. In contrast, GM's then president was in firm support of the perspectives put forward by the head of GM China, believing that strategic positioning was paramount, especially in light of the burgeoning automotive market in China's third and fourth-tier cities. Rick Wagoner, the CEO at the time, along with John F. Smith Jr., the then chairman of the board of directors, faced intense scrutiny from Wall Street analysts. Despite this, they staunchly defended their investment in China's automotive sector. Armed with a profound understanding of the Chinese market's potential, they drew comparisons to Poland, where, despite a population of less than 40 million, sedan sales in 1999 reached 500,000 units. In contrast, China's coastal population alone accounted for 400 million people, yet sedan sales were only marginally higher at 650,000 units[1]. This disparity highlighted China as an immense, untapped market. GM's leadership astutely recognized that the ascendancy of the Chinese automotive century necessitated a focus on the domestic market—a signal they captured and held in high regard during their strategic deliberations.

GM harbored an additional strategic ambition: to foray into the realm of low-cost automobiles, a move requiring meticulous consideration in the global automotive context. Liuzhou Wuling, with its established strengths, presented itself as an ideal foundation for this venture. The mini-vehicle segment, an unoccupied niche in GM's product portfolio, garnered heightened attention during this period as international manufacturers scrutinized every segment of the Chinese automobile market with precision. GM, already engaged in the production of mid-to-high-end sedans in Shanghai, and multi-purpose vehicles like the Jinbei in Shenyang, Liaoning Province, acknowledged that incorporating mini-vehicles into their lineup would enable comprehensive coverage across all vehicle categories.

---

[1] Li An'ding. *A Tale of Cars in China: 30 Years, from Start to Fast Lane*[M]. SDX Joint Publishing Company, 2017, 126.

April 1999 marked the unfolding of a pivotal meeting as Shen Yang, armed with thorough preparation and determination, journeyed to Shanghai for a significant rendezvous with Lawrence B. Zahner, the then president of GM China. Clutching a thick ledger outlining Liuzhou Wuling's future development plans and equipped with a compelling cache of arguments, he was ready for an exhaustive dialogue. Lawrence B. Zahner, renowned for his eloquence and profound grasp of cultural nuances, had amassed a wealth of experience in bridging Eastern and Western cultural divides, which was particularly evident from his involvement in the initial joint venture discussions between SAIC Motor and GM. This background naturally set high expectations for the meeting with Shen Yang. However, the conversation took an unexpected turn mere minutes after it began, with Lawrence B. Zahner reaching into his pocket, signaling an unforeseen twist in the discussion.

Taken aback by Lawrence B. Zahner's unexpected gesture, Shen Yang braced for the possibility that their meeting might be cut short—a prospect he found disconcerting. However, Lawrence B. Zahner's actions took an unanticipated turn. Rather than an abrupt dismissal, he produced a slim business card. With a tone of candid sincerity, he addressed Shen Yang, "Shen, we've conducted a comprehensive evaluation of your company. You can jot down your valuation, and we'll consider purchasing it." In a symbolic gesture, he then tore the business card in half, offering one fragment to Shen Yang. Holding the other piece, he briefly brandished it before Shen Yang's eyes and then tucked it back into his pocket, remarking quietly, "If we close this deal, we'll reunite these halves". In that moment, Shen Yang managed to maintain his outward composure, but internally, he was awash with a torrent of emotions. The fragment he held was more than just a piece of card; it symbolized a potential gateway to a monumental partnership.

The prospect of establishing a joint venture with a global automotive titan like GM necessitated expansive and supportive involvement from the local government. The People's Government of Guangxi Zhuang Autonomous Region had long been committed to actively attracting foreign investment, driven not only merely by the desire for capital but also by a strategic goal to refine and upgrade the local industrial framework. From the onset of economic reforms until 1999, Liuzhou had not seen investment from any Fortune Global 500 company, a stark contrast to Shanghai, where over 400 such corporations had set up operations. Recognizing this disparity and the opportunity at hand, the autonomous regional government convened a special meeting with a clear agenda: to encourage an open-minded approach and collective effort in welcoming GM into the region.

As May 1999 drew to a close, Liuzhou welcomed its rainy season, the air thick with growing humidity. Amid this climate, a palpable sense of excitement and joy permeated the atmosphere at Liuzhou Wuling. The workforce buzzed with anticipation, eagerly awaiting the arrival of distinguished visitors. This excitement stemmed from developments that had unfolded rapidly since Shen Yang's meeting with Lawrence B. Zahner in Shanghai. Less than a fortnight after their pivotal discussion, a delegation from GM China made their way to Liuzhou, marking the initiation of official negotiations for the joint venture, a significant milestone for Liuzhou Wuling. In a bid to expedite the process, an array of due diligence investigations was promptly launched, underlining the commitment to efficiency and speed.

The due diligence undertaken by GM spanned an extensive six months. This process went far beyond mere financial verification; it was akin to an in-depth professional management training for the team at Liuzhou Wuling. Initially taken aback and somewhat confounded by the breadth and depth of materials requested by GM, the management at Liuzhou Wuling grappled with a lack of requisite financial data and struggled to furnish the detailed written documentation demanded. This exhaustive and rigorous investigation laid bare the inner mechanisms of Liuzhou Wuling, serving as a revelatory experience for its management. It brought about a profound realization of the importance of managing enterprise data with meticulous precision. For the team at Liuzhou Wuling, this experience was transformative, much like a person who, after a long journey devoid of water, finally submerges in a hot bath, emerging refreshed and renewed.

Despite the initial rapport and enthusiasm surrounding the potential partnership, certain regulatory constraints loomed large and could not be overlooked. In accordance with China's automotive industry policy at the time, a foreign enterprise was allowed to establish joint ventures with a maximum of two domestic companies. GM was already engaged in two such projects in China—one with SAIC Motor in Shanghai and another with Jinbei GM in Shenyang. Consequently, due to these existing commitments and in compliance with the stipulated policy, it was unfeasible for GM to initiate an additional joint venture with Liuzhou Wuling.

The adage "where there's a will, there's a way" held true in the case of GM and Liuzhou Wuling. Despite the stringent regulatory landscape, both entities displayed adaptability and creativity in finding a viable solution. After thorough deliberations,

GM China decided to venture into Liuzhou Wuling's management sphere through a stock acquisition strategy, which involved acquiring a 34% stake in Liuzhou Wuling, equating to an investment of USD 90 million. For GM, holding a 33% stake in a subsidiary enabled it to consolidate its financial statements within the parent company's automotive industry system.

In July 1999, addressing the joint venture's identity complexities, Liuzhou Wuling Automobile Co., Ltd. was officially established. This new entity comprised the four essential workshops vital for car manufacturing: stamping, welding, painting, and assembly. The strategy, as per the joint venture negotiations, was to capitalize on the then-current "recovery growth" of the securities market, which entailed swiftly completing the prospectus and reporting processes, with the aim of securing a B-share listing by the end of 1999. Following this, GM would have the opportunity to subscribe to Liuzhou Wuling's B-shares, cementing their collaborative partnership.

It sounded like a perfectly crafted framework, a well-orchestrated strategy. However, before the B-share listing could come to fruition, it encountered a critical obstacle.

By the end of 1999, GM China's ambitious plan to acquire a stake in Liuzhou Wuling was vetoed by its Detroit headquarters. The decision rested on clear-cut reasoning: Liuzhou Wuling's profitability levels did not meet the standards set by GM. Additionally, GM did not have mini-car models in its portfolio, rendering it unable to support Liuzhou Wuling's product development endeavors.

Caught between policy constraints and the veto from GM headquarters, Liuzhou Wuling's aspirations for a foreign joint venture hit an impasse. Within a span of two years, the company's hopes for a B-share listing were not only dashed once but twice.

However, the industrious and pragmatic ethos of Liuzhou Wuling meant that they did not limit themselves to just one avenue. Concurrently with their efforts to forge ties with foreign investors, they were also exploring collaborations with domestic automotive powerhouses.

Dongfeng Motor Corporation, headquartered in Hubei, emerged as a prospective partner for Liuzhou Wuling. This potential for collaboration had deep roots, dating back to 1981 when Dongfeng entered into a joint venture with the Liuzhou Automobile Manufacturing Factory that developed and produced Guangxi's first vehicle, Liujiang cargo truck. This joint venture culminated in the establishment of Dongfeng Liuzhou Automobile Co., Ltd. in 1997, which laid the groundwork for a potential partnership.

Against the backdrop of this historical connection, the People's Government of Guangxi Zhuang Autonomous Region took proactive steps in early 1999 to facilitate potential collaboration between Liuzhou Wuling and Dongfeng. This collaboration, especially considering Dongfeng's expertise in sedan manufacturing, presented an opportunity for Liuzhou Wuling to venture into sedan production. However, the model offered by Dongfeng to Liuzhou was the Dongfeng Little Prince, a vehicle that fell short of the Renault models Liuzhou Wuling had aspired to introduce from France. Additionally, Dongfeng's proposition to relocate some of Liuzhou Wuling's mini-vehicle production to Shiyan in Hubei Province was met with resistance from Liuzhou's management team. How could they justify such a shift to their local employees, who had invested their labor and loyalty in the company? And how could the enterprise's roots, deeply embedded in Liuzhou's soil and nurtured with the sweat of generations, endure being uprooted halfway through their growth?

The prospect of relocating part of their operations felt like a betrayal of the legacy left by their predecessors.

Amid mounting pressure from various government entities, some of which were eager to witness the fruition of a joint venture, the management team at Liuzhou Wuling, directly involved in the negotiations, bore significant stress. Over the course of just a few months, the discussions spanned from Guangxi to Hubei, and ultimately to Beijing, involving a series of repetitive dialogues. These talks ranged from formal meetings at national ministries and high-level discussions in Wuhan to interactions at the Guangzhou Baiyun Hotel. Despite the nearly half-year of intense efforts, it seemed that the divergences were not converging toward resolution.

By May 1999, it became evident to both sides that the negotiations had reached an impasse. Despite hopes and encouragement from the municipal government, there was a unanimous consensus among the factory leaders opposing the signing of the agreement.

Local governments exert significant influence over the automobile manufacturing industry within their jurisdictions, posing unique challenges for entrepreneurs at local state-owned enterprises. Navigating this landscape requires astuteness and strategic finesse. Following the Central Government's 1998 initiative to alleviate the burdens on state-owned enterprises, local governments, eager to stimulate regional economies, have formed dynamic partnerships with entrepreneurs looking to inject vitality into their businesses. However, these collaborations involve nuanced, often unspoken, strategic games. These delicate maneuvers, which hinge on intentions and tactics, are pivotal in determining whether a company can reverse its fortunes. The intricate relationships between local governments and major corporations exemplify this dynamic. Instances such as the interactions between the Sanshui District Government and Jianlibao beverages, the Shunde District Government and Kelon refrigerators, and the subsequent development of the relationship between the Shenyang Municipal Government and Brilliance Auto Group, are emblematic of the ongoing fluctuations in the reform of state-owned enterprises.

The leadership at Liuzhou Wuling, although somewhat resolute, keenly sensed the urgency as time slipped away. Their options were dwindling rapidly, resembling a diminishing reservoir, highlighting the imminent crisis. The structure of China's automotive industry, known as the "Big Three, Small Three, Mini Two", was officially established as early as 1992[①]. This framework included the three major sedan manufacturers: FAW Group, Dongfeng, and SAIC Motor; three smaller manufacturers: Beijing Jeep Corporation, Tianjin Xiali, and Guangzhou Peugeot; and two mini-vehicle producers: Chang'an-Suzuki Alto and Yungque-Subaru, both military enterprises that had transitioned to mini-vehicle manufacturing and were key beneficiaries of government support. The pressures induced by policies were increasingly evident. Fuji Heavy Industries, for instance, had initially provided technology to Guizhou Aircraft Industry Corporation and by 1998, formalized a joint venture with them. In contrast, Liuzhou Wuling found itself isolated, like a lone wolf in the wilderness. The imperative to find a means of survival and growth for the company was immediate and critical.

Amidst the mounting pressure, the management team at Liuzhou Wuling explored the possibility of another domestic partner, SAIC Motor, for a joint venture. The industrial prowess of Shanghai Municipality had a longstanding impact on Liuzhou. Notably, Guangxi LiuGong Machinery had its origins in the Shanghai Huadong Steel Factory, and in 1960, several other factories had relocated from Shanghai to Liuzhou, encompassing industries such as knitting, enamelware, and towel manufacturing. Additionally, the collaborative bond between the two cities was further solidified by the partnership in the production of Forever bicycles. These stories, though gradually fading, lingered in the memories of some individuals. Parallel to the ongoing talks with GM, Liuzhou Wuling also harbored aspirations to

① China Association of Automobile Manufacturers. *30 Years of Reform and Opening-up in China's Automobile Industry (1978–2008): A Retrospective and Outlook*[M]. China Logistics Publishing House, 2009, 121.

leverage its relationship with GM to establish a collaboration with SAIC Motor.

In the strategic game of business, skillfully playing one's cards is crucial. Recognizing this, GM initiated efforts to encourage SAIC Motor to consider a collaboration with Liuzhou Wuling. However, at that time, SAIC Motor showed tepid interest in mini-vehicles, as their primary focus was on sedans and mid-to-high-end commercial vehicles, including models like the Regal, GL8, and Buick New Century. Despite their initial lack of interest in the mini-vehicle sector, SAIC Motor responded to GM's strong recommendation, dispatching a team of senior consultants to evaluate Liuzhou Wuling. During this inspection, the cohesive and spirited ethos of Liuzhou Wuling left a positive impression on the SAIC Motor experts.

In a situation akin to attempting to revive a seemingly lifeless endeavor, optimists at Liuzhou Wuling clung to a sliver of hope amid an apparently hopeless scenario, actively pursuing breakthroughs in their deadlock. They found themselves navigating between SAIC Motor and GM, diligently exploring avenues for collaboration. During this period, GM was engaged in dual discussions: on the one hand, they were in talks with Liuzhou Wuling regarding subscribing to the company's public shares, while on the other, negotiations were underway with SAIC Motor to establish a tripartite cooperation framework and formulate a viable plan for joint action.

With the veto of the B-share listing plan by GM headquarters, a more defined strategy began to take shape in early 2000. GM proposed an innovative approach that received active support from the People's Government of Guangxi Zhuang Autonomous Region: SAIC Motor would initially establish a joint venture with Liuzhou Wuling, with SAIC Motor as the majority stakeholder. Subsequently, this joint venture would partner with GM, transforming the bilateral collaboration to a Sino–Sino–Foreign tripartite model. Additionally, facilitated by high-level government communications, the Shanghai municipal government expressed its backing for SAIC Motor's venture into Guangxi to engage in this tripartite cooperation.

Throughout the tripartite negotiations, the most extensively discussed and revised document was the production plan, a pivotal document focused on strategizing the production output, starting from the existing capacity of 100,000 units and outlining a growth trajectory for future production. Ultimately, in a move marked by boldness, the parties agreed on an ambitious target: to escalate the annual sales volume to 300,000 units over the next decade. This twofold increase was the pinnacle of what the stakeholders envisioned for the future of the new joint venture. The substantial growth was set against the backdrop of Liuzhou Wuling being a regional enterprise situated in a relatively remote area, lacking a robust automotive industrial base, and grappling with limitations in transportation and talent. While GM acknowledged the importance of a comprehensive market landscape and strategic positioning, they appeared to maintain a cautious stance regarding Liuzhou Wuling's developmental prospects.

In March 2000, a significant revelation came to light through an interview with Xu Kuangdi, the then Mayor of Shanghai Municipality, on CCTV. He announced that SAIC Motor, Liuzhou Wuling, and GM were on the cusp of establishing a joint venture company, with an ambitious production target of 1 million units. At the time, such a target was considered astronomical, especially within the Chinese automotive market, where the total annual production hovered around just 2 million units.

The unexpected announcement from Shanghai Municipality regarding the joint venture, previously a closely guarded secret known only to a select few in management, caught many off guard. Employees of Liuzhou Wuling, engrossed in their daily production and sales efforts, were particularly surprised to learn that their leaders, while focused on boosting the company's operational performance, were also orchestrating a strategic endeavor on a much grander scale. This revelation led to a flurry of questions, especially given Liuzhou Wuling's remarkable performance improvement in 1999, leaving many wondering about the necessity for such a significant collaboration at a time when the company was already on a positive growth trajectory.

The announcement about the joint venture triggered a complex mix of emotions among those involved. Surprise, confusion, suspicion, worry, bewilderment, and even anger permeated the atmosphere, leading to unrest.

At the ideological and political work conference of Liuzhou Wuling held in April 2000, Shen Yang, having just returned from negotiations in Shanghai, proceeded directly to the meeting in Wuling Hotel's annex building, luggage in tow, to elucidate the significance of the tripartite joint venture to the employees.

In an effort to address employees' concerns, Liuzhou Wuling arranged for an economist to deliver an insightful lecture, who creatively depicted the domestic automotive landscape as a realm of "three big dogs, seven small dogs, and a pack of wild dogs". Here, the "three big dogs" symbolized the industry powerhouses—FAW Group, Dongfeng, and SAIC Motor; the "seven small dogs" referred to more formal, yet smaller manufacturers like Chang'an and Liuzhou Wuling, adept but not as dominant; and the "pack of wild dogs" represented the numerous small, disorganized entities with limited output scattered across the industry. The domestic automotive industry was generally disorganized and lacked significant scale. In contrast, foreign companies were likened to "wolves", far more formidable and organized. In this scenario, the smaller contenders, despite their agility and skill, could not stand alone against these wolves. The key to survival and resistance to market risks was in forming larger, more powerful alliances. For Liuzhou Wuling, then just a "small dog" in this grand scheme, facing the impact of the wolves after China's entry into the World Trade Organization (WTO) posed a daunting prospect. Their best strategy was to dance with the wolves—to collaborate and adapt, rather than risk being overrun in the automotive market.

Joint ventures emerged as the primary avenue for progress. In this tripartite partnership, SAIC Motor embodied an advanced cultural ethos, GM represented the pinnacle of productive forces, and Liuzhou Wuling symbolized the aspirations of the people—a fundamental bottom line that the management was determined to safeguard. This strategic approach was unequivocally considered the optimal path for Liuzhou Wuling's future. In pursuit of clarity and relatability, the management team diligently worked to demystify complex principles and make intricate concepts more accessible. Through persistent efforts in work mobilizations, they endeavored to enlighten employees about broader market trends and the critical choices confronting every enterprise.

4.3 The Widest Road Ever Crossed

Around the turn of the millennium, China was witnessing a significant wave of state-owned enterprise reform, coinciding with the impending opening of the door to the WTO. Amidst this transformative period, the People's Government of Guangxi Zhuang Autonomous Region was deeply engaged in formulating strategies to elevate the region's automotive industry, and one key focus laid on how prominent manufacturers in the area could integrate modern management systems and advanced technology.

Confronted with the proposition of a tripartite joint venture, the People's

Government of Guangxi Zhuang Autonomous Region demonstrated remarkable determination and courage, throwing its unwavering support behind Liuzhou Wuling in its endeavor to attract strategic investors. To maximize benefits for the local enterprise post-joint venture, officials from the regional government to the Liuzhou Municipal Committee played a pivotal role in the negotiation process. Eminent figures such as Wang Hanmin, then Member of the Standing Committee of the Party Committee of Guangxi Zhuang Autonomous Region and the Vice-Chairman of the People's Government of the Guangxi Zhuang Autonomous Region; Shen Beihai, then Secretary of Liuzhou Municipal Committee of the Communist Party of China and Director of the Standing Committee of Liuzhou Municipal People's Congress; and Wang Yuefei, then Member of the Standing Committee of the Party Committee of Liuzhou Municipality and Deputy Mayor of Liuzhou City, constituted the core team representing the government in the negotiations, during which they were consistently at the frontlines. During the most intense periods of negotiation, Wang Hanmin's commitment was particularly notable, necessitating frequent travels to Shanghai, sometimes as many as four times within a month. On one occasion, faced with overlapping commitments, he had to make a whirlwind trip to Shanghai for morning negotiations and return to Nanning in the afternoon. With no direct flights available at the time from Shanghai to Nanning, he had to fly to Guilin and then make the journey back to Nanning by road.

Throughout the negotiation process, the People's Government of Guangxi Zhuang Autonomous Region made a strategic and audacious decision: rather than rigidly fixating on shareholding proportions, their focus was on firmly establishing the automotive industry within the local region. This insightful approach played a key role in assuaging the concerns of the two major stakeholders, SAIC Motor and GM. In a pivotal move, the People's Government of Guangxi Zhuang Autonomous Region initially transferred most of the company's shares to SAIC Motor, in a non-compensatory allocation of state assets, while retaining only a minority equity stake for the local region. With SAIC Motor emerging as the controlling shareholder, they then strategically increased and expanded their shares under the pretext of technological upgrades within the newly established SAIC-Wuling company, which paved the way for bringing GM into the fold. This bold move toward mixed-ownership reform, exemplifying both strategic foresight and adaptability, was subsequently presented for approval to the then State Economic and Trade Commission.

On July 19, 2001, a pivotal asset transfer agreement was signed in Nanning between SAIC Motor and Liuzhou Wuling. Under the terms of this agreement, Liuzhou Wuling transferred a significant 75.9% of its state-owned legal person shares to SAIC Motor, noteworthy for its absence of any compensation. This transaction resulted in the bifurcation of the original Wuling company into two distinct entities: Liuzhou Wuling and SAIC Wuling. As part of this division, the four major process workshops—stamping, welding, painting, and assembly—along with their corresponding management departments, were integrated into the SAIC joint venture company. This strategic move set the stage for the entrance of GM, culminating in the establishment of SGMW. Concurrently, other departments, including those overseeing power, machinery repair, mold workshops, and the technical center, as well as the security and armed forces department and four subsidiaries not implicated in the shareholding arrangement, came together to form Liuzhou Wuling Automobile.

The method of asset allocation adopted during this period sparked considerable debate and concern, with many questioning the rationale behind Liuzhou Wuling, a prospering company, surrendering its most valuable resources—essentially its core manufacturing workshops and management departments. What remained in the hands of Liuzhou Wuling were primarily component processing workshops and support units. This move prompted widespread speculation and apprehension, as stakeholders pondered whether this decision signaled a substantial loss for the city of Liuzhou.

As a result, there emerged a pressing need for comprehensive explanations and assurances to address these apprehensions. The situation, laden with uncertainty, left many to wonder whether this move was a daring strategic play or a risky bet that could potentially jeopardize the future of a local enterprise. The decision carried immense weight, necessitating a high degree of accountability and courage from those at the helm. Upon close scrutiny, it became apparent that Liuzhou Wuling's options were inherently constrained within the rapidly evolving landscape of joint ventures in the Chinese market. The chosen strategy, involving the division and formation of joint ventures, operated on a principle akin to leading with a "locomotive" and subsequently pulling along the rest of the "train". Given the challenges and opportunities present at the time, this approach was arguably the most viable and strategic route for Liuzhou Wuling.

Among those likely experiencing the greatest disappointment was Shen Yang. He had wholeheartedly dedicated himself to driving corporate reform and engaged in relentless negotiations to facilitate the establishment of the joint venture company.

Despite his tireless efforts and commitment, Shen Yang ultimately found himself marginalized in the final arrangements, as another individual was appointed to the pivotal role of general manager with the formation of the SAIC-Wuling joint venture.

The sidelining of Shen Yang came as a surprise to many. As the chief negotiator, he had weathered immense pressure during the intense and complex negotiation process. On the one hand, the People's Government of Guangxi Zhuang Autonomous Region was consistently pushing for a swift conclusion of the joint venture project. On the other, GM often expressed dissatisfaction with the specific terms and conditions Shen Yang proposed. At times, the negotiations became so fraught that GM initiated a retreat for all involved parties, effectively putting a temporary halt to the discussions. Throughout this process, Shen Yang played the role of a strategic chess player, meticulously evaluating his moves and attempting to discern the motives of the opposition, all while seeking the most advantageous position on each aspect of the agreement. During one particularly heated negotiation session, Shen Yang's frustration reached a boiling point. He forcefully slammed down his pen and declared, "No more talks! I might as well retreat back to the mountains and become a guerrilla fighter". This unexpected outburst was a surprising tension breaker, leading to GM humorously dubbing Shen Yang as the "guerrilla leader". This light-hearted moment, shared with a round of laughter, saw the negotiators—now nicknamed the "American Captain" and the "Guerrilla Leader"—returning to the task at hand with renewed vigor, sifting through the clauses. Even amidst these dramatic episodes, the gravity and earnestness of the negotiation process remained resolutely in focus.

The conclusion of the negotiations marked a bittersweet turn of events for Shen Yang. Despite his pivotal role in the successful establishment of the joint venture, he found himself on the outside looking in. Instead of assuming a leadership position within the newly formed SAIC-Wuling, Shen Yang was appointed as the general manager of Liuzhou Wuling Automobile, a separate entity positioned just across the street from the SAIC-Wuling facility. This new assignment effectively severed a longstanding partnership, as his colleague Yao Zuoping continued within the joint venture company. The once-cohesive team was now split into two entities: SAIC-Wuling and Liuzhou Wuling, separated only by a narrow road. In a scene laden with symbolism, Shen Yang, carrying the weight of disappointment, led the departments excluded from the joint venture. Metaphorically, this situation weighed on him like carrying a load of scrap metal, along with the responsibility for the old, weak, sick, and disabled. Crossing the road to establish a new base felt more than just a physical relocation.

For Shen Yang, crossing this particular road might have felt like the longest and widest path he had ever walked in his life.

Fate often weaves its narrative like a parabola, artfully elevating individuals to the heights of excitement, only to subsequently plunge them into the downward arc of its trajectory. The path to ascend from such a descent is a journey each person must navigate and discover for themselves.

Despite his initial dejection, Shen Yang recognized that dwelling in disappointment was not an option. His team looked up to him for leadership and reassurance during these times of change. Rallying his spirits, he began to chart a new course of action, and by August 2001, he had reframed the situation with a renewed perspective. In a discussion, he put forth a fresh interpretation, drawing a distinction between the two entities: "We are a limited company, while the entity across the street is a shareholding company. The 'division' between us is not a 'splitting of the family' but rather as a strategic 'demerger.' This distinction is crucial for fulfilling the joint venture requirements of our shareholders and seeking greater development for the joint-stock company."

Shen Yang possessed a deep understanding of the extensive employment spillover effect intrinsic to automobile manufacturing. He knew that an OEM could significantly influence employment not only in upstream sectors, including component and raw material suppliers, but also in downstream industries such as finance, sales, and service. This holistic perspective enabled him to see that the success of the SGMW could swiftly translate into opportunities for Liuzhou Wuling Automobile. Understanding this intricate interconnectivity, Shen Yang saw an opportunity for mutual growth and advancement, an insightful perspective that kindled a new ambition within him, fueling a renewed sense of purpose and direction.

Across the road, a growing sense of unease began to permeate among the employees. As both SAIC Motor and GM China deployed their management personnel to integrate into the leadership of SGMW, the initial excitement surrounding the formation of the joint venture started to wane. This shift in atmosphere was largely due to the increasingly prominent and influential role of GM within the joint venture.

With the family now split and the essential arrangements settled, the wait for approval from the State Economic and Trade Commission turned into a prolonged and arduous ordeal. This period of limbo was marked by stagnation in sales and a noticeable lack of improvement in the company's overall performance, making it an exceptionally challenging phase.

The management team of the joint venture, comprising representatives from all three parties, frequently found themselves mired in exasperating disputes. Both SAIC Motor and GM struggled with a lack of deep understanding of Wuling's unique dynamics. Yao Zuoping, although appointed to oversee manufacturing, faced considerable constraints in his decision-making authority, with most significant decisions dictated by the shareholders, leaving him with minimal latitude for independent action. The staff composition further complicated the situation, comprising Shanghai personnel representing SAIC Motor and GM, with occasional assistance from foreign employees. Consequently, tensions within the team arose not just from Sino-American cultural differences but also from the divergent perspectives of individuals hailing from metropolitan areas and those from more inland, regional backgrounds.

In the midst of what could be likened to the clamorous sound of pots and pans symbolizing the chaotic and tense atmosphere, a defining moment emerged. On June 4, 2002, in Nanning, Guangxi, a significant breakthrough was achieved. Wuling Motors, SAIC Motor, and GM came to a consensus and signed a tripartite cooperation agreement, officially establishing the Sino–Sino–Foreign joint venture company— SAIC-GM-Wuling Automobile Co., Ltd. (SGMW). This landmark agreement outlined the shareholding structure of the new entity: SAIC Motor held a majority stake of 50.1%, GM owned 34%, and Liuzhou Wuling retained 15.9%.

The equity structure of the SGMW joint venture was, at the time, viewed as a pioneering and bold move, testing the resolve of the People's Government of Guangxi Zhuang Autonomous Region. While some deemed this structure overly radical, advocating for greater control over shareholding, Wang Hanmin, then Member of the Standing Committee of the Party Committee of Guangxi Zhuang Autonomous Region and the Vice-Chairman of the People's Government of the Guangxi Zhuang Autonomous Region, held a different perspective. As a key proponent for Wuling's collaboration with SAIC Motor and GM, he underscored the imperative of rapid development in Guangxi, a region with a modest economic volume and a nascent industrial base. He perceived the collaboration as a vital opportunity for Guangxi to expand its industrial landscape and foster growth. Championing the joint venture initiative, he urged government leaders to adopt a more liberal mindset while attracting investment. His goal was to introduce advanced manufacturing systems and leading industrial concepts to the region. Wang Hanmin's steadfastness paved the way for a fresh perspective on industrial collaboration, where shareholding was crucial, but not as critical as preserving the industrial "green mountains". This philosophy was encapsulated in the Guangxi government's innovative development approach of "Less the possession, more the value of the company in the society". While some interpreted this as a concession, others saw it as a demonstration of astute judgment, reflecting a pragmatic focus on the welfare of the people. The decision to leverage the joint venture to boost local employment was seen as a prudent choice. By keeping the original brand and independent R&D capability, Wuling's business could persistently thrive, invigorating Liuzhou's automotive industry. For Guangxi, the establishment of SGMW represented more than a new business venture; it symbolized the stimulation of the entire upstream and downstream industrial chain, illustrating the profound impact of maintaining a strategic presence in the industry.

The visionary foundation upon which SGMW was built stands as a monumental testament to its founders. The underlying principle of this venture was to maintain a long-term perspective, echoing the adage, "So long as the green mountains are preserved, there will be no shortage of firewood supply". This philosophy has resonated powerfully over the years, underscoring the importance of sustainable development. The rapid progress of SGMW not only stimulated local employment in Liuzhou by generating demand for parts manufacturers but also spurred the growth of its counterpart, Liuzhou Wuling Automobile. In 2015, Liuzhou Wuling Automobile underwent a significant transformation, a direct outcome of the "ensuring presence" philosophy, leading to a surge in local employment opportunities. However, human nature tends toward forgetfulness, and historical facts can be easily overshadowed. Occasionally, the notion that Liuzhou Wuling could have thrived independently resurfaces, despite the limited options available at the time. The decision to form a joint venture was not simply a division among siblings but a calculated and strategic choice for optimal progress, laying the groundwork for numerous other opportunities. Viewing the joint venture and the local government's earnest efforts to enhance the welfare of its people as merely a division of assets is a historical misinterpretation.

4.4　A Lamb in the Wolf's Embrace?

During the 10th Five-Year Plan (2001–2005), China's significant opening to the world had a profound global impact, with the pivotal accession to the WTO in 2001 marking a transformative moment. This momentous occasion set China irrevocably on the path of globalized manufacturing, heralding a major economic transition. For the automotive industry, 2001 was a whirlwind of intense emotions and rapid changes, an era marked by a tumultuous blend of hesitation and decisiveness, dejection and excitement, fear and courage, as well as gloom and glory, encapsulating the industry's complex response to the new challenges in the wake of globalization. The State Council's government work report in March 2001, highlighting the encouragement of private car ownership, stood out as a particularly bold initiative.

The automotive industry in China experienced its second wave of joint ventures, this time with a more intense and broad-based approach. Unlike earlier phases, where joint ventures typically focused on single models or specific projects, the period following China's entry into the WTO witnessed an influx of major multinational corporations establishing a presence in China[1], seeking comprehensive collaborations spanning entire vehicle lineups. Previously, foreign automotive brands had extended the lifespan of existing models through CKD assembly, reaping profits from older models. However, starting from 2001, these companies shifted their strategy to introducing synchronized new models. Contemporary versions began replacing the "Old Three"—Jetta, Santana, and Citroën Fukang—which had long dominated the Chinese market. Brands like Buick Sail gained prominence, signaling the introduction of affordable cars for the general populace. Sedans transitioned from being luxury items to more accessible goods, marking the beginning of an all-out marketization battle within the automotive industry.

By this time, the global automotive landscape had largely crystallized into an oligopoly, dominated by six major automotive groups, supplemented by three additional players. These leading entities were producing vehicles on a massive scale, with annual outputs ranging from a minimum of 4 million to as much as 8.7 million vehicles. In stark contrast, China's total automotive production in the year 2000 stood at just 2.069 million vehicles, with sedans accounting for only 605,000 of those[2]. Among domestic car manufacturers in China, the highest production volume achieved was a mere 400,000 units.

---

① China Association of Automobile Manufacturers, China Automotive Industry Advisory Committee. *History of China Automotive Industry, 1991–2010*[M]. China Machine Press, 2014, 165.

② Continuous Growth in China's Automobile Production[J]. *Trade Information of World Machinelectronics*, 2001.

The trajectory of the automotive industry was evident, and time was of the essence. By the close of December 2000, China's automotive landscape boasted a staggering 825 foreign-invested enterprises[①]. The influx of foreign investment and the surging trend of joint ventures appeared relentless. For city decision-makers focused on developing their local automotive industries, the period from 2000 to 2001 presented itself as a critical window of opportunity.

Liuzhou city, harnessing collective effort and strategic vision, successfully seized this pivotal window of opportunity. However, the venture through this "window" was not entirely a journey into an idyllic landscape.

Joint ventures, while often strategic, do not invariably lead to reliable alliance or a bright future. Cultural discrepancies and conflicts stand as some of the most significant challenges that can impede the success of mergers and collaborations. GM, with a century of history, had cultivated its own comprehensive business philosophies and systematic manufacturing concepts. Similarly, SAIC Motor, as one of China's top three automotive enterprises, had developed its own distinct cultural philosophy. Whereas Wuling brought to the table over 40 years of development and experience, having cultivated a corporate culture tailored to its growth, which was characterized by a low-cost, minimalist, and differentiated operational management model that had been integral to its success prior to the joint venture.

The three stakeholders in the joint venture—GM, SAIC Motor, and Wuling—each contributed their own distinct management philosophies, styles, and practices, deeply ingrained in their diverse regional cultures. These varied backgrounds led to intense conflicts, both before and after the establishment of the joint venture, turning even the smallest issues into conflicts so profound and widespread that they could be likened to a "world war" within the company. Points of contention varied widely, ranging from personnel decisions to car models, and even down to seemingly trivial details such as a bell.

Situated at No. 18 Hexi Road in Liuzhou City, SGMW had, despite years of evolution, retained much of its original exterior. A distinctive feature was the wall near its entrance bearing the motto "Perseverance with Self-Strengthening", beneath which hung a large iron bell marking the beginning and end of each workday. Upon the establishment of SGMW, personnel from SAIC Motor, newly arrived in Liuzhou,

---

① China Association of Automobile Manufacturers. *30 Years of Reform and Opening-up in China's Automobile Industry (1978–2008): A Retrospective and Outlook*[M]. China Logistics Publishing House, 2009, 129.

proposed removing both the inscription and the bell, citing aesthetic reasons. Yao Zuoping, however, stood firmly against this suggestion. He saw the inscription as a reflection of Wuling's enduring ethos and core corporate spirit, and the iron bell, more than just a timekeeper, a continual call to vigilance and motivation for Wuling's workforce. The very soul of a company, its unique essence, demands protection; its genetic core, woven into its being, is not something to be casually redefined. After considerable debate, it was decided that the inscription would remain. Its bold characters continued to greet everyone at the company's entrance, symbolizing the enduring spirit of Wuling. In times of significant events or challenges, employees often gathered for group photos in front of this inspiring inscription, reinforcing their commitment and enthusiasm. The large bell, meanwhile, found a new home just inside the gate, continuing to toll every day. Its sound served as a constant source of inspiration, fostering diligence and aspiration among all those who were part of Wuling.

Following the formation of SGMW, the company became a battleground for profound ideological confrontations, fueled by the arrival of personnel from each of the three collaborating entities. These clashes, characterized by their depth and frequent detriment, unfolded like intense "world wars" within the organization, occurring frequently and with substantial impact.

During the nascent stages of the joint venture, executive committee meetings at SGMW were often day-long affairs steeped in tension, arising from differences in communication styles, management philosophies, and vested interests. These gatherings often bore witness to significant divergence in crucial corporate decisions, with Chinese and foreign personnel typically seated separately, each articulating their perspectives from distinct vantage points. Initially, some foreign staff members displayed a somewhat condescending demeanor, eliciting resistance from Wuling employees who firmly held their ground, driven by strong self-esteem. This dynamic often led to heated exchanges, sometimes escalating to physical manifestation of frustration through table slamming, chair kicking, and verbal confrontations. Email communication was no less challenging; there were instances where the Chinese side did not respond to emails from their foreign counterparts, and conversely, times when the foreign side struggled to understand emails from the Chinese team. Essentially, this was a scenario marked by a mutual lack of understanding, resulting in the accumulation of unresolved issues.

The staff at Wuling grappled with complex emotional upheaval and a collective sense of distress, finding themselves entangled in a dilemma, wrestling with the challenge of reconciling with the demeanor of their joint venture partners, all the while acknowledging the value inherent in the innovative ideas introduced by these partners. This emotional conundrum, however, proved to be not exclusive to Wuling; rather, it mirrored situations encountered elsewhere in the global automotive industry. A noteworthy parallel can be drawn with Chrysler's experience following its unexpected acquisition by Daimler-Benz in 1998. Employees at Chrysler in the United States similarly perceived a sense of condescension from the luxury German automaker, concluding that despite the ostensible agreement on equal partnership, the Germans effectively assumed control of the American company. Executives from Benz appointed to Chrysler often exhibited an air of superiority, particularly regarding mass-market vehicles and the trucks used by the blue-collar workforce[1], thereby exacerbating the discord and cultural clash.

Notwithstanding the myriad frustrations encountered, the resilience exhibited by the Wuling staff was not to be underestimated. Despite grappling with their frustrations, they adeptly suppressed any resentment, positioning themselves to showcase their capabilities, echoing the sentiment encapsulated in the words of the renowned Chinese poet Li Bai: "Looking up at the sky, I laugh aloud and go. Am I a man to crawl amid the brambles low?"

4.5 A Pot of Traditional Chinese Medicine

Confronted with the conflicts and cultural clashes post-joint venture, the management team realized the imperative of directly tackling these issues to facilitate cultural integration. Despite concerted efforts by teams deployed by the shareholders, effective harnessing and unification of the strengths of all three parties seemingly remained elusive. In response to these persistent challenges spanning over a year, the president of GM China, in 2002, proposed a strategic move to SAIC Motor: the appointment of Shen Yang as the general manager of SGMW. However, compliance with the joint venture agreement necessitated that the general manager be an employee of SAIC Motor. To fulfill this requirement, Shen Yang needed to be

---

① Bill Vlasic. *Once Upon a Car: The Fall and Resurrection of America's Big Three Automakers—GM, Ford, and Chrysler*, trans. Guo Li[M]. China CITIC Press, 2011, 52.

officially transferred to SAIC Motor, which would then enable him to assume the role of general manager at SGMW. This proposal, extending beyond a tactical adjustment, received the endorsement of relevant governmental departments in the Guangxi Zhuang Autonomous Region, which recognized the substantial benefits associated with having a local figure like Shen Yang in a key leadership position, especially considering the potential advantages for regional development.

With the structural elements of the joint venture established, the subsequent crucial step was to harmonize the diverse cultures involved. The persistent disputes proved counterproductive to fostering a harmonious joint venture environment. In fact, the collaboration between SAIC Motor and GM had already laid a foundation for overcoming cultural barriers. At the inception of their joint venture, Chinese leadership introduced the concept of "individual behavioral constraints within the organization",[1] which encapsulated the principles of "Study, Standardization, Spring, and Prioritize SAIC-GM's interests".[2] The objective was to amalgamate the distinctive cultural attributes of the joint venture partners, seeking common ground where a shared set of values could be established.

The philosophy that had underpinned the successful collaboration between SAIC Motor and GM once again emerged as a valuable asset in the context of the newly established tripartite joint venture factory. Guided by pivotal figures like Shen Yang and Yao Zuoping, the management team wholeheartedly embraced and championed the principle of prioritizing the joint venture's interests, emanating from the executive committee and cascading down through the ranks of middle management.

At SGMW, the executive committee functioned as the apex decision-making body. Comprising seven members, four of whom held the authority to endorse decisions, the committee included two representatives from SAIC Motor—the general manager and deputy general manager—and one each from GM—the chief financial officer—and Wuling—the deputy general manager. The committee's mandate was to review all project proposals and materials before submission to the board of directors, convening weekly meetings for this purpose. These sessions predominantly focused on what was termed "the three important and one large"—covering important decision-making, significant personnel appointments and dismissals, major project

---

① Jia Chunlan. "SAIC-GM: A Corporate Culture Embracing Market Competition," *Chinese and Foreign Corporate Culture*. No. 11 (2002).

② The 4S principle: Study, Standardization, Spring, and Prioritize SAIC-GM's interests.

investment decisions, and large-scale utilization of funding. Integral to the committee's operation was the implementation of the one-vote veto system, which empowered the executives of SGMW to exert substantial influence and consistently integrate their perspectives into the decision-making process.

In an effort to circumvent the airing of conflicts in public forums, SGMW adopted a nuanced approach to decision-making, through which issues were first discussed and consensus reached among all members of the executive committee. Following this, the proposals underwent scrutiny and approval by the deputy general manager of the relevant department. This method departed from conventional decision-making models prevalent in state-owned enterprises. Despite the diverse interests reflected in the executive committee's composition, the guiding principle of prioritizing the joint venture's interests gradually facilitated a harmonious convergence of perspectives, fostering a spirit of seeking common ground while respecting individual differences among shareholders.

The executive committee's efficiency steadily improved, with meticulously focused meetings, even those spanning an entire day, ensuring that every decision made aligned with the long-term development and interests of the enterprise.

A notable incident unfolded in one of the workshops when a batch quality issue surfaced. Despite the problem originating from a subcontractor, the workshop head, appointed by GM, stepped up and willingly took responsibility. His approach was empathetic, emphasizing, "Let's be gentle with our employees; allowing them to learn and grow from this experience is what truly matters". Some executives volunteered their time to teach at the joint venture's English club. These acts of kindness and engagement were met with immediate reciprocation by Wuling employees, illustrating the notion that touching people's hearts often does not require grandiose actions.

Efforts were also made to enhance non-organizational interactions with foreign personnel within the company. A key initiative in this regard was the annual organization of Christmas parties, graced by the company's main leaders. These events played a pivotal role in reinforcing the organization's culture, instilling a sense of unity reminiscent of the warmth of sunshine.

Adhering to the guiding principle of prioritizing the joint venture's interests, the staff from the three different parties—representing the diverse cultures and backgrounds of the company—gradually transitioned from a stance of mutual exclusion and misunderstanding to one of proactive learning and integration.

SGMW's corporate governance structure underwent a significant transformation. Operating within the framework of Corporate Law and Corporate Charter, the company implemented a new meeting system characteristic of modern corporate management. This system comprised the Shareholders' Meeting, Board of Directors, Supervisory Committee, and Executive Committee. Concurrently, it retained certain traditions typical of state-owned enterprises, including the presence of the Party Committee, the Labor Union, and the Staff and Workers' Representative Congress. This dual system was meticulously designed to ensure a seamless integration of new and traditional approaches.

A noteworthy change in this evolved structure was the heightened emphasis on the role of the "professional manager" within the Executive Committee, replacing the earlier focus on the "entrepreneur". Appointments to managerial positions were now determined by the Board of Directors, aligning with the broader trend toward de-administration. Managers, irrespective of the shareholder they represented, were encouraged to adopt a philosophy that prioritized the company's development.

As the joint venture evolved, a strategic framework termed "one steering wheel, four wheels" began to take shape. The "four wheels" represented key aspects of the business: the first wheel stood for human resources, the second the capability to acquire and integrate excellent resources, the third a commitment to technological transformation and innovation, and the fourth the capital, whereas the "steering wheel" in this analogy was the corporate culture [①] . This culture effectively communicated the leadership's vision, subtly infiltrating the mindset of every employee, much like a gentle spring rain nurturing growth.

Amidst these transformations, there was a constancy in Wuling's approach. The management firmly believed in a localized strategy tailored to the domestic market. While tactically open to learning from GM, strategically, they remained grounded in national realities. Wuling's extensive engagement with local customers provided them with profound insights into their specific emotional needs, diverging notably from GM's global perspective. While Wuling prioritized market and customer orientation, GM leaned toward technology and process-driven approaches. This milieu fostered both understanding and the necessity for strategic navigation, striking a balance

① Yao Zuoping, Wan Junkang, and Wang Hui. "Development Strategy of 'One Steering Wheel, Four Wheels' in Dual-Chinese and Foreign Cooperative Enterprises[J]. *Journal of Wuhan University of Technology Information & Management Engineering*, 2005.

between global insights and local imperatives.

The decision regarding which brand to use for the development of mini-vehicles presented a significant challenge. Initially, GM hesitated to continue with Wuling, showing a preference for the Chevrolet trademark instead. The management of SGMW chose not to directly oppose this idea. Instead, they presented a compelling and vivid scenario to illustrate their point. Many of the car buyers at the time were local farmers who had recently prospered, and were accustomed to carrying their money in traditional snakeskin bags, often feeling out of place in overly lavish settings. The SGMW management suggested that a dealership branded with the more upscale Chevrolet might intimidate these customers, potentially preventing them from even entering the store. In essence, opting for Chevrolet could risk alienating a significant portion of the mini-vehicle market. GM appreciated the humorous yet insightful nature of this analogy. Understanding the cultural nuances and market dynamics at play, they agreed to retain the Wuling brand, averting the potential marginalization of Wuling in its first major crisis.

The Americans involved in the joint venture displayed their unique approach to cultural adaptation. At a New Year tea party, Phil Murtaugh, then president of GM China, greeted the attendees with a traditional Chinese bow. He expressed his gratitude, acknowledging that his learning experience in China extended beyond Shen Yang to include the older leaders as well. His impromptu speech took everyone by surprise, especially the factory's former leaders who felt acknowledged and deeply appreciated. Phil Murtaugh's action indicated that American managers were also putting effort into understanding and respecting the cultural nuances and relationship dynamics with former leaders.

Yao Zuoping, reflecting on the collaboration among the three parties, eloquently likened it to the process of brewing traditional Chinese medicine. This analogy encapsulates the essence of cultural integration, portraying it as a distillation of the best aspects while discarding the unnecessary. In this metaphor, SAIC Motor, GM, and Wuling collectively constituted a blend comparable to a pot of Chinese herbal medicine. GM assumed the role of an enhancer, augmenting the effectiveness of the mixture, while SAIC Motor ensured the right conditions, akin to maintaining the perfect brewing temperature. Their combined efforts helped to unlock and amplify the intrinsic qualities of the fundamental ingredients—Wuling's spirit of "Perseverance with Self-Strengthening". Through the seamless integration of these components, without differentiating between "you" and "me", the collaboration was able to yield fruitful results, much like the harmonious blend achieved in an expertly prepared traditional medicinal concoction.

4.6 Gains for All Parties

The "traditional Chinese medicine" approach to joint ventures, critically evaluated for its effectiveness, held particular significance for GM, given the strategic importance of this partnership in China's expansive market. This approach demanded a Go game mindset, striving for an equitable distribution of influence across the board, coinciding with GM's urgent need for a localized, networked distribution system in China. The Sino–Sino–Foreign joint venture model, crafted with SAIC Motor and Wuling, provided GM the opportunity to strategically extend its footprint across China. Following the tripartite agreement in June 2002, GM replicated this model in other ventures, including gaining control over the Yantai Daewoo project and Yantai Autobody Co., Ltd. in Shandong with SAIC Motor, ultimately leading to the establishment of Shanghai GM Dong Yue Motors Co., Ltd.[1]. This strategic move enabled GM to establish a comprehensive network: SAIC-GM in East China, Shanghai GM Dong Yue Motors in North China, Jinbei GM in Northeast China, and SGMW in South China. Initially perceived as a serendipitous coincidence, this Sino–Sino–Foreign mixed ownership reform model, in hindsight, showcased a profound understanding of globalization and the adaptability and wisdom inherent in the Chinese approach. In the intricate realm of unspoken rules, this strategy unlocked a realm of new possibilities.

On November 18, 2002, SAIC-GM-Wuling Automobile Co., Ltd., a joint venture co-founded by SAIC Motor, GM China, and Liuzhou Wuling, celebrated its official inauguration.

The highlight of this day was the debut of the company's first product—Wuling Sunshine. As it gracefully rolled off the assembly line, its progression seemed to pay homage to an entire era and honor the founders of SGMW.

This year marked a watershed moment in the history of China's automotive industry, witnessing an explosive surge in growth. Total vehicle production leaped

---

① China Association of Automobile Manufacturers. *30 Years of Reform and Opening-up in China's Automobile Industry (1978–2008): A Retrospective and Outlook*[M]. China Logistics Publishing House, 2009, 137.

from 2.33 million to 3.25 million units, catapulting China's global rank in car production from eighth in 2000 to fifth in 2002. For automotive entrepreneurs who had strategically positioned their companies, this period was one of genuine exhilaration. Steering their businesses from the driver's seat, they could distinctly feel the thrust of acceleration, propelling them into a new epoch of industrial growth.

Ready?
Go!

Chapter 5 The Age of Iconic Vehicles
2003–2008

5.1 Farewell to Flat-Fronted Vehicles

Originally inspired by Japanese mini-commercial vehicles, mini-vehicles in China initially served as mini-trucks, but later evolved to extend their utility well beyond their initial design intent as China progressed through stages of modernization.

Mini-vehicles in China notably carved their niche as urban taxis, particularly gaining prominence in the early 1990s. Manufacturers such as Tianjin Daihatsu and Hafei capitalized on the surging demand and limited supply of vehicles, successfully breaking into the urban taxi market, with Beijing and Tianjin leading this burgeoning trend. The thoroughfares of Beijing soon teemed with yellow, flat-fronted minivans, affectionately known as "bread-loaf cabs", which, due to their cost-effectiveness and widespread availability, quickly became an integral fixture and an early symbol in the annals of the country's automotive history. By the end of 1991, Beijing's taxi fleet had grown to 13,000, with bread-loaf cabs constituting a modest 18%. However, by the end of 1994, the number of taxis in Beijing skyrocketed to over 60,000, with bread-loaf cabs accounting for nearly 35,000, representing almost 60% of the entire fleet. Concurrently, during this period when Beijing was plagued by severe sandstorms, people in their haste to reach destinations often sought refuge in these bread-loaf cabs, hailing them as a safe haven from the harsh elements, almost as if escaping a calamity.

The widespread presence of bread-loaf cabs, which originated in Beijing and Tianjin, swiftly proliferated to other provincial capitals and smaller cities across China. Cities like Xi'an, Zhengzhou, Jinan, and Taiyuan soon embraced these minivans, turning them into highly coveted assets in the market. By the end of 1997, these distinctive cabs represented a quarter of the country's entire taxi fleet[1].

Nevertheless, concerns over safety and environmental impact, particularly due to

---

[1] Liu Yuan and Li Lin. Taxi Market: A Battleground for Automobile Manufacturers[J]. *Beijing Automotive Engineering*, 1999.

their significant pollution footprint, marked these vehicles as merely a transitional phase in urban development. In 1998, Beijing initiated the phasing out of these low-end, environmentally unfriendly bread-loaf cabs. Their presence, akin to a comet briefly illuminating the sky, gradually faded from the historical stage. While Tianjin Xiali's hatchback sedan swiftly filled the void left by bread-loaf cabs as the predominant taxi model in Beijing, a miscalculation of market demands led to its rapid decline. The low-end configuration of these models significantly underestimated the evolving quality expectations of Chinese cities. By 1999, Beijing's taxi market had entirely transitioned away from bread-loaf cabs toward more environmentally friendly models with features like electrical fuel injection and three-way catalytic converters, such as the Jetta, Citroën Fukang, and Xiali, signaling the end of Beijing's bread-loaf cab era. In an interesting twist of fate, just as the rise of these cabs began in Beijing and quickly spread nationwide, their decline, too, started in Beijing and swiftly enveloped the entire country[①].

The urban bread-loaf cabs, once a ubiquitous sight, emerged as a unique outcome of the considerable disparity between China's developing automotive industry and the sudden surge in consumer demand. These cabs epitomized a market anomaly, thriving momentarily but lacking sustainability over the long term.

Intriguingly, mini-vehicles discovered a renewed niche at the desakota regions, enjoying a lifespan far exceeding that of their urban taxi counterparts. The grassroots vitality like wild grasses flourishing in these regions, provided them with a longer-term mission.

Both urban and rural regions in China were relatively underdeveloped during the early 1990s, relying on a mix of human-powered vehicles, motorcycles, motorized tricycles, and tractors for transportation. Minivans, evolving from mini-truck technology and serving as dual-purpose tools for production and personal transport, progressively assumed a pivotal role in urban-rural transit. They were primarily used for business and operational purposes, adeptly handling both cargo and passenger transport.

Between 1980 and 2000, China's population grew from 990 million to 1.27 billion, with the urban populace increasing from 190 million to 460 million and the urbanization rate from 19% to 36%. Despite this near twofold increase in urbanization over two decades, the rural population remained substantial, increasing from 800

---

① Yang Yunlong. Taxi Industry: A New Era Unfolds[J]. *China Business Times*, 2000.

million in 1980 to 840 million in 1990, before slightly decreasing to 810 million by 2000, highlighting that urban-rural integration was still in its nascent stages as the century drew to a close. Rural residents were gradually embracing dual identities as both farmers and entrepreneurs or workers, a societal shift reflected in the versatile role of mini-vehicles. With their practical utility and symbolic significance, these vehicles not only expedited the pace of China's urbanization but also subtly mirrored the dynamic era of rapid urban development. Their enduring presence and evolving role in China's transportation landscape served as a nuanced metaphor for the country's unique social structure during this transformative period.

As the 20th century drew to a close, minivans and agricultural vehicles, which had initially flourished in China's urban and rural landscapes, began to face developmental challenges. Major cities phased out bread-loaf cabs, signaling a shift in urban areas from a closed, low-consumption state under the planned economy to an era of commercialization and internationalization. This transformative period coincided with global automotive giants actively pursuing joint ventures in China. Concurrently, restrictions were imposed on agricultural vehicles, barring them from urban areas and highways, signifying the deepening integration of rural life with urban development. These changes reflected two major trends of the era: those not aligning with the prevailing tide were phased out, while those adapting experienced their zenith.

The mini-vehicle market in China was always characterized by fierce competition, and the government regulation was relatively lenient. From 1995 to 2000, Chang'an and Liuzhou Wuling each produced over 500,000 vehicles, while Hafei and Changhe manufactured over 400,000, and Tianjin Automobile produced just over 250,000. The competition among Chang'an, Liuzhou Wuling, Hafei, and Changhe was particularly intense and unresolved, with the next decade set to determine the market leader. On the contrary, Tianjin Automobile lagged behind, with the gap progressively widening. By 2000, these four leading companies collectively commanded 90% of the national mini-vehicle production, making it the most concentrated sector in China's automotive industry[1]. Vehicles from these prominent mini-vehicle brands became omnipresent, shuttling between urban and rural areas, emerging as one of the most dynamic elements in the capillaries of China's

---

[1] The cited data is derived from the annual *China Automotive Industry Yearbook*, providing insights into the production output and product structure of the eight major mini-vehicle manufacturers in China spanning from 1995 to 2000.

economy.

Nevertheless, the honeymoon period for any industry is finite, constrained by a window of opportunity, and the automotive market is no exception.

Regulations were tightening, ushering in new benchmarks for vehicle safety. Starting in January 2003, all automotive companies were mandated to cease the production of mini-vehicles that failed to meet the frontal collision occupant protection standards. While a grace period of six months allowed these companies to sell their existing inventory[1], any non-compliant mini-vehicles were subject to mandatory delisting, posing a significant challenge for many mini-vehicle manufacturers. The flat-fronted vehicles, such as bread-loaf cabs, characterized by vertically aligned windshields and short front crumple zones, were susceptible to severe deformation in accidents, presenting a considerable risk to driver and passenger safety. Compliance with collision tests for such designs was highly unlikely. Consequently, mini-vehicle enterprises were compelled to develop models capable of withstanding these rigorous tests. Failure to introduce new, compliant products within the stipulated deadline would leave dealers without cars to sell.

Regulations have perennially steered the path of the automotive industry, acting as a catalyst for progress and consistently nudging it onto new trajectories, particularly in the engine sector. This time, the regulatory pressure on mini-vehicles posed a formidable challenge, thrusting them into a critical battle for survival.

The question then arose: How could the rapid growth in mini-vehicle production and sales be sustained? What lies ahead for mini-vehicle manufacturing companies? Confronted with this dilemma, mini-vehicle enterprises urgently adjusted their strategies, grappling with the strain imposed by the new regulations. Early industry adopters, such as Chang'an Star, gained a significant advantage[2]. Equipped with Suzuki's technology and a mid-mounted engine, the Chang'an Star, featuring an extended front, was fully compliant with collision regulations and, having successfully passed tests at Tsinghua University's automotive collision laboratory in 1999, was among the first to hit the market, evoking envy from its competitors.

---

[1] State Economic and Trade Commission and Ministry of Public Security, Circular on Relevant Issues on Further Strengthening Administration of Public Notice and Registration of Vehicles, No. 768, 2002.

[2] China Association of Automobile Manufacturers, China Automotive Industry Advisory Committee. *History of China Automotive Industry, 1991–2010*[M]. China Machine Press, 2014, 209.

Various other mini-vehicle manufacturers were also navigating the changing automotive landscape, akin to hunters exploring new territories. Models such as Changhe Beidouxing, derived from Japanese designs, and Hafei Baili and Saima shifted their focus toward urban families, pivoting away from their predominantly rural orientation. While this dual-track approach appeared to effectively spread risk, it revealed strategic drawbacks. In urban areas, these models faced stiff competition from established names like Santana, Jetta, and Fukang, while in rural regions, their emphasis on passenger comfort was somewhat premature. This attempt to straddle both markets led to a diffusion of focus. For companies like Changhe and Hafei, venturing into passenger cars seemed overly ambitious, indicating a hasty and perhaps premature entry into the passenger car market.

The allure of passenger cars has always enticed automakers, symbolizing glamor and prestige. Yet, venturing into this segment without a well-defined strategic focus can yield dire consequences. As companies like Songhuajiang, Changhe, and Tianjin Daihatsu ventured into the competitive urban market of bread-loaf cabs, they were captivated by the allure of the city, confidently believing they could maintain a significant presence on urban streets. In the automotive industry, the determination and vision of a company's leader play a pivotal role in steering its strategic course. SGMW, however, opted for a different trajectory. Instead of pursuing the glittering urban market, they remained steadfast in their focus on rural areas and the urban fringes, catering to the mid-to-low-income demographic in rapidly urbanizing regions.

In the vast and dynamic Chinese market, where global car brands fiercely compete, success demands dedication and perseverance akin to a farmer tilling the land diligently. This stands in contrast to the approach of a hunter, constantly on the lookout for immediate opportunities but lacking a long-term commitment.

5.2 First Strike in the Auto Wars

As 2002 drew to a close, the Wuling Sunshine, fully compliant with the new collision regulations, started rolling off the production line at the Liuzhou factory. This vehicle model, the inaugural product of the joint venture forged through the united efforts of the tripartite shareholders, debuted to an audience of expectant and scrutinizing eyes—its arrival was greeted with a mix of blessings and skepticism.

The establishment of Liuzhou Wuling's Technical Development Center in early 1999 represented a transformative shift in the company's approach to management. Evolving from the original design department, it amalgamated various functions such as process engineering, standardization, and new product prototyping, forming a robust team of nearly 200 members. A notable innovation in this organizational structure was the inclusion of manufacturing engineering within the design and development department, effectively merging the product center with the manufacturing center. In many manufacturing companies, product design engineers and manufacturing engineers often face tension due to divergent priorities: one emphasizes functionality, while the other focuses on manufacturability, creating a dynamic akin to two pendulum balls in perpetual collision. In day-to-day operations, this tension manifests in frequent encroachments on each other's domains, with one side pushing for design changes and the other resisting alterations. By binding these two roles together, the "body-centered" R&D and manufacturing model was enforced[①]. Years later, this approach, which prioritized manufacturing-oriented design, would be lauded as an innovative trend. It ensured the seamless integration of design and manufacturing processes, embodying a forward-thinking strategy that harmoniously blended two traditionally separate areas of expertise.

During that period, the Technical Development Center operated with basic design tools and manufacturing methods. The processes for producing single- and double-row trucks, as well as flat-front vehicles, involved scaling from actual models. It began with physical measurements of models and proceeded to create two-dimensional drawings using simple design software. Skilled workers in the prototype workshop then brought these designs to life, with a primary focus on single- and double-row trucks.

In reality, the Technical Development Center's capabilities were limited to modifying existing models rather than developing entirely new ones. The notion of

---

① Body-centered product development refers to a strategic approach adopted by automotive companies, where the core technology and primary area of expertise revolve around body engineering, aligning with their vehicle platform strategies. This approach incorporates advanced concepts and methodologies such as concurrent engineering, lean production, design for x (DFX), and computer-aided technologies (CAX), aiming to establish a comprehensive organizational system and management model that encompasses the entire process of vehicle body styling, engineering design, product validation, and production preparation. Ultimately, this strategy intends to enhance the overall product R&D capabilities of automotive companies, enabling them to swiftly respond to market demands and achieve the goals of developing automotive products within shorter cycles, at lower costs, and with higher quality.

starting from scratch on a blank sheet to design a car far exceeded its capacity at the time, a limitation that became evident during discussions on the departmental composition of SGMW, where stakeholders chose not to include the technical center in the contract clauses, effectively excluding it from the joint venture's core structure.

Despite Liuzhou Wuling's leading position in the mini-vehicle market in 1998 and the Technical Development Center's decade-long experience, it did not receive significant respect from the representatives of SAIC Motor and GM during negotiations. However, as the new joint venture lacked its own R&D center, the Technical Development Center was still, to a certain degree, of significance, continuing to provide R&D services for the joint venture. The employees remained in their offices, yet the team was excluded from the joint venture's core activities, creating a disheartening and somewhat isolating environment at the Technical Development Center.

On the other hand, SAIC Motor and GM were committed to the development of the Pan Asia Technical Automotive Center (PATAC), a joint endeavor aligned with their venture, and they held high expectations for its impact. PATAC was envisioned to introduce a new-generation, fully-equipped design into China's automotive industry. Given that SGMW was a nascent joint venture, new product development tasks were, naturally, anticipated to be assigned to PATAC.

In parallel, while SAIC Motor, GM, and Wuling navigated complex negotiations, Wuling was actively working on its next-generation products. Their primary, non-negotiable goal was to develop a new model compliant with the upcoming safety collision regulations, a crusade for the company's very existence.

Another project under consideration was the localization of a Daihatsu model named "Urban Breeze" that involved the utilization of domestic components to craft a new vehicle model for the Chinese market. While efforts were underway to introduce this model, GM, as part of the joint venture discussions, staunchly opposed the project. The competitive dynamics between Daihatsu and Suzuki, coupled with GM holding a stake in Suzuki, rendered the introduction of a Daihatsu model in conflict with corporate alliances. This situation was further compounded by Suzuki lacking a viable alternative model, presenting a complex challenge in the joint venture's product strategy.

Confronted with these intricate challenges, and driven by a sense of urgency, Shen Yang firmly advocated for the development of an entirely new vehicle tailored for the joint venture, one that would meet the impending safety collision regulations.

Despite his conviction, SAIC Motor and GM expressed reservations regarding Wuling's R&D capability and questioned the strategic timing of such a venture. From their perspective, Wuling's management team appeared overly eager and impulsive, resembling ambitious yet relatively unseasoned aspirants in the complex arena of automotive development.

Shen Yang's commitment to research and development, while steadfast, did not guarantee success. Known for his composure, he rarely displayed signs of agitation, concealing the wavering determination within. He adhered to the principle of "going with the flow", believing that, as long as the overarching direction remained sound, even if it involved additional steps or detours, it would ultimately yield opportunities.

In this context, "going with the flow" is referred to as a commitment to independent development, meticulously crafting products that conform to legal regulations.

Amidst intense negotiations among stakeholders, SAIC Motor and GM eventually acquiesced, allowing Wuling's Technical Development Center to present a development plan. They also solicited proposals from the PATAC and the British HORIBA MIRA Ltd.

As the time to make a decision approached, management teams from all involved parties convened in Shanghai. The proposals from the three entities placed SAIC Motor and GM's decision-makers in a quandary, as, judging from the engineering timelines, MIRA required 36 months, PATAC proposed 30 months, while Wuling's Technical Development Center suggested an ambitious 18 months. The cost differentials were even more pronounced, with PATAC's costs double those of Wuling, and MIRA's costs twice those of PATAC. The board, acknowledging the gravity of the decision, entrusted Shen Yang with the final call, but with the precondition that he was confident that the car's production would be within the set timeline and budget, essentially making it a binding commitment akin to a military order.

Under immense pressure, Shen Yang found himself wrestling with sleepless nights. One crucial evening at the hotel of the SAIC Retired Cadres Activity Center, around eleven, he felt the need to make a pivotal call to Zhang Zhengxiang, then Deputy Director of Wuling's Technical Development Center. With a grave demeanor, Shen Yang asked, "The prevailing trend leans toward entrusting foreign companies with safety collision improvements. I need to know—can we truly manage it on our own?"

Until this point, Wuling's Technical Development Center had not forayed into the realm of independent vehicle development, as their expertise had been confined to adapting introduced models.

The question "Can we manage it on our own?" struck Zhang Zhengxiang like a lightning bolt, rousing a latent passion often dormant in many technicians. At these moments, the leader's recognition and trust act as a catalyst for this latent fervor, marking a turning point. The newly sparked passion evolved into a formidable force, empowering technicians to transcend their usual limits and tackle challenges with newfound vigor.

Zhang Zhengxiang's response was swift and resolute: "I want to take on this challenge!"

He promptly reached out to his colleagues in Liuzhou, sparking a lively discussion about the prospect of charting an independent path through independent development. As they deliberated, a surge of collective enthusiasm swept through the team, rapidly spreading and culminating in a unanimous and spirited resolution: they would take the reins and spearhead the project themselves.

Once again, a knock echoed at Shen Yang's door.

"We can do it ourselves!"

"Will time be an issue?"

"Absolutely not."

"And the cost?"

"Absolutely not."

Steeped in a tone of familiar resilience, this exchange encapsulated the essence of Shen Yang's longstanding rapport with his team. Their dialogue, marked by calm assurance and reliability, had become their signature. To an outsider, these direct and unembellished exchanges might seem inconsequential. Even Shen Yang pondered the audacity of such absolute certainties at times. A misstep in this venture could jeopardize their cherished autonomy in design. The dual aspirations he held dear—keeping the original brand and independent R&D capability—hung precariously in the balance, contingent on the success of this pivotal undertaking.

On that night in Shanghai, beneath the steady glow of a lit window, a maelstrom of wavering, hesitation, and resolve intertwined. The process by which these thoughts crystallized into a final decision remained shrouded in ambiguity. However, one truth stood clear: courage is not an isolated endeavor but a collective symphony of emotions, ignited and amplified within the team through shared encouragement and support.

The following day brought a transformative call from Shanghai to Wuling's Technical Development Center, granting them an unequivocal green light. This news electrified the team in Liuzhou, unleashing two years' worth of pent-up frustration in a torrential outpouring of emotion. The atmosphere was charged with an almost palpable intensity, akin to troops rallying for a critical charge, poised on the brink of a battle where the outcome was uncertain yet the resolve to strike first was undiminished[1]. It was a fiery surge of spirit, yet the road ahead remained veiled in uncertainty.

In a prudent move, the management of SGMW proposed a joint meeting between PATAC and Wuling's Technical Development Center to deliberate on decisions regarding the vehicle model. While the management harbored hopes of PATAC taking the lead, the Technical Development Center remained steadfast in its commitment to success. Even before the meeting commenced, it was laden with underlying tensions and high stakes—a battlefield of hidden currents where much more than just technical decisions were in play.

On the scheduled day, the meeting room crackled with heightened emotions as representatives from both PATAC and Wuling's Technical Development Center gathered. Intended to be a collaborative session, the meeting quickly devolved into a tense confrontation, fueled by the precise and unvarnished nature of technical language. The debate rapidly escalated, transforming the meeting into a verbal skirmish. The real battleground emerged around the whiteboard, where technicians from both sides fervently sketched out their concepts for collision safety design, each vying to demonstrate the superiority of their approach. The whiteboard marker became the focal point of contention, with both parties eager to visualize and assert their ideas. This intense clash of perspectives eventually prompted the moderator to temporarily halt the proceedings.

In the aftermath of this "battle for the marker", the proposal put forth by Wuling's Technical Development Center left a lasting impression on both GM and SAIC Motor. For Wuling, this meeting transcended mere technical discussions; it was akin to a struggle for a vital weapon in the battlefield of independent research and development, where authority and influence are often determined by the weapon of one's ability to lead and develop independently.

In this decisive moment, Wuling triumphantly reclaimed a potent submachine

---

① Ge Bangning. The Wuling Gene[J]. *Auto Business Review*, 2014.

gun—a bold affirmation of their capability and resolve to lead in the creation of the new vehicle.

5.3 A Spring's Ambition

During that era, two key models served as benchmarks for designing vehicles compliant with automotive collision safety regulations: the Japanese Mitsubishi flat-front vehicles and the distinctively designed Chang'an Star. At the Liuzhou Wuling Hexi base, a Chang'an Star was strategically placed in every workshop, serving both as a practical learning tool for the staff and as a catalyst to ignite their competitive zeal. Having such a tangible benchmark proved empowering, fueling determination and a drive to excel.

In a bid to save both cost and time, Wuling's Technical Development Center swiftly developed a prototype within just three months, drawing inspiration from the Chang'an Star. However, the initial reaction to the prototype from the leadership was one of stark surprise. The design was rudimentary, bearing an unrefined resemblance to a lengthy, slender sausage—far from aesthetically pleasing. The design philosophy had remained largely unaltered, primarily involving an extension of the vehicle's front. This was achieved by a simple yet significant modification: adding a "nose" to the front, which extended the front suspension from the modest original 0.6 meters to a more pronounced 1 meter. To further increase space, the body of the vehicle was elongated beyond that of the Chang'an Star, resulting in an overall appearance that was, regrettably, markedly unappealing.

The realization dawned that mere imitation of the Chang'an Star's design was insufficient; innovation was imperative. Therefore, the Technical Development Center embarked on a journey to reimagine their design strategy from the ground up. Previously, the team had conducted extensive field research in rural regions, delving into Chang'an Star's user experience, revealing a critical flaw—the spatial constraints, a characteristic inherent to Japanese mini-vehicles adopted by the Chang'an Star through Suzuki's technology from Japan.

Space emerged as the linchpin of Wuling's design breakthrough. Given that the Chang'an Star reigned supreme in the mini-vehicle segment during this era, the design ethos at Wuling was clear-cut: outclass the Chang'an Star to captivate the market. Consequently, the Technical Development Center meticulously examined the

Chang'an Star, probing into the reasoning behind each facet of its design, with an acute focus on optimizing space utilization. One notable design aspect of the Chang'an Star was its trapezoidal rear door frame—broader at the base and tapering toward the top. This design, while enhancing strength and rigidity, often posed challenges during overhead loading of cargo. Furthermore, the elevated threshold of the door, intended to prevent water ingress, proved to be a hindrance in the loading and unloading process, compromising spatial efficiency.

These intricate details were scrutinized with meticulous attention, as the design team diligently cataloged their observations, seamlessly integrating them into their design paradigms. An exemplar of this approach was the augmentation of the dimensions of the rear door opening, recognizing that the rear, rather than the side doors, was the primary conduit for loading and unloading. Conceptualizing the rear door as the "front yard" of a house, the design called for ample space to facilitate easy access. A square-shaped door frame was adopted to streamline the placement of goods, complemented by a threshold lower than the vehicle's floor, enabling direct placement of goods onto the floor. In addition, the interior two-level step was removed, creating a seamless and uniform floor extending from the front to the back of the vehicle. Wuling's goal was clear: they intended to not only match but surpass the Chang'an Star by offering superior space and convenience for cargo handling.

Another crucial aspect of the design lay in the vehicle's proportions. In the realm of automotive aesthetics, where appearance holds paramount importance, proportion is a key determinant of a vehicle's visual appeal. Recognizing the need to extend the car body, it became evident that widening the wheelbase was imperative to achieve a harmonious balance in the vehicle's overall proportions.

Interestingly, the elegance of these proportions hinged on something as seemingly mundane as a spring.

The Chang'an Star utilized a coil spring in its rear suspension, complemented by a multi-link system. This configuration adeptly mitigated both longitudinal and lateral oscillations during driving[①], effectively smoothing out road surface irregularities. However, this semi-independent rear suspension, while enhancing ride comfort, encroached upon interior space, necessitating a raised, two-level floor design.

In contrast, the team at Wuling's Technical Development Center advocated for

---

① Xiang Shengyin. Introduction to the Chang'an Star SC6350/SC1015X Mini-cars[J]. *Automobile and Parts*, 1999.

the adoption of leaf springs in the rear suspension, aligning more closely with user needs. While leaf springs are typically firmer and offer less comfort compared to coil springs, they excel in maximizing interior space. This viewpoint, however, met with resistance from PATAC, which was reluctant to embrace what they perceived as an antiquated technology more suited for trucks than passenger cars. The prevailing industry standard for passenger vehicles emphasized independent suspension, with a semi-independent suspension deemed as the bare minimum to strike a balance between comfort and load-bearing capacity. This divergence of opinions came to a head during a critical development meeting, where a senior technician from SAIC Motor vehemently critiqued the leaf spring proposal, questioning its relevance in modern car design. Faced with this challenge, Shen Yang, known for his meticulous attention to technical detail and active involvement in design discussions, felt compelled to intervene. He passionately defended the distinctiveness and significance of deviating from the Chang'an Star's model. Above all, Shen Yang emphasized that user needs were paramount and should be the guiding principle in the vehicle's design process.

In their conclusive presentation, the Technical Development Center laid out a stark and unequivocal comparison. The semi-independent suspension system, enhanced with coil springs, indeed delivered superior comfort. However, this design proved incompatible with the vehicle's intended dual-purpose role for both commercial and passenger use. The necessity for a raised floor in this design resulted in a higher rear section, leading to a three-tiered rear floor layout with distinct height variations between the second and third rows, and the front. Wuling's evaluation determined that the primary market demand revolved around cargo-carrying capacity, with secondary importance placed on intricate details and comfort. Leaf springs, traditionally associated with single- and double-row trucks, were deemed sufficiently versatile for this application.

The presentation's conclusion was met with an uncomfortable silence rather than applause. Despite the palpable tension, the leaf spring design was ultimately selected.

This design decision was soon translated into a significant manufacturing challenge. A design's success is contingent on its manufacturability. Throughout the prototype phase, each design element and dimension was replicated with exacting precision. The vehicle's tuning demanded extensive performance testing, a task that lacked a dedicated department at that time; therefore, such meticulous responsibilities fell to the more broadly-focused chassis department. The team of seven technicians dedicated nearly a month to rigorous road testing, committing every parameter and speed for different highway segments to memory. Their coordination resembled well-oiled machinery, functioning in perfect harmony, often without the need for verbal cues. For example, adjustments to the front suspension were executed in mere minutes, resembling a choreographed routine more than a testing procedure. In the same vein, the efficiency and teamwork displayed in Formula One (F1) pit stops epitomize the zenith of collaborative specialization. In these scenarios, a team of 21 professionals can change four tires and replenish 60 liters of petrol in just seven seconds. The precision and rapidity with which 14 individuals change tires mirrors a powerful chord struck on a piano. Inspired by this level of expertise, the young members of the chassis department approached their test track duties with an intensity and precision mirroring that of an F1 team, transforming their work into a high-octane, precision-driven endeavor.

In the critical road-testing phase, a visit to the testing grounds in Hainan Province was indispensable. Here, the team could simultaneously make adjustments and conduct tests, typically concluding within a week. However, given the imperative to conserve time, achieving success on the first attempt was crucial, necessitating extensive preparations beforehand. The Technical Development Center ingeniously repurposed a cement sports field from a driving school in Liuzhou for preliminary trials. In the absence of a gyroscope, the team employed an ingenious yet rudimentary technique: a large water bottle filled with ink, suspended by a hose at the center of the road, served as an improvised device to measure the turning radius and steering angle[1]. This unconventional method drew curious glances from many driving school students who paused to observe the innovative use of the spinning bottle in the testing process. Remarkably, when this vehicle later underwent rigorous assessment with an actual gyroscope at the facility in Hainan, it excelled, achieving top scores in every category and passing the tests in just half a day. After the tests, the team promptly returned to Liuzhou to continue their work, as they had no leisure to indulge in Hainan's charm despite the allure of its scenic beauty.

The entire endeavor resembled a race against time, a relentless relay where each minute and second were pivotal, propelling the team toward the next critical juncture.

---

[1] Ge Bangning, "The Wuling Gene", *Auto Business Review* no. 1 (2014).

5.4 From Joke to Jewel

The development of the Wuling Sunshine was a period marked by an unprecedented commitment to meticulousness among the engineers. The disassembly of the Chang'an Star proved particularly enlightening, revealing the intricate attention to detail inherent in Japanese automobile manufacturing—a standard that the team at Wuling aspired to match.

The head of body manufacturing at the Technical Development Center was known for his innate fascination with machinery, a trait that became even more pronounced following the company's joint venture. His keen interest in GM's lean manufacturing system prompted him to embark on a quest for knowledge, leading him to numerous international factories where he observed and studied their processes. His dedication to learning was so profound that he devoted countless hours to immersing himself in technical documentation, whether in libraries or data rooms. On one occasion, his complete absorption in the technical materials at a GM-owned Daewoo factory in Republic of Korea resulted in his detention by security, almost leading to a premature return to China. It was in these immersive environments that the engineers at Wuling honed their automotive craftsmanship. Named for the grease that marked their hands from tireless work in the workshop, the "black hand engineers" were the unsung heroes driving the evolution of automobile manufacturing. Regrettably, their critical role in the ascent of Chinese manufacturing is often eclipsed. Many global analysts overlooked the innovative strides being made within these workshops, attributing China's manufacturing surge solely to its lower labor costs. While the innovations emerging from these workshops may not have been groundbreaking or patented in the traditional sense, likened to unheralded diamonds hidden in the mountains, it was the engineers' unwavering pursuit of knowledge and their inherent discontentment with the current state that elevated this "black hand innovation" a cornerstone of a factory's success.

The initial phase of the Wuling Sunshine project spanned approximately four months, while the subsequent stages, encompassing development, refinement, and production, transpired in a remarkably swift 14 months, resulting in an 18-month total timeline. By November 2002, this car was ceremonially unveiled, in commemoration of the establishment of SGMW. The company's burgeoning core competency lay in its low-cost manufacturing approach. A critical aspect of this strategy was self-manufacturing, a key element in securing cost leadership. The "black hands" of the workshop played a pivotal role, successfully compressing R&D expenses to over RMB 60 million, encompassing the entire project cost. This figure included a substantial investment of RMB 18 million in the production line and an additional RMB 20 million to 30 million allocated for mold investments. Other expenditures, such as tooling development and prototype manufacturing, necessitated the direct involvement of Wuling's dedicated team.

This car's journey could be likened to a child's first foray into mud sculpting or pottery.

During a workshop visit by senior executives from GM China, the vehicle resembled a clay pot in their eyes. Their surprise mirrored those of someone admiring a child's clay creation. However, during the inspection, the car door began to wobble, emitting a jarring, tearing sound that resonated above the din of the workshop's machinery. Swiftly, an alert engineer from the back of the group hastened forward to firmly shut the door.

The initial astonishment quickly morphed into disappointment, and curiosity turned to disdain. The manufacturing output, falling perhaps even below expectations, was precisely what GM China's management had anticipated from the joint venture.

The market's pre-sales response echoed this sentiment. Despite the car's spacious interior, concerns such as the unexpected swinging open of the rear door during transit, posing a risk to passenger safety, marred its reception. Criticisms poured in, with certain regional dealers expressing a preference for the original Liuzhou Wuling over the SGMW venture. Some even advocated for a suspension of sales for the new model.

GM was engulfed in frustration. The shareholders' board convened a pivotal meeting to deliberate the potential discontinuation of the Wuling Sunshine project, motivated by apprehensions of detrimental effects on the reputations of the involved stakeholders. The president of GM China starkly echoed a sentiment expressed by a Japanese executive, denouncing the vehicle as "nothing more than a pile of crap". The prevailing sentiment in the boardroom was harsh and unforgiving, viewing the product as an inferior result from a backward team situated in a less developed province and city, which had heaped considerable pressure on the senior management of SGMW.

In April 2003, the traditional Double Third Festival, also known as the Shangsi Festival, unfolded with customary enthusiasm among the Zhuang people in Guangxi. The lively ambiance of festive songs resonating under Yufeng Mountain and the bustling markets stood in stark contrast to the grim mood of Phil Murtaugh, then president of GM China, who was visiting to express his concerns. Disinclined to partake in the local celebrations, Phil Murtaugh promptly proceeded from the airport to the factory in Hexi, bypassing formalities, and emphatically called for the discontinuation of the Wuling Sunshine's production. Anticipating such a directive, Yao Zuoping had prepared a comprehensive report, meticulously presenting it with in-depth explanations that traced the quality issues back to factors such as tight deadlines, budget constraints on tooling, and deviations in dimensional control. Methodically laying out the facts, he confidently concluded that these issues were not insurmountable. Noticing Phil Murtaugh's skepticism, Yao Zuoping reassured him that within three months, the Wuling Sunshine could be transformed into a commendable vehicle. He further proposed that GM dispatch additional quality experts, particularly those specialized in dimensional control, to assist in the endeavor. In this crucial moment, it was Yao Zuoping who offered assurances to the concerned American executive, pledging substantial improvements in the near future.

Confronted with formidable challenges, the manufacturing department had to rise to the occasion. Taking charge, Yao Zuoping spearheaded the establishment of a Quality Improvement Command Center on the second floor of the main office building, affectionately referred to as the Red Building. This command center meticulously listed and prominently displayed all identified problems on its walls, transforming the space into a "quality problems extermination zone". An exhaustive review revealed a staggering number of over 1,800 problems, ranging from roof leaks to self-opening rear doors. The situation resembled a contest of defects, revealing layers of deviations stemming from gaps in knowledge across design, manufacturing, and the supply chain. Each identified problem was assigned to a specific individual, held accountable for its resolution. The devised strategy also involved daily progress meetings and on-site brainstorming sessions, all aimed at addressing issues on a day-to-day basis. The urgency and gravity of the situation were evident to all involved: a failure to rectify the car's flaws would mark the premature end of what had recently begun, leaving no room for redemption or the next step.

To tackle the immediate quality challenges, the manufacturing engineering department at Wuling embraced a strategy known as "star absorption". Imbued with rich cultural connotations drawn from Chinese martial arts novels, this term symbolized a proactive approach to learning from and collaborating with established suppliers. Despite lacking relevant prior experience, the team frequently organized technical discussions with suppliers and made visits to other factories to observe their assembly lines. Learning from these suppliers often proved to be the most efficient means of enhancing their own capabilities, emblematic of Wuling's evolutionary journey in manufacturing. The process entailed first understanding and adopting a solution from one supplier, then, while engaging with a second supplier, assimilating its strengths, identifying weaknesses, and juxtaposing it with the approach of the first. This iterative cycle of learning and integration to absorb diverse insights and practices, consistently applied with each new supplier, created a dynamic process of continuous improvement, through which Wuling's manufacturing capabilities underwent significant enhancement.

This strategy significantly contributed to the rapid advancement of China's manufacturing capabilities, as many industry leaders adopted the humble approach of learning from suppliers, thereby markedly reducing their learning curve. In situations where knowledge is a scarce commodity, the eager assimilation and application of external expertise become pivotal methods for transformation. This knowledge, often residing within the realms of quality suppliers, requires manufacturers to actively acquire, comprehend, and integrate it.

GM's global manufacturing standards also played a crucial role in this evolution. While they may not have directly addressed specific issues, they were foundational in establishing a robust systemic management framework. The methodology, centered around process logic rather than purely technical management, provided a structured approach to prioritize issues, determine methods, assign responsibilities, and set deadlines.

In contrast, Japanese experts tend to focus more on the logic of technology. When Japanese experts, contracted for three months, were invited to SGMW, they excelled in problem diagnosis but often fell short in providing pragmatic solutions. This disparity proved to be a perfect complement to the capabilities of Wuling's "black hand engineers". With extensive on-site experience, these engineers could swiftly implement and test the Japanese consultants' recommendations, which had proven to be enlightening for the team at Wuling, whose enthusiasm and engagement were notably appreciated by one of the Japanese experts sent by GM. Knowledge absorption is a synchronized chemical reaction between the storyteller and the listener, and the palpable intensity of this reaction among the Wuling team on the ground served as a source of inspiration for all involved.

Within the Quality Improvement Command Center, nestled on the second floor of the iconic Red Building, a tangible transformation was underway. The walls, once cluttered with countless notes highlighting quality problems, gradually cleared, making way for accolades and words of praise and marking a rejuvenation of energy and purpose throughout the factory. By the latter half of 2003, the production of the Wuling Sunshine saw a significant upswing. It was during a market visit to Hebei that Phil Murtaugh and his team witnessed firsthand the vehicle's flourishing sales. Impressed by what he saw, Phil Murtaugh wasted no time in reaching out to Yao Zuoping. Over the phone, a spirited Phil Murtaugh showered compliments on the Wuling Sunshine, celebrating its growing triumph. With a chuckle, he asked good-naturedly, "Hey, no hard feelings, right?"

At this moment, any lingering doubts about the car's appeal were swept away in the tide of shared achievement.

The Wuling Sunshine's journey, however, was not solitary on China's automotive highways. In the broader landscape of the Chinese automotive market, the velocity and vigor of cars were conjuring a formidable tempest. The year 2001 marked a pivotal moment, especially for Chinese sedans, as the State Planning Commission currently named as National Development and Reform Commission, eliminated national price controls on automobiles. From that year onward, a plethora of car models, akin to unleashed racehorses, began captivating urban residents and fueling their consumer desires, signaling a new era in the automotive landscape.

At the crossroads of urban and rural life, where aspirations for prosperity intersect with the realities of country living, people stood on the threshold of embracing a brighter future. The Wuling Sunshine, owing to the meticulous craftsmanship of the artisans at the manufacturing site, had seen a marked improvement in quality. Its key design features began to assert their importance: the strategic space planning, effortlessly accommodating both cargo and passengers, aligned perfectly with the demands of the time. To enhance driving accessibility, the Wuling Sunshine introduced a car-type flexible shaft gear-shifting mechanism, effectively addressing the common issue of unclear and challenging gear shifting in previous mini-cars. Serving as the inaugural vehicle for many, it transcended its role as merely a family car or a tool for startups, evolving into a communal asset for transporting friends and family. Its capacious interior not only accommodated passengers but also carried their dreams and aspirations toward a prosperous future.

In the grand narrative of an era, the most successful products are those that resonate with its rhythm. The Wuling Sunshine embodied the prevailing struggle during that particular era. Like a magnet in motion, it drew an ever-growing number of people transitioning to urban life, captivated by its promise to improve their quality of life.

5.5 The Sky Is the Limit

The automotive industry resembles an immense ocean, where waves of innovation and surprising surges continually ripple through its vast expanse, embodying both leadership and unpredictability in the endless blue. For those navigating this industry, motion is perpetual, with little room for pause or rest.

With the dawn of 2004, the Chinese automotive sector embarked on a youthful era, marked by the appointment of internationally-minded young leaders across various automotive groups. These leaders brought with them a refreshing outlook, infusing the industry with new ideas and visions. On 2005 New Year's Day, Chen Hong, the newly appointed president of SAIC Motor and chairman of SGMW at the time, visited Liuzhou. Struck by the dynamic energy he encountered, his engagement with the company's plans led to a moment of revelation. He boldly challenged the joint venture's initial goal of producing 300,000 vehicles annually, and proposed an audacious target of 1 million vehicles per year, aiming to not only lead but also transform the industry.

An annual output of 1 million vehicles!

This bold proposal of achieving an annual output of 1 million vehicles cast a stunned silence over the room, pushing the boundaries of what was previously deemed imaginable. While the original tripartite agreement had set an ambitious target of 300,000 vehicles by 2010—a goal considered the zenith of achievement by the previous board—organizations often inadvertently limit their own growth potential. Chen Hong's audacious vision effectively shattered these self-imposed ceilings, unveiling previously unimagined opportunities and casting new light on the potential of SGMW through the lens of economies of scale. This revelatory insight held the promise of unlocking a transformative and elevated trajectory for the enterprise.

The spring of 2005 brought forth contrasting emotions, particularly with the unexpected resignation of Phil Murtaugh, president of GM China. A driving force behind the establishment and prosperity of the joint venture, he made significant contributions to GM's collaborative endeavors in China. His pivotal role as a key negotiator for the Pudong sedan project with SAIC Motor in 1996, coupled with his optimistic view of the Chinese market and his deep integration into Chinese culture, proved instrumental. Furthermore, his promotion of "empathetic thinking" and a pragmatic approach that bridged ideological divides[1] had been crucial in fostering SAIC-GM's expansive growth. Over his five-year presidency at GM China, he played a crucial role in expanding the company's influence, notably elevating SGMW into one of the most dynamic joint ventures in the automotive industry. This project, in which he took immense pride and demonstrated deep involvement, continually drew his attention to the burgeoning mini-vehicle sector. Nonetheless, the decision by GM in early 2005 to move its Asia-Pacific headquarters from Singapore to Shanghai, resulting in overlapping roles and functions between the Asian and Chinese divisions, might have influenced Phil Murtaugh's decision to step down.

Throughout his tenure, Phil Murtaugh had consistently exhibited a supportive stance toward the joint venture. In a memorable interaction with the government, he humbly acknowledged the collective effort behind SGMW's success, highlighting the contributions of figures like Wang Hanmin, the vice-chairman of the People's Government of the Guangxi Zhuang Autonomous Region, and praising the capabilities of team members such as Shen Yang and Yao Zuoping, whom he believed would thrive in any global automotive enterprise.

Phil Murtaugh's departure cast a shadow of melancholy over the management team at SGMW. Nonetheless, the subsequent appointment of a new chairman, who not only trusted the joint venture but also raised its strategic importance within the group, provided a silver lining. From this vantage point, amidst the winds of change, SGMW found itself in a fortunate position, continuing its journey of growth and progress.

Navigating the developmental path of joint ventures is often fraught with challenges, as exemplified by Jinbei GM in Shenyang. Reflecting on this tumultuous

---

① Li An'ding. *A Tale of Cars in China: 30 Years, from Start to Fast Lane*[M]. SDX Joint Publishing Company, 2017, 313.

period, the president of GM Asia Pacific acknowledged that Jinbei GM's primary misstep was a miscalculation in market analysis. The joint venture partners proceeded without comprehensive market research, assuming a robust market for pickup trucks. This oversight resulted in a significant disconnect when the completed vehicles failed to align with market demands[①]. Further exacerbating the situation, GM pointed out deficiencies in their Chinese counterparts' understanding of consumer needs and brand concepts—a critique that nearly led to a premature dissolution of the partnership. While clashes between a joint venture's board of directors and management are not uncommon, the key lies in navigating these differences constructively. Cultivating trust and mutual appreciation is essential for the harmony and success of such partnerships.

In the realm of automobile manufacturing, where vehicles typically serve consumers for 15 to 20 years, the pressure on manufacturers to develop successors and new models remains incessant. Inspired by the ambitious goals set by the new chairman, the management team at SGMW was driven to aim even higher, raising the pivotal question: What is the next significant leap, and from where will the next wave of innovation emerge?

A journey to Japan was imminent, given that it is the birthplace of the concept of mini-car, also known as kei cars. The term "K-Car" first appeared in documents from the Ministry of Transport of Japan in 1949, denoting four-wheeled lightweight vehicles. However, it was not until 1955 that Japan's production of mini-vehicles notably reached a few hundred units. In that pivotal year, the Ministry of International Trade and Industry of Japan introduced the "national car" concept and established specific standards for these vehicles. This move was soon followed by the enactment of the Regulations for Four-Wheeled Lightweight Vehicles, significantly bolstering the development of the mini-vehicle sector in Japan, with the vehicles designed to navigate the country's narrow and elongated terrain, perfectly suited for traversing fields and villages. Their small engine size not only meant lower taxes but also exempted owners from the need to have a designated parking space, a necessity for larger cars in Japan. These conveniences played a key role in nurturing Japan's mini-vehicle industry, catapulting companies like Daihatsu and Suzuki to the forefront of the global market in this segment. Governmental policies further facilitated the

---

① Jia Xinguang. *The Grand Reshuffling: Dominance in the Ebb and Flow of China's Automotive Sector*[M]. China Machine Press, 2010, 132.

transition of Japan's mini-vehicles into mass production. From 1955 to 1980, despite fluctuations in market trends for mini sedans, the demand for mini-commercial vehicles remained notably steady, suggesting a robust and consistent market need[1]. Japan's pronounced edge in mini-vehicle production and the adaptability of these vehicles to both urban and rural markets in East Asian countries resulted in Japanese models and engines, particularly from manufacturers like Suzuki, Daihatsu, Mitsubishi, and Honda, becoming primary templates for Chinese mini-vehicle producers.

In late November 2005, Shen Yang and his team attended the Tokyo Motor Show, upholding a tradition of seeking international exploration and exposure. The goal was to broaden their global outlook by immersing themselves in a diverse range of international automotive innovations. However, the models showcased at the event failed to make a significant impression. The team's brief visit, lasting less than half a day, underscored the realization that the pursuit of inspiration and novel ideas would need to extend beyond the confines of this single exhibition.

While savoring their boxed lunches by the roadside outside the exhibition hall, the team engaged in a lively discussion about the Tokyo Motor Show and the future trajectory of product planning. The trip to Tokyo had proven somewhat underwhelming, with the once-vibrant Japanese mini-vehicle industry appearing to lose its former dynamism. The models on display showed little advancement, potentially stifled by the Regulations for Four-Wheeled Lightweight Vehicles. This stagnation suggested that mini-vehicles had hit a developmental ceiling, with their spatial innovation hamstrung by these stringent rules—a classic case of a factor that both fosters and impedes progress. In stark contrast, Chinese automotive companies were navigating a market free from such regulatory shackles, begging the question: Why adhere strictly to Japanese models?

The more pragmatic approach was to forge ahead, tailoring designs to the preferences and needs of domestic users. With evolving consumer demands, it became apparent that cars could not continue to indefinitely reduce in size. If that option was off the table, the only viable alternative was expansion. Therefore, building upon and enhancing the existing framework of the Wuling Sunshine seemed a more practical strategy than starting anew.

Size became a focal point to consider. Recognizing that traditional models were

---

① Furukawa Akira. An Overview of Mini-cars and Their Body Design[J]. trans. Dong Yiqing, *World Auto*, 1983.

proving inadequate, a counterintuitive approach—upsizing minivans—emerged as a trend worth exploring. In the midst of this animated discussion, the seed of a new product concept was planted. By the conclusion of their roadside meal, the dimensions for Wuling's next-generation vehicle were set impromptu: an enlarged design measuring 4.0 meters in length and 1.7 meters in width.

The team's deliberations on the dimensions of a mini-vehicle, conducted on Japanese soil—the very birthplace of the concept—served as an unintended yet poignant metaphor. During that period, China's standards and policies for mini-vehicles were still in their infancy, marked by a lack of clarity and definition. Until 2005, China's automotive policies closely mirrored Japanese norms, where the length of minivans typically did not exceed 3.5 meters, and vehicles over 4.0 meters (4.0 to 6.0 meters) were categorized as light vehicles, creating a gap between 3.5 meters and 4.0 meters, a segment yet to be explored or defined.

The question arose: What type of vehicle could effectively fill this void? SGMW had previously contemplated extending its popular early model, the LZ110, to 4.0 meters in response to the market's increasing demand for "more cargo, faster transport." Now, the opportunity to explore this idea presented itself once again.

Upon their return to China, the core technical team made a beeline for the China Automotive Technology and Research Center in Tianjin to delve into the standards governing Chinese mini-vehicles. Their objective was ambitious yet clear: to redefine the length of mini-vehicles from the existing 3.5 meters to a more expansive 4.0 meters.

This seemingly modest extension of 0.5 meters, in reality, marked a pivotal transition with the potential to herald a new epoch for larger minivans. The Chinese mini-vehicle, emancipating itself from the constraints of Japanese technical regulations, was on the cusp of a significant challenge against the globally acclaimed Japanese light vehicles. In the ensuing years, this uniquely Chinese variant of the minivan would weave its own legendary narrative, one that triumphs over the established Japanese model.

Entrusted with the ambitious task of developing a prototype for the internal project code-named N300, the Technical Development Center embarked on a remarkably swift operation. Within a mere 14 days, a mock-up of the car materialized, followed by the completion of a concept car design in just 45 days, and subsequently, the formulation of the exterior design scheme. This rapid sequence of developments culminated in the readiness of the prototype for the large-size minivan by 2006 New

Year's Day, poised for a groundbreaking inspection.

Notably, the expansion of the car's dimensions was not confined to its length alone; its width also increased by a substantial 10 centimeters. While extending the length and elongating the wheelbase did not necessitate the development of a new chassis, the increase in width entailed far-reaching implications. A broader track mandated a comprehensive overhaul of the chassis design, marking a major leap in design and development capabilities for SGMW's Technical Development Center and venturing into previously unexplored territory. Despite the scale of this undertaking, GM's management appeared relatively unconcerned with these intricate details, allowing the project to progress smoothly.

The impromptu decision made during a roadside discussion was then propelling the project down the fast track of development.

Before the initiation of the N300 project, another minivan, the Wuling Hongtu, had been launched, a collaborative effort between SGMW and PATAC. This model adhered strictly to GMS standards, incorporating elements of sedan design that reflected a more standardized development process and a streamlined design approach. Personnel from the Wuling Technical Development Center were dispatched to PATAC in Shanghai to contribute to the development of the Wuling Hongtu, and many of SGMW's supervisors and managers who began their careers in fundamental engineering roles were intricately involved in every step of the process. These mid-level staff members demonstrated a voracious appetite for knowledge, encompassing control, verification, process, and manufacturing. They eagerly assimilated the rich expertise accumulated over a century by GM, adapting advanced processes to their factory's conditions and continuously honing their skills. This approach, drawing from the modular thinking employed in Wuling Hongtu's development at PATAC, likewise accelerated the N300's development process. Within this framework, lagging behind was not perceived as a failure but rather as an opportunity for learning. A perpetual cycle of learning, action, and further learning remained in motion, nurturing the emergence of a new and dynamic entity in the automotive world.

Vehicle design is an intricate balancing act that juggles with multiple factors such as quality, body weight, and cost, requiring these elements to be meticulously cross-referenced and carefully balanced. The N300, geared toward the commercial market, catered to consumers seeking durable, cost-effective vehicles capable of transporting heavy loads. The enhanced spatial dimensions of the N300 inevitably led to an increase in weight. To counter this, designers embarked on a painstaking process, thoroughly analyzing every dimension and scrupulously shaving off millimeters and grams wherever feasible. They rigorously calculated the dimensions of joints and weld edges within the three-dimensional digital model, ensuring the necessity of each retained millimeter.

The N300's development journey saw the continually refined prototype subjected to numerous road tests and a myriad of other evaluations. Among the most challenging were the high-altitude tests conducted in the Kunlun Mountains, at elevations reaching 5,000 meters. Test personnel faced the formidable challenge of altitude sickness, enduring symptoms such as chest tightness, shortness of breath, dizziness, nausea, fatigue, and swelling. Despite these physical hurdles, the team persevered, driven by the determination to understand the vehicle's potential responses at high altitudes. Sleep eluded many, with some resorting to the aid of oxygen tanks for rest. Each night, the test supervisor would diligently check every team member's pulse and breathing before they retired for the night. Both the team and the vehicle withstood the rigors of these extreme environmental conditions under a sky studded with stars. Against the moonlit grandeur of the mountains, this testing phase transcended technical exploration, evolving into a profound display of human resilience.

5.6 Quality's Quantum Leap

Within the company, each department faced its own set of distinct challenges, with the Quality Department undergoing a particularly demanding journey of transformation and rejuvenation. Following the joint venture, the department pivoted its focus from external procurement and collaboration to encompass the entire manufacturing process. It was during this phase that the philosophy "quality is crafted in the process" firmly took root. Leveraging this foundation, the company, in an effort to align its operational realities with the best practices of both GM and SAIC Motor, compiled its inaugural edition of a manufacturing quality manual, introducing the stringent "triple no" principle of quality: accept no defects, manufacture no defects, and pass on no defects.

In 2002, SGMW established a robust production and maintenance system, complemented by a preventive maintenance framework. Guided by Yao Zuoping, technical engineers authored and published a specialized book *Statistical Process Control*, and devised over 1,900 standardized operation sheets for various process stations, more than 150 quality control operating systems, as well as over 400 error-proofing projects, collectively leading to a significantly high first-time pass rate in product quality.

Embracing the ethos that "quality is crafted in the process", the company launched a comprehensive quality improvement project for the Wuling Sunshine. Despite facing numerous quality issues during the initial phases of market introduction, the company internalized an awareness to build a "customer chain", categorizing customers into internal and external groups. Internally, each subsequent manufacturing process was perceived as the customer, emphasizing the critical importance of preventing defects from being passed down the line. This period marked the full implementation and integration of the principle that "quality is a collective commitment" into the very fabric of the company's culture.

Employees from across various departments, including design and procurement, actively participated in a deliberately slowed-down car manufacturing process. This approach, focused on producing cars at a reduced speed, effectively highlighted and magnified issues related to safety, quality, and production rhythm. The participation of staff from different sectors allowed for rapid identification and resolution of problems, ensuring that no issue was overlooked or carried forward into subsequent stages. In 2006, Yao Zuoping introduced the innovative "ball on a ramp" theory in automotive quality management. This theory visualizes car quality formation through four distinct stages, represented as the "ramp," encompassing four quality modules, symbolized as the "ball", with the quality system acting as the "wedge".[1] With this theory as a guiding principle and considering the company's specific situation and unique traits, SGMW meticulously crafted its exclusive SGMW-GMS quality management system.

While these methodologies proved applicable to the N300 project, SGMW acknowledged the talent scarcity arising from its location in the north-central region of Guangxi, posing challenges to its development efforts. To address this, the

---

① Yao Zuoping, Wan Junkang, Li Huawei. Features and Management Integration of Automobile Quality[J]. *Development and Innovation of Machinery and Electrical Products*, 2006.

company urgently needed a mechanism to catalyze a surge in knowledge acquisition and infuse the organization with essential expertise, a strategy crucial for fostering the enterprise's dynamic growth and sustainability. Therefore, SGMW sought to harness scientific research resources from universities, pioneering a R&D approach centered on "leading with our strengths, integrating resources, and fostering innovation". Under the guidance of the company's R&D team, experts from distinguished institutions such as Hunan University, Jilin University, and Shanghai Jiao Tong University were invited to contribute to the development process. For example, Zhong Zhihua's team from Hunan University specialized in body safety and reliability; Guo Konghui's team from Jilin University focused on chassis performance; Lin Zhongqin's team from Shanghai Jiao Tong University concentrated on body precision and engine development. Additionally, collaborations were established with Baosteel Group for material forming analysis, PATAC for virtual assembly and test validation, and the China Automotive Technology and Research Center for handling standards, regulations, and overall vehicle certification.

Confronting challenges such as suboptimal driving experiences, vibrations, and noise due to issues related to vehicle weight and load, SGMW identified a significant gap in its R&D capability in these domains. Eager to remedy this, the company sought collaboration with Academician Zhong Zhihua from Hunan University, specifically for conducting crash tests. In an exceptional undertaking, a team from Hunan University swiftly mobilized to Liuzhou in April 2006, initiating work in the laboratory even prior to formalizing a business contract. Academician Zhong Zhihua's dedication was particularly evident during the vehicle collision test phase, wherein he personally inspected the cars' undersides. Displaying a remarkable commitment, he conducted these thorough examinations directly on the ground without the use of protective mats, leaving a lasting impression on observers.

He meticulously developed various plans, including diverse test rigs that progressed from individual component testing to comprehensive full-vehicle crash tests. These examinations, encompassing welding points, cross-sectional sizes, and other factors, were conducted both at the university and in the Liuzhou factory. For example, real-vehicle trials were employed to determine the optimal shape for the vehicle's frame, with the goal of identifying the most effective configuration. The frequent train trips between Changsha and Liuzhou became emblematic of the dynamic collaboration between an academic institution committed to practical application and an industrious enterprise seeking to enhance its expertise.

In an era where China's bullet trains epitomize unparalleled efficiency, reflecting on a time dominated by the leisurely pace of green-skinned trains chugging along at 80 kilometers per hour feels almost inconceivable. The journey from Changsha to Liuzhou, beginning in the evening, would extend into the following afternoon. On a notable occasion, Academician Zhong Zhihua, equipped with only a bag, remarkably managed to bring with him a full-sized automobile frame in a sleeper carriage. The task of transporting this unwieldy frame to the Wuling factory was herculean for the two young men who met him at the station. To optimize the use of lab equipment in Changsha, Academician Zhong Zhihua prepared the frame at the university, then journeyed over a thousand kilometers to the Wuling factory for reassembly and subsequent collision and vibration tests. Knowledge, much like automobile parts, was rudimentarily pieced together and then widely disseminated.

In the domain of chassis performance structure and spring technology, a team led by Academician Guo Konghui from Jilin University played a pivotal role in providing essential technical performance verification. The complex challenges faced by the factory were methodically addressed through focused research by university professors, who strategically divided and tackled each obstacle. SGMW forged a symbiotic collaboration model with academic institutions, wherein the company presented real-world challenges as examination tasks for students and collaborated on postgraduate programs with universities. The universities, in turn, would periodically release the results of these challenges and deploy staff to be stationed at the factory. This approach effectively cultivated talent in both academic and industrial realms, ensuring that whether pursuing master's degree or doctoral degree, students rooted their research in tangible, real-world challenges. Upon completing their studies, these students often secured preferential consideration for employment opportunities within the company. The implementation of this integrated strategy had effortlessly bridged the gap between academic theory and the pragmatic exigencies of the Liuzhou factory.

5.7 Bridging North and South: A Tale of Two Bases

The Liuzhou factory's vision extended beyond its immediate vicinity, reaching out to the northeastern coast.

In June 2005, SGMW and Etsong (Qingdao) Vehicle Manufacturing Co., Ltd. conducted a signing ceremony for asset transfer, integrating Etsong (Qingdao) into SGMW's northern production base. This transition marked the end of Etsong (Qingdao)'s ambitious but challenging eight-year journey in automotive endeavors, culminating in an acquisition. During this period, major automotive groups across China were vying to establish their presence nationwide. Qingdao, historically aligned with FAW and serving as a key truck base for FAW Jiefang Qingdao Automobile[①], was expected to be under FAW's influence. Therefore, SGMW's entry into Qingdao surprised many industry observers.

For numerous cities, automobile manufacturing has long been a cherished aspiration. When Qingdao was designated as one of China's 16 sub-provincial cities in February 1994, automotive manufacturing rapidly ascended as a top priority. The automotive industry became the buzzword across the Chinese mainland, inspiring passion and aspirations. Local governments and entrepreneurs, captivated by the allure of the automotive sector, eagerly invested in various capacities. This bustling scene attracted a diverse array of entrants. In 1997, Etsong (Qingdao), originally a tobacco company, forayed into car manufacturing by acquiring second-hand equipment from the United Kingdom's "declining aristocrat" Rover. However, the reality of car manufacturing extends beyond passion; the substantial capital requirements often dampen investors' enthusiasm. With limited brand recognition and experience, Etsong (Qingdao) struggled to achieve mass automobile production or secure the necessary manufacturing qualifications. Following the national automotive plan's establishment of the "Big Three and Small Three" joint venture sedan framework, other aspiring manufacturers adopted a "produce first, seek approval later" strategy, hoping to gain market entry permits. As a mix of proactiveness and reluctance, this approach became a common path for many hopeful players in the

---

① Ban Weidong. The Story Behind SGMW's Restructuring of Etsong (Qingdao)[J]. *China Automotive News*, June 20, 2005.

automotive field.

For Etsong (Qingdao), the core challenge stemmed from its inability to produce a market-worthy car. Even after FAW's acquisition in 2001, the company struggled to develop a viable car model, given FAW's primary focus on its truck base in Qingdao, leaving Etsong (Qingdao)'s sedan aspirations somewhat neglected.

The narrative took a turn in 2003, as FAW recognized the need for a robust response to the burgeoning sedan market in China. Etsong (Qingdao) emerged as a potential base for FAW's Mazda 9 sedan project, sparking considerable enthusiasm in Qingdao about the prospect of sedan production. However, this optimism was short-lived. During an inspection visit, Mazda representatives expressed profound disappointment, sharply critiquing Etsong (Qingdao)'s factory as nothing more than a glorified car repair shop, lacking genuine car manufacturing expertise. This scathing assessment prompted FAW to reassess their involvement, and the downturn in China's sedan market in early 2004 accelerated Etsong (Qingdao)'s decline.

FAW's subsequent withdrawal plunged Etsong (Qingdao) into desperation, leading them to seek partnerships with other automakers, including Dongfeng, SAIC Motor, and Chery, which showed little interest in acquiring the beleaguered firm, while SGMW believed otherwise.

SGMW's entry came as a critical lifeline for Etsong (Qingdao) and a strategic opportunity for itself. An agreement was swiftly reached between the two parties. In early 2005, propelled by Chairman Chen Hong's ambitious inspection tour goals, SGMW revised its 2010 target upward from 300,000 to 500,000 units. However, the Liuzhou factory's maximum production capacity was capped at about 220,000 units, underscoring the imperative for expansion. Given its southern location, SGMW recognized the necessity of a broader geographical footprint for auto manufacturing that demands substantial material throughput, expanding northward emerged as the only logical course of action.

Geographically speaking, Qingdao's strategic location, characterized by its service radius and population density, made it more conducive to whole vehicle sales than Liuzhou, providing a tactical advantage in terms of space utilization. As a mini-vehicle production base, Qingdao presented distinct locational benefits; its advanced national road network facilitated expedited access to provinces such as Henan, Shanxi, and the Beijing–Tianjin–Hebei region. Additionally, its waterways were instrumental in enabling rapid vehicle transportation to the Northeast. At the time, the majority of SGMW's sales were concentrated in North China, specifically in Henan, Hebei, and

Shandong, making both North and East China prime regions for mini-vehicle market expansion. In terms of sales density, within a radius of 1,000 kilometers from Qingdao, SGMW could secure a market share of 75%. In contrast, its market share in its Guangxi base remained below 45%.

During the 2005 Spring Festival, SGMW initiated its preliminary assessment and negotiation with Etsong (Qingdao), and deployed the heads of four major workshops for an on-site evaluation to ascertain production capacity. Etsong (Qingdao)'s facility, at the time, was in a state of disrepair, lacking essential amenities like water, electricity, and heating, and was devoid of staff. The negotiation room was as frigid as an ice cellar, presenting a substantial endurance challenge for those visiting from warmer southern regions. Within this confined space, marked by intense discussions and people seeking warmth in close proximity, topics were adeptly addressed and resolved with remarkable efficiency.

The next crucial step for SGMW was the selection of equipment for the Qingdao facility. The factory had already compiled a comprehensive equipment list based on their specific requirements, which was to be scrutinized by the directors of the four major workshops from SGMW, who subsequently identified the essential equipment while marking others for removal by the team in Qingdao. Following this crucial meeting, the directors were scheduled to personally inspect the equipment in the workshops. The journey from the meeting room to the workshops, spanning roughly 200 meters, unfolded against a backdrop of a stark, colorless seascape. The sky loomed heavy and overcast, with dense, motionless clouds. The elongated, mournful waves of the sea contributed to an overall somber atmosphere. Solitary seagulls soared at angles, their haunting cries almost serving as a warning to newcomers that they were encroaching upon their domain. The entire area exuded a sense of bleakness and abandonment, with the icy sea breeze slicing through the desolate factory structures. Without hats, the cold stung everyone's ears, prompting a brisk dash to the workshops. Inside, the semi-old equipment of the long-unused factory felt even colder, resembling more a forsaken warehouse than an active production facility.

This scene evokes memories of 1984 when Volkswagen initiated a groundbreaking partnership with the Shanghai Automobile & Tractor Company (predecessor of SAIC Motor) in Beijing, laying the groundwork for a joint venture. Martin Posth, one of Volkswagen's pioneer managers in China, detailed his initial visit to the primitive sheds in Anting, Shanghai, in his book *1,000 Days in Shanghai: The Volkswagen Story - The First Chinese-German Car Factory*. The conditions he encountered were almost beyond belief[①]—drafty windows, pervasive humidity, lack of heating, scattered metal scraps, and an overall ambiance reminiscent of a ravaged wasteland. Additionally, manual assembly of Shanghai cars took place within the factory, juxtaposing two industrial eras under one roof with a technological gap spanning fifty years—a sight profoundly overwhelming for the German team, the trailblazers of SAIC Volkswagen Automotive.

In that defining moment, the middle managers from SGMW, each assuming a role akin to Martin Posth, were struck with a mix of astonishment and apprehension upon witnessing the state of the facility.

However, they wisely acknowledged the importance of tempering their critique. Etsong(Qingdao)'s industrial park, located in the Qingdao Economic and Technological Development Zone in Huangdao District, showcased well-established basic infrastructure facilities. Not merely a mature factory site, it also possessed additional land for future expansion. Its favorable location, accessible by both land and water and strategically positioned to connect the north and south, made it an ideal production base for SGMW, which was situated inland in South China. A vast opportunity awaited for a protagonist to take center stage.

In strategic endeavors, intent often supersedes the need for meticulous planning. With a clear direction, actions naturally adapt and refine the unexpected details encountered along the way.

From the initial spark of ambition to the meticulous factory inspection and equipment evaluation, the negotiations between the two entities progressed almost seamlessly. Commencing in early 2005 and culminating after three months of thorough deliberation, a preliminary acquisition agreement was inked. SGMW committed RMB 300 million to acquire the plant assets of Etsong (Qingdao), with plans to initiate factory construction in the near future. This strategic move also brought relief to the Qingdao Municipal Government, as the once-dormant factory area, land, and industrial park could now be revitalized after eight years of stagnation.

For SAIC-GM, which had previously acquired the Dong Yue vehicle manufacturing facility in Yantai, Shandong two years earlier, this development was warmly welcomed. The synergy between Yantai and Qingdao, by operating in tandem yet independently, facilitated a more flexible allocation of components and customer

---

① Martin Posth. *1,000 Days in Shanghai: The Volkswagen Story - The First Chinese-German Car Factory*[M]. trans. Xiang Wei. China CITIC Press, 2008, 4.

resources.

Navigating the grand strategy on the automotive industry's chessboard involves critical considerations for every automotive group, resembling a military operation on a sand table, where each strategically positioned flag serves a distinct purpose. During that era, many automotive groups were expanding their footprints across multiple regions; a multi-location strategy was a distinctive and deliberate choice for these automotive conglomerates.

Certain entities, including the Liuzhou Municipal Government, harbored reservations about SGMW's establishment of a new base in Qingdao. Their concerns revolved around the potential for this venture to foster an autonomous entity growing and seeking independence. Despite being a joint venture, SGMW still bore the lineage and shares of a local state-owned enterprise, making the perspective of the local government a crucial factor. To allay these concerns, SGMW's management promptly reassured them with a proactive pledge. Upholding the ethos of "Less the possession, more the value of the company in the society", the Qingdao base was positioned as an extension of the manufacturing capabilities of SGMW, rather than an independent entity.

The manufacturing engineering team at SGMW also rallied support for establishing the new facility in Qingdao. In April 2005, a ceremony in the iconic Red Building at their headquarters in Liuzhou marked the formation of the first 22-member pioneering team, with the head of the manufacturing department appointed as the leader for this initiative. Shen Yang's stirring mobilization speech underscored the challenge ahead: "We hail from the mountains. Now, as we embark toward the sea, we face the challenge of adapting, surviving, and ultimately thriving in Qingdao. Can we do it? I believe so. Our red flag, deeply anchored in the mountainous karst, can surely find its stand on the beach as well."

The paramount goal for this pioneering team was to plant the red flag on the beach—a metaphor for establishing a strong presence in Qingdao. Despite Etsong (Qingdao)'s factory possessing a complete production line, it fell short of meeting the current enterprise requirements. The integration of existing Etsong (Qingdao) employees into the Wuling culture posed a significant challenge. Moreover, the scarcity of supporting manufacturers in Qingdao raised concerns about excessive logistics costs for components, a critical factor that could potentially constrain the development of an automotive enterprise in a new location. For regions aspiring to foster their automotive industries, it is imperative to take into consideration the local layout of component industries, as mere transplantation of a few large entities without a supportive ecosystem often leads to eventual stagnation.

The principle of self-reliance was crucial, with essential equipment transported from Liuzhou to Qingdao. The pioneering team displayed remarkable efficiency, completing the modification and relocation of equipment within just two months. The human resources department, in parallel, managed to accomplish the herculean task of recruiting, training, and initiating production within a three-month period. This operational start was indeed a race against time.

Nevertheless, the challenges encountered were formidable. Developing a robust automotive manufacturing supply chain in Qingdao would take a considerable amount of time. The production ramp-up at the Qingdao factory faced hindrances due to its sluggish pace, and the necessity of transporting many materials from Liuzhou incurred hefty logistics costs. Furthermore, a noticeable scarcity of human resources added to the complexity. At one point, the situation necessitated a complete halt in production, leading to operators being sent home on leave, while workshop directors and team leaders traveled to the headquarters in Liuzhou for intensive training.

Four years prior, when SGMW was established as a joint venture, representatives from Shanghai, symbolizing advanced culture, had traveled to inland Liuzhou to impart their knowledge and expertise. Now, another coastal city found itself in the position of seeking cultural and operational insight from Liuzhou, epitomizing a return to the roots culture that resonates with the enduring spirit of "Perseverance with Self-Strengthening." The office building at the Qingdao plant, a mirror image of the Liuzhou headquarters, stood as a modest four-story red-brick structure. While it may not have many stories to tell, it undeniably and tangibly reaffirmed and perpetuated a legacy of resilience and determination.

5.8 Crazy Gambit, Winning Hand

The ultimate resolution was to manufacture the innovative N300 model at the Qingdao base.

It was a decision that caught many by surprise. Until then, the Qingdao base had primarily focused on producing the Wuling Dragon, a model predating the joint venture with SGMW. This sizable bumper minivan, priced just above RMB 30,000, had enjoyed its share of success, particularly due to its robust front beam that adeptly met the early 21st-century mandatory crash test requirements. This phase served as a preparatory period for the Qingdao base, enabling it to refine and enhance its manufacturing capabilities.

During this juncture, Wuling's Liuzhou Hexi base was not operating at full production capacity, presenting a quandary: whether to continue the production of the new N300 model in Liuzhou or to set up a new production line in Qingdao specifically for this upcoming model.

Opting for the latter was a bold, almost audacious move. The production of a new vehicle model is typically fraught with unforeseen challenges, and establishing a new production line demands an extensive period of adaptation and fine-tuning. Generally, combining these two formidable tasks is not recommended. Given its relatively nascent stage of development, the Qingdao base appeared an unlikely candidate to bear such a significant responsibility, a perspective reflected in the reluctance of both the shareholders and SGMW's internal management to embrace such a risky undertaking.

Yao Zuoping was among the few steadfast believers that the success of the new Qingdao base rested on the introduction of new products, contending that without fresh offerings, the base risked becoming unsustainable, potentially reducing the strategic layout to a precarious structure akin to a sand castle. Since the N300 initially targeted markets in North and Northeast China, Yao Zuoping passionately advocated for production to be located as close as possible to the target sales markets and consumers.

His logical and consistent reasoning eventually overcame the technical hesitations. Once the decision was made, it was time to confront a plethora of challenges head-on. Yao Zuoping personally led an expansive team of over 200 individuals to Qingdao. Huangdao Hotel, situated nearby the factory, and other hotels in the area were swiftly occupied by the influx from Liuzhou, which marked the beginning of an intense operational phase in Huangdao, characterized by a hive of activity and an unmistakable dynamism, akin to the rapid growth of bamboo shoots.

In 2006, as the Qingdao branch transitioned into full-scale production, embarking on a transformative journey, technicians found themselves in constant transit between the two locations. During this critical phase of mass production, the Qingdao base grappled with a shortage of engineers proficient in equipment calibration, exemplified by the consistent failure of frame mold production to meet design specifications. To mitigate this, components were initially crafted in Liuzhou, then swiftly airlifted to Qingdao. Upon their arrival, they were promptly sent to the frame supplier for essential welding, and by the next morning, these vital parts were delivered back to the factory, ready to be integrated into the production of key test vehicles.

Amidst a whirlwind of activities spanning various locations, the year concluded with uplifting news for SGMW as it reclaimed its position as the leading seller in the mini-vehicle segment. The Wuling Sunshine triumphantly ended the eight-year reign of the best-selling Chang'an Star. This achievement was a significant morale booster for the joint venture's employees, who had grappled with feelings of misunderstanding, distrust, and discontentment for over four years. The success of the independently developed models brought immense joy and a profound sense of fulfillment, validating the company's perseverance and its decision to rely on its own strengths and judgment.

With everything falling into place, July 2007 saw the groundbreaking for the Qingdao engine factory. Subsequently, in September of the same year, the SGMW Liuzhou engine factory was not only completed but also commenced operations, marking the most extensive investment project since the joint venture's establishment, with a dedicated focus on developing and producing the advanced B-series engines. These engines served as the much-needed "heart" for SGMW's vehicles, addressing the congenital "heart disease" that had plagued its predecessor, the Liuzhou Tractor Factory, for over two decades. The B-series engines not only overcame technological challenges but also alleviated cost-related concerns[1]. The substantial RMB 2 billion investment in the Liuzhou engine factory was directed not just toward advancing engine technology and quality but also toward reducing costs through the adoption of cutting-edge equipment and large-scale production.

The Qingdao engine factory adeptly leveraged experiences gained from the construction of the Liuzhou factory, making adjustments to the height, space, and overall facility utilization. For a precision machining factory, stringent requirements for temperature and humidity control for the machinery and components were paramount. The Qingdao engine factory had a lower building height to enhance energy efficiency, and the project team implemented a series of exhaust measures to sequentially resolve air quality concerns resulting from the reduced height.

---

① Yao Wei. Behind the Mass Production of the B-Series New Engines[J]. *Commercial Vehicle News*, 2007.

Meanwhile, the introduction of the Daewoo 1.2-liter engine at the Qingdao engine factory, arriving at an opportune time, addressed the power matching issue for Qingdao's new cars. The promising synergy between the two entities held the potential for a significant impact in future market endeavors.

Nevertheless, some regrets lingered. Despite the subsequent introduction of engines with a 1.5-liter displacement and other varieties, the lack of complete independence in design posed challenges for designers striving for extensive optimization. This introduced a potential hurdle for SGMW's future development of passenger cars. Into a realm of a thousand hills, each summit crossed only reveals another's will. Such is the destined path for those who forge the trail in the automotive landscape.

In 2007, SGMW achieved annual sales of 550,000 units, once again securing its position at the top of the mini-vehicle market. At this juncture, the mini-vehicle market had undergone profound changes, with the Wuling Sunshine beginning to embody the demeanor of a market leader. By the year's end, it had reached a milestone of over one million units in circulation, elevating itself into the ranks of the top ten best-selling single-platform models globally. SGMW led the market with a 43% share, followed by Chang'an at 30%, and Hafei at 14%, while other mini-vehicle manufacturers could only achieve a maximum market share of around 5%. This surge in sales volumes led to a competitive duopoly in the mini-vehicle market.

The new N300 model started to make its mark, significantly contributing to the rapid growth of the Qingdao base. As SGMW's factories expanded, many component manufacturers also set up their facilities in proximity. The presence of an OEM inevitably attracted component suppliers, creating a cascading effect where one factory spurred the growth of another, forming a supply chain akin to planting trees one after another. The surrounding neighborhoods also proliferated. The once desolate Qingdao west coast, previously the exclusive domain of seagulls, was no longer theirs alone. They had to make room for the increasing number of people coming to stroll along the seaside.

5.9 Battle for the Discourse of Power

The dynamics of the discourse of power in joint ventures is one of the concerns of interests in the automobile industry, particularly in the context of whether late-developing countries can achieve autonomy in their automotive sectors through external collaborations. The evolution of the automotive industry in these countries is aptly encapsulated by the three-door model[①]: the Korean model, exemplifying a closed door approach; the Mexican model, illustrating a fully opened door approach; and the Chinese model, a strategy resembling a half-opened door.

The Korean model is an archetype of autonomous development for follower countries, relying predominantly on domestic resources to build a comprehensive automotive industry system. This approach is marked by significant government intervention. However, the post-Asian financial crisis era revealed flaws in Korea's inward-looking development model, misaligned with global automotive trends, prompting a shift toward a more open and internationalized strategy.

In contrast, the Mexican model is distinguished by its openness. The country's primary goal is to boost tax revenue, imposing minimal constraints on brand control and domestication rates. Similarly, other countries like Spain and Canada have adopted an open-door policy toward foreign investment in their automotive sectors.

The Chinese model, on the other hand, holds particular significance, embodying the potential to not only become the world's largest manufacturer but also a massive consumer market. Initially emulating the Korean model, China aimed to establish a comprehensive automotive industry system. However, following the landmark Beidaihe automotive development conference in 1987, China opted for a hybrid approach—safeguarding its industry while embracing opportunities for opening-up, engaging deeply in international competition and cooperation.

While the fully closed-door Korean model, justifiable in its early development stages due to a small domestic market, faced limitations on the global stage, and the fully open-door Mexican model struggled with the development of independent brands, China's more nuanced half-opened door approach offers greater flexibility. However, it also complicates regulatory mechanisms, raising concerns about the potential loss of independent development capacity in joint ventures.

In this context, SGMW pioneered a fourth model for Sino-foreign joint ventures: a joint operation at first glance, but independent in terms of two aspects at its core. This innovative strategy positioned SGMW as the only joint venture car manufacturer in China to keep its original brand and independent R&D capability—a significant

---

① China Association of Automobile Manufacturers. *Research on China's Automobile Development Strategy*[M]. China Machine Press, 2014, 1272.

attainment of discourse of power won through frontline perseverance.

In 2003, SGMW ventured into passenger car production with the Chevrolet Spark (Lechi), a model introduced by GM enriched with global resources and Daewoo technology. The leadership at SGMW envisioned great potential for the youth-oriented Lechi. However, despite selling over 200,000 units, production was eventually halted. One contributing factor was the challenge of integrating GM and Daewoo technology with SGMW's design and manufacturing strengths, resulting in elevated costs. Furthermore, Lechi faced intense competition; Chery Automobile, by replicating Lechi's design, introduced the more affordable QQ car, swiftly gaining market popularity. This patent dispute left SAIC Motor in a dilemma. The ordeal with Chery Automobile had a precedent. In 2001, Chery Automobile, initially facing difficulties securing a car manufacturing license, swiftly formed an alliance with SAIC Motor through a stock swap, gaining entry into the sedan market. However, a subsequent Chery model sparked a patent dispute with Volkswagen, souring relations with SAIC Motor in Germany. Following this dispute, SAIC Motor chose to terminate its collaboration with Chery Automobile. But just as one challenge seemed to abate, another loomed on the horizon.

This hasty foray into importing sedan models from abroad served as a stark reminder that relying on foreign designs was far from a strategic shortcut. Despite this realization, efforts to collaborate with international partners continued. The Suzuki light four-wheel MPV mini-car LANDY, coupled with its compact yet powerful K14 engine, was seen as a potential boon from GM to SGMW. Supported by GM, executives from SGMW visited Suzuki five times. While they found the vehicle and engine impressive, they noted necessary design modifications for its success in China, such as enlarging the door openings to better suit the Chinese market. However, the Japanese counterparts, confident in their global leadership in mini-vehicles, firmly opposed any such alterations, leaving scant room for input from the Chinese team. Amid these disagreements, the plan to introduce the Suzuki model was ultimately shelved. Consequently, SGMW resolved to proceed with model innovation and the independent development of the N300.

Later, the LANDY mini-car was introduced by Changhe, rebranded as Changhe Suzuki Landy, featuring the 1.4-liter K14 engine. For Changhe, beyond their older vans, the Changhe Suzuki Landy represented their hope for a new generation of mini-vehicles. Upon its market debut in 2007, the Landy enjoyed a phase of robust sales. However, constrained by a lack of independent design capability, Changhe could only make minor tweaks and adjustments to this model, proving insufficient for substantial improvements.

In contrast, Wuling's unwavering dedication to strengthening its independent R&D capability facilitated the development of successive product series that systematically targeted market niches. This strategic approach initiated a consistent offensive, which eventually caused the sales of Changhe Suzuki Landy to falter, demonstrating a lack of resilience and a discernible decline in market presence.

Had SGMW succumbed to the initial temptation of replicating Japanese car models, it might have witnessed the erosion of its independent R&D capability—a narrative all too familiar in the annals of China's automotive best-sellers. While market hits can momentarily capture the spotlight, their long-term viability often wanes. A singular model may temporarily satisfy market demands, but establishing a brand's legacy demands a commitment to ongoing model innovation.

Prior to the N300, the company had already launched a series of successful products, including the Wuling Sunshine, Wuling Yangguang, Wuling Xingwang, and Wuling Hongtu. When deliberating on the naming of the N300, unanimous agreement favored continuing with the "光" ("light" in Chinese) series, deemed both catchy and auspicious. As a larger-sized minivan, expected to mark the dawn of a new era for large-size minivans, radiating a glorious light, the N300 was christened Wuling Rongguang (Wuling Glory).

In June 2008, the Wuling Rongguang transitioned into mass production in Qingdao and made its debut at the Beijing Motor Show. Departing from convention, SGMW eschewed the typical background music for a lion dance troupe at its launch, infusing the event with the vibrancy of local culture. Amidst the resonant beats, an assembly of VIPs—including then CEO of GM, then chairman of SAIC Motor, and then president of SAIC Motor—bore witness to this landmark occasion. The Wuling Rongguang not only introduced a new category of vehicle but also carved out a niche market for large minivans. Even within niche markets, vast opportunities abound, awaiting those with the insight to identify and exploit them.

By the end of 2008, Wuling Rongguang had achieved sales of 37,500 units, with monthly production and sales surpassing 10,000 units. The launch of Wuling Rongguang had enabled SGMW to successfully enter the Northeast market. Previously, the company's market focus had been mainly on regions such as Central China, North China, and the Pearl River Delta. This new product launch transformed the Qingdao branch into a solid strategic pivot, extending the reach of the Liuzhou headquarters northward into Northeast China.

Wuling Rongguang, the newly defined large minivan model, thoroughly demonstrated the technical center's capabilities, from defining the vehicle model to establishing its platform, and from system integration to the complete vehicle, immediately garnering attention and attracting followers. The Chinese market is perennially filled with trend-chasers. Even the fastest strides by leaders can only secure a half-step lead, as peers quickly swarm to catch up. What was once an empty new track can become crowded in the blink of an eye. Pursuers and imitators are akin to echoes in a valley, not requiring much time to resonate. Where someone sets a trend, others follow. There is no room for anyone to afford to stop and rest.

In contrast to the three-year development process of Wuling Hongtu, Wuling Rongguang had a more direct lineage from the Wuling Sunshine. It was designed to fulfill the dual purpose of cargo and passenger transport with its elongated and broadened structure, while its manufacturing standards were rigorously aligned with GM's global benchmarks. Wuling Hongtu, from its inception, displayed lackluster performance, representing GM's final foray into the mini-commercial vehicle segment as a shareholder. Developed under the guidance of PATAC, Wuling Hongtu integrated numerous sedan design features to cater to a range of commercial and passenger needs, skewing toward PV-oriented development. Despite these efforts, it failed to resonate with consumers. This PV-orientation in Wuling Hongtu reflected a broader speculation on social trends; GM surmised that the evolution of mini-vehicles was plateauing and necessitated a pivot toward more sedan-like qualities. Conversely, SGMW's management contended that, given China's nascent urbanization phase, mini-vehicles were poised for a prolonged lifecycle. The divergent philosophies surrounding these two models underscored differing interpretations of broader social consumption trends. Wuling Hongtu's underperformance further tilted the balance of power of discourse within the joint venture, emphasizing the market's decisive preference. Mini-vehicles, as the market verdict revealed, are not simply scaled-down sedans but form a distinct category with their own market niche, entirely separate from that of sedans.

The discourse of power surrounding product development remains a contentious topic in Chinese automotive joint ventures, with some attributing challenges to the 50 : 50 equity ratio and its perceived impact on decision-making dynamics. However, this perspective might oversimplify the complexities inherent in joint venture management. Established by China's *Automotive Industry Policy* in 1994, this equity ratio is also a manifestation of equilibrium[1], significantly influencing the trajectory and policy orientation of joint ventures for well over a decade[2]. It served as a foundational blueprint, providing strategic guidance for foreign investments and technological integrations that followed. Amid the uncertain future of joint ventures, both parties often preferred the other to shoulder greater risk. For instance, at the inception of SAIC Volkswagen Automotive, Volkswagen Germany initially ceded sales rights in a market whose sales potential was highly speculative. Likewise, the establishment of an independent sales company by FAW Group and FAW-Volkswagen in 1997 adhered to a 50∶50 equity structure. In this context, shareholding resembled a burdensome obligation, with foreign partners not necessarily keen on increasing their stake. It is clear that a 50∶50 shareholding ratio does not necessarily constrain the decision-making autonomy of the Chinese entities. Dominance within joint ventures materializes through a market-driven counter-selection mechanism, wherein authority is derived from market success rather than merely delegated.

SGMW's journey exemplifies this principle. By the end of 2008, the Wuling Sunshine had sold over 1.4 million units, just six years since its launch, solidifying its standing as a legendary vehicle. Wuling Sunshine's structural integrity and Wuling Rongguang's spacious design serve as quintessential embodiments of the core principles that propelled these independently developed and branded models to garner consumer acclaim.

---

[1] Li An'ding. *A Tale of Cars in China: 30 Years, from Start to Fast Lane*[M]. SDX Joint Publishing Company, 2017, 402.

[2] China Association of Automobile Manufacturers. *30 Years of Reform and Opening-up in China's Automobile Industry (1978–2008): A Retrospective and Outlook*[M]. China Logistics Publishing House, 2009, 27.

Chapter 6 The Million Milestone Unveiled
2009–2010

6.1 Global Spotlight

Soichiro Honda, the founder of Honda Motor Co., Ltd. in Japan, harbored a profound passion for design, earning him the endearing title of "Head of Design" among his design room staff. His steadfast belief was that design should resonate with the spirit of the times and align with the aesthetic preferences of the broader public[①].

Design is paralleled to a strategic bet on prevailing trends, where designers assume the role of weather forecasters—positioned slightly in the past yet leaning into the future, navigating through the elusive and ever-changing currents of style and preference. Understanding trends is akin to deciphering a Picasso cubist painting: rich in hints and fragile logic, yet lacking definitive attributes. Automotive designers, tasked with conceptualizing a brand-new vehicle, face challenges comparable to interpreting a cubist masterpiece, a task that the next generation of Wuling Rongguang designers embraced with vigor.

A hint of a clue came in early 2007 when Shen Yang and his team, during a business trip to Indonesia, observed the popularity of Japanese minivans. One particular seven-seater model caught Shen Yang's attention, with its design seemingly tailor-made for Chinese consumers—ideal for family reunions during festivals or group outings on sunny days, offering ample space to comfortably accommodate everyone.

In anticipation of the imminent launch of the Wuling Rongguang, the team recognized the pressing need for the development of a new product. The focal point of their design deliberations once again gravitated toward the seven-seater Japanese

---

① Ikujiro Nonaka. *Soichiro Honda: An Intellectual Barbarian Following His Dreams*[M]. trans. Chen Di. New Star Press, 2019, 57.

vehicle, which had been lingering in their minds.

No sooner had the idea been proposed than SGMW expedited the import of a Japanese Toyota Avanza from Indonesia for an in-depth study. At that time, the absence of such a seven-seater and capacious vehicle in the Chinese market underscored a pivotal decision for the Technical Development Center: to emulate or to innovate. Nevertheless, the choice of emulation posed a pivotal quandary: Could they surpass their Japanese counterparts in terms of quality, performance, and affordability?

Met with resounding negative responses to these critical queries, the team recognized that their only option was to forge a new path.

The Toyota Avanza underwent a scrupulous examination. Its modest dimensions, rear-wheel drive, and a "2+3+2" seating arrangement across three rows initially made it enticing, but its classification as a passenger vehicle revealed significant shortcomings. The semi-independent rear suspension, a tiered floor complicating spatial utilization, and a cramped middle row highlighted its emphasis on passenger orientation at the expense of rear space and third-row comfort.

As the brainstorming sessions progressed, the Toyota Avanza's role in the development process evolved. Rather than a direct model for emulation, it served as a conceptual benchmark, guiding the designers to consolidate their vision. The vehicle's limitations spurred the team to transcend its design, leading to the crystallization of the new model's structure: seven seats, ample space, enhanced comfort, and a front-engine rear-wheel-drive layout.

Just as a soccer coach tactically positions the 11 players in various formations to counter different opponents on the soccer field, SGMW opted for a strategic pivot. In urban landscapes, the commercial vehicle market for models seating more than seven was dominated by JAC Refine, SAIC-GM Buick GL8, and GAC Honda Odyssey. The design team posited that vehicles serving dual purposes—catering to both business and personal use—would more aptly meet the evolving demands of China's urban and rural development. Consequently, the traditional "2+3+2" seating arrangement was revamped into a "2+2+3" layout, strategically placing the most populous row in the rear to optimize seating comfort. In contrast to the Toyota Avanza, where accessing the third row required flipping the second-row seats, the new design introduced a passageway between the two seats in the second row, streamlining access to the back. This adjustment in the rear seat arrangement inherently impacted the vehicle's width; the Wuling Hongguang's body would be widened by 6 centimeters compared to its predecessor, the Wuling Rongguang.

This seemingly straightforward reconfiguration signifies a profound transformation in the vehicle's structure, compelling a comprehensive redesign to accommodate these structural shifts.

The team's initial choice leaned toward rear-wheel drive after a meticulous examination of drivers' commuting patterns. Front-wheel drive presented challenges, particularly during restarts and accelerations on inclines, often leading to a "nose-lift" effect and making the front wheels susceptible to slipping. In contrast, rear-wheel drive provided a solution by ensuring increased friction for the rear wheels under similar conditions, reducing the likelihood of slipping and enhancing hill-start performance. This insight was gleaned from thorough on-site evaluations, acknowledging that many drivers reside at the desakota. Often, their final approach home might involve navigating streams or modest inclines, underscoring the necessity for a vehicle with robust acceleration, efficient hill-start capability, and superior load capacity to meet the practical everyday needs of individuals. For those residing on hillsides, a rear-wheel-drive vehicle could streamline the journey home, ensuring a seamless experience for the driver.

Considerations about interior space followed. The Toyota Avanza's interior floor, molded by its chassis structure, resembled a three-tier waterfall; therefore, it became imperative to eliminate unnecessary elevation changes to maximize the interior space. The challenge lay in transforming a three-step floor into a more manageable two-step configuration. Addressing these spatial dilemmas turned car design into an intricate game, akin to sculpting with modeling clay—elongating, widening, and elevating. It required a careful balance of proportions and interior space, immersing automotive designers in a world of geometric complexities that consumed their days and fueled their creativity.

In the intricate dance of automotive design, even the smallest component can significantly impact the overall harmony of geometric space. This time, the designers focused their attention on the position of the vehicle's springs. The transition from traditional leaf springs to coil springs, commonly found in passenger cars, underscores a profound evolution in design philosophy aimed at enhancing human comfort.

This transition in spring technology symbolizes a broader societal shift toward prioritizing comfort and user experience.

The suspension system, crucial for ride comfort, places the choice of springs at the forefront of design considerations. While many international models position coil springs beneath the frame, this configuration compromises interior space and raises the vehicle's height, potentially skewing the balance between length and height and detracting the vehicle's aesthetic appeal. To achieve a flat interior floor and improve the vehicle's proportions and stance, it was imperative to reduce the overall height, precluding the placement of coil springs under the frame. After extensive deliberation, the designers decided to locate the coil springs along the sides of the frame, a strategic move aimed at lowering the floor height, expanding interior space, and refining the vehicle's visual profile.

This daring innovation, however, was met with skepticism from the Korean designers employed by SGMW at the time, who deemed the risk too substantial and, thus, opposed the strategy.

Conversely, the local design team, fueled by ambition and a readiness to embrace risk, resolved to proceed. This risk-taking ethos had become deeply embedded within the culture of the Technical Development Center. Despite a partnership spanning over five years with SAIC Motor and GM, Wuling's Technical Development Center found itself under pressure, eager for a significant breakthrough. Much like inquisitive youth challenging norms during their formative years, questioning the status quo became their primary drive. Against the backdrop of the joint venture's formidable prowess and extensive expertise, they grew accustomed to making audacious moves as a testament to their capabilities.

Guided by a straightforward principle that prioritized user needs, the designers sought to augment the Wuling Hongguang's interior dimensions and space beyond what was achieved with the Wuling Rongguang. Additionally, the vehicle's design required refined curvatures to minimize air resistance and fuel consumption.

The innovative rear suspension design, featuring coil springs, was swiftly developed and successfully passed all requisite tests.

In comparison to models featuring tiered floors, the interior space of Wuling Hongguang underwent meticulous optimization, resembling a well-tended expanse of fertile land—vast and level. The advantages of a flat floor were tangible and unmistakable, not only expanding the rear space but also maintaining a respectable vehicle height.

The pursuit of these design innovations introduced strategic undercurrents. At SGMW, initiating a new project required board approval, prompting a tendency to downplay enhancements in project proposals to streamline the approval process. The

Wuling Hongguang lineup held particular significance for the company, marking its inaugural venture into a front-engine, rear-wheel-drive configuration. This marked a significant departure from previous models that featured mid-mounted engines beneath the driver's seat, leading to uncomfortably high temperatures during summer drives. Shifting the engine to the front alleviated the notorious discomfort of "sitting on a furnace", rectifying a notable flaw associated with the Wuling Sunshine. Furthermore, embedded within this shift was a more strategic breakthrough: the adoption of a front-engine layout not only addressed immediate concerns but also paved the way for future sedan development. The dynamics of the discourse of power within the joint venture was a nuanced affair, replete with intellectual and strategic maneuvering.

The joint venture's board, however, glossed over the significance of the front-engine, rear-wheel-drive layout presented in the project proposal, perceiving it merely as an incremental improvement. The success of the Wuling Sunshine buoyed SGMW's management with optimism. As pioneers in the mini-vehicle sector, it appeared that future design initiatives for mini-vehicles would face fewer hurdles from shareholders. The dynamics of the discourse of power within the joint venture resembled water flowing beneath ice, gradually eroding resistance with persistent force.

Embodied in SGMW's subtle ambition to serve the passenger vehicle market, the Wuling Hongguang emerged as a bold leap toward sedan development, ready to navigate the competitive terrain of the automobile market. Could it replicate or even surpass the achievements of its forerunners?

6.2 Quality-Crowned Legendary

The challenges confronting the Wuling Hongguang proved to be more formidable than initially anticipated. Historically, structural modifications in mini-commercial vehicles were relatively minor, with the engine compartment distinctly isolated from the passenger area by the vehicle's floor. However, with the evolving focus on PV-oriented development, comfort emerged as a critical priority. This paradigm shift necessitated the incorporation of front bulkheads to segregate the engine from the passenger compartment, introducing a new layer of complexity to the vehicle's structure, demanding substantial advancements in manufacturing processes. Furthermore, the precision requirements for passenger cars diverged markedly from those for mini-commercial vehicles. It was during this period that the notion of perceived quality, heavily influenced by user experience, began to take shape. To thoroughly comprehend the nuances differentiating these two vehicle categories, in-depth internal dialogues were convened to dissect variances in design, technology, and quality benchmarks.

In defining essential technical specifications, Shen Yang and Yao Zuoping spearheaded the effort, orchestrating a strategic session with three distinguished experts—Guo Konghui from Jilin University, Zhong Zhihua from Hunan University, and Lin Zhongqin from Shanghai Jiao Tong University—at the Liuzhou base. Collaboratively, they meticulously established concrete metrics pertaining to chassis and body structure, as well as body precision, charting a course for the vehicle's development.

In comparison to its predecessor, the Wuling Sunshine, the Wuling Hongguang experienced substantial modifications to its exterior, notably featuring the development of new, larger doors. However, the increase in door size presented challenges in terms of rigidity, leading to issues such as uneven surfaces on door panels during static quality assessments. Even minor discrepancies, or slight inconsistencies, in stamping molds and presses could result in irregularities on the exterior body panels. Upholding stringent quality standards, the quality department steadfastly prohibited vehicles with such flaws from leaving the factory.

Stones from other hills can polish our jade. Recognizing the value in learning from others to deepen their expertise, SGMW extended invitations to several Japanese and Korean specialists renowned for their proficiency in stamping and welding. These experts demonstrated exceptional diligence and caution in their work, offering guarded and action-oriented responses to inquiries from the technical staff. However, the Wuling team discovered an alternative route to gain insights. In less formal settings, these Japanese and Korean experts were surprisingly forthcoming, generously sharing valuable knowledge and insights during casual interactions and social gatherings. This knowledge was gradually assimilated and disseminated, enriching the local expertise. The amalgamation of external knowledge with internal curiosity fostered an environment ripe for the exchange and growth of technical understanding, illustrating the synergistic potential of combining diverse talents.

The Wuling Hongguang marks a new zenith that Wuling Manufacturing aspires to reach, striving not only for the comfort synonymous with passenger vehicles but also for a significant leap in quality.

Persistent challenges with quality have long haunted Chinese manufacturers, particularly in the realm of bodywork. At Wuling, the vexing issue of frequently warped and contorted doors, requiring post-production hammer adjustments for a proper fit, posed a considerable conundrum—even for the head of the quality department. The joint venture with SAIC Motor and GM was a gateway to global benchmarks for a company that once operated in relative isolation. In 2000, when Yao Zuoping stepped into the SAIC-GM assembly workshop, he was immediately struck by the markedly superior door assembly quality—seamless at just a glance, prompting a crucial question: What secret technique had been employed to achieve such excellence?

This conundrum was not unique to China; it also loomed large in Detroit, the United States, during the early 1980s. As Japanese cars gained dominance in the American market, the big three automakers in Detroit found themselves in a position compelled to learn from their Japanese rivals to enhance the quality of their automobiles. Historically, American cars were synonymous with robustness and power rather than precision. The gaps between body panels were notably generous, often ranging from 3 to 4 millimeters with considerable inconsistency. In stark contrast, Japanese vehicles boasted a consistent panel gap of approximately 2 millimeters, setting a new standard for body precision. Given that numerous components are affixed to the car body, imprecision in this area could escalate into significant issues during the final assembly phase, adversely impacting key quality metrics such as appearance, sealing, and noise reduction. In response to this challenge, Professor Shien-Ming Wu at the University of Michigan, backed by the big three automakers, spearheaded a project in the early 1990s aimed at enhancing body precision, dubbed the 2-mm Program. Leveraging a data-driven methodology, this initiative successfully melded statistical analysis with manufacturing engineering practices, leading to marked improvements in the quality of American automobile manufacturing. This project not only addressed the immediate quality issues but also set a precedent for incorporating rigorous data analysis into the automotive manufacturing process, resulting in significant quality advancements in American cars.

As the 21st century dawned and global automakers hastened to establish joint venture factories in China, there emerged a pressing need to enhance the manufacturing quality of automobiles. Despite utilizing identical equipment to their overseas production facilities, both SAIC Volkswagen Automotive and SAIC-GM grappled with notable quality discrepancies in comparison to imported vehicles, attributed to the proficiency of technical workers and the level of supplier support. Body precision in these factories often fluctuated between 4 and 6 millimeters, significantly undermining vehicle quality. It was during this period that Detroit's 2-mm Program began to gain recognition. However, the application of this project encountered challenges; its reliance on costly laser online inspection and a lack of sophisticated data analysis capabilities limited its impact within the joint ventures.

Nonetheless, at the SAIC-GM plant, Yao Zuoping saw the remarkably precise door gaps—a testament to the burgeoning efforts within the Chinese automotive sector to tackle this quality issue. Professor Lin Zhongqin's team from Shanghai Jiao Tong University, innovating beyond the original 2-mm Program, departed from expensive laser testing in favor of a hybrid data collection model. This model encompassed both online and offline data gathering, each with its distinct advantages and limitations. While laser online inspection offered large sample sizes and rapid processing at the expense of limited measurement points, coordinate measuring machine (CMM) offline inspection provided detailed measurements at the cost of smaller sample sizes and longer processing times. Employing a data integration strategy, the team from Shanghai Jiao Tong University devised an offline, small-sample quality control technique that capitalized on the strengths of both data sources. This innovative approach effectively tailored the 2-mm Program for the Chinese context, eschewing the original's heavy reliance on online inspection to embrace a model well-suited to China's cost-sensitive manufacturing landscape. This methodology propelled models like the Santana 2000 and Passat of SAIC Volkswagen Automotive to the pinnacle of Volkswagen's global quality rankings. Additionally, SAIC-GM's Buick, Sail, and Cadillac models also adopted this strategy, heralding a new era of widespread adoption and quality enhancement in Chinese automobile manufacturing.

Yao Zuoping's discovery of both the solution and the ideal collaborator, Professor Lin Zhongqin from Shanghai Jiao Tong University, led to a prompt invitation for him to visit Liuzhou. This visit unveiled an unconventional approach to car manufacturing—a factory characterized by bustling labor, minimal automation, and a notable absence of contemporary measuring tools. The workshop floors, chaotic with scattered parts and materials, featured storage racks without wheels, requiring manual relocation by workers. The earthen ground became muddy in the rain, and inadequate ventilation made the workshops oppressively hot in the summer.

The team from Shanghai Jiao Tong University did not rush to advocate for the implementation of the 2-mm Program, acknowledging that the factory's conditions were not yet conducive. Nevertheless, they committed to providing personnel support. During this period, the team made several visits to Liuzhou, offering improvement recommendations and consultancy, while also conveying SGMW's challenges to the university's research team, which initiated a robust exchange of knowledge between the academic institution and the enterprise.

The perfect moment soon presented itself in 2006, when SGMW and Shanghai Jiao Tong University inaugurated the Joint Research Center for Modern Auto Body Technology, marking the beginning of academic-industrial technical collaborations, including the ambitious body 2-mm Program. Young faculty, postdoctoral researchers, and graduate students from the university were enlisted for the project, signifying the official launch of SGMW's quest for enhanced body precision. That very year, SGMW regained its leading status as the country's top producer and seller of minivans. To uphold this position, the company understood the importance of embodying the essence of being the first. Quality emerged as the champion, setting the stage for a new era of manufacturing excellence.

Upon entering the workshop, the researchers from Shanghai Jiao Tong University were greeted not with ceremonial welcomes but rather with the resonant clamor of hammers in action. Along the body adjustment line, seasoned yet nimble experts busied themselves with car doors, their hammers in constant motion. Assigned specifically to this task for their exceptional skill, these craftsmen demonstrated their artistry, with each tap of the hammer on the hinges serving as a testament to their meticulous approach to door adjustment.

This period marked a pivotal phase in the development of Wuling Rongguang. Heeding the Shanghai Jiao Tong University team's counsel on the unresolved issue of door noise, a specialized task force was formed, facilitating a collaborative effort across multiple roles. Led by the university team, SGMW mobilized efforts across various departments, involving key participants from the quality department, as well as process and product engineers. Whenever data consultation was required, engineers delved into databases, and workshop personnel were granted access to compare actual parts against their designs on computers.

The on-site adjustments entailed a blend of technical precision and craftsmanship. The 2-mm Program ventured into the nuanced evaluation of part quality, navigating the complexities of establishing acceptable tolerances among numerous components[①]. Interestingly, not every part deemed "good", in the conventional sense, was retained. Larger parts that fell short of tolerance standards might require the adjustment of more precise smaller parts to ensure compatibility, emphasizing surface matching over mere error correction. This pragmatic approach, geared toward optimizing project outcomes and prioritizing cost-efficiency and timely delivery while upholding functionality, demanded a reevaluation of traditional quality perspectives.

Propelled by the 2-mm Program, SGMW underwent a transformative organizational restructuring to include a dimensional team, adopting what was then an innovative strategy. In a departure from the previous paradigm where measurement points solely fell under the purview of the quality department, the scope expanded to involve designers. This fostered a seamless integration between process engineers at the factory, designers at the technical center, and the university research team. Eager for swift and efficient assimilation with "exobrains", SGMW prioritized direct integration to bridge the knowledge gap prevalent in geographically isolated enterprises, making dimensional engineering a widely adopted practice. By 2007, dimensional engineering had become a foundational pillar for Chinese domestic car brands, ushering in an era characterized by a systematic, engineering-driven approach that propelled these brands to ascend.

While SGMW's 2-mm Program may seem to echo the experiences of the Shanghai Jiao Tong University team with SAIC Volkswagen and SAIC-GM, the reality diverged significantly, particularly in terms of car design rights. Within a joint venture, the concept of modifying design drawings typically faces daunting barriers, necessitating multilevel approvals and often involving overseas headquarters, where the response is usually negative. Consequently, prior implementations of the 2-mm Program were largely confined to workshop initiatives. However, SGMW enjoyed broader authority and influence, spanning manufacturing to design, including decisions on structure and tolerance specifications. The principle of "change as desired" not only highlights the advantages of possessing autonomous design rights but also stands as an element crucial in cost-effective manufacturing.

---

① Note: The extent of quality tolerance values, sometimes colloquially labeled as "bad" and "good", actually falls within the permissible error range, often considered equivalent.

Design, constituting about 15% of total costs, exerts a disproportionate influence of 75% on quality defect costs, underscoring the critical need to delve into the upstream design phase for substantial quality enhancements. While the exacting standards of quality in mini-commercial vehicles might not align with those of GM and Volkswagen's passenger vehicles, SGMW was committed to achieving remarkable progress through the 2-mm Program, which, unlike its initial focus on body manufacturing and dimensional analysis in the United States, broadened its scope to include the design phase.

The impact was profound. Initially, the implementation of the 2-mm Program saw SGMW's body manufacturing quality continuous improvement index[①] range between 8 and 12 millimeters—a figure alarmingly high for any automaker, comparable to a human enduring a fever of 42°C. However, by 2008, this figure had been narrowed down to 6 to 8 millimeters. The essence of the 2-mm Program lies in its systematic approach to continuous improvement, methodically addressing defects in sequence. The initial phase targets and eliminates the most prominent defects, followed by a refinement of processes and a strategic focus on lesser defects, systematically eliminating each one. Instead of attempting to rectify all issues at once, the program prioritizes tackling major problems first, thereby methodically eradicating the most severe defects at each iteration and setting sights on new goals thereafter.

The remarkable strategy of "low cost, high value" at SGMW is rooted in a unique amalgamation of the company's pre-joint venture excellence in management, lean production principles honed by generations at Wuling, and the distinct Wuling culture. This synergy resulted in the creation of the Lean Production Wuling-ization system, underscoring the company's commitment to continuous improvement and leveraging its inherent strengths. Post the joint venture, SGMW wholeheartedly embraced GM's global manufacturing system, augmenting it with the introduction of three comprehensive BOP and BOE standard systems tailored to mini-vehicles, family cars, and passenger vehicles. The hallmark of this innovative approach lies in its emphasis on manufacturing vehicles that align with market demand and user needs, departing from rigid adherence to uniform standards. This departure from GM's conventional single BOP and BOE standards allowed the manufacturing system to authentically embody the philosophy of "low cost, high value", establishing it as a

---

① The Continuous Improvement Index (CII) serves as a metric for quality evaluation.

defining characteristic of SGMW's production ethos.

In 2007, commemorating the fifth anniversary of the joint venture, Rick Wagoner, then chairman and CEO of GM, visited Liuzhou, frequently expressing his endorsement. Acting on his directive, GM dispatched observers from its 45 global factories to Liuzhou in a phased manner. Subsequently, Yao Zuoping was invited to travel to Detroit, Michigan, to deliver a lecture to over 300 executives from GM worldwide. In that pivotal moment, the Karst mountains of Guangxi, where SGMW is headquartered, were metaphorically illuminated, signifying that manufacturing prowess developed in this region had set a global standard.

In August 2009, Shen Yang from SGMW was honored with the prestigious Manufacturing Leadership Award in Detroit, an accolade established by the Shien-Ming Wu Foundation in 1999 and annually awarded to a distinguished business leader. This occasion marked the first time, a decade after its inception, that the award was conferred upon a Chinese entrepreneur. The symbolism was clear: the pursuit of quality within a factory begins with the general manager. Only when the principle of quality deeply resonates with leadership can it truly proliferate throughout the organization. By 2010, SGMW had achieved a body manufacturing quality continuous improvement index of 3 to 4 millimeters, representing the "normal temperature" indicative of a mature and robust automaker's health.

6.3 Excellence Evolved in the 4S Store Saga

Toyota's exceptional success is not solely attributed to the Toyota Production System (TPS) but also to the visionary sales strategy initiated by Shotaro Kamiya, a sales genius who revolutionized car sales in Japan. Shotaro Kamiya's approach replaced the conventional image of sales employees in work attire with a professional sales force clad in suits, transforming the appearance and atmosphere of sales dealerships from "greasy spots" into professional spaces. More critically, he reengineered the sales system to align production with sales volume, making the latter a key driver for manufacturing decisions. This strategic innovation in sales provided Toyota's manufacturing with a "precise clock", tuned to the voices of consumers, highlighting that innovation in understanding and catering to user needs is as impactful as technological advancements in production.

The sales channel, thus, functions as a direct conduit for manufacturers to gather and respond to consumer feedback.

In 2009, SGMW achieved a significant milestone by selling 1.06 million units, becoming the first single car company in China to surpass the annual threshold of 1 million vehicles produced and sold. This achievement also coincided with China overtaking the United States as the world's largest automobile market for the first time. In the midst of this significant market evolution, smaller yet impactful trends came to the forefront. National initiatives like "automobile to the countryside" in that same year notably propelled the market. SGMW found its stronghold in these towns and villages, leveraging an extensive sales network that reached even the most remote areas, akin to capillaries stretching into distant corners, and national policies acted as vital nutrients within these networks, swiftly embraced by consumers in rural settings.

For SGMW, this pivotal moment was a decade in the making. In October 2001, during the joint venture discussions between SAIC Motor, GM, and Wuling, a modest marketing team of four was established. They embarked on an extensive field research journey across more than 20 cities, many straddling the desakota. The findings startled the researchers from SAIC Motor and GM, revealing a rudimentary car sales environment and simplistic organizational setups they had not anticipated. The majority of these dealerships, ranging from 80% to 90%, were small-scale private entities, including individual proprietorships and family-run operations. They not only sold Wuling vehicles but also represented other brands like Anhui Flying Tiger, Shaanxi Hanjiang, and Nanjing Triumph. Typically operating out of temporary spaces leased from factories or construction sites, offered to dealers at no cost, these sales points displayed cars festooned with big red flowers alongside miscellaneous items like cushions, tires, and even cooking stoves. Nevertheless, what truly astounded the researchers was the indomitable spirit exhibited by the dealers, particularly evident in Rui'an, Wenzhou, where seven dealerships stood in close proximity, each modestly peddling Wuling cars without a hint of surrender.

The most profound impact was witnessed within Wuling's own sales team, who experienced the deepest revelation from this exploratory and exhaustive journey, exposed for the first time to GM's sophisticated dealer management concepts and methods. It felt as if a window had been abruptly opened, ushering in a gust of fresh insights. Inspired by these new perspectives, Wuling resolved to foster specialization within its dealerships, mandating that dealers exclusively sell its products and forgo offering vehicles from other brands. This strategy marked a deliberate transition toward more focused operations and brand-centric development, laying the foundation for transformative changes in how Wuling approached its market presence.

The formulation of rational criteria for dealer recruitment, separation, and motivation gradually became standardized. Initially, applying a universal policy proved impractical; the transition needed to begin with embracing "specialization" to encourage outlets to evolve into dedicated dealerships. For instance, it became mandatory for dealers to prominently feature the official Wuling logo, identifying them as "Wuling Exclusive" stores.

While changing the storefront's appearance might seem superficial, the real crux of transformation lies in redefining the business relationship between dealers and the manufacturing plant. In an era marked by explosive growth in China's automotive market, acquiring vehicles for dealerships often equated to assured profits, making the business relationship a pivotal command chain. Despite the term "relationship" carrying a human touch, it conceals the nuanced dynamics of favoritism. A robust relationship could secure advantageous dealership terms, while a weaker one might result in the abrupt termination of vehicle distribution rights. With over 200 dealers nationwide, each navigating their unique strategy, these business connections held the potential to either empower or leave them feeling anxious and uncertain.

To achieve substantial progress, eliminating ambiguity and distrust within the dealership network was paramount. SGMW set out to introduce clear and transparent business policies, wielding reform with one hand and offering incentives with the other. These policies explicitly articulated the company's principles, detailing what was encouraged and what was discouraged, all while presenting highly attractive incentives. However, these policies encountered considerable pushback from the finance department, where significant discord emerged, particularly concerning the extent and tiered structure of vehicle wholesale rebates, and presented a precarious balance, as adjustments in one area could potentially result in disproportionate impacts elsewhere. Budget control was a major concern.

To invigorate dealer motivation, the initial policies leaned toward generously rewarding high performers, while underperformers primarily faced verbal reprimands. Following robust debates, a consensus was reached to address both high achievers and underperformers, with the objective of cultivating a more resilient dealership network and gradually phasing out less productive agencies.

Given the nature of these business policies, clarity and directiveness were imperative to ensure that rewards and consequences were transparent and equitable across all dealerships. With the comprehensive rollout of these detailed policies and guidelines, dealers began to regain confidence, recognizing that adherence to these rules would mutually benefit both parties in a prosperous relationship. SGMW's annual dealer meetings became eagerly anticipated events where keynote presentations detailing future strategies and policies provided valuable insights into the company's direction. Furthermore, to instill advanced sales methodologies among dealers, SGMW launched extensive training programs that offered up to three months of education for dealership and service station managers, focusing on policy interpretation, human nature, and service excellence.

Learning from SAIC-GM's strategy provided an invaluable shortcut. The 2002 launch of the Buick Regal is a prime example of how SAIC-GM harnessed feedback from sales channels, tailoring its offerings to the preferences of Chinese consumers. This model boasted luxurious interiors akin to those in Japanese cars—right down to the seat materials, color schemes, and the craftsmanship of the steering wheel—setting it apart from its American Buick counterparts. These localization efforts, grounded in market demand, underpinned the Buick series' triumph in China. Dealers were treated as integral allies by SAIC-GM, who equipped them with sophisticated management techniques and robust financial support, thereby shaping SGMW's approach to dealer network development.

In 2003, SGMW made a pivotal move, transitioning its dealers from specialized operations to exclusive outlets, thereby initiating the cultivation of a cohesive brand identity across its retail landscape, playing a central role in the broader commercial policy framework established for dealers.

This approach marked a revolutionary departure. Despite the prevalence of joint-venture brand sales outlets, which had become more common since GAC Honda introduced the first 4S shop four years prior, the appearance of commercial vehicle stores remained rudimentary, often resembling makeshift street stalls. The concept of exclusive dealerships was still finding its footing.

Through these initiatives aimed at standardizing the dealership channel, SGMW embarked on a more in-depth quest to forge a robust brand presence, seeking to understand the impressions and emotions a brand evokes in consumers, the dealership visiting experience, and the enduring impressions formed. The focus was on transforming car sales locations into welcoming environments where consumers felt at ease and were inclined to linger.

The sales department at SGMW assiduously pondered these questions.

Recognizing the importance of a cohesive brand presence in nurturing the brand's growth, specifications for exclusive dealership spaces were refined and articulated. Consequently, SGMW introduced four sets of showroom standards, advocating for entirely independent showrooms and tiered subsidies to dealers who pioneered this initiative.

Between 2004 and 2005, following an extensive effort to revamp storefront images, SGMW approached a pivotal moment in its retail strategy by transitioning toward the 4S store model.

However, the substantial investment required for establishing 4S stores raised concerns among some dealers. In response, the SGMW sales team undertook a comprehensive effort to bolster dealer confidence. In addition to providing pricing support, they offered strategic advice to help dealers overcome the initial investment hurdle and initiated stricter pricing policies to prioritize the development of 4S stores.

The effectiveness of the 4S store model in enhancing the consumer experience and differentiating Wuling from its competitors in the mini-vehicle market was undeniable, leading to consistent sales growth. By 2006, the strategic establishment of 4S store channels had been instrumental in propelling SGMW to the forefront of the domestic mini-vehicle market in terms of sales volume.

Refinement in management practices became a priority on the agenda. The accurate ascertainment of sales figures at the endpoints has perennially posed a challenge in the dynamic between car manufacturers and their sales channels. Historically, manufacturers had to depend on sales data provided by dealers, the authenticity of which was often challenging to verify. It was not uncommon for sales channels to manipulate these figures to meet the criteria for promotional policies from manufacturers, resulting in discrepancies where vehicles ostensibly sold remained in dealers' inventory. This perpetual cat-and-mouse game frequently left manufacturers bewildered, with decisions on regional sales appearing somewhat arbitrary.

Around 2005, SGMW began to be able to obtain vehicle registration data from various regions, providing the most accurate reflection of actual sales. This breakthrough empowered manufacturers to base their strategic decisions on precise data for the first time, encouraging dealers to establish their sub-networks and expand further into towns and villages. Leveraging regional sales data, manufacturers engaged in dialogues with underperforming dealers to enhance market penetration. By the close of 2008, SGMW's sales outlets nationwide had expanded to 845, complemented by an increase in service outlets to 934.

The launch of the "automobiles to the countryside" policy in 2009 unexpectedly ignited the market, leading to an impressive 83% surge in annual sales of cross passenger minivans, reaching a total of 1.95 million units. SGMW expanded its network, surpassing 1,000 sales and service outlets nationwide, with an additional 300 county-level service points added in just one year, achieving a 40% coverage rate. This initiative not only extended services into rural areas but also introduced innovative "flight service" models for remote locations, where service teams delivered spare parts directly to villages. Additionally, SGMW tapped into preferred communication channels in second and third-tier markets with its "movies to the countryside" campaign, hosting over 20,000 screenings across the country in 2009 alone. Each film started with short automotive maintenance videos, educating farmers on vehicle care[①].

This strategic effort to deepen channels, stretching into China's vast rural areas, positioned each storefront as a welcoming beacon, symbolizing SGMW's commitment to being the first friendly face for consumers.

6.4 The Perceived Quality

At the 2010 Beijing Motor Show, the Wuling Hongguang debuted with aspirations to transition to PV-oriented development. Initially, it did not evoke much enthusiasm among dealers, who were accustomed to the success of the Wuling Sunshine and Wuling Rongguang, viewing the new model with tepid interest. During a dinner event, amidst toasts and clinks, Yao Zuoping sought to uplift the spirits of the dealers, who were skeptical of the Hongguang's potential, predicting a modest sales figure of 5,000 units a month. Boldly contending, "I'll wager that this car will sell no less than 20,000 units a month", Yao Zuoping's declaration, more a gesture of encouragement than a firm prediction and accompanied by a decisive swig of his drink, was met with skepticism as dealers took his words with a grain of salt.

Despite plans for the Wuling Hongguang to launch a post-motor show, prevailing negative feedback—chiefly, its lack of a commercial vehicle feel—prompted Shen Yang to delay its debut and immediately direct the Technical Development Center to undertake necessary adjustments.

---

① Tong Zheng, "Driving Mini-cars into the Rural Market", *Economic Daily*, 2010-05-28 (016).

The Wuling Hongguang, striving to carve out its niche as a compact commercial vehicle, necessitated a design overhaul to move away from the typical van image. This endeavor led to the formation of a swift decision-making team dedicated to refining the vehicle's overall "feel". Key design considerations included ensuring the B-pillar remained slender upon the front door's opening, avoiding overly rounded corners to prevent a bulky, armored car appearance. The redesign extended to the side panels and the vehicle's rear, which demanded a slanted rather than a straight finish, with careful consideration of aesthetic details like the fender's and engine hood's height to achieve a more appealing look.

This meticulous attention to design nuances marked SGMW's formal adoption of the "perceived quality" concept, shifting focus toward the user experience beyond functional quality and dimensional accuracy. With GM's support in styling, design, product, and process aspects, SGMW embarked on a journey to enhance the perceived quality, aiming to resonate more profoundly with users' experiential feelings.

Equipped with a magnifying glass and sticky notes, technicians at the Technical Development Center meticulously examined the prototype, attaching notes to any identified issues. This first evaluation blanketed the prototype with hundreds of sticky notes, each indicating a problem that demanded a solution.

The crux of their challenge revolved around the necessity for new molds—a substantial financial undertaking, given that molds could cost millions of RMB each. Balancing cost-efficiency, enhanced functionality, and the desired "feel" posed an unprecedented challenge for the Technical Development Center. Suppliers, wary of the risks, were reluctant to deviate from proven models like the Wuling Sunshine, which reliably generated sales of several hundred thousand units annually, ensuring mold costs were quickly recouped. Consequently, the Technical Development Center found itself in direct negotiations with suppliers, advocating for the project with promises of volume sales and subsidies. Despite initial skepticism, suppliers were persistently reminded that embracing PV-orientation was not just the future but a collective stride toward upgrading the local supply chain.

With strategic adjustments swiftly made, the Technical Development Center bridged the identified gaps. Following an intensive four-month period of non-stop effort, the Wuling Hongguang was launched in September 2010. Initial sales figures were modest, averaging around 6,000 units per month, stirring some apprehension. Nonetheless, the management remained convinced that the pivotal shift toward PV-orientation was on the horizon and that the Wuling Hongguang was in step with the evolving market demands.

As 2011 unfolded, the market response surged. Wuling Hongguang's sales skyrocketed to 220,000 units for the year, with dealers frequently calling to press for expanded production capabilities. The bold prediction made over glasses of wine was coming to fruition.

In a parallel development, Daihatsu, in collaboration with FAW Jilin, rolled out the Xenia in China in 2007, a rebadged Toyota Avanza. Despite its success in Indonesia, the Xenia experienced tepid reception in the Chinese market, sharply contrasting with the burgeoning success of the Wuling Hongguang.

Even if we could replay history and mirror every detail, the world would still unfold differently. A direct replication of the Toyota Avanza for the Wuling Hongguang might have resulted in failure. Despite apparent similarities, the two models are grounded in distinctly different design philosophies. SGMW conducted an X-ray-like detailed examination of its user base, immersing into various scenarios in which consumers use their vehicles, to fully comprehend the significance of navigating a river, traversing a mountain path, loading cargo, or facilitating a social gathering, all through the lens of the users. The external appearance of a vehicle is just the tip of the iceberg; underneath lies a rich tapestry of social psychology. Simply imitating another model falls short of capturing the essence that distinguishes a legendary car.

6.5 The Most Important Car in the World

The triple Wuling symphony, a classic overlay, took place in 2011. With the Wuling Sunshine, an eight-year market stalwart, displaying signs of decline, Wuling Rongguang orchestrated a sales resurgence, while the freshly introduced Wuling Hongguang surged to the forefront. This confluence of success propelled Chinese mini-vehicles to outperform their Japanese mentors, such as Daihatsu and Suzuki, which, despite their dominance in Southeast Asia, experienced a downturn in the competitive Chinese market. In 2001, during the development phase of the Wuling Sunshine, GM's senior management inquired about the vehicle's potential, and Yao Zuoping expressed the belief that the Wuling Sunshine could garner popularity in

China for a minimum of ten years. Although seemingly an offhand remark, it insightfully captured the zeitgeist of the era. Entering the 21st century, minivans became ubiquitous, diligently navigating between small towns and rural markets, serving as the best companions for the striving class.

From 2001 to 2010, China's GDP grew from RMB 10 trillion to RMB 40 trillion, doubling within a decade. Concurrently, the average net income of rural residents increased from less than RMB 2,500 to nearly RMB 6,000[1]. This substantial increase in income meant that the net earnings of a farmer's family over two years were roughly equivalent to the cost of a mini-car, making these vehicles affordable and practical tools for increasingly prosperous farmers. At the beginning of the 21st century, China had about 20 million agricultural vehicles, with 10% of farming households owning one. As these households considered upgrading their vehicles, mini-cars undeniably held considerable allure.

The surge in farmers' incomes, on the one hand, and the extensive development of rural roads, on the other, played a significant role in the expansion of the rural market. The strategic enhancement of expressways and main trunk roads, recognized as the lifelines of the national economy, significantly improved long-distance transport capacities. Meanwhile, ordinary roads, weaving through both urban and rural landscapes like capillaries, became indispensable for local transportation. Between 2001 and 2010, China's expressways grew from under 20,000 kilometers to 74,000 kilometers, and the overall road length increased from 1.7 million kilometers to 4 million kilometers across the 12 national trunk roads famously referred to as the "five verticals and seven horizontals". This expansion translated into a significant rise in road network density, escalating from 17.8 kilometers per hundred square kilometers to 41.8 kilometers over the course of a decade[2]. The latter half of the 11th Five-Year Plan period witnessed a rapid acceleration in highway development, further catalyzed by a RMB 4 trillion stimulus package following the 2008 global financial crisis, aimed at bolstering domestic demand and channeling investments into infrastructure. Notably, this two-pronged approach to highway expansion, concentrating on major arteries and local networks, not only met the demands of the heavy-duty truck market but also spurred the growth of the light and minivan transport market.

---

[1] Data source: *China Statistical Yearbook* from 2010 to 2021, China Statistics Press.

[2] Data source: *China Automotive Industry Yearbook* over the years.

This era stood out as a golden decade for China's mini-vehicle industry, propelled by the country's robust economic growth and supportive policies. Minivans and mini-trucks, renowned for their affordability and versatility, saw unprecedented development. SGMW, implementing a focused strategy, became a trendsetter in the mini-vehicle segment, while those who wavered missed out on a significant opportunity.

In March 2009, the State Council officially unveiled the *Automobile Industry Adjustment and Revitalization Plan*, introducing 11 policy measures, two of which had a pronounced impact on mini-vehicle sales. The first measure halved the vehicle purchase tax for passenger cars with engines of 1.6 liters or smaller. The second launched the "automobiles to the countryside" initiative, providing a one-time financial subsidy for farmers purchasing minivans with engines up to 1.3 liters, or for those replacing three-wheeled vehicles or low-speed trucks with light trucks. Owing to these national policy subsidies, China's mini-vehicle production and sales in 2009 exceeded that of low-speed vehicles for the first time. By 2010, production and sales volumes crossed the 3 million mark, with minivans alone accounting for over 2.5 million units, surpassing China's total automotive production and sales in 2001.

From a market share standpoint, only a select few mini-vehicle manufacturers truly reaped the benefits of China's economic boom during this era, with notable successes seen in SGMW and Chang'an. SGMW experienced a meteoric rise in the production and sales of mini-vehicles, with its 2010 figures registering a staggering tenfold increase compared to 2001. Simultaneously, Chang'an also experienced rapid growth, but the leadership in the mini-vehicle segment shifted, presenting Chang'an with a formidable challenge to reclaim its once-established foothold.

The two remaining contenders among the top four, Hafei and Changhe, experienced vastly different destinies. The 2008 global financial crisis, which significantly impacted the American Big Three automakers, sent ripples across the global auto industry. In response to heightened risk awareness, the fourth among the eight objectives outlined in the Automobile Industry Adjustment and Revitalization Plan emphasized substantial advancements in mergers and reorganizations. This strategic initiative sought to establish two to three large automotive enterprise groups, each surpassing a production and sales volume of 2 million units, and four to five groups exceeding the 1-million-unit threshold. Ultimately, the goal was to reduce the number of automotive enterprise groups capturing over 90% of the market from 14 to fewer than $10^{①}$. According to data from the China Association of Automobile Manufacturers on previous year's car sales, none of the top three automotive groups—SAIC Motor, FAW Group, and Dongfeng Motor Corporation—had achieved sales exceeding 2 million units, while Chang'an Automobile, in fourth place, had not yet reached the 1-million-unit sales mark. This triggered a substantial restructuring within the automotive industry, symbolized by the signing of a cooperation agreement between China South Industries Group Corporation (CSGC) and Aviation Industry Corporation of China, which led to the integration of Changhe and Hafei into Chang'an Automobile[②], effectively segregating Chang'an's automotive sector from its military and other affiliated business sectors. Consequently, the three mini-vehicle enterprises, all formerly associated with the national defense and military industry system, were amalgamated under the Chang'an banner, consolidating the top four mini-vehicle powers into two.

This merger notably strengthened Chang'an Automobile's stature as a formidable contender within the automotive industry, standing alongside SAIC Motor, FAW Group, and Dongfeng Motor Corporation. In the mini-vehicle segment, the competitive landscape shifted from a four-way rivalry to a dual confrontation.

However, the market soon demonstrated its unforgiving nature toward mini-vehicles. By the close of 2010, the cessation of financial incentives for farmers purchasing minivans with an engine displacement of 1.3 liters or less precipitated the minivan market's rapid contraction, resembling the swift release of air from a punctured tire. The repercussions were swift, with external pressures mounting and internal challenges intensifying. Despite Chang'an Automobile housing three major mini-vehicle brands after the merger, their market positioning suffered from significant overlap, and the diverse array of passenger and commercial vehicle options dispersed consumer interest. Far from merging into a synergistic entity, the trio of brands weighed heavily on each other. Hafei and Changhe struggled to recuperate, with Hafei witnessing a sharp nosedive in sales and Changhe eventually becoming part of the BAIC Group. Each narrative had its unique elements, yet a common thread of disappointment echoed, paralleling the destinies of Tianjin

---

① The General Office of the State Council[J]. *Automobile Industry Adjustment and Revitalization Plan*. March 20, 2009.

② China Association of Automobile Manufacturers, China Automotive Industry Advisory Committee. *History of China Automotive Industry, 1991–2010*[M]. China Machine Press, 2014, 256.

Daihatsu and Yunque-Subaru as they gradually faded from the competitive landscape.

These sobering tales underscore the paramount importance of management stability. Between 2001 and 2010, among the elite mini-vehicle contenders, only SGMW could pride itself on remarkably stable leadership. In stark contrast, other entities experienced frequent turnovers in leadership: Hafei's chairmanship changed five times over the decade, while Changhe saw its leadership change hands six times. Each change at the helm disrupted the accumulated energy within the company. For leaders at state-owned enterprises, the art often lies not just in choosing paths to pursue but also in identifying ventures to avoid—a true measure of their strategic insight and determination.

Unlike other mini-vehicle manufacturers that adopted a diversified approach, anchoring mini-vehicles as the bedrock while simultaneously venturing into sedans, SGMW honed its focus exclusively on its core category, demonstrating unwavering strategic precision. While Hafei and Changhe explored a broad product strategy, evenly distributing their attention between sedans and mini-vehicles, SGMW dedicated itself solely to the mini-vehicle niche, embracing a product strategy marked by an "expansive range, diverse offerings, and distinct differentiation." Throughout the initial decade of the 21st century, SGMW's strategic dedication remained firmly rooted in the mini-vehicle domain. With its sights set on becoming the undisputed leader in mini-commercial vehicles, it consistently broadened its mini-vehicle portfolio, constructing bastions and waging long-term strategies, steadfast against the tide of external changes.

Since their introduction into the Chinese market, mini-vehicles have navigated over two decades of intense competition, witnessing the rise and fall of contenders and the gradual waning of initial allure, embodying the vicissitudes of fortune over the years. In the 1980s, eight formidable competitors vied for dominance in China's mini-vehicle arena; by the late 1990s, this number had dwindled to four; and a decade later, the competition had narrowed to a solitary standoff between two titans. The market remains in perpetual flux, akin to the ruthless dynamics of a football knockout tournament. SGMW ultimately triumphed over numerous adversaries, clinching a leading stance in the mini-vehicle marketplace and shaping a near-monopolistic competitive landscape. Over a span of a decade, with three flagship products, each iteration arrived in perfect harmony with the zeitgeist. The Wuling Sunshine earned accolades for its design, the Wuling Rongguang for its spaciousness, and the Wuling Hongguang marked a pivotal leap toward catering to passenger needs.

In 2010, the Wuling Sunshine graced the cover of the American business magazine *Forbes*, celebrated as "the most important car on earth". Esteemed for championing the global entrepreneurial spirit and offering astute insights into business models, the magazine lauded, "the no-frills Sunshine is by far China's bestselling vehicle, with 597,000 purchased last year. The bestselling car in the United States, the Ford F-series pickup, no longer comes close to that sales level."[①]

These extraordinary sales numbers unveil a narrative far more profound than the mere sum of its parts; they encapsulate the aspirations and relentless toil of countless entrepreneurs who have crafted their fortunes from the ground up. However, this story transcends individual success, shedding light on the ascending force of Chinese manufacturing. A beacon for the determined, the Wuling Sunshine, alongside its counterparts, the Wuling Rongguang and Wuling Hongguang, emerges as a symbol of the indomitable spirit of ambition. They epitomize the vitality of the grassroots, flourishing with vigor, and embracing every moment to soar.

Together, they journey forward. SGMW sails resolutely through the epochs, emboldened by a spirit of perseverance that defines the age.

6.6 Global Strategy: GM's Calculated Moves

After formalizing the joint venture in 2002, SGMW swiftly blossomed into a beacon of success for GM, the reigning titan of the global automotive industry at the time. By 2005, sales surged to 337,000 units, and in 2006, they vaulted to 460,000 units, catapulting the company to the zenith of China's mini-vehicle market. In that year, even GM's president marveled at how SGMW's meteoric rise had surpassed all expectations.

By 2009, SGMW had gracefully scaled the million-unit peak, etching its name in history as China's first car company to eclipse the milestone of annual production and sales of 1 million units. However, amidst this monumental achievement, GM, as a pivotal shareholder, found itself, too, entangled in financial turmoil, unable to partake in the festivities; it was like being mired in a quagmire, with its machinery defiantly roaring against the bind, yet unable to inch forward.

This era was fraught with adversity for the colossi of the automotive world.

---

① Tu Yanping. The Regal Triumph of Wuling Hongguang[J]. *Auto Business Review*, 2017.

In 2008, Toyota suffered its first annual loss in seven decades, a staggering setback that prompted the resignation of its president after only three years in office. Akio Toyoda, the progeny of the company's founder, was abruptly thrust into leadership. In his inaugural address, he poignantly declared, "I am sounding the horn to signal to everyone that we are on the edge of a cliff",[1] a stark wake-up call to the dire straits facing the automotive giant.

GM found itself navigating through the most tumultuous and protracted crisis in its storied history. In March 2009, Rick Wagoner, then chairman and CEO of GM, stepped down, and by June, the automotive giant had plunged into bankruptcy. Faced with a blend of responsibility and urgency, the US government deemed it necessary to inject an additional USD 30 billion into the company, securing a 60% ownership stake, which is an intervention that effectively transformed GM into a government-owned entity.

Chrysler Corporation, another stalwart among the Big Three, encountered similar challenges and was ultimately taken under the wing and revitalized by Italy's Fiat Automobiles. After its own roller-coaster journey that included a brief association with Nanjing Automobile, Fiat Automobiles became a transient figure in the dynamic saga of China's automotive industry, eventually assuming the role of a sideline spectator. In Europe, however, Fiat Automobiles thrived under astute leadership and its prowess in low-cost manufacturing, earning the title of the "King of Small Cars". The leadership at Fiat Automobiles harbored a clear-eyed perspective on the auto industry's transition toward thinner profit margins, a vision succinctly encapsulated in his words: "The automotive industry is now more like Walmart's retail world; treating cars as luxury items is a recipe for adversity."

In the throes of its most challenging period, GM found a steadfast ally in SAIC Motor, which emerged as a critical support pillar. In a strategic move to secure their partnership, SAIC Motor acquired an additional 1% of GM's shares in the SAIC-GM joint venture, thereby becoming the majority shareholder with a 51% stake, up from 50%. In a surprising twist, GM expressed a desire to boost its stake in SGMW by 10%. In a landscape where larger entities aimed to divest and smaller ones looked to deepen their investments, this maneuver of strategic retreat and advance carried profound implications.

The aggregate output of vehicles from joint ventures in China holds paramount

---

[1] Cost Above All: Toyota's Century-Long Drive to the Edge of a Cliff[J]. *The Beijing News*, March 2, 2010.

importance for multinational corporations, with the Chinese market acting as a crucial bulwark. As of 2003, only Volkswagen, after years of concerted effort, had managed to secure more than 10% of China's production share, while other global automotive giants hovered below the 4% mark. However, by 2011, GM had surged from a modest 0.8% in 2001 to an impressive 27.4%, claiming the top spot[①] and outpacing Volkswagen's 25.9%. This extraordinary feat was largely attributed to the sales performance of SGMW, acting as a pivotal balancing force. This underlying strength of SGMW was precisely why GM sought to augment its shareholding in the venture.

In the Japanese market, GM's strategy oscillated between engagement and withdrawal. By 2005, in alignment with a global contraction strategy, GM significantly dialed back its operations in Japan, terminating its partnerships with Suzuki and Subaru. The association between the American automaker and Suzuki began in 1981, with subsequent years seeing an uptick in its investment. However, by 2006, GM divested a substantial portion of its Suzuki shares, retaining only a 3% interest. The rationale for its continued alliance with Suzuki waned as the appeal of compact cars began to diminish. Despite Suzuki's strong presence in burgeoning markets like China and India, GM saw an opportunity to leverage its Korean subsidiary to establish a foothold in these regions. Furthermore, GM's interest in Fuji Heavy Industries dwindled, culminating in the transfer of its shares to Toyota.

GM was guided by broader objectives; its dual global strategies of downsizing and prioritizing emerging markets were intrinsically linked to SGMW, underpinning GM's intent to amplify its stake in the SGMW joint venture.

By this time, Detroit in the United States painted a picture of stark desolation. Yet, as the adage goes, Rome was not built in a day. Despite this, the unfolding crisis and its myriad of warnings did not go unnoticed by the management. As early as November 2005, Rick Wagoner, in a bold move, announced a global layoff of 30,000 employees and the closure of 11 factories. A mere month before this drastic announcement, he had journeyed to Liuzhou, Guangxi, captivated by Wuling's "low-cost manufacturing" ethos. He proclaimed, "I'm not here to lecture but to absorb. The lean operation of SGMW stands as a beacon, a model worthy of replication across GM's global network."[②] This expression of humility was not mere showmanship; it

---

① Lu Yuebing, Jiang Xuewei, Ren Rongwei. *Growth Strategy of China's Automotive Industry*[M]. Tsinghua University Press, 2014, 122.

② Shattering the Limits: The Ten-Year Legend of SGMW[J]. *China Youth Daily*, 2012-11-19 (05).

was a genuine acknowledgment of the innovative, cost-effective manufacturing strategies he witnessed nestled in the mountains of Liuzhou. Weary from years of tough negotiations with the United Auto Workers (UAW), Rick Wagoner recognized that the escalating production costs in the United States were irreversible, signaling the diminishing competitiveness of American automobiles.

Leadership roles are often transient, susceptible to the unpredictable forces of change. Yet, the insights and decisions made by these American executives have consistently provided GM with clear directives, particularly during challenging periods. To GM, SGMW represented more than a mere joint venture; it was a global bastion of manufacturing excellence, embodying efficiencies that proved elusive within the United States. The imperative to preserve these manufacturing edges was paramount, even amidst the tumultuous landscape of 2009, where GM's leadership remained profoundly attuned to the core values of manufacturing excellence.

China's automotive market has emerged as a towering beacon of optimism on the global stage, casting a steadfast glow across the industry. In that pivotal year, the robust performance of China's market alleviated numerous global automotive behemoths from experiencing a tide of restless nights. The battle for a foothold in the Chinese market has intensified, evolving into a linchpin for both survival and growth.

In a bid to coax Chinese stakeholders into relinquishing 10% of the shares, GM extended three compelling gestures of goodwill.

The first gesture saw the proposal to integrate its esteemed global supplier network into Liuzhou, a move that promised to significantly boost the burgeoning automotive city's development and stimulate local job creation. The second olive branch involved weaving Liuzhou Wuling Automobile (subsequently rebranded as Guangxi Automobile Group) into its intricate global supply chain, thereby introducing the group to the expansive realm of global commerce. These offers presented enticing prospects for fostering local economic progress.

However, it was the final proposition that truly set hearts aflutter across Liuzhou's OEM hubs. GM dangled the prospect of launching a new passenger car brand to be produced right in Liuzhou. While the Spark Lechi had been previously introduced, it was a direct transplant from Daewoo, lacking in localized innovation. The management team at SGMW, buoyed by a streak of robust growth, harbored a particular fondness for passenger vehicles. The aspiration to manufacture sedans is an indelible dream shared by all within the automotive field. In this industry, the foreheads of company leaders are perennially creased with concern. Even amidst the triumph of a model's success, they find themselves immediately entrapped in the anticipation of the next competitive fray. A successful car model enjoys a prime selling window of about four to five years. Nevertheless, even the most fortunate automotive entrepreneurs find themselves incessantly pursued by the inexorable advance of time, subject to its cyclical evaluations.

In the wake of the meteoric rise of the Wuling Hongguang, a pivotal question loomed: what lay ahead on the horizon? By 2010, China's minivan sector was pushing its boundaries. To enhance the purchasing power of farmers, at the year's outset, seven national ministries extended the "automobiles to the countryside" initiative until December 31, injecting a final boost into the mini-vehicle market and significantly bolstering the rural economy. Nevertheless, the mini-commercial vehicle sector, inherently a niche market with its own set of limitations, was projected to reach its zenith by year-end. Venturing into the passenger car domain emerged as the only tangible pathway forward. The leadership at SGMW was not merely open but poised to embrace this challenge, bringing them closer than ever to realizing their longstanding dream of manufacturing sedans. While the future remained as uncertain as a mist-veiled lake, they gazed into the horizon with optimism.

Simultaneously, the People's Government of Guangxi Zhuang Autonomous Region found itself once again caught in a whirlwind of strategic deliberations. The hybrid ownership reform initiated eight years prior had proven its efficacy in revitalizing the local economy. However, in the face of GM's fresh propositions, the question loomed: Was this an overreach, a classic case of giving an inch and taking a mile? Was it prudent to adhere to established practices, or was it time to explore new territories? The allure of GM's proposal to invest in a state-of-the-art sedan manufacturing base in Liuzhou's Hedong District was tantalizingly appealing. If shares could be traded for the development of a local industrial hub, promising heightened employment and economic growth, then reducing the government's shareholding might just be a sacrifice worth making. After all, the prospect of infusing the local economy with new, dynamic energy was an opportunity too lucrative to forgo.

In the governance sphere, any policy promoting local growth is celebrated as a beacon of progress. Anchored in this philosophy, the government of the autonomous region made a pivotal decision to uphold its foundational pledge, relinquishing 10% of its shares to GM. Consequently, the stake of Liuzhou Wuling Automobile Co., Ltd. in the venture diminished from 15.9% to a mere 5.9%. The landscape of valuation had undergone a dramatic transformation since the turn of the millennium. In the negotiations of 2000, GM allocated USD 30 million for a 34% stake; fast forward to the present, an additional 10% share commanded an investment of USD 51 million. Seven years of cumulative experience had metamorphosed the erstwhile humble pheasant into a resplendent golden phoenix, with Liuzhou's soil bearing witness to this manufacturing marvel and surge in value.

The mixed-ownership reform model, pivotal in overhauling state-owned enterprises and steered by the ethos of "Less the possession, more the value of the company in the society", once again proved its mettle. A strategic compromise catalyzed significant advancements. The Liuzhou government, steadfast in its commitment to serve the people's welfare, welcomed the establishment of a new passenger car R&D base, fortifying automotive infrastructure in Liuzhou, Guangxi.

In a moment of profound adversity, a venerated centenarian in the automotive industry bestowed its blessings upon a nascent local marque. However, the onus now rests on this fledgling entity to chart its own destiny.

As one chapter unfolded, so did the other narrative. The *Automobile Industry Adjustment and Revitalization Plan*, introduced in 2009, discreetly opened a gateway, allowing slivers of light to filter through. At its core, the sixth goal outlined a trajectory for the future of electric vehicles, earmarking a production ambition of 500,000 electric and other new energy vehicles. It urged major passenger vehicle manufacturers to prominently feature certified new energy vehicle offerings. For the first time, electric vehicles timidly introduced themselves to the world. Riding on the momentum of the electric vehicle pilot initiative for the Beijing Olympics, the "Ten Cities, Thousand Vehicles" project, a collaborative effort spearheaded by the Ministry of Science and Technology of the People's Republic of China along with three other ministries, was set in motion. This initiative was destined to fuel the flames of burgeoning electric vehicle development across China, and automakers took note. SGMW began the deployment of investigative teams to navigate this emerging domain.

In the following year, Tesla, the American electric vehicle pioneer perennially operating at a deficit, embarked on a landmark journey by becoming a publicly traded company on the Nasdaq.

Everywhere one looked, seeds of new beginnings were germinating.

Chapter 7 Passenger Cars: From Cocoon to Butterfly 2011–2019

7.1 Dawn of Autonomy

The march toward automotive independence was well underway, with joint ventures actively developing indigenous brands while simultaneously engaging in partnerships with established foreign entities. In 2004, the State Council heralded a new era by advocating for "independent innovation", catalyzing a robust movement toward the cultivation of domestic car brands, with companies such as Geely, BYD, Chery, and Great Wall harnessing this momentum. Against this backdrop, joint ventures also began navigating toward greater self-reliance, seeking to carve out their identities. In 2006, SAIC Motor took a significant stride in this direction by launching Roewe, incorporating the intellectual property and technology of the British brand Rover 75. This push toward brand autonomy gained further momentum in 2007 when SAIC Motor, committed to the cause, integrated the iconic British brand MG— renowned for its high-performance sports cars—into its portfolio through the acquisition of Nanjing Automobile. This period also witnessed the emergence of new brands such as Besturn and Aeolus, alongside GAC Honda's Everus, Dongfeng Nissan's Venucia, and FAW-Volkswagen's Carely, sparking widespread discourse on the autonomy and identity of these burgeoning brands.

During this transformative era, debates flared over the blurred lines between foreign and domestic brands. With joint ventures typically operating under a 50:50 equity ratio, the autonomy of emerging brands became a contentious topic. Many partnerships hesitated to venture into new brand territories[①], occasionally choosing to rebrand outdated models from their international counterparts as independent

---

① Li An'ding. *A Tale of Cars in China: 30 Years, from Start to Fast Lane*[M]. SDX Joint Publishing Company, 2017, 215.

offerings. This dilemma underscored a more profound ambition among joint ventures for autonomous innovation and research capabilities, transcending their conventional roles as mere profit generators.

Concurrently, domestic brands experienced a meteoric rise, charting new territories with unforeseen success. A watershed moment occurred in 2010 with Geely's acquisition of the esteemed global luxury marque, Volvo, from Ford—an impactful move reverberating throughout the industry. This acquisition not only signified a significant leap in global stature for Chinese automotive firms but also highlighted the industry's matured entrepreneurial spirit and its readiness to challenge global norms. The Chinese automotive sector, once emerging, had firmly established itself on the world stage.

While operating within the framework of a joint venture, SGMW proudly champions the Wuling brand, a name epitomizing the ethos of "Perseverance with Self-Strengthening", serving as a testament to the resilience of the esteemed state-owned enterprise. As the dominant partner in this collaboration, SAIC Motor wields significant influence, positioning Wuling as a proprietary brand distinguished by autonomy.

The ambition to carve out a new niche and introduce a distinct, independent sedan brand has been simmering for years.

A decade prior, the mini-vehicle segment was dominated by the top four manufacturers, collectively commanding a staggering 90% market share, eclipsing their competitors. Chang'an, Changhe, and Hafei, deeply rooted in the defense and military sector, along with Liuzhou Wuling, are unified by a shared zeal for pioneering sedan innovations. At the dawn of the new millennium, Chang'an, boasting a production prowess of 150,000 Alto units annually, unveiled the Chang'an Suzuki Antelope, engaged in strategic dialogues with Ford, and had a suite of strategic sedan offerings. With a strategic and measured approach, the company's efforts extended to fortifying its footprint in the mini-vehicle domain, setting its sights on Hebei and Nanjing, thereby solidifying their leadership position. Concurrently, Changhe, in collaboration with Suzuki, pioneered the small multi-purpose vehicle market with the Beidouxing, while Hafei, transitioning from partnerships with Suzuki to collaborations with Italian firms, and then Daewoo and Mitsubishi, positioned itself as a formidable contender within the upper echelons of the mini-vehicle segment with a diversified product lineup. The mini-vehicle sector was a dynamic arena of fierce competition and innovation, wherein each player crafted a unique narrative and vied for prominence. However, even with its partnerships with SAIC Motor and GM, Liuzhou Wuling had not embraced any prominent foreign sedan brands.

Why do mini-vehicle enterprises, particularly those entrenched in the defense and military domains, manifest a notable predilection for sedan production? This inclination was succinctly expressed by the former deputy director of the Commission for Science, Technology, and Industry for National Defense (COSTIND) during an automotive forum in 2003, stating, "The essence of the automotive industry's evolution is epitomized by sedan development",[1] encapsulating the shared zeal among industry leaders for sedan innovation solutions—a pursuit nearly akin to an obsession. Liuzhou Wuling, formerly known as the Liuzhou Mini Vehicle Factory, saw its collaborative endeavor with French automaker Citroën on a sedan project abruptly curtailed. Nevertheless, mini-vehicle firms with military lineage demonstrated ingenuity in navigating stringent regulations, leveraging their distinctive networks to carve niches in sedan production. Chang'an Automobile, distinguished among its peers for receiving substantial policy support, held a unique position, authorized to manufacture both minivans and subcompact sedans within the defense and military echelons. Conversely, local state-owned enterprises, hampered by resource limitations, were forced to operate within restricted spheres.

The past decade has witnessed an impressive surge in the mini-vehicle market, reflecting China's broader economic narrative characterized by gradual urban-rural integration and a rapid increase in urbanization. In 2001, China's urbanization rate stood at 38%, a figure that soared to 49.9% by the close of 2010. This period marked a pivotal transition in the balance between urban and agricultural domains, with 2010 serving as the final year dominated by the agricultural paradigm. By the conclusion of 2011, a significant milestone was achieved as China's urban permanent population outstripped its rural counterpart for the first time, with the urbanization rate escalating to 51.8%[2], marking a new chapter in the country's demographic and socio-economic evolution.

En route to major urban centers, a plethora of mini-vehicles faced restrictions from entering city limits, driven by environmental and safety considerations. Consequently, they congregated in desakota regions, an intermediary zone that

---

① Zhang Guangqin. Accelerating the Development of the Military Automotive Industry[J]. *Defence Science & Technology Industry*, 2003.

② The referenced data is sourced from the official website of National Bureau of Statistics.

evolved into a sanctuary for mini-vehicles, attracting not only these vehicles but also a dynamic mix of mobile populations and self-owned business entrepreneurs. Around the turn of the millennium, Beijing began enforcing restrictions on mini-vehicles within city roads, leading brands like Hafei to strategically target individual business owners situated beyond the Fourth Ring Road for promotional activities[①]. If the expanse beyond the Fourth Ring could still be classified as the desakota region in 2000, by 2010, this demarcation had edged closer to the Fifth Ring. The transformation was significant: agricultural lands vanished, factories either closed or relocated, and the demographic straddling the Fourth and Fifth Rings pivoted predominantly toward the service sector. This transition underscored the ascendancy of micro and small enterprises as the vanguard of urban encroachment into rural economies, characterized more by individual businesses than by large-scale industrial operations. The micro and small business sector not only facilitated an orderly shift from China's bifurcated urban-rural economy but also emerged as a fertile ground for the continuous genesis of social innovation cells.

As societal paradigms shifted, so too did the zeitgeist. The pivotal moment of 2010 signaled a demand within urban economies and landscapes for superior vehicular options. The once-appealing minivans saw a diminishing allure, while sedans maintained their timeless appeal. Entrepreneurs, guided by astute instincts, capitalized on the subtle cues of the times. For SGMW, having firmly established its presence, the moment was opportune to cultivate the aspirations it had harbored.

The drive toward PV-oriented development and embracing independent branding posed a dual challenge at the forefront of the industry's evolution.

7.2 Baojun's Debut Bout

GM harbored distinct ambitions for charting its own path in the competitive landscape of passenger vehicle innovation.

Within the glittering realm of mini-commercial vehicles, SGMW had already secured a dominant position, demonstrating exceptional prowess in both design innovation and cost-effective production. However, in the passenger vehicle domain,

---

① Li Miaomiao. My Dream Is to Empower China's Auto Sector: Interview with Cui Xuewen, Chairman and President of Harbin Aircraft Industry Group[J]. *China Business News*, 2002.

it remained an emerging player. The Wuling Hongguang, a compact MPV with a front-engine, rear-wheel-drive configuration, offered handling akin to that of a sporty sedan and marked a foray into the realm of perceived quality and family-oriented design aesthetics. Despite these advancements, the venture's shareholders still perceived SGMW primarily as a manufacturer specialized in mini-commercial vehicles.

From the initiation of joint venture discussions with SAIC Motor and GM, Wuling's Technical Development Center was relegated to a subsidiary role. By the time the joint venture materialized in 2002, the Technical Development Center had yet to be integrated into the joint venture's operational framework. This local R&D entity was viewed by GM as a "negative-value local specialty", deemed expendable in the broader corporate strategy.

The long-standing discontent among the team at Wuling's Technical Development Center was palpable, facing what seemed to be an unjust battle, especially considering PATAC scarcely viewed them as competitors. The development of the Wuling Sunshine model marked the beginning of this contest, with the Technical Development Center triumphing over PATAC for the project's helm, albeit being somewhat dismissively branded as merely "more cost-effective". Initially met with skepticism rather than praise within GM, the Wuling Sunshine nonetheless gained market strength, notching remarkable sales that bolstered the standing of Wuling's Technical Development Center in this competitive display.

The saga's subsequent chapter saw PATAC roll out a new mini-vehicle platform, giving rise to the high-end Wuling Hongtu, which catered to both commercial and passenger needs. Despite its appealing design, it faced sales challenges. In stark contrast, the Wuling Rongguang, a brainchild of Wuling's Technical Development Center, sustained the sales momentum sparked by the Wuling Sunshine, affirming the center's prowess in capturing market demand.

Following two decisive rounds, the outcome unequivocally shifted the balance, dispelling PATAC's claim to design supremacy over mini-commercial vehicles within the SGMW alliance. Time, acting as a meticulous arbiter, gradually corrected prevailing biases. Eight years of unwavering effort cemented SGMW's reputation for independent research and development in the commercial vehicle sphere.

This era heralded a new wave of dynamics in passenger vehicle development, a domain traditionally dominated by PATAC. Despite being stereotyped as specialists in commercial vehicles, the Technical Development Center at SGMW was determined to showcase its capabilities. An undercurrent of rivalry and unvoiced complaints simmered between the two entities.

The conflict precipitated the formation of a dedicated sedan development team within the joint venture, with initial design leadership remaining under PATAC's purview. In an effort to quell tensions and foster cooperation, Chen Hong, the president of SAIC Motor, suggested a novel approach: the creation of PATAC's Liuzhou Branch. This move would facilitate direct collaboration between PATAC staff and the Technical Development Center at Wuling on passenger vehicle projects. This proposal received universal acclaim, underscoring the necessity for flexibility and a human-centric approach to resolving corporate disputes.

Afterall, this venture marked the inception of SGMW's first independently branded sedan, imbuing the project with profound significance.

During this period, GM unveiled a new platform architecture that extended the vehicle design process to 36 months, presenting PATAC with a prime opportunity to showcase its capabilities. Leveraging Buick Excelle's platform, PATAC embarked on a comprehensive overhaul of its exterior design and technological features. PATAC's Liuzhou Branch, situated within SGMW's complex, initially welcomed a management team of nearly 30 from PATAC, supplemented by its own recruitment efforts, growing the team to two to three hundred members. In contrast, Wuling's Technical Development Center contributed fewer than 10 individuals, adopting a stance of learning and observation. PATAC enforced stringent confidentiality protocols, limiting interactions between its team and Wuling's staff, complete with separate access controls for their respective offices. The acquisition of knowledge evolved into an individualized endeavor, impeded by entrenched procedural rigidity. Each proposed enhancement to the vehicle required approval from GM's North American headquarters, introducing delays at every modification point.

Confronted with such a protracted approval process, the management of SGMW found itself in a quandary, disheartened yet powerless. The idea of regaining design autonomy flickered through their minds, tantalizingly close yet elusive. For the time being, the autonomy to design sedans remained just out of reach for SGMW.

In April 2011, the Baojun 630, a sedan celebrated for its dynamic qualities, made its debut at the Automobile Shanghai, eliciting a polarized reception. Observers noted that from its side profile, the vehicle boasted an allure suggesting a value of RMB 120,000. However, a closer examination of the rear compartment diminished its perceived worth by RMB 20,000, and the interior experience, reminiscent of a van, further depreciated its perceived value to that of a van's price range. While externally promising luxury, the interior failed to uphold this expectation, leading to a progressive decrease in its psychological valuation. This disparity indicated a fundamental misunderstanding of the sedan's market positioning.

A revision of the model was clearly necessary, prompting an immediate and direct challenge.

The need for the model change was unquestionable; the contention lay in the timing of its implementation.

The interior of the Baojun 630 was deemed in need of an extensive revamp, necessitating more than mere aesthetic adjustments but encompassing fundamental structural changes. The primary obstacle lay in the requirement for new molds, a venture marked by both significant expense and complexity. PATAC's initial estimates suggested such a model revision would span a minimum of six months, but the rapidly evolving Chinese car market, having secured its status as the world's largest by sales volume since 2009, brooked no delays. The proliferation of private vehicles in urban areas had outpaced the capacity of city planning, leading to unprecedented traffic congestion. By the end of 2010, Beijing had enacted stringent car purchase restrictions to mitigate the swelling tide of small passenger vehicles. Against this backdrop of intense demand juxtaposed with rigorous regulatory measures, any postponement of the car's launch was untenable.

Confronted with a market demanding swift action, the timeframe for the Baojun 630's redesign was compressed to an ambitious two months—a seemingly unfathomable challenge for PATAC. The process of creating preliminary design renderings alone could occupy the entire period, not to mention the demands of actual production. However, in the unforgiving competitive landscape, excuses held no currency, presenting a stark choice: to accomplish what is possible or to concede defeat. Opting for the path of possibility, Wuling's Technical Development Center stepped up to the challenge, ready to tackle the daunting task ahead.

Working diligently through the night, the Technical Development Center compiled a comprehensive list of 27 necessary modifications, which was promptly shared with PATAC for confirmation. Surprisingly, PATAC agreed to take responsibility for only the car key, leaving the bulk of the intricate tasks to Wuling's Technical Development Center, which, demonstrating exceptional efficiency, managed to finalize the design renderings within an astonishing two days. Throughout the approval process for the general manager's endorsement, the technicians pragmatically suggested bypassing an in-depth review to expedite matters for rapid approval, underscoring the audacity and initiative of a youthful and bold team.

The pivotal challenge was to drastically reduce the time required for mold development. Traditionally, mold creation spans four months, and Wuling's proposal to halve this timeline faced skepticism and reluctance from mold suppliers. Doubts arose regarding the feasibility of such an accelerated schedule. Confronted with an immovable deadline, how could the Technical Development Center surmount the considerable obstacle of navigating this critical bottleneck within the constrained two-month period?

Following an intense overnight brainstorming session, the breakthrough came with a bold proposition: to request mold suppliers to operate without any safety margins, implementing a zero-tolerance policy for errors, under the assurance that SGMW would bear full responsibility for potential issues. The caveat emphasized transparency; any problems encountered had to be reported immediately, bypassing the usual procedural niceties and pushing the limits of conventional processes. Communication channels were streamlined to an unprecedented degree, effectively creating a direct line for immediate problem-solving. Miraculously, this high-stakes strategy paid off, with the molds completed in a mere 40 days, enabling the car's redesign to adhere to the stringent two-month deadline and setting the stage for imminent mass production.

By mid-2011, a silent yet potent demonstration unfolded at the entrance of SAIC-GM's headquarters. Two vehicles, each bearing the same logo but conceived by different teams—PATAC and Wuling's Technical Development Center—were showcased side by side, serving as a quiet yet impactful testament to the capabilities within SGMW, leaving GM's executives in awe. Until this moment, the venture's design prowess had been overlooked in GM's global strategy for passenger vehicles, which typically involved harnessing global resources for model design and chassis provision, often from places like Brazil, while tapping into SGMW's manufacturing excellence. This event, however, unveiled a new competency within the joint venture: an ability for independent design, albeit based on an existing framework, unmistakably highlighting SGMW's design autonomy.

This episode represented yet another covert battle in the ongoing struggle for autonomy in R&D within the framework of a Sino-foreign joint venture. SGMW, through concrete evidence of its product innovations, once again showcased its prowess in sedan design and manufacturing to its stakeholder, GM. Such a persuasive demonstration, a hallmark of Wuling's ethos, has deep roots. A notable instance occurred in 1982 during a mini-vehicle construction meeting organized by CNAIC in Tianjin. The Liuzhou Tractor Factory, uninvited, audaciously drove a mini-truck thousands of miles to the venue, securing its place in the meeting and ensuring its inclusion in the subsequent year's list of designated factories. This act epitomized the belief that actions profoundly surpass words, and that the spirit of innovation is critical to triumph in any venture.

For the stakeholders of SGMW, the internal competition between the two teams was but a preliminary stage. The ultimate arbiter of success would be the vast consumer market, not merely the conviction of the company's management. The true test lay in garnering the endorsement of end-users, whose approval would seal the product's fate.

Baojun emerged as an entirely new entity, necessitating the establishment of a novel distribution network from scratch. Absent a precedent in sales and service, a proactive decision was made to immerse a significant portion of the sales force in SAIC-GM's 4S shops for a comprehensive two-month training. Concurrently, criteria for 4S shop construction and business strategies were swiftly formulated.

In delineating franchise standards, the strategy involved not only tapping into some of SGMW's large strategic dealers but also, more importantly, prioritizing the induction of new dealers, with a particular emphasis on those boasting expertise in passenger car sales. The ambition was to sculpt a superior brand image for Baojun, warranting a channel development strategy that markedly diverged from prevailing network systems.

The inception phase of the Baojun brand was characterized by an intensive commitment to consumer feedback, with each team member diligently focused on understanding consumer insights. Shen Yang took to "Autohome", a prominent automotive forum at the time, creating an account to closely monitor and collect feedback on the Baojun. Similarly, Yao Zuoping engaged directly with the brand's clientele, participating in meetups with car enthusiasts organized by the company to gain firsthand and genuine perspectives from users.

Dedicating an entire year to the meticulous crafting of an independent new dealer system, SGMW successfully expanded its presence to the farthest reaches of the market, an effort culminating in the establishment of over 400 dealerships, all singularly devoted to the Baojun brand, with the Baojun 630 leading the way in this endeavor.

Despite the robust establishment of distribution channels, the anticipated surge in consumer demand did not materialize. The Baojun brand confronted a sobering reality as monthly sales hovered below 10,000 units—a figure that paled in comparison to the dealers' experiences with the high-velocity sales of Wuling's commercial vehicles. In December 2011, when Wuling commercial vehicles were soaring at a monthly sales of 150,000 units, the Baojun 630's performance seemed to make only modest strides alongside the rapid pace set by seasoned competitors.

Relative to its performance, the pricing of the Baojun 630 was high, suggesting a lapse in fully understanding consumer sentiment. The sluggish sales figures for the Baojun 630 were, in part, attributed to a lethargic response to consumer feedback. Efforts by SGMW to collect and act on consumer insights faced bureaucratic inertia; proposed changes required approval from PATAC, with even minor modifications like altering a groove on the engine hood necessitating consultations with GM's design headquarters. This cumbersome process demonstrated a lack of agility in implementing adjustments, diluting the directness and impact of consumer feedback. The transition from consumer feedback to actionable measures by the manufacturer appeared muffled, with the urgency and clarity of the message fading into the background, leaving behind a trail of missed opportunities to truly connect with the market's pulse.

As the relentless march of time pressed on, its unforgiving nature became all too apparent. PATAC's next venture, the Baojun 610, experienced a similar lag in its market debut, underscoring the inherent risks of automotive innovation. The development of a new car model is a substantial gamble, with thousands of team members pouring years of blood, sweat, and tears into a project shrouded in uncertainty. The market's reception—be it a dismissive shrug or an enthusiastic embrace—remains an enigma until significant financial resources are committed. Unfortunately, this particular gamble did not pay off as hoped. The market's lukewarm response sent ripples of concern through the network of dealers specializing in Baojun vehicles. The situation grew dire; 4S shops found themselves in urgent need of support, and the Baojun brand itself teetered on the brink, necessitating prompt intervention.

Amidst these challenges, a palpable sense of anxiety began to pervade the atmosphere.

At this critical juncture, Shen Yang found himself navigating a dichotomy as stark as the contrast between a cup of bitter, scalding coffee and another of sweet, refreshing orange juice. Since its debut in 2010, the Wuling Hongguang had ascended to remarkable heights, perpetuating the legacy of success established by the Wuling Sunshine and Wuling Rongguang. Over the years, the Wuling brand had evolved into an emblem of legendary status, instilling a sense of invincibility and ease of triumph among its ranks. However, the underwhelming performance of the Baojun 630 introduced a jarring dissonance into this harmonious narrative of victories.

For automobile manufacturers, the specter of a crisis is ever-present, lurking in the shadows, ready to disrupt the status quo without warning. Leaders in the automotive realm often find themselves straddling a fine line between triumph and turmoil, their emotions swaying with the vicissitudes of sales trends.

The pressing question then becomes: How does one arrest the downturn of a fledgling brand and model?

7.3 The Unity of Squads

In January 2012, Shen Yang, in his capacity as the general manager, delivered a visionary New Year message that introduced a partnership model into the corporate culture. He envisioned a partnership as more than just a collaboration; it was about being fellow travelers on a collective journey, sharing the road toward a common goal. This approach aimed to invigorate employee engagement, harness human potential to the fullest, and elevate achievements across the board. The message also served as a preemptive measure against the encroaching rigidity threatening to calcify the organization's dynamic spirit. The backdrop to this initiative was a challenging year in the mini-vehicle market, witnessing a 10% decline in 2011[1], signaling a potential saturation point. Despite this downturn, SGMW managed to expand its market share by an impressive 6 percentage points, approaching dominance in nearly half of the mini-vehicle segment. However, this growth came at a time of overall market contraction, highlighting the dangers of resting on laurels in a rapidly evolving industry. As the joint venture celebrated its decade of operation—a decade marked by exponential production growth from hundreds of thousands to millions and workforce expansion from 4,000 to 20,000—the specter of "big company syndrome" loomed large, threatening to stifle the organization's vibrant spirit.

---

[1] Yu Yue. SGMW: Breaking Through Capacity Bottlenecks[J]. *China Business Journal*, 2012-04-23 (042).

Shen Yang underscored the peril of allowing procedural rigidity and impersonal communication methods, such as PowerPoint presentations and emails, to erode the essence of interpersonal connections within the company. Reflecting on the transformation undergone by the state-owned enterprise over four decades and its rejuvenation following the joint venture, he reminded everyone that SGMW, despite its youthful 10 years of existence, stood at a critical juncture. It was imperative to avoid the pitfalls of "big company syndrome", characterized by a loss of agility and a diminishing sense of curiosity and eagerness to learn.

Embodying the ethos, "Alone, one may sprint swiftly, yet united, we journey far beyond the horizon", Shen Yang's message sought to empower employees, imbuing them with renewed vigor to collectively navigate the challenges that lay ahead.

The ethos of mutual support was not just understood but wholeheartedly embraced by the workforce. In the year that saw the revitalization of the Wuling Sunshine, a critical need arose for the aggregation of component data. On the day of the deadline, as data from the body, frame, and door teams were meticulously uploaded, an unexpected snag halted the floor team's data submission, funneling all eyes and pressure onto them. However, as the clock marked the end of the regular workday, solidarity shone brightly; no one left for home. They stayed, a testament to their unity, waiting for the pivotal data. By the evening's cloak at 19:00, volunteers from other teams stepped forward, offering to dive into the data depths to unearth the discrepancy. The Technical Development Center building buzzed with activity well into the night, its numerous rooms illuminated as a collective force joined hands in problem-solving. When the breakthrough came at 4 o'clock in the morning, the body and accessories design department triumphantly met the deadline, with prompt notification to the leadership. The immediate flood of supportive messages from the project director and the chief engineer, seemingly in eager anticipation, raised the intriguing question: Had they, too, been vigilantly awake, awaiting the resolution? Despite the tight timeline for the rejuvenated Wuling Sunshine, employees, bound by a partnership ethos, resolutely adhered to each deadline. Challenges faced by an individual were swiftly met with the support of many, and hurdles for a team summoned the strength of the entire department. Fueled by this culture of mutual encouragement, the team's collective resilience was significantly fortified.

Now, the collective ambition was laser-focused on conquering the domain of passenger cars, akin to seeds poised at the brink of spring, eager and ready to burst forth into vigorous growth.

The evolution of SGMW from mastering the mini-vehicle realm to venturing into the passenger car domain was subtly heralded by the development of the Wuling Hongguang, serving as a formative initiation into this new territory. By the time 2011 rolled around and the development of its enhanced version, the Wuling Hongguang S, was underway, SGMW had already secured a firm grasp on design quality. The company methodically dissected the project into 10 pivotal performance categories, pinpointing essential components, critical dimensions, and parameters, along with fundamental requirements to direct its focus, thereby significantly elevating both performance and design quality. Meanwhile, the meticulous approach during the Baojun 630's design and manufacturing journey contributed to SGMW's growing proficiency in navigating the nuanced transition from utility to passenger vehicles.

In this vein, the Technical Development Center embarked on an exploratory journey into passenger car research and development, utilizing intensive brainstorming sessions as the crucible for innovation. Staff members were grouped and assigned the task of dissecting how the Wuling Hongguang stacked up against traditional passenger cars, closely scrutinizing body structure, capabilities, and standard specifications to bridge any disparities. This exercise of "intensive debates and profound revelations" fostered a unified direction and a robust drive towards enhancing perceived quality and precision in design. Consequently, the once straightforward design ethos gradually evolved, assimilating modern design principles and innovative thinking.

The leap from the mini-vehicle segment to the realm of passenger cars introduced SGMW to a new set of stringent quality expectations, particularly in terms of exterior perceived quality and noise performance. The standards that were once deemed satisfactory for models like the Sunshine, Rongguang, and Hongguang now had to be reevaluated and elevated. For example, while commercial vehicles could accommodate door gaps of up to 5 millimeters, passenger cars mandated these gaps to be no more than 3.5 millimeters, demanding uniform and seamlessly rounded edges. Similarly, the visibility of welding spots faced stricter scrutiny in passenger cars, with visible marks deemed permissible in commercial vehicles now considered unacceptable, demanding a flawless finish. Furthermore, the structural aesthetics of commercial vehicles, where functional reinforcement ribs, like its veins and arteries, might be exposed, cannot meet the sleeker, more refined expectations of passenger car design. Dimensional tolerances witnessed a significant tightening as well; what was previously acceptable at a variance of up to 10 millimeters in welding must now be meticulously controlled within a mere 1.5 millimeters. These heightened quality standards necessitate rigorous controls and, in many instances, the development of new molds to ensure compliance with the exacting demands of passenger car production.

To bridge the knowledge gap between commercial and passenger vehicle standards, the Technical Development Center's chief engineer spearheaded an exhaustive training initiative targeting workshop directors and middle management. This educational endeavor was anchored in meticulously crafted presentations that delineated the nuanced differences in design and manufacturing processes between the two vehicle categories, illuminating every detail of passenger cars, contextualized against the backdrop of commercial vehicle practices. In preparation for these enlightening sessions, the courseware development team embarked on an in-depth exploration, conducting on-site photography to enrich their narrative. This visual documentation served as a precursor to more immersive, hands-on workshops where actual vehicle components were employed to vividly illustrate distinctions. For example, the nuanced art of sealant application—a crucial operation where precision ensures the integrity of passenger vehicles against water ingress and noise pollution—was thoroughly examined. Unlike the more forgiving standards for commercial vehicles, where a liberal application of sealant sufficed, passenger cars demanded meticulous attention to ensure no potential entry points for water or avenues for noise disturbance were overlooked. This included a comprehensive review of critical areas such as engine and cabin partitions, flooring, side panels, roofs, and doors, many of which required a combination of welding and precise sealant application for optimal sealing. To augment this hands-on learning, the team compiled extensive video footage of finished vehicles, creating a looped visual aid that underscored best practices and highlighted potential pitfalls. In an innovative move, medical endoscopes were procured to facilitate inspections of those challenging-to-view sealant applications deep within the vehicle's structure, turning every nook and cranny inside out for scrutiny. Magnifying glasses became ubiquitous, transforming into an indispensable tool for every participant.

SGMW's journey toward excellency was a testament to the meticulous refinement of its processes—a reality highlighting the deep and gradual assimilation of textbook principles into practical manufacturing. Contrary to the misconception that joint ventures can effortlessly transplant foreign blueprints and methodologies to streamline production and resolve challenges in a cookie-cutter fashion, the truth on the factory floor often paints a different picture. The recalibration of machinery and adaptation to the nuances of local production demands cannot be achieved by simply mirroring foreign practices.

The genesis of a vehicle, particularly in its nascent stages, is marked by a series of trials and a plethora of disparate ideas. Depending solely on external R&D and design entities, in the absence of in-house capabilities, frequently results in inefficacy. Even renowned design firms can find themselves at a loss, unable to deliver compelling solutions when confronted with the client's evolving visions. It is through independent development that these initial, amorphous ideas are refined, shaped, and polished into tangible innovations. For automotive joint ventures to keep their original brands and independent R&D capability, it is imperative to cultivate robust design capabilities that can transform vague ideas into concrete, market-ready models. Some joint ventures, despite financial success, may find themselves on a path of innovation stagnation, often defaulting to an OEM model due to a lack of creative expression and design acumen.

As the team at SGMW navigated the journey of learning and enhancement, they simultaneously forged ahead with a groundbreaking endeavor—the inception of a passenger car, discreetly dubbed CN200. Shifting gears from their traditional focus on minivans, characterized by rear-wheel drive and a notable absence of comfort, this venture aimed at a paradigm shift. The team set out to pioneer a front-engine, front-wheel-drive platform, complete with a reimagined chassis and suspension system, tailored explicitly for the passenger car segment. Initially, the decision was to adorn this new vehicle with the "Wuling" red emblem, sidestepping the "Baojun" marque. It appeared that sedan development under Baojun had not yet fallen under the ambit of Wuling's Technical Development Center. Despite a decade-long collaboration, GM chose to reserve this privilege exclusively for PATAC. Nevertheless, there was unanimous agreement among GM's executives regarding the Technical Development Center's foray into passenger car design under the Wuling banner.

Thus, the stage was set for the introduction of this new Wuling model.

On the eve of a crucial board meeting, Shen Yang and Yao Zuoping met to strategize the presentation of the Wuling-branded passenger car. However, the discussion was overshadowed by the pressing conundrum of the Baojun brand's dearth of new models and lukewarm market reception. In the quiet of the night, illuminated only by the occasional glow of their cigarettes, an audacious idea took form amidst the haze of lingering smoke and an ashtray filled with cigarette butts:

What if this vehicle, initially envisioned for the Wuling, were to be transitioned to the Baojun?

In the predawn silence, a phone call jolted SGMW's sales executive from sleep, prompting an urgent, overnight overhaul of the presentation slated for the next day. The pivotal decision made in those early hours was to rebrand CN200 under the Baojun marque.

During the presentation, GM's executives were surprised by the revelation of a car fully conceptualized by SGMW bearing the Baojun insignia. Despite initial hesitations stemming from the underwhelming debut of the first vehicle launched under the Baojun, the decision to proceed with the Baojun branding for this new model was, albeit reluctantly, sanctioned by GM's management.

This development marked a serendipitous victory.

The process of forming impressions or conclusions is rarely instantaneous. Often, the significance of details witnessed firsthand unfolds over time, revealing insights and nuances previously overlooked. This board meeting crystallized a pivotal realization: SGMW possessed the capability to independently design sedans, a prospect previously unimaginable for GM's executives. Throughout the decade-long partnership, autonomy over design and development had scarcely been considered attainable. However, in a quiet and unexpected turn of events, it became a reality.

In the world of joint venture automotive companies, securing the right to independent research and development transcends mere argumentation or the volume of one's voice. It is not purely about logical reasoning but rather entails a nuanced blend of courage, intellect, and the delicate art of relationship management, all while navigating the complex landscape without causing lasting rifts. It extends beyond mere strength to include meticulous attention to detail, challenging decision-makers to apply their wisdom and timing adeptly—conditions pivotal in achieving meaningful autonomy for the company.

The model that SGMW ultimately brought to fruition, blessed with the shareholders' approval, was christened the Baojun 730. In the lexicon of the Chinese automotive sector, the number "7" is imbued with fortune. According to China's vehicle certification directory, vehicles prefixed with "7" are recognized as sedans, while those beginning with "6" are identified as passenger vehicles. Circa 2001, as China's sedan market gained momentum, many automotive novices, not initially designated in the country's official vehicle manufacturing plan, often navigated regulations with a "6" prefix qualification. Their journey started on the industry's periphery, aiming for the coveted "7" prefix, symbolizing sedan status.

With the number "7" leading the charge, a promising dream began to take shape.

7.4 The Chief Test Driver

With the brand firmly established, designs finalized, and prototype vehicles ready, the only remaining hurdle before initiating mass production for the highly anticipated Baojun 730 was the general manager's thorough evaluation. This final assessment, a hallmark of Shen Yang's leadership, was both a ritual and a formidable challenge for every new Wuling vehicle, with the Baojun 730 being the latest subject. Shen Yang, leading the technical team, deliberately selected a notoriously uneven road to test the vehicle's mettle.

Shen Yang's method in these evaluations was straightforward and uncompromising, resembling an assessor armed with three decisive axes, casting a shadow of intense anticipation over the team. The inaugural test demanded the vehicle start smoothly in third gear—an unconventional ask simulating the conditions of a novice driver pushing the vehicle beyond its usual limits. The initial hiccup arose from an evident power discrepancy, as the vehicle faltered while attempting to overtake on secondary roads without downshifting to second gear. The subsequent test scrutinized the vehicle's acoustic insulation, aiming to ascertain if conversations at the front of the cabin remained audible at the rear—an acknowledged challenge for rear-wheel-drive configurations. This time, noise intrusion from the roof became apparent, producing a disconcerting drumming sound while in motion. The final ordeal tested the vehicle's suspension against the harshness of potholes, a true test of comfort and build. The lead designer, seated at the back, nearly collided with the roof during one such encounter, and his reaction and reddened complexion spoke volumes to Shen Yang, who found no need for words.

Regrettably, the Baojun 730 failed to meet the stringent criteria set forth in these tests.

Navigating the intricate landscape of automotive design without a predefined roadmap, SGMW had historically leaned into the sturdy pillars of self-education and introspection to carve its path of learning and innovation.

This self-discovery journey of accumulating wisdom through trial and error is epitomized in the evolution of the Wuling Sunshine. Upon its market introduction, the

Wuling Sunshine faced its fair share of tribulations, notably manifested in consumer reports citing unexpected rear door lock openings. This issue prompted Wuling dealerships to frequently replace rear doors for consumers, leading to the perplexing and disheartening situation of discarding nearly new original doors. Intriguingly, this problem rarely surfaced during the factory's testing phases. It was not until a fortuitous conversation with a GM engineer that a breakthrough was achieved: tailgate rigidity played a pivotal role in the lock mechanism's reliability. This insight marked a watershed moment for Wuling's Technical Development Center, illuminating the path forward by establishing an important threshold for tailgate rigidity to preemptively address the issue.

Emboldened by this epiphany, the Technical Development Center embarked on a meticulous quest to master the quantification of rigidity, delving into the intricacies of modes, bending stiffness, and beyond. This process entailed correlating simulation data with empirical test results, coupled with rigorous endurance testing, to cultivate a comprehensive database of performance indicators. Refinements were made to better align with real-world user conditions, enhancing vehicle durability.

This represents a broader ethos of collective enlightenment and adaptive learning within SGMW's automotive design endeavors.

In the realm of commercial vehicle development, priorities were conventionally given to structural integrity, reliability, and collision safety. However, the foray into passenger cars introduced an additional layer of complexity, demanding careful attention to aerodynamics, body torsional rigidity, deflection, and modal analysis as part of the perceptual evaluation. Neglecting these aspects may result in vehicular noise during motion, much like the impact of drum skin tightness on the sound's consistency. SGMW's breakthrough came with the establishment of an advanced computer simulation laboratory and the implementation of sophisticated software analysis, identifying over 500 crucial performance indicators. These milestones were achieved gradually, not only symbolizing the company's evolution but also echoing the broader narrative of a country's journey toward industrialization.

Despite an initial setback during the general manager's test drive, the Technical Development Center was not without recourse. Solutions were swiftly identified, including addressing powertrain mismatch through gear ratio adjustments and recalibration, mitigating roof noise by refining modal analyses for vibration and redesigning the roof's structure and enhancing ride comfort by overhauling the rear suspension system, transitioning from leaf to coil springs. These adaptations underscored the center's adeptness in translating learned skills into actionable solutions. While drawing on the expertise of GM America in design and manufacturing provided a foundational blueprint, the essence of SGMW's competitive edge was forged through meticulous attention to industrial nuances and a proactive approach to bridging knowledge gaps through self-driven inquiry.

The chief test driver's role transcended simple technical evaluation, embodying a deep-seated interest in understanding user psychology.

Back in 2011, amidst the surging sales success of the Wuling Hongguang, a noticeable trend emerged: consumers were increasingly gravitating toward its higher-end configurations, signaling a growing aspiration for progress, akin to the keen anticipation one experiences observing a child's first teeth emerge—curiosity was in the air. In an informal tearoom setting, Shen Yang stumbled upon the Technical Development Center's product manager, sparking an impromptu dialogue about potential enhancements to the Wuling Hongguang. The product manager, with fervor, outlined the existing design and configuration constraints, and, as the steam from their tea dispersed, Shen Yang, inspired by the conversation, pledged an additional budget to explore the feasibility of an upgraded version.

"How much budget can we allocate for the upgrade?"

"Let's earmark an extra RMB 3,000 for each set of wheels. What magic can we make happen?"

"Deal! We'll put together a plan."

This negotiation epitomized the center's established budgeting dialogue. Here, increasing the budget was synonymous with fostering innovation within a culture characterized by thriftiness and diligence. The design team, adept at pinpointing crucial enhancements, dove into exhaustive discussions, and they presented an ambitious upgrade plan within a mere three days, with costs totaling RMB 2,900, necessitating collaboration with suppliers. Each model enhancement required suppliers to streamline processes further, perpetually in pursuit of cost efficiencies. Reflecting on the proposal's ambition, Shen Yang humorously lamented, "Are we truly pushing it to the limit at RMB 3,000?" In the end, the final budget for the upgrade was meticulously calibrated to RMB 2,500.

In 2013, the introduction of the revamped Wuling Hongguang S marked a strategic pivot toward a more PV-oriented and comfortable offering, receiving a warm reception from the market. Buoyed by the sterling reputation of its predecessor, the Wuling Hongguang, this new iteration, too, made an impressive debut. During that year, the Wuling Hongguang series achieved a significant sales milestone, reaching 530,000 units, with sales sharply ascending as the year drew to a close. By January 2014, monthly sales astonishingly surpassed 80,000 units, giving rise to the "Hongguang Phenomenon" and cementing the Wuling Hongguang's position as a national icon.

This successful upgrade underscored a fundamental truth: unraveling consumer desires is akin to deciphering a mystery. The key to winning consumer affection lies in discerning insights that extend beyond the mere calculation of sales figures and data. Experienced market navigators know well that the essence of true insight is found not just in spreadsheets but in the lived experiences and aspirations of their customers.

As this narrative unfolded, a broader vision began to take shape. By the end of 2013, the inauguration of the SGMW Chongqing base heralded a new chapter, amalgamating GM's global manufacturing prowess with the distinctive operational ethos of SGMW. Situated in Chongqing, home to Chang'an Automobile, this strategic move placed long-standing rivals within the same city's bounds. Here, two giants, often vying for dominance in the mini-vehicle market and trading places on the sales leaderboard, found themselves co-located in the same urban landscape, setting the stage for an enthralling chapter in their ongoing market saga.

With the commencement of operations at the Baojun Base in Liuzhou's Hedong District the previous year, SGMW achieved a strategic milestone in its manufacturing footprint, spanning three key cities—Liuzhou, Qingdao, and Chongqing—and housing a quartet of production facilities. This strategic arrangement, reminiscent of a golden triangle, not only optimized production flexibility but also synergized geographical advantages, laying a robust foundation for limitless creative aspirations.

Shen Yang, an automotive enthusiast with deep roots in the mountains, has embarked on a journey of discovery and inspiration throughout his career. In 2005, he was entranced by the coastal vistas of Qingdao, featuring expansive seas and sandy beaches. His adventures continued in 2007 as he immersed himself in the cultural tapestries of Egypt and India. Now, he found himself embraced by an even larger mountainous city, with each experience electrifying his soul and broadening the horizons of his imagination. For individuals like Shen Yang, who cast their gaze beyond their immediate surroundings, their vision will not be hemmed in by urban sprawl or the natural barriers that stand in their way.

7.5 Sharing a Ride to Navigate Uncharted Waters

In the autumn of 2013, China introduced the Belt and Road Initiative, unveiling a vision to collaboratively establish the New Silk Road Economic Belt and the 21st Century Maritime Silk Road. This ambitious plan aimed to nurture the development of a global economic community, creating a new frontier for international strategies among prominent manufacturers. In this spirit of global outreach, SGMW ventured into India and Egypt, charting a course toward the internationalization of Chinese automotive prowess.

In 2004, just two years after the joint venture's inception, SGMW began to capitalize on the international networks of both GM and SAIC Motor, seeking opportunities to export complete vehicles to regions such as South America, the Middle East, and Africa, and cultivating a specialized team dedicated to navigating the complexities of overseas markets. In 2008, SGMW articulated three strategic pillars, elevating its overseas operations to stand alongside its mini-vehicle and passenger car divisions as a core area of focus.

Following GM's reorganization in 2009, a new strategy for the global market emerged. The company, preferring collaboration over solitary ventures in emerging markets, sought to leverage the strengths of its partners, an approach influenced by both internal constraints and an acknowledgment of Chinese manufacturing's competitive edge. Concurrently, SAIC Motor was navigating its own international challenges, particularly with its acquisition of Republic of Korea's SsangYong Motor. The path to internationalization demanded versatility and adaptability, and SGMW was emerging as a pivotal player in the global strategy.

In the pursuit of a strategic 50-50 joint venture alliance, SAIC Motor and GM established General Motors SAIC Investment Ltd. in Hong Kong, creating a nexus for investment and collaboration that would catapult them into the burgeoning markets of Southeast Asia. Their primary focus was on India, marking it as the inaugural destination and positioning SGMW at the forefront of this ambitious venture.

India, a country pulsating with potential and creativity, stands as a beacon for the rapidly evolving automotive sector. The year 2010 witnessed a remarkable surge in car sales within India, escalating by 31% from the previous year to hit 1.87 million units, with small cars constituting roughly three-quarters of this volume[1]. In emerging economies, the initial growth spurt in the automotive sector often favors mini-vehicles, especially minivans, due to the general populace's modest purchasing power. However, as the economic landscape matures, market dynamics shift, gradually phasing out minivans in favor of a diverse array of automotive offerings, relegating minivans to a niche segment within the mini-vehicle market. During this period, India experienced an upswing in mini-vehicle development, coinciding with the onset of a declining trend in China's minivan segment.

As the "King of Mini-cars", Japanese brands had firmly established their dominance in India. Suzuki, a brand synonymous with expertise in mini vehicle manufacturing, commanded nearly half of the Indian market share. Osamu Suzuki, the president of Suzuki, encapsulated this phenomenon in his book *I Am the Ruler of Small Company*, noting, "In the vast global car market, India's dedication to small cars stands out as a unique patch. Trying to weave in larger models that have found success in other lands into this distinct market usually falls flat. But for a company like Suzuki, with its roots and expertise deeply entrenched in crafting small vehicles, India emerges as an extraordinary window of opportunity".[2] Against this backdrop, SAIC Motor and GM, acknowledging the unique position of SGMW—a powerhouse in China's mini-vehicle sector known for its "low cost, high value" proposition and manufacturing prowess—saw it as the ideal candidate to challenge Japanese supremacy in India.

GM had already laid foundational assets in India, including two vehicle manufacturing facilities, an engine plant, and the Chevrolet sales division, all integrated into the newly established General Motors India Private Limited. With this infrastructure in place, the introduction of SGMW's models and expertise was poised to start anew, inaugurating a fresh chapter in the competitive landscape.

The question of leadership in the Indian market loomed large.

The individual has to master the art of manufacturing to unlock the benefits of cost-efficient production, dive deep into the essence of Wuling's culture for the company to take root and flourish, and there is more…

Indeed, he is the embodiment of such knowledge and innovation.

In recent years of development, SGMW has embraced an approach akin to

---

① Wang Chao. Is India's Auto Industry Set to Outpace China[J]. *China Youth Daily*, 2011-02-24 (010).

② Ge Bangning. First Foray into India[J]. *Auto Business Review*, 2011.

"encircling the cities from the countryside". Rather than simply adhering to the beaten path of GM's manufacturing guidelines, the approach crafts vehicles that resonate with the heartbeat of the market's demand. While SAIC-GM aligns with the high standards set by GM North America, Yao Zuoping has charted a pioneering course, redefining equipment and process standards to etch a unique manufacturing ethos distinct to SGMW. This bold move has given rise to an engine production operation that operates on just a fraction—a mere one-fifth—of the operational costs of its North American counterparts, positioning SGMW as a standout exception within GM's global manufacturing framework.

GM and SAIC Motor, inspired by the triumphant narrative of SGMW, decided to transplant this model of efficiency and innovation onto Indian soil. Back in 2003, the decision by GM India to construct a new factory sparked a global consultation among GM's manufacturing entities, each eager to contribute their blueprint for the future. Amidst this competitive landscape, SGMW, still in its infancy as a joint venture, entered the fray. Led by Yao Zuoping, the proposal derived from the blueprint of the Liuzhou factory distinguished itself for its pragmatism and leadership in cost-effectiveness, propelling Yao Zuoping to prominence within GM's global manufacturing community. Faced with the ambitious venture in India, SAIC Motor and GM unanimously turned to Yao Zuoping to spearhead the project. Consequently, relevant departments approached Yao Zuoping for discussions.

"Your contributions to SGMW have been pivotal..."

"It's imperative, however, for our leaders to embrace new horizons and challenges..."

"We firmly believe that India presents the most fitting stage for your next stage..."

"..."

However, the Guangxi Zhuang Autonomous Region, Yao Zuoping's home base, was reluctant to let go of such a vital figure. With SGMW on an upward trajectory, the prospect of parting ways with one of its foundational pillars was daunting. How could they entertain such a move amidst a period of vigorous expansion?

For Yao Zuoping, the decision to transition from Liuzhou to India initially felt like an insurmountable leap. After dedicating a quarter century to the company, the thought of navigating the unknown terrain of India to establish new footholds stirred a mix of excitement and trepidation. His deep-rooted connection to his homeland, coupled with the formidable "golden partnership". He had cultivated with Shen Yang, infused the prospect of departure with poignant significance. Yao Zuoping, three years Shen Yang's junior and a fellow native of Guangxi, had not only joined the company around the same time but had also lived through the formative years of their careers side by side. With countless conversations, shared victories, challenges, and memories, their bond was forged strong within the iconic red walls of their office.

After thoughtful deliberation, a middle ground was reached: Yao Zuoping would helm the role of general manager at GM India while retaining his position as the vice general manager at SGMW.

As autumn's breath whispered change and nostalgia intertwined, the moment for bold beginnings dawned. In September 2010, under the emblematic banner of "Perseverance with Self-Strengthening" at the entrance of the SGMW factory, Shen Yang bid a heartfelt farewell to the 13 pioneers embarking on this new venture. Yao Zuoping's mission was clear: to transplant the cost-effective business ethos and esteemed models of SGMW, like the Wuling Hongguang, into the Indian landscape, where they would don the Chevrolet badge in a bold bid to captivate the Indian market.

Under the frosty adornment of the night and the moon's glow reminiscent of their distant hometowns, Yao Zuoping and his team were not greeted with fanfare but with a workshop filled with doubtful glances in India. The task at hand—transplanting the essence of Chinese manufacturing excellence onto foreign soil—aroused curiosity as much as skepticism. Beneath the luminous gaze of the moon, they sought solace in poetry, their resolve unwavering, and their spirits buoyant.

The moon on Mid-Autumn, with affection bright,

Illuminates foreign lands as home at night.

Let's trade the flatbread for our mooncakes' taste,

Amidst the sandalwood, that Indian embraces.

Into India's depths, a tiger's den we dare,

Only by seizing cubs, can we truly fare.

Sailing the seas, in pursuit of a grand feat,

In bravery's dance, who but us can compete?

GM's factory in India was a showcase of modernity, boasting cutting-edge technology and adhering rigorously to the global manufacturing standards set by GM. The processes were meticulously defined, ensuring a standardized approach to production. Despite these strengths, the facility lagged significantly behind in production efficiency, resulting in manufacturing costs that were three to five times higher than those incurred by SGMW. With a production target of 30,000 vehicles annually under a single-shift operation, the Indian facility required a workforce of nearly 1,600 per shift to meet its targets—a stark contrast to Liuzhou's lean operation, where similar production figures were achieved with just 300 people. This disparity not only highlighted differences in operational efficiency but also unveiled a complex organizational structure within the manufacturing entity.

Upon a close examination of the operational dynamics at the Indian factory, Yao Zuoping was struck by the inefficiencies, likening the organization to "a soaked towel, each squeeze releasing torrents". For Yao Zuoping, whose career was dedicated to refining manufacturing systems and elevating quality, the evident wastefulness he encountered was almost unbearable.

At the welcome party in India, Yao Zuoping, armed with his newly acquired Hindi greeting, "namaste", instantly bridged cultural gaps. Waste no time, he delved straight into his mission statement: "My purpose here is to reduce costs." Playfully gesturing towards his towering British colleague, he quipped, "Among the two of us, he's the taller one. Therefore, he stands for quality, and I, for cost..." This blend of candor and humor not only broke the ice but also elicited waves of laughter and applause from the assembled employees.

Yao Zuoping was resolute in his commitment to slashing costs. He meticulously analyzed and refined GM's global manufacturing system with a disarmingly straightforward strategy, tailoring processes to align with local standards and customs. In assembling the Indian management team, his unconventional icebreaker often was, "Are you comfortable diving into a meal with just your hands?" underscoring his belief that standardization cannot effectively bridge cultural gaps. While GM initially harbored reservations about deviating from established norms, any opposition proved tepid. It became evident to GM's leadership that in the era of globalization, a one-size-fits-all approach was inadequate. Embracing the Wuling model represented a tangible pathway to navigating the complexities of global markets.

A substantial domestic production percentage is greatly valued by governments worldwide, and SGMW tapped into this expectation by bringing its Liuzhou-based suppliers to India, marking a concerted effort by a Chinese enterprise and a significant stride forward for the national supply chain. Baosteel Group began its production of cut steel plates on Indian soil, while Shanghai Yanfeng introduced its automotive interiors for local sourcing, even extending its supply chain to include Tata Motors in

India, thereby securing a strategic position in the market. This collaborative endeavor resulted in the Chevrolet Enjoy, a rebranded Wuling Hongguang, achieving an impressive domestic production percentage of over 50% for its parts. Ironically, as Chinese component manufacturers established a stronghold in India, the overarching entity, GM, gradually phased out its operations in the Indian market.

The year 2010 heralded India as a burgeoning market for automotive giants like Ford, GM, and Toyota, all witnessing significant sales upticks. Ford's sales in India for the year soared to 84,000 units, almost doubling the previous year's figures; GM enjoyed a 59% surge in its Indian car sales, reaching 110,000 units; and Toyota's sales climbed to 75,000 units, marking a 38% increase[①]. This surge in sales was attributed to the expanding appetite for new vehicles in the Indian automotive market and the introduction of several new models by these companies.

GM, with global vision and ambition, found its capabilities substantially bolstered through its partnership with SGMW. As initiatives gained momentum in India, parallel progress unfolded in the venture in Egypt, which stands as GM's bastion in North Africa. In a groundbreaking development in November 2011, the president of GM North Africa, on behalf of GM Egypt, inked both a technology transfer agreement and an engineering service agreement with Shen Yang in Liuzhou. This event heralded the Chinese automotive industry's inaugural foray into intellectual property exportation. In a noteworthy departure from the historical norm, where SGMW compensated GM for intellectual property and branding rights, the tables turned a decade into their collaboration, with GM now remunerating SGMW in dollars for these privileges. Reflecting on this pivotal milestone, Shen Yang commented, "Now, our talents can venture overseas to earn technology management fees, reversing the previous flow where we were the ones making payments." True internationalization, he believed, was anchored in the export of expertise. This venture saw the export of SGMW's flagship model, the Wuling Rongguang, from its Qingdao branch to Egypt in a CKD format. There, it was rebranded as the Chevrolet Move, marking the debut of a Chinese car model assembled by GM in Egypt, which symbolizes a pioneering collaboration between the century-old American corporation and indigenous Chinese technology on Egyptian soil.

In 2011, as Daniel Francis Akerson assumed the role of global chairman at GM, his tenure commenced with a period marked by enthusiasm and high aspirations. This

---

① 2010 Asian Auto Boom: Global Giants Scramble for a Slice of the Asian Market[J]. *China Auto Market*, 2011.

was evident during the completion ceremony of the second phase of capacity expansion at SGMW's Qingdao branch, where he confidently asserted that the Qingdao factory was destined to become an important export hub to tap into future overseas markets. The successful launch of the Chevrolet Move in 2012 propelled GM's market share in Egypt to 34%, achieving parity with Suzuki and commanding a price premium of EGP 10,000 over Suzuki's offerings. This milestone not only galvanized the team but also left a lasting impression on shareholders.

By May 2013, the Indian passenger car market welcomed the Chevrolet Enjoy, a rebranded version of the Wuling Hongguang tailored to suit local preferences. Adaptations included a right-hand drive configuration and the introduction of a diesel engine option to cater to Indian consumers. The Chevrolet Enjoy exceeded expectations, carving out a niche in a sea of European, American, and Japanese contenders. It quickly ascended to the second spot in the Indian MPV segment, challenging Suzuki's longstanding market hegemony. Its remarkable performance was further cemented by the model winning the MPV of the Year award at the prestigious Autocar-India Awards 2013, an event co-hosted by the renowned British automotive magazine Autocar and Bloomberg News, marking a significant achievement for SGMW in the international automotive arena.

Leveraging the extensive channel expertise of GM and SAIC Motor, SGMW had honed its strategy for international expansion. In the competitive Egyptian passenger car market, it successfully generated income through technical services, a testament to the efficacy of its knowledge-based strategy. Meanwhile, the launch of the Chevrolet Enjoy in India represented a groundbreaking achievement for a Chinese automotive company, exemplifying a comprehensive export strategy encompassing knowledge, team, and management export in its overseas ventures.

This strategic approach marks a pivotal step in the trajectory of Chinese passenger vehicles as they navigate the intricate maze of global market dynamics, piecing together the puzzle of international success.

7.6 The Baptism of Independence

In April 2014, the moment arrived for the apprentice to forge their own path. SGMW's Technical Development Center, showcasing commendable sales achievements, demonstrated its full capability to operate autonomously. In a voluntary move, PATAC's Liuzhou Branch embarked on a "functional transition" to integrate into SGMW's Technical Development Center, marking not a conclusion but the dawn of a new phase of growth. The combined sales of the Baojun 630 and the subsequent Baojun 610 soared to 250,000 units, a success that was rather noteworthy. Crucially, PATAC's contribution to SGMW proved invaluable, infusing the Liuzhou team with the intellectual resources it most needed.

The essence of this joint venture extended beyond mere capital or car models; it fundamentally revolved around the transference of automotive manufacturing expertise. GM, with its global manufacturing standards, had perfected a system ensuring operational quality across different geographies. Yet, standardization alone does not spell market victory. The success of a car in any given market is deeply intertwined with local consumer behavior. Localization adjustments are not mere appendages but thoughtfully crafted enhancements. PATAC's meticulous product adjustments were tightly governed by procedural standards, a discipline that, while refining product quality, occasionally impeded the agility to promptly respond to the market's dynamic demands.

The landscape of manufacturing is witnessing a subtle yet significant transformation. Within the core of factory operations, a dedicated space has been established for global consumer reviews, where frontline workers step into the shoes of consumers, scrutinizing the products with a critical eye. This innovative area is outfitted with an array of specialized tools designed to pinpoint quality concerns that hold paramount importance for consumers, such as the uniformity of paint thickness and the precision of gap widths, the findings of which lay the groundwork for continuous enhancements. This approach, aligned with GM's rigorous global quality assessment criteria, is a standardized practice implemented across all its factories, including SGMW. To underscore its commitment to excellence, GM has stationed a quality expert in Liuzhou to relay the facility's quality performance directly to the corporate board.

In a strategic move during the Baojun 730's development phase, a model of SAIC-GM's flagship MPV, the Buick GL8, was conspicuously placed at the entrance of every workshop. This deliberate placement ensured that it was the first thing anyone saw upon entering, with its doors always left unlocked, an accessibility encouraging regular and thorough inspections by managers and section chiefs, leveraging the Buick GL8 as a benchmark. This process was instrumental in guiding the team on how to craft a compact MPV that not only meets but exceeds established standards.

To push the envelope on quality, SGMW embarked on an ambitious learning initiative, sending a significant contingent of its workforce to glean insights at Jinbei GM in Shenyang. Surprisingly, the early production lines for the Buick GL8 were not as technologically advanced as one might anticipate. Nevertheless, products emerging from these relatively humble assembly lines were remarkably defect-free. This experience served as a powerful lesson for SGMW's engineers, reinforcing the understanding that the essence of quality transcends the sophistication of equipment, instead rooted in a deep-seated culture of quality awareness among the workforce.

The pursuit of excellence soon presented a significant challenge for SGMW engineers: the task of universally applying a single set of quality standards across diverse markets, user bases, and product types. It became apparent that adopting a one-size-fits-all approach to global standards was impractical. The solution lay in a pivot toward a more nuanced strategy—one involving a closer connection with end-users and the customization of offerings to meet their specific demands. Building upon the groundwork laid by GM's global consumer review initiatives, SGMW ventured into the domain of perceived quality reviews, crafting bespoke vehicle evaluation criteria that resonated more closely with user expectations. This paradigm shift marked a transition from a product-centered mindset to a user-centered philosophy, introducing engineering methodologies designed to simulate actual user scenarios. At its core, this strategy sought to illuminate the real-world contexts in which vehicles are used, thereby enriching the perspectives of both designers and manufacturers, and ensuring that the final products not only meet but anticipate the needs and preferences of users.

These collective efforts culminated in the arrival of the model codenamed CN200, which had received the board's auspicious approval. On July 30, 2014, a landmark moment unfolded as SGMW unveiled its first independently developed passenger car, the Baojun 730, featuring a front-engine, front-wheel-drive sedan platform.

Concurrently, the longstanding challenge of harmonizing the sales channels for the Wuling and Baojun brands was finally overcome. At the dealers' conference, SGMW heralded a new era with the announcement, "One system, two brands, one team". This declaration resonated enthusiastically with dealers, particularly those who had previously focused exclusively on the Baojun brand. The past two years had seen them grapple with challenges and voice their frustrations; now, they were empowered to showcase both brands under one roof, safeguarding their investments. This consolidation of sales networks facilitated a smooth transition, embracing brand synergy and breaking through in county networks. This strategic move expanded distribution across over 2,000 county and township outlets nationwide, ensuring uniform pricing and sales strategies, which not only fortified the dealer network but also allowed SGMW to streamline its marketing efforts, rendering traditional new product launch media events unnecessary.

On the day of the Baojun 730's unveiling, Shen Yang and Yao Zuoping were among the first to arrive at the company's nerve center located within the red administrative building, their anticipation palpable. Together, they leaned into the glow of a computer screen with the intensity of spectators at a live football match, Yao Zuoping's sport of choice. On this occasion, however, the unfolding action was not played out on a grassy field but displayed through the vigorous dance of numbers across the screen. Orders surged, mimicking the enthusiastic leap of a bull market index, ascending with unwavering momentum. By the time the clock had yet to strike nine, the tally of orders had already breezed past the 10,000 mark.

Success flourished in their midst, radiant and teeming with vitality, reflecting the exuberance of summer blossoms.

The launch of the Baojun 730 sparked widespread jubilation across the board. Within a mere three months, monthly sales skyrocketed to 30,000 units, and before half a year had passed, cumulative sales reached an astounding 120,000 units, crowning it the most rapidly ascending star in the automotive sky of that period. During this time, the Chinese MPV market was abuzz with activity, with veterans like SAIC-GM's Buick GL8, GAC Honda Odyssey, and JAC Refine, a Hyundai adaptation, having long dominated the scene. Beneath these titans, the compact MPV segment remained wide open—a market opportunity ripe for the taking. In this era of automotive evolution, the Baojun 730's arrival could not have been more impeccably timed.

Positioned as a compact MPV, the Baojun 730 emerges as a diminutive sibling to the Buick GL8, tailored to meet the needs of large families. It stands as a testament to practicality, offering seating for seven, and embodies a design ethos that emphasizes straightforward, PV-oriented attributes. The front-engine, front-wheel-drive configuration in its design is a deliberate choice to enhance comfort without compromising the spacious reputation associated with the Wuling series. Throughout its design and development, meticulous attention was devoted to ensuring ample headroom and height across all three rows of seating. Ingenious adjustments to the interior floor—subtle lowering and leveling without altering the chassis—were made to incrementally enhance space, often by mere millimeters. In the realm of automotive design, the quest for the perfect balance of dimensions, costs, and weight is akin to an art form, with designers acting as meticulous sculptors of space and efficiency. The width of each seat and the precision of cushion edging were calculated with exacting detail, factoring in every contour. Additionally, the necessity for generous legroom prompted the strategic outward placement of chassis components, subsequently influencing the positioning of both the fuel tank and spare tire. This meticulous orchestration of interior space is akin to a masterclass in optimization, pushing the boundaries of perceived dimensions to their very limits, all in the pursuit of creating a vehicle that maximizes utility and comfort within its compact form.

Within the company's fabric, a profound sense of unity and a shared purpose wove together the ambitions, awareness, and endeavors of each employee. Shortly after the Baojun 730 hit the market, consumer feedback quickly highlighted a notable usability issue with the door handle switches. Responding promptly and effectively, the company dedicated four months to reengineering the handle, crafting new molds, and implementing the improved design across the board, all while ensuring measures were taken to offer upgrades to those who had already purchased the model. Venturing into uncharted territory in car design is like navigating the unknown, akin to a blind person piecing together an elephant's form; it demands a holistic grasp to glean accurate insights. The Baojun 730, without squandering resources, managed to enhance its performance and quality beyond its predecessors.

Precision in every facet underscored the company's strategic foresight and its knack for capitalizing on automotive trends. Two years prior, the Baojun base in eastern Liuzhou had commenced operations. Just a year before, the first phase of the engine factory at the Baojun base was constructed and put into operation. Subsequently, in a sequence of strategic expansions that mirrored a satellite adjusting its trajectory in orbit, the Baojun base executed three consecutive capacity increases, guided by the mantra of "pursuing innovation, embracing change, and testing limits". This strategic escalation aligned perfectly with the burgeoning demand for the Baojun 730. Upon its launch, the vehicle swiftly ascended to the zenith of its potential, heralding a golden era for the model.

Either lead in cost-effectiveness or stand out with distinctiveness. To truly enhance a company's competitive edge, it necessitates mastery of both.

Buoyed by the stellar user experience of the Baojun 730, the SGMW team experienced an unprecedented morale boost, marking the first time in the 12-year history of the joint venture where it genuinely asserted ownership over its design team. From the outset, Shen Yang had been a fervent advocate for keeping the original brand and independent R&D capability—a vision that has now materialized, affirming years of unwavering dedication. Shen Yang's steadfast belief in the potency of innovation and entrepreneurship, the conviction that creativity and continuous improvement hinge on the autonomy to design and innovate, has been resoundingly validated. The Baojun 730, a manifestation of this philosophy, has finally garnered well-deserved accolades for a principle long championed by Shen Yang.

In 2014, as China implemented restrictive policies on car purchases and usage in major cities like Hangzhou and Shenzhen, consumers became increasingly discerning in their vehicle choices. This shift, coupled with joint venture manufacturers' strategy adjustments—such as price reductions and a focus on second- and third-tier cities where small displacement models found favor—intensified competition for domestic brands. Amidst these challenging dynamics, SGMW stood out within SAIC Motor for its exceptional performance, surpassing even SAIC Volkswagen Automotive in annual car production and sales[1]. Despite the overall decline in the minivan market in favor of sedans and MPVs, a trend continuing from 2013, SGMW's offerings, particularly the minivan lineup, retained more than half the market share. The company's strategic acumen was further evidenced in the MPV market, where the Wuling Hongguang reigned supreme with annual sales of 750,000 units, capturing nearly 40% of the market share, and the newly introduced Baojun 730 quickly climbed the ranks to fourth[2]. This combined success of its models not only underscored SGMW's market dominance but also marked a significant shift at SAIC Motor's annual summary meeting, with SGMW's management taking their well-deserved place at the forefront.

Central to SGMW's strategy in PV-oriented development, the Baojun 730 emerged as a linchpin, clinching a significant triumph for the company. The sustained popularity of the model, evidenced by annual sales consistently exceeding 20,000

---

① *SAIC Motor Corporation Limited Annual Report, 2014.*

② In 2014, the Baojun 730 achieved sales of 120,000 units, while SGMW's minivan sales reached 650,000 units, capturing a market share of 53%. Starting from 2013, models such as the Wuling Hongguang were reclassified by the China Association of Automobile Manufacturers from the minivan category to the MPV market for statistical purposes. Data source: China Automotive Technology and Research Center and China Association of Automobile Manufacturers [K]. *China Automotive Industry Yearbook 2015*, 217–218.

units several years after its launch, attested to its lasting appeal and strategic importance, transforming what was initially an overlooked model into a resilient, enduring success story.

7.7 Crafting a Unique Essence

To some extent, the Baojun 730 can be seen as both a continuation of the legacy established by the Wuling Hongguang and a victory for the core user base traditionally served by Wuling. By leveraging the well-established sales network of the Wuling brand, the Baojun marque managed to secure a solid foothold for its launch. The process of building a car brand necessitates unwavering and consistent effort. Therefore, the introduction of a new model benefits significantly from the goodwill and loyalty generated by preceding models, facilitating a smoother path to climbing sales figures. In contrast, targeting an entirely new consumer segment can present significant challenges.

During this period, the burgeoning SUV market commanded the industry's attention. In China, passenger vehicles are categorized into four segments: sedans, multi-purpose vehicles (MPVs), cross passenger cars (early minivans), and sport utility vehicles (SUVs). SUVs, prized for their off-road capabilities, suitability for family leisure activities, and overall versatility, gained substantial popularity among consumers. With over 100 domestic SUV models vying for market share and the continuous introduction of new entrants, the competition became exceptionally intense.

The BAIC Group stands as a cornerstone in the development of off-road vehicles in China. The Beijing 212, synonymous with military-exclusive vehicles since the 1960s, has not only observed but also played a pivotal role in shaping crucial moments in Chinese automotive history. In 2015, the BAIC Group doubled down on its commitment to SUVs, pouring substantial investments into the creation of intelligent, compact, and high-end SUV models[1].

Great Wall Motors, originating from Hebei, weaves a distinctive narrative in the annals of Chinese automotive evolution. Beginning its journey in the modified car

---

① Yu Maojun, Lei Li. Paving the Way for SUVs: China SUV Trend Development Forum and Award Gala[J]. *Auto Time*, 2015.

segment, it expanded into rural pickup trucks before ultimately establishing its stronghold in the SUV market, where it solidified its status as a formidable contender. By 2015, Great Wall Motors found itself navigating a crowded field of rivals. It was not just up against international collaborations such as SAIC Volkswagen's Tiguan and GAC Honda's CR-V but also faced competition from domestic brands like JAC Refine S3 and Chang'an CS75. Despite this, the Haval H6 emerged as a standout, clinching the top spot in sales and securing a significant lead over its closest domestic competitors[①].

SGMW, with the precision of radar detection in the SUV market, identified a surprising gap: the absence of SUVs priced below RMB 100,000. At that juncture, popular SUV models from industry giants like Great Wall and Chang'an were tagged above RMB 120,000. With a longstanding commitment to affordability, SGMW saw an opportunity and decided to test the waters.

This strategic approach was not unprecedented. During the developmental phase of the Baojun 730, a compact MPV, the groundwork for a mid-size SUV was concurrently being laid on the design tables, heralding the arrival of the Baojun 560. This new model was envisioned to share the Baojun 730's platform, utilizing the same chassis to curtail design and development expenditures while boosting production efficiency. When it came to engine selection, designers initially faced a decision. The Baojun 730 was offered with either a 1.5-liter or a 1.8-liter gasoline engine, both delivering commendable power. However, prototype testing of the Baojun 560 revealed that the 1.5-liter engine fell short on performance, prompting the definitive choice of the 1.8-liter engine for the final model.

In the automotive manufacturing process, the design and modeling phases play a crucial role, involving the iterative crafting of 1:1 scale clay models, a step essential to faithfully translate the design concept into a tangible and manufacturable form. The development of the Baojun 560's clay model saw it undergo upwards of a dozen iterations, with continuous adjustments to data until the vehicle's H-point and B-pillar were precisely defined. Noise, an ever-persistent challenge, posed significant hurdles. For instance, an issue with noise leakage through the front bulkhead was identified during the prototype review phase, prompting an urgent need for design optimization, mold redevelopment, and the inaugural application of soundproof glass in the model,

---

① Zhou Lei. Review of the 2015 SUV Market: Unbeatable Chinese Brands Make Their Mark[J]. Phoenix New Media, January 28, 2016.

which led to a 2-decibel reduction in overall vehicle noise.

The test drive for the Baojun 560 was conducted on the extended incline of Lianhua Mountain in Liuzhou City, aligning closely with General Manager Shen Yang's ethos of "subjecting ordinary vehicles to extraordinary conditions". In pursuit of versatile vehicles capable across varied terrains, SGMW identified slopes across Guangxi, Chongqing, Yunnan, and beyond to establish test driving circuits. In Chongqing, for example, a specific slope was chosen to evaluate transmission slippage, assessing its impact on and potential damage to the gearbox. This testing approach under typical road conditions mirrors the actual driving experiences of users, supplemented by rigorous, specialized extreme condition testing conducted at dedicated facilities in Beijing, Hainan, and other locations.

In July 2015, adhering to its hallmark approach of simplicity and authenticity in market entry strategies, SGMW launched the Baojun 560, entering the fiercely competitive SUV arena. Forgoing a flamboyant launch event, the introduction was heralded by a straightforward tagline: "A family SUV from Wuling." The prior success of the Baojun 730 had set high expectations for the Baojun marque. For two years running, SGMW introduced standout models that held their own in the marketplace, signaling a significant stride in its PV-oriented development.

Designed as a five-seater family vehicle, the Baojun 560 initially featured a manual transmission and was priced under RMB 100,000, showcasing SGMW's deep-seated expertise in optimizing interior space. Despite its primary goal of establishing a niche in the SUV market, the Baojun 560 did not compromise on interior spaciousness. It boasted a wheelbase of 2,750 millimeters, on par with the seven-seater MPV, the Baojun 730, ensuring generous legroom for rear-seat passengers. The vehicle's flat floor design also eliminated any central hump, enhancing the comfort of those seated in the rear. From the outset, the ambition was clear: to feature the longest wheelbase and provide the best legroom in its segment, setting a new standard for compact SUVs.

A notable feature of the Baojun 560 is its versatile second-row seating, which can be divided and folded in a 60/40 ratio to lie flush with the trunk's floor, thereby expanding the cargo space from 460 liters to an impressive 1015 liters. This design significantly expands interior space, allowing for an extension of the length from the back of the front seats to the rear door threshold up to 1,790 millimeters, which offers ample room for relaxation during long journeys or for transporting a greater volume of goods[1], making a lasting impression on users.

To collect feedback on the Baojun 560, SGMW orchestrated a test drive event at a 4S dealership in Qingdao, inviting existing consumers to participate. The event elicited overwhelmingly positive responses from more than 20 participants. Buoyed by the success in Qingdao, SGMW promptly initiated a nationwide two-month-long test drive campaign. Sales teams were deployed to various shopping malls and residential areas, specifically targeting potential buyers and prioritizing outreach to previous Wuling consumers. Sales representatives were also directed to approach individuals driving older vehicles, offering them a test drive of the Baojun 560. This innovative promotional approach sparked a surge in consumer interest, turning what appeared to be a straightforward strategy into a remarkably effective method of captivating consumer hearts.

The Baojun 560's spacious design, affordable price of under RMB 100,000, and its inventive grassroots marketing approach swiftly catapulted it into the spotlight of public attention. Upon its entry into the SUV market, the Baojun 560 made a splash, rapidly gaining momentum and experiencing a sharp increase in sales. It emerged as an unexpected contender against established names, with its performance at one point rivaling the monthly sales figures of the perennial market leader, the Great Wall Haval H6.

The year 2016 witnessed a notable upswing in SUV sales within China, with a total of 9.047 million units sold, marking a year-on-year increase of 44.59%, nearly equalling the sales figures for passenger cars. This trend signaled a shifting landscape in favor of SUVs, poised to dominate the market over passenger cars. Amidst this sales boom, the competition intensified; the sales rankings saw significant shifts, with three of the top five models changing from the previous year[2]. The Baojun 560 emerged as a formidable player, securing the third spot and narrowly missing the second, a stark contrast to its absence from the rankings just a year before. That year, SAIC Motor stood out as the most successful entity, with three of its brands claiming positions in the top five SUVs. Notably, the Baojun 560, a creation of SGMW, was hailed as the most significant breakthrough of the year.

Establishing itself as a robust contender, the Baojun 560 distinguished itself in

---

① Wei Dong. SGMW Baojun 560[J]. *Evo China*, 2015.

② "Top Ten Passenger Car Brands by Sales in 2015" and "Top Ten Passenger Car Brands by Sales in 2016", China Association of Automobile Manufacturers.

the highly competitive SUV market, a "red ocean" teeming with rivals. The model's appeal, rooted in its spacious interior and extended wheelbase, resonated with consumers on a psychological level influenced by social factors, positioning SGMW as the tacit "King of Space".

In the landscape of cross passenger cars, SGMW emerged as a dominant force, claiming more than half of the market share. Alongside Chang'an Automobile and Dongfeng Sokon Automobile, which together accounted for an additional quarter[①], these entities collectively commanded a significant majority of the market, even amidst signs of contraction. This market trend mirrored broader economic shifts, as the rural reforms outlined in the 13th Five-Year Plan led to increased rural incomes and agricultural intensification, thereby diminishing the urban-rural market dividend that had previously fueled growth. This tightening grip on the cross passenger car market, a trend emerging around 2010, saw MPVs increasingly encroaching on the segment's territory. It was against this backdrop that SGMW strategically expanded its portfolio with the development of new MPV models, adapting to the evolving market dynamics.

Every action sets the stage for its consequence, yet the bridge between cause and effect often spans a lengthy journey. On this temporal continuum, one end is fraught with anxious speculations and the agony of decision-making. Nevertheless, with precise timing and unwavering resolve, the interlude of anticipation eventually unfolds into a moment of joy, waiting on the other side of time's revolving door.

As sunlight bathes the Liujiang River, a testament to enduring success shines in the 2016 MPV market. SGMW, with its perennial favorites—the Wuling Hongguang and the Baojun 730—claimed more than 40% of the market share. In the realm of SUVs, the remarkable surge of the Baojun 560 catapulted it to third place, placing SGMW at the forefront across three out of the four major passenger vehicle segments, securing two top positions and a commendable third. This remarkable achievement, akin to winning two golds and a bronze in a highly competitive field, naturally elevated SGMW into the elite circle of companies boasting over RMB 100 billion in revenue.

By this time, SGMW had embraced a rhythm of rapid development, introducing a new model each year from 2014 through 2017. This strategic initiative encompassed

---

① China Automotive Technology and Research Center and China Association of Automobile Manufacturers[R]. *China Automotive Industry Yearbook 2017*, 244.

both commercial and passenger vehicles, with the company maintaining a competitive edge in both cost-efficiency and uniqueness. In 2016, the compact hatchback Baojun 310 made its debut, followed by the introduction of the small SUV Baojun 510 in 2017. For a joint venture company committed to independent research and development, the launch of each new model entailed a detailed strategic deliberation with its shareholders.

The Baojun 310's debut as a compact hatchback captured the attention of GM's executives, aligning with their interests and aspirations in this segment. The company was an active participant in the initial stages of the product's development, providing numerous alternative designs and strategies. Ultimately, the decision to take the lead with SGMW in the design and development phases was influenced by the significant cost development advantages and profound understanding of consumer preferences demonstrated by the latter. This cost-leadership approach, perhaps uniquely achievable in the Chinese context, positioned the Baojun 310 as a popular choice among the youth, solidifying its status as the preferred vehicle for a new generation.

With the introduction of the Baojun 310, the Baojun brand strategically shifted its focus toward a younger audience, emphasizing designs, features, pricing, and marketing initiatives that resonate with this demographic's tastes. The launch of the subcompact SUV Baojun 510 in Shenzhen in 2017 was marked by a vibrant event themed "Play to the Fullest". The launch party was a spectacle of vividly painted vehicles, dynamic light shows, and immersive VR driving simulations, meticulously curated to captivate the interests of young consumers. Subsequently, the Baojun 510 went on a nationwide tour, making stops in major cities to directly engage with the youth. This strategic approach reaped significant rewards, propelling the Baojun 510 to the forefront of the SUV market, clinching the second position on the sales chart for the year with an impressive tally of 360,000 units sold. In December alone, sales soared to 54,100 units, narrowly missing the top spot by just 1,000 units and nearly matching the monthly sales figures of the perennial favorite SUV, the Haval H6[1].

The Baojun 510 identified an opportunity as conspicuous and expansive as a truck on a miniature battlefield, marked by numerous little red flags. This was a niche that only those adept at cost-efficient strategies could effectively exploit. If the

---

[1] "Top Ten Passenger Car Brands by Sales in 2017" and "Top Ten Passenger Car Brands by Sales in December 2017", China Association of Automobile Manufacturers.

Baojun 560 had crafted a legacy within the realm of mid-size SUVs, the Baojun 510 was poised to redefine expectations for its smaller counterparts. Venturing into the subcompact SUV market required a precarious balance of pricing and cost management—an arena where raising prices posed a challenge without corresponding decreases in costs, a veritable tightrope walk of financial strategy. Japanese manufacturers and India's Tata Motors had adeptly navigated this balance, paving the way for Chinese firms to make their mark.

Few manufacturers were eager to venture into this segment, primarily due to the daunting challenge of maintaining a manufacturing system capable of supporting such aggressive pricing strategies. The subcompact SUV market was a battleground where only those equipped with superior cost-control measures could not only survive but also thrive. Armed with a proficiency in low-cost production, SGMW was ready to leverage this strength. In a deliberate departure from the conventional rugged aesthetics associated with SUVs in terms of design and marketing strategy, the company molded the Baojun 510 into a distinct contender in the market.

Initially facing internal rejection among six alternative designs for a subcompact SUV, none of which met Yao Zuoping's expectations due to a perceived lack of essence, the model that eventually became the Baojun 510 was on the brink of being overlooked. Driven by necessity, Yao Zuoping requested a review of previously discarded designs, recognizing that aesthetic appreciation can sometimes be both instantaneous and challenging to articulate. To the surprise of the technical center staff, management instantly favored one of these discarded designs after further debate, allowing intuition to guide their decision. This pivotal choice resurrected the Baojun 510 from the rejected proposals, which later, unexpectedly, earned the moniker "Aesthetics Beast", swiftly becoming the annual game-changer in the SUV market.

7.8 Peaks and Valleys: Mastering the Balance

The Baojun 510 and 310 series emerged as notable successes within their respective segments, defying the pronounced decline of the mini-vehicle market. Even facing this downturn, the once-dubbed "King of Mini-cars" adeptly managed its product portfolio, achieving sustained rapid growth. Fueled by the momentum of the

Baojun brand and supported by the enduring popularity of traditional commercial vehicles like the Wuling Sunshine, Rongguang, and Hongguang, SGMW distinguished itself as the first domestic automaker to surpass an annual production and sales volume of 2 million units in 2015, and the entity in the Guangxi Zhuang Autonomous Region to record over RMB 100 billion in sales revenue in the subsequent year.

This success catalyzed the dynamic expansion of Liuzhou's automotive industry chain. As a key supplier to SGMW, Guangxi Automobile Group Co., Ltd., revolving around Liuzhou Wuling Automobile, was inaugurated in 2015 and ascended to the RMB 20 billion output league by the next year. By this time, Liuzhou had become home to five major vehicle enterprises: SGMW, Guangxi Automobile Group, Dongfeng Liuzhou Automobile, FAW Jiefang Liuzhou Special Automobile, and Sinotruk Liuzhou Yunli Special Purpose Vehicle Co., Ltd., fostering a robust automotive industry ecosystem. Inspired by SGMW, numerous local manufacturers in Liuzhou seamlessly transitioned into and integrated within the global supply chain, embodying the strategic vision articulated 14 years earlier by the government of the Guangxi Zhuang Autonomous Region. This vision, encapsulated by the principle of "Less the possession, more the value of the company in the society", resonates anew, akin to the main theme in a symphony.

The year 2017 stood as a zenith for SGMW, boasting an impressive annual sales volume of 2.15 million units that cast a luminous spotlight on the company within China's automotive sales rankings. The Baojun brand, in particular, celebrated a significant milestone, surpassing 1 million units in annual sales. This accomplishment traced a trajectory of success, beginning with the Baojun 630 sedan, progressing through the triumph of the compact MPV Baojun 730, and witnessing the growing popularity of the mid-size SUV Baojun 560 and the subcompact SUV Baojun 510, reflecting seven years of diligent effort reaping abundant rewards. The introduction of the Baojun E100, SGMW's first electric vehicle, heralded the company's burgeoning presence in the new energy vehicle sector. This era was marked by exultation and magnificence, with the perseverance of previous years crystallizing into tears of joy.

In the same year, China's automobile sales escalated to 28.879 million units, achieving a 3% growth over the previous year and establishing a new historical high. This sustained China's status as the world's largest automobile market for the ninth consecutive year[①]. Notably, SUV sales reached unprecedented levels, surpassing 10 million units and dwarfing global car sales figures. SUVs, with their spacious interiors, elevated chassis, and dynamic appeal, adeptly catered to the preferences of both urban and rural consumers. Once again, this era subtly exerted its influence, reflecting shifts in demography and economic frameworks in the evolution of automotive offerings.

As 2017 drew to a close, the automotive industry witnessed the expansive potential of the Chinese market, where car ownership soared to 217 million units, signaling a new phase of stock replacement. With an assumed vehicle lifespan of 10 years, maintaining an annual sales figure of 30 million units became imperative[②]. The push toward automotive innovation was unmistakable, as trends in smart connectivity, new energy vehicles, and shared mobility drew a fresh wave of entrants to the sector.

The automotive landscape transformed into a proving ground for internet companies, with autonomous driving emerging as a standout innovation. The synergy of "Internet + Automobile", a collaboration between automakers and IT firms, captured the public's imagination. Particularly compelling were the ambitious efforts of new car brands like NIO, XPeng, and Li Auto, transitioning from conceptual pitches on presentation stages to the reality of production lines, and moving from the dream of PowerPoint-based car design to the tangible challenge of mass production, earning them acclaim as the "New Forces of Car Making". Despite the turbulence caused by the downfall of LeEco's automotive project, which had entered the industry with much fanfare only for its founders to hastily exit, the emergence of these new players seemed to dispel any lingering doubts, lighting up the industry with vibrant energy. This scene mirrored the historical influx into the mini-vehicle market, now replayed with notable success among these emerging brands. The atmosphere was buoyant among these new automakers, their discourse filled with determination, poised as if awaiting the imminent eclipse of traditional vehicles.

As the calendar turned, the Chinese automotive market faced an unprecedented downturn, recording its first sales decline in 28 years. The preceding period of rapid growth had been tumultuous, with warning indicators manifesting in various guises, but the signs foretelling impending trouble were largely disregarded amid the

---

① Ministry of Commerce. Regular Press Conference of the Ministry of Commerce, January 18, 2018.

② China Automotive Technology and Research Center and China Association of Automobile Manufacturers[R]. *China Automotive Industry Yearbook 2017*, 14.

pervasive wave of overwhelming optimism.

In 2018, the vitality of the Chinese automotive market waned, enduring its first contraction in nearly three decades. The chill was palpable, much like cold winds stripping trees bare and frost seizing the orchids in the courtyard. Passenger vehicles bore the brunt of the downturn, with all categories, especially crossover utility vehicles catering to both commercial and personal use, experiencing significant sales reductions[1]. This contrasted sharply with previous years, a period when the market blossomed like spring. Chang'an Automobile, a domestic powerhouse, had surpassed the 2 million sales threshold in 2013, reaching a zenith of 3.06 million units in 2016[2]. SGMW celebrated a historic high with 2.15 million units sold in 2017. Yet, as the echoes of celebration lingered, a succession of setbacks began to emerge, with the initial signs of a cooling market evident as early as the spring of 2018.

Within this broad downturn, automakers witnessed varying rates of sales erosion. The launches of the Baojun brand in spring 2018, including the compact SUV Baojun 530 and the six-seater MPV Baojun 360, failed to replicate the explosive success of their forerunners.

In a stark departure from the prevailing downward trajectory of 2018, the automotive industry saw Tesla buck the trend of previous years, which had been characterized by high interest but modest sales, to enter a phase of rapid global market growth, with sales hitting 245,000 units in 2018. This marked a dramatic increase in electric vehicle sales, matching the total number delivered since its inception in 2003. While this upsurge in electric vehicle development, spearheaded by Tesla, significantly influenced consumer sentiment toward electric vehicles, it stopped short of triggering a buying frenzy.

The perennial challenge of identifying the direction for future product enhancements and iterations persists for every car manufacturer, as they annually seek the next "fertile ground" for innovation.

Despite the Baojun brand achieving the landmark sales figure of over 1 million units and Wuling's commercial vehicles demonstrating robust potential, the distinction between the Wuling and Baojun appears to still require further definition.

---

① *China's Auto Market Review in 2018 and Outlook for 2019*. China Association of Automobile Manufacturers, February 22, 2019.

② *Three Million Milestones: The Journey to New Horizons—New Year Message 2017*. Chang'an Automobile, December 30, 2016.

Moreover, the powertrain remains a consistent hurdle, with shareholders finding the available choices less than ideal. These challenges intensify in the face of unfavorable market trends. Shen Yang has consistently adopted a proactive stance in identifying potential risks, even during prosperous times. Reflecting on this, his New Year's message to employees a few years back underscored the necessity of fostering a culture of crisis awareness and vigilance.

7.9 Navigating the Smart Innovation Maze

By this juncture, SGMW had successfully realized its three foundational strategies: establishing dominance in the mini-vehicle arena, emerging as a formidable presence in the passenger vehicle market, and solidifying its position on the global stage. The pressing question then arose: what comes next? Smart connectivity swiftly took center stage as a key focus. Following comprehensive discussions, it seamlessly integrated into SGMW's refreshed tri-fold strategy, emphasizing "PV-oriented development, internationalization, and the new four features (electrification, connectivity, shared mobility, and intelligence)". This marked a strategic pivot toward a new dimension of vehicle development. Concurrently, the Baojun brand underwent a transformative rebranding, now known as New Baojun, embodying a youthful, technological, intelligent, and connected brand DNA, championing a novel lifestyle of mobility. Geared toward becoming the preferred choice for young consumers, especially those born in the 1990s with disposable income, it sought to resonate with a vibrant demographic.

The evolution of the brand's identity also featured a significant logo change. Acknowledging that the original horse head emblem lacked distinction for some, New Baojun introduced a diamond-shaped logo, celebrating the allure of geometric design. This dual shift, both in the brand name and logo, represented a bold departure. While automotive brand logos often undergo evolution, as demonstrated by industry giants like Volkswagen, Mercedes-Benz, and BMW, their names typically remain constant.

The marketing framework for the New Baojun underwent a comprehensive overhaul. Out of a network of over 2,000 dealerships, SGMW handpicked 100 to pilot the New Baojun concept. This initiative radically transformed the dealership experience across the board, from staff training and operational processes to the interior ambiance and sales techniques, all reengineered to offer a dynamic and engaging car-buying journey tailored to the preferences of young consumers in both small towns and metropolitan areas.

In 2019, the inaugural appearance of the New Baojun brand took center stage with the launch of the intelligent SUV, the New Baojun RS-5. This model, building upon the Baojun 530, introduced a comprehensive suite of smart driving capabilities. Meanwhile, the Baojun 530 itself saw continuous enhancements, including a chassis redesign and ongoing improvements to its exterior design and interior seating configuration. Hot on its heels, the New Baojun lineup expanded swiftly with the introduction of the RM-5, RC-6, and RS-3 models, launched in quick succession much like dumplings being briskly prepared, showcasing the brand's aggressive strategy of refreshing and diversifying its product offerings.

Each newly introduced model under the New Baojun banner was equipped with advanced smart connectivity technology, incorporating a wealth of innovative features. Despite this, the vehicles came with a significant price increase, surpassing even the price points of leading SUVs in the market. Nevertheless, SGMW remained optimistic, banking on the vehicles' appealing design and diverse configurations to attract buyers.

However, the market response fell short of expectations. Despite extensive training for the selected 4S dealerships, the sales approach retained a conventional outlook and did not swiftly adapt to the revamped store experience. The distinctive selling proposition of New Baojun's smart features encountered challenges in gaining quick traction among consumers. In some cases, dealers were so entrenched in the traditional Wuling sales system that changing perceptions proved difficult. A striking example occurred in SGMW's Northeast region, where a myna bird, trained to say phrases like "Not cheap" and "Next one", humorously highlighted the entrenched market challenges faced by the newer, pricier models.

Initially, the Baojun and Wuling brands were marketed together, maintaining a clear distinction between sedans and commercial vehicles. However, the delineation between brands began to blur as vehicles from Baojun, New Baojun, and Wuling were all retailed under the same roof, leading to a confusing amalgamation of offerings.

Recognizing the importance of distinct brand identities, as each brand caters to unique market segments and consumer preferences, becomes apparent. For instance, when Toyota was gearing up to introduce its luxury brand Lexus, it opted for a dedicated sales network. Toyota 4S dealerships interested in selling Lexus models were required to undergo extensive retraining, relearning, and assessments, covering various operational aspects.

The issue of brand amalgamation prompts a deeper inquiry into the root cause of New Baojun's disappointing sales figures. Seeking insights, SGMW's management discreetly conducted visits to its 4S dealership network, and observations revealed that the sales staff rarely highlighted the vehicles' smart features. Despite positioning New Baojun models at price points RMB 2,000 to 3,000 above their Baojun counterparts, sales discussions predominantly focused on aesthetics and build quality, neglecting the advanced intelligence aspect. Only in response to a barrage of direct inquiries did sales personnel briefly mention, "This car offers connectivity; it can connect to a smartphone". Furthermore, potential buyers expressing interest in experiencing the touted smart connectivity features encountered a hurdle: ordinary smartphones were incompatible, necessitating the use of a specific phone provided by the 4S dealership for demonstrations, which further complicated the consumer experience.

After a period of sales, dealers found themselves grappling with emerging challenges as consumers encountered new issues. Traditionally centered around mechanical repairs, the landscape had shifted to addressing electronic components and troubleshooting software glitches. Some technicians, uncertain about resolving these new problems, inadvertently recommended part replacements, inflating costs and inciting additional complaints. The sales staff's hesitance to promote New Baojun stemmed from the complexity of articulating its features, compounded by a myriad of operational problems post-sale, which led to accountability dilemmas and subsequent resignations within the sales force.

The nature of smart connected vehicles stands in stark contrast to that of traditional automobiles, posing a unique challenge that all automotive manufacturers are acutely aware of and actively endeavoring to overcome: the substantial need for technical knowledge. The formidable barrier of educating consumers on the adept utilization of these advanced features has come to the forefront. William Edwards Deming, an American quality control pioneer, once introduced "the three corners of quality"[1], asserting that a product's quality is a composite of the product itself, the

---

① William Edwards Deming. *Out of the Crisis*, trans. Zhong Hanqing[M]. China Machine Press, 2017, 145.

provision of training to customers (such as user manuals), and the manner in which customers use the product. This framework underscores the impact of customer training on the perceived quality of new products, emphasizing the importance of setting realistic customer expectations. It is crucial to recognize that frustration during usage can lead users to abandon a product, underscoring that quality transcends the product in isolation. Applying William Edwards Deming's theory to the realm of intelligent car sales underlines the critical role of in-store sales in conveying the value of smart features. If sales personnel lack the expertise to effectively communicate the advantages of smart vehicles, the quality triangle collapses, dissuading potential purchases. This precipitated an introspective initiative at SGMW to enhance the quality of the customer experience in response to the premature push into smart connected vehicles.

SGMW's leap into integrating intelligent features into the New Baojun lineup might have been slightly ahead of its time, especially considering that a portion of their consumer base still used feature phones. Despite the New Baojun vehicles boasting advanced connectivity options and driver assistance systems, including automatic following and steering, backend data revealed a notable underutilization of these features by consumers.

The gap between user expectations and automakers' projections proved to be significant. It became evident that there was a noticeable "inertia" among users toward embracing smart connectivity for several reasons. Firstly, due to unfamiliarity, about 30% of users were at a loss on how to utilize these smart features; secondly, the cumbersome registration process and frequent disconnections discouraged nearly a third of the users from engaging with these functionalities. More importantly, there was a discernible lack of interest among users in using these features, as the perceived value addition of smart connectivity failed to strongly resonate with them.

Racing ahead in the realm of innovation can sometimes bring unforeseen challenges. The inclusion of cutting-edge smart technologies into vehicles necessitates the simultaneous evolution of both sales and service frameworks to support these advancements. It is apparent that the transition from traditional to smart connected vehicles involves a more significant shift than initially presumed. Convincing consumers of the benefits of these technological innovations may necessitate an extended period of education and adaptation. In the domain of intelligent vehicles, SGMW found itself at the forefront early on but faced the challenge of market readiness.

The year 2019 was marked by pervasive challenges within the automotive industry, transcending the confines of any singular company. The sector was beleaguered by a confluence of adverse factors, including a deteriorating macroeconomic environment, escalating trade tensions between China and the United States, waning consumer confidence, the premature enforcement of National Phase VI Motor Vehicle Pollutant Emission Standards, and substantial reductions in subsidies for new energy vehicles, which collectively precipitated a lackluster demand within the Chinese automotive market. Consequently, China's production and sales figures for passenger cars experienced a year-over-year decrease of 9.2% and 9.6%, standing at 21.36 million and 21.444 million units, respectively.

Chang'an Automobile's sales trajectory epitomized the broader industry downturn, with sales declining for three consecutive years from a zenith of 3.06 million units. By 2019, Chang'an reported sales of a mere 1.76 million units, marking a 15% decline from the previous year, which itself followed a 25% decrease from 2018[①]. This scenario was representative of a widespread downturn across the sector. In such challenging times, it becomes imperative for every automaker to introspect on the resilience of its brand and the diversity of its product portfolio.

The assortment of products under an automotive brand acts as distinct units within a battalion, providing mutual support in addressing various consumer segments and collectively fortifying brand presence, akin to a human pyramid, where each layer supports the next. For instance, launching a product priced above RMB 100,000 necessitates the presence of another in the RMB 80,000 to 100,000 bracket to ensure robust sales backing. Stability is the bedrock of every offering. While products that initially capture the market as standalone successes often enjoy a fleeting period of exclusivity, a singular focus on individual models or blockbuster hits proves unsustainable for long-term growth and stability.

GAC Group's proprietary brand, Trumpchi SUV, once celebrated a significant sales achievement. The Trumpchi GS4, its flagship model, achieved a cumulative sales volume of 1 million units within just 41 months from its launch until September 2018, setting a record as the fastest Chinese brand SUV to hit this milestone. However, 2019 marked a stark reversal of fortune, with sales experiencing a sharp decline. Unlike the gradual and controlled maturation process of joint venture brands,

---

① "Chongqing Chang'an Automobile Company Limited 2019 Annual Report" and "Chongqing Chang'an Automobile Company Limited 2018 Annual Report", 15.

managing an independent brand often resembles tightrope walking, where each new model launch is fraught with risk.

In the highly competitive automotive landscape, it is imperative for brands to confront challenges head-on, ensuring that their product offerings have no inherent weaknesses. Continuous innovation and updates are crucial to retain a loyal customer base and safeguard new products as they venture into uncharted markets. Given the perpetual flux of the market, a product in development today may encounter a vastly different landscape by the time it reaches production in the following year. Typically, automotive products undergo a two-year development cycle before reaching market readiness. Establishing a robust base model provides a safety net for newly launched models, helping to avert irreversible errors. In the case of New Baojun, which launched amid the onset of a downturn in the Chinese automotive market, plunging the brand into a particularly challenging period marked by declining sales.

Wuling's commercial vehicles, including the Wuling Sunshine, Rongguang, and Hongguang, have demonstrated the ability to sustain a longer life cycle, marked by their distinct appeal. The sales zenith of these models typically unfolds over three to five years, encompassing several product iterations. In contrast, SGMW's passenger vehicles experience a surge in sales within a relatively brief span of one to three years. This discrepancy prompts an inquiry into the root causes of this phenomenon.

Societal trends often exhibit a rhythmic oscillation, creating an emotional vacuum that continually seeks new sources of excitement. Wuling's commercial vehicles have thrived by adeptly tapping into this vacuum, showcasing an ability to preemptively identify and capitalize on shifting societal dynamics—a testament to their strategic foresight. However, the transition into the passenger vehicle segment reveals a trend toward abbreviated product lifecycles, attributable in part to the rapid pace of societal evolution and changing consumer preferences. Yet, it also underscores the necessity for Wuling's passenger cars to establish a distinct identity or "temperament". Achieving success in this domain demands a meticulous effort to grasp consumer desires and to sculpt a unique brand persona that transcends the mere aggregation of market demands. It is through such dedicated endeavors that avenues for growth and development emerge, enabling brands to resonate deeply with their audience.

In the mature landscape of China's automotive market, where local brands have thrived, relying solely on features without a clear intrinsic rationale for a car inevitably leads to failure. The evolution of China's independent automotive brands has been significantly influenced by early policy planning. Prior to its accession to the WTO, state support for the "Big Three and Small Three" auto joint ventures effectively granted foreign cars a robust foundation of brand recognition among Chinese consumers.

Cultivating independent automobile brands in China is fraught with challenges. Even the most successful or "miraculous" cars can quickly become obsolete in the face of the market's relentless evolution. For example, Brilliance Auto Group's once-celebrated Jinbei and Zhonghua models, as well as JAC Group, which opted to avoid joint ventures, have all navigated through turbulent times.

This raises the question: Can the automotive industry experience a paradigm shift akin to the transformative developments witnessed in the smartphone sector, where flagship products drive brand growth? Huawei, for instance, achieved a noteworthy breakthrough by enhancing its photography capabilities through a strategic partnership with Leica, transitioning from the mid-tier market to challenging the high-end dominance of Apple and Samsung. While Apple championed authenticity, Huawei focused on beautification, an innovative approach that has left a significant mark. Given that smartphones are considered fast-moving consumer goods, with consumers regularly upgrading to the latest models, the market dynamics provide opportunities for new entrants. This fluidity, allowing for strategic insertion into market gaps, has facilitated the rapid ascent of domestic smartphone brands.

Automobiles, being durable goods, have significantly longer usage cycles in comparison to other products, fostering a more cautious approach among consumers toward changing vehicles. This inherent characteristic of the automotive sector means that car users are not able to frequently update their vehicles to benefit from the latest brand innovations, which poses a challenge to the growth prospects of emerging automobile brands, as the brand effect within the automotive industry tends to be more enduring and deeply ingrained than in other sectors.

The team at SGMW, alongside the broader automotive industry, finds itself in dire need for rejuvenation. The automotive landscape in China, and, in fact, globally, has been facing a period of desolation, calling for a concerted effort to reinvigorate the sector. Carl Philipp Gottfried von Clausewitz, in *On War*, underscored the importance of leadership during times of confusion, suggesting that the role of the general is to act as a guiding light in darkness, inspiring his troops to advance. This analogy resonates with the current state of the automotive industry, where conviction and direction are crucial. As 2019 drew to a close, many within the industry likely reflected on what felt like an interminably long year, welcoming its end with a sigh of relief. In the lead-up to the Spring Festival of 2020, Shen Yang, like many others, reflected on the accomplishments and setbacks of the past year, and prepared for the opportunities and challenges ahead.

However, on the brink of a new dawn, an unforeseen tempest loomed, poised to reshape the very fabric of the industry's future.

Chapter 8 Minimalism Redefined 2020

8.1 The "950" Initiative: Saving Wuling!

On January 25, 2020, the first day of the Chinese New Year, traditionally a time of widespread celebrations during the Spring Festival, Shen Yang and Yao Zuoping exchanged New Year greetings over the phone, their voices laden with concern amidst the festive ambiance. Despite SGMW's proactive establishment of a specialized task force aimed at controlling and preventing the spread of COVID-19, the origins of the pandemic, the extent of its threat, and the precise actions required remained shrouded in uncertainty.

Amid the prevailing sense of unease, the imperative for life and industry to press forward persisted. With the factory's operations hanging in the balance, Yao Zuoping, driven by a sense of duty, left his family home on the third day of the Chinese New Year to make his way back to the production site. The State Council had by then issued a directive to extend the Spring Festival holiday, indicating the unlikelihood of resuming standard factory operations and underscoring the necessity for heightened emergency preparedness. The factory was slated to resume production on January 31, 2020 (the seventh day of the Chinese New Year), necessitating prior arrangements for essential pandemic prevention supplies. However, in the throes of preparation, the task force confronted a daunting revelation: masks, crucial for effective pandemic prevention, were acutely scarce and beyond reach.

The necessity to produce masks became a critical factor in facilitating an expedited resumption of work at SGMW.

Initially considered mere peripherals, masks sparked innovation within the core technical team at SGMW's factories, who were already strategizing in their offices in response to the urgent call to action. Engineers, who had never before needed to delve into the intricacies of mask manufacturing, began an intensive online search to understand the composition and production processes involved. Their research revealed that a mask's fundamental structure comprises two layers of non-woven fabric with a layer of melt-blown fabric in between, all crafted from polypropylene. To their astonishment, the process of making masks closely resembled an assembly line operation with which they were already familiar: layering the three fabric pieces, precision-cutting and pressing them into shape inside a mold, and then sealing them together with heat.

This revelation was a turning point. The engineers realized that the soundproofing cotton used in car interiors, made from materials similar to those in melt-blown and non-woven fabrics, could serve as a viable substitute. Moreover, the assembly process aligned with their existing proficiency, positioning them uniquely to meet the urgent demand for masks.

After thoroughly confirming the viability of procuring the necessary raw materials and quickly assessing their production capabilities, SGMW officially declared on February 6 its intent to collaborate with suppliers of automotive soundproofing cotton for mask production. Immediately following this announcement, on February 7, a collaborative effort was initiated, with a joint team from SGMW stepping in to support the supplier's factory in scaling up mask production, focusing on enhancing both output volume and product quality. The designated machinery for this urgent task sprang to life, operating at full throttle. Initially, the production process yielded "bare masks", formed through direct stamping using hard molds, with the manual attachment of the two ear straps left to end-users.

However, complications surfaced on the very day slated for kickstarting production, as a new order mandated that 70% of the mask output be appropriated by the People's Government of Guangxi Zhuang Autonomous Region. In the face of a global pandemic, masks had been deemed critical resources, warranting centralized distribution by governmental authorities, which suggested that SGMW might confront a renewed scarcity of masks for its operational needs.

As the ticking clock heightened anxiety, emphasizing the need for decisive action to alleviate fear and counteract inactivity, SGMW took a pivotal step on February 8 to confront the crisis head-on, convening a meeting to strategize work resumption, culminating in the decision to initiate in-house mask production. Promptly, a command center was established on February 9, marking the official initiation of the project, aptly named "950"—a clever play on words in Chinese, phonetically echoing "救五菱" (Save Wuling). This nomenclature symbolically embodied the mission to safeguard the company. The chosen slogan, with its grassroots appeal, encapsulated the distinctive and spirited culture of SGMW, serving as a clarion call to action and aligning the workforce toward a common objective. The urgency of the situation mobilized all procurement staff to leverage every available resource to address two critical needs: securing polypropylene for the masks and acquiring the necessary manufacturing equipment.

The transformation was swift at SGMW's Liudong base workshop. Employing homemade molds, the factory's steel plate stamping machinery was repurposed to cut and shape mask fabric. Despite the equipment's adaptability and fine-tuning, the transition from cutting steel to the more yielding fabric proved less than seamless; the masks' edges were haphazardly incised, necessitating considerable manual refinement. Adding to the complexity, the manual welding of the ear straps presented another challenge, requiring delicate handling and precision—qualities in which the company's female workforce demonstrated exceptional proficiency. A formidable "women's commando" swiftly coalesced, featuring volunteers from various departments within the company. Ranging from workshop operators to personnel in logistics and the technical center, anyone in Liuzhou was eager to contribute. The factory hummed with relentless activity, operating around the clock in three shifts to produce simple, flat masks—a tangible testament to the company's resolve and solidarity.

Amid the continuous barrage of daily news updates, decisions within SGMW had to be made swiftly, often relying on split-second intuition rather than protracted deliberation. Decision-makers found themselves in a constant race against time, contending with unseen challenges at every turn. A notable milestone was reached on February 10 with the completion of the Class 100,000 cleanroom renovation. The following day saw the arrival of mask-making machines from Wuxi, Jiangsu Province, heralding the introduction of a modern production line to the factory. However, the initial fanfare was dampened when these machines were discovered to be in a deplorable state of neglect, rusted from years of disuse, missing critical parts, and appearing nearly beyond salvage.

Confronted by this formidable situation, the engineering team ingeniously decided to amalgamate the two ailing machines into a singular, functional unit, allowing production to commence on one while the team meticulously refurbished the parts necessary for the second. They sprang into action, leveraging their collective knowledge and resources at their disposal. Despite their relative unfamiliarity with mask production machinery, they embarked on a rapid online research expedition to understand the intricacies of a mask production line, and, identifying each necessary component from online images, sourced the required parts overnight. Miraculously, the first "antique" mask machine was resurrected and operational as daylight broke, a mere eight hours after its arrival in a dire condition. The factory buzzed with revitalized energy as the machine sprang back to life, ready to contribute to the urgent mask production efforts.

While one contingent of engineers diligently worked on restoring the initial batch of mask-making machines to operational status, another group embarked on an ambitious project with a different set of equipment. Within a span of less than two days, leveraging the existing machinery as a template, these on-site engineers ingeniously reverse-engineered and crafted a duplicate mask machine. These two machines, working in tandem like siblings, significantly accelerated mask production. Methodically, they churned out masks that not only fulfilled a practical need but also served as a symbol of hope for many during those uncertain times. Despite their efficiency, these machines were semi-automated, heavily reliant on manual intervention for tasks such as threading the ear straps, highlighting the pressing necessity for a fully automated solution to enhance production capabilities and address the escalating demand for masks.

Confronted with this challenge, the team reverted to the conceptual phase, tasked with deconstructing and comprehending the intricate manufacturing processes underpinning mask machinery. Astonishingly, a comprehensive mask machine design involved over 170 schematics, encompassing 43 distinct types of electrical, pneumatic, and mechanical systems, and necessitating the selection of more than 800 components. Yet, the determination to forge ahead remained unwavering. On February 11, 2020, SGMW resolved to develop its proprietary mask machine, promptly establishing a dedicated task force under Yao Zuoping's direct leadership. Faced with the daunting task of determining the machine's model and production capacity, the leadership team did not hesitate to set an ambitious target: a daily output of two million masks.

"Two million masks?"

At that juncture, a single machine's daily output was capped at merely 20,000 masks. Nevertheless, the ambitious target set by the leadership did not elicit skepticism; instead, it quickly crystallized into a resolute collective commitment. The directive to scale up production to two million masks daily cascaded down the ranks with a sense of urgency, and task forces were promptly assembled, each assigned a specific role. The preparation team spearheaded the design efforts and scrambled to procure necessary materials, while the debugging and delivery teams pooled technical expertise to expedite the machine tuning process, ensuring their timely deployment to the production lines.

This endeavor was more than a race against time; it was a battle for life itself. The design department embarked on an unrelenting 24-hour operation to finalize blueprints and configurations. In an extraordinary display of dedication, many team members pushed themselves beyond human limits, working for 28 to over 36 hours straight without breaks for food, water, or rest. Simultaneously, procurement efforts intensified, with staff members tirelessly contacting suppliers to secure the essential machinery and components needed for mask production. Among these, the ultrasonic welding machine emerged as a pivotal bottleneck. With escalating demand, the cost of these machines ballooned unexpectedly, leaping from an initial rate of around RMB 2,000 each to a staggering online quote of RMB 18,000 by the time SGMW entered the market. And when a viable supplier was eventually identified, the price had further escalated to RMB 25,000 per unit.

"Alright, deal!"

The decisive clinching of the deal unfolded in one swift motion. In such critical moments, decisions needed to be made instantaneously, without a second's delay, as hesitation could potentially mean losing ground to competitors in a fiercely competitive procurement race. This heightened atmosphere was charged with the immediacy of securing essential equipment, knowing that prices could skyrocket to RMB 100,000 per unit within a week due to such demand pressures.

In a further development, an additional request was made: to emboss the Wuling logo on the masks. Acknowledging the significance of expressing solidarity during these trying times, the responsibility for conceptualizing a marking machine was delegated. Rising to the challenge, the interior trim tooling team swiftly finalized the structural design of the plan within a two-hour timeframe. Subsequently, utilizing lathes, grinders, and drills, and employing meticulous precision in machining, assembly, wiring, and debugging, the team successfully crafted the inaugural handmade prototype in an impressive six-hour span. Working cohesively like cogs in a well-oiled machine, each team member contributed seamlessly, united by a collective determination to beat the clock.

In parallel, SGMW mobilized its extensive dealership network to source vital components, focusing primarily on Guangzhou—the central hub for pneumatic actuators and essential parts for mask machines. Empowering its dealers to procure these components at any cost, Wuling found its trust well-placed. Wuling's dealers proved their dedication by stationing themselves at warehouse entrances overnight, ensuring they were the first to secure and dispatch the crucial parts as soon as the warehouses opened the following day.

In the high-stakes landscape of this operation, the paramount importance of trust and responsibility shared between partners became unmistakably apparent, uniting them in a collective mission.

Following an unyielding 76-hour stretch, the engineering team, visibly fatigued with red eyes bearing witness to their tireless efforts, witnessed a continuous influx of external components into the Liuzhou factory. The atmosphere within the workshops and offices resonated with the vibrancy of engineers engrossed in debugging and assembling tasks. Machines, once semi-automated, hummed incessantly, maintaining uninterrupted operation even as their human counterparts took breaks. This relentless drive transformed the entire factory into a beacon of ceaseless productivity, pulsating with activity through day and night.

On February 16, Guangxi witnessed the launch of its first fully automated mask machine bearing the Wuling brand, signaling the commencement of large-scale automated mask production. Boxes featuring the distinctive Wuling logo started their continuous journey from the workshop, symbolizing a monumental shift. Transitioning from its initial status as a newcomer in the industry, SGMW rapidly ascended to become a pivotal player in mask production. The journey was marked by an initial phase of panic, superseded by a series of triumphs amid chaos, characterized by prompt decision-making and the preemptive procurement of raw materials, equipment, and essential components—even from locations far removed from Liuzhou. Rapid assessments compensated for geographical challenges, ushering in an era of speed and efficiency that pushed the limits of the lean production system. This phase was defined by the incorporation of standardized production operations, material management, and mask distribution protocols into an overarching strategy aimed at boosting production capacity. By the close of February, SGMW had successfully manufactured 16 mask slicing machines and 35 ear band machines for the fully automated mask production line. On March 1, the factory achieved an output of one million masks per day, and by March 17, daily production triumphantly surpassed the two million mark.

As masks evolved into an indispensable commodity, SGMW leveraged its adeptness in adapting to production changes, initiating substantial donations of masks. This philanthropic gesture did not go unnoticed, as people across the country, confined to their homes, began to recognize the emergence of this unforeseen yet formidable player in the mask manufacturing arena.

The surge of attention acted as a catalyst for decisive action. Capitalizing on this momentum, SGMW introduced the impactful slogan, "Wuling builds what people need". This resonant message struck a chord, profoundly inspiring all individuals associated with the brand.

Far more than a mere rallying cry, this slogan served as a guiding light that reinvigorated the company's production ethos and kindled a profound zeal within the hearts of the Wuling community. The pervasive shadows of pessimism that had loomed over the automotive market for the past two years were suddenly dispelled, infusing the Wuling workforce with a renewed sense of purpose and determination.

The outbreak, officially designated as COVID-19 by the World Health Organization on February 11, 2020, was initially underestimated globally in terms of its eventual ramifications. However, as the spring of 2020 unfolded, it became increasingly evident that this crisis was set to become a global calamity of unprecedented scale, destined to fundamentally reshape societal norms, manufacturing paradigms, and the intricate web of global supply chains.

As the world retreated indoors to curb the virus's spread, the public's focus increasingly gravitated toward short-form video content, signifying a transformative shift in the attention economy and cementing short videos as a dominant force in capturing viewership. Amidst this digital pivot, SGMW's foray into the mask market captured the public's attention. Similarly, when luosifen, a Chinese noodle soup specialty from Liuzhou, emerged as a culinary phenomenon, quickly selling out due to high demand, SGMW capitalized on this trend and introduced its own branded version of the delicacy. The Wuling-branded masks and luosifen became significant traffic magnets, channeling a considerable influx of viewers to SGMW's digital platforms, including Douyin, Bilibili, Xiaohongshu, Kuaishou, Weibo, and Weixin official accounts. The team responsible for managing these platforms was astounded as their follower count experienced a dramatic surge virtually overnight, which positioned SGMW at the center of public attention, establishing the company as a central figure in the digital landscape.

Concurrently, SGMW was in the advanced stages of pre-launch testing for its second-generation electric vehicle. This development process unfolded as two distinct narratives—the company's viral success in the consumer goods market and its pioneering strides in electric vehicle technology—unexpectedly converged.

8.2 Pursuing Success without Subsidies

SGMW's journey into the realm of electric vehicles traces back to the inspiration drawn during the 2008 Beijing Olympics. The subsequent launch of the "Ten Cities, Thousand Vehicles" electric vehicle demonstration project by the country marked a cautious yet forward-looking step toward electrification. By 2009, the Ministry of Science and Technology had delineated development objectives for China's burgeoning electric vehicle industry, charting a course through the prevailing skepticism at the time.

Amid the dominion of gasoline-powered vehicles, a fresh wave of innovation began to stir, symbolized by a gentle breeze heralding transformation. Despite the prevalence of skepticism, a contingent of visionaries and entrepreneurs maintained faith in the transformative potential of electric mobility. Among them, Shen Yang envisioned a specialized unit dedicated to spearheading SGMW's venture into the electric vehicle market. This incipient team, ignited by the passion and ambition of its members, was modest in size but abundant in determination, led by a newly minted doctoral graduate co-educated by SGMW and Hunan University.

Embarking on a new chapter of innovation, SGMW's electric vehicle team advanced through exploration, crafting a distinctive narrative of entrepreneurial endeavor.

In 2012, the State Council unveiled *Development Plan for Energy Efficient and New Energy Automobile Industry (2012–2020)*, laying out a comprehensive policy framework. At this juncture, China's new energy vehicle fleet barely exceeded 4,000, indicating the sector's nascent stage. The plan's ambitious goal of achieving a cumulative production and sales figure of 500,000 pure electric and plug-in hybrid vehicles by 2015 seemed almost fantastical.

During this period, SGMW, from its Chongqing base, was scaling up its manufacturing capabilities. The electric vehicle pioneer team there initiated the design of an electric vehicle model based on the Wuling Sunshine. While this specific model never reached mass production, it sparked a broader interest in electric vehicles within Wuling.

The concept of what the car should embody proved somewhat elusive. The industry predominantly believed that pure electric vehicles would instigate a competition between large and small car segments. Supported by national subsidies, new energy vehicles initially found their niche in public transportation and buses, subsequently making their way into urban commuting scenarios, such as A0-class small cars. This progression played a critical role in reshaping consumer perceptions and gradually steering new energy vehicles toward mainstream acceptance.

After profound contemplation, Shen Yang arrived at a critical realization: a market buoyed only by policy subsidies might experience only ephemeral success. He recognized that the true litmus test for the electric vehicle market would emerge once these subsidies receded, revealing genuine consumer interest. The mission became clear—to engineer an electric vehicle that could enchant the market based on its inherent merits, independent of policy incentives.

What, then, would define such a vehicle, independent of subsidy influence? Embarking on the creation of a compact electric vehicle seemed a prudent choice. The vision was established, yet outlining the specifics of this compact electric vehicle called for a thorough investigation. For Shen Yang, who had steered the joint venture through a decade of evolution, a formidable challenge presented itself: engaging with the leadership at GM. From the outset, GM's executives had shown reticence toward SGMW's aspiration to innovate within the compact electric vehicle domain, as GM aimed to lead the development of small, particularly electric, vehicles for the future.

By 2015, the Technical Development Center at SGMW had amassed considerable expertise in the electric vehicle sector, yet their project proposal for electric vehicles faced rejection twice by the board of directors. The recurring argument from GM's top brass was rooted in the belief that SGMW lacked the requisite knowledge of electric vehicles, suggesting instead that GM's own R&D team should lead the endeavor. Given GM's global stature and history of developing iconic vehicles, such skepticism held some merit. However, considering SGMW's keen insight into the Chinese automotive market, understanding of consumer preferences, and its distinctive approach to blending low cost with high value in manufacturing, GM found itself compelled to reevaluate during each round of discussions about new platforms and products. Witnessing Shen Yang's unwavering advocacy for electric vehicle development rights, shareholders were once again reminded of his steadfast resolve.

Mastering the art of negotiation requires finding common ground. By revising the projected sales figures for the future, the board eventually gave its nod to SGMW's proposal for an electric vehicle project. Shen Yang, demonstrating his characteristic all-in commitment, positioned himself and the company at a point of no return.

Amid this uncertainty, discussions proliferated among the Technical Development Center's staff regarding the ideal electric vehicle to conceive. Shen Yang posed a cryptic challenge: "A new breed of urban mobility independent of subsidies," setting the stage for the project's inception and leaving the team to decipher his puzzle.

At that juncture, the supply chain's development was still in its early stages, and the compact yet spirited development team lacked familiarity with conventional gasoline-powered vehicles; even the design team was relatively inexperienced. Nonetheless, these young visionaries undertook the formidable task of orchestrating a solution, navigating through over 500 regulatory mandates and leveraging existing supply chain conditions. By mid-2016, SGMW unveiled its inaugural electric vehicle, the Baojun E100, a model essentially conjured into existence through a collective display of ingenuity and determination.

The Baojun E100's target audience remained an enigma, posing a new challenge for the sales team. Entrusted with the task of promoting this innovative vehicle, they grappled with identifying the ideal consumer and understanding who would truly appreciate its unique value. Initially envisioned as a modern alternative to electric bicycles, catering to short city commutes or school runs, the potential conversion of even a modest fraction of Liuzhou's 700,000 and Nanning's one million electric bike users into E100 drivers was deemed a noteworthy prospect.

However, reality proved more complex than initial projections. Feedback garnered during the test drive phase revealed concerns over the vehicle's limited interior space, deemed inadequate for family use, and its range, considered insufficient for longer journeys to neighboring cities. These critiques reflected conventional expectations regarding the offerings of a vehicle, exposing a mismatch between the original target demographic of electric bike users and the actual prospective users of the Baojun E100.

This discrepancy led to a critical impasse in the market strategy.

8.3 "Three-Good Student" Meets Liuzhou Model

In 2017, SGMW's leadership addresses were marked by the recurring themes of being "catchy, clever, and convenient". These addresses, particularly the annual New Year message delivered by the general manager, have become hallmark events, setting the tone for the company's direction each year. Within the Wuling community, these speeches transcend mere communication; they are imbued with eloquence and persuasive power, adeptly encapsulating the company's annual goals and focal points. SGMW's proficiency in articulating strategic intentions with clarity, method, and warmth has played a pivotal role in galvanizing a collective ambition toward achieving tangible objectives.

The journey to crafting a legendary vehicle is governed by a unique fusion of magic and logic, deeply rooted in the enduring and adaptable spirit of the enterprise. This process is a transformation of minute details into compelling narratives, narratives into legends, and legends into myths that stand as the highest expression of culture, encapsulating the collective aspirations and positive dynamism of a flourishing community, and signifying more than mere accomplishments but rather embodying the very ethos of SGMW.

The Baojun E100, personifying the spirit of innovation, ventured into the electric vehicle market with a clear mission. Its design philosophy was encapsulated in three appealing traits: "Catchy, Clever, Convenient." "Catchy" highlights its unique and eye-catching design, "Clever" celebrates its straightforward and enjoyable handling, and "Convenient" underscores its compact size, easy parking, and the cost-effectiveness of recharging for less than RMB 100 monthly. These qualities collectively distilled the essence of the E100, sparking interest and forging connections without delving into the complexities of space optimization, subsystem integration, or high-voltage safety. Therefore, the Baojun E100 emerged as the quintessence of a "three-good student" car for the modern era.

Addressing the challenge of accurately identifying the target demographic for electric vehicles, SGMW adopted a novel strategy, moving away from speculative market predictions and embracing direct market feedback. In a groundbreaking initiative, the company introduced 2,000 to 3,000 Baojun E100 electric vehicles into the market in Liuzhou, offering free trials spanning two months. This approach, significantly surpassing conventional test drives that offer limited exposure to a select few, marked the advent of widespread and authentic user engagement in vehicle testing.

This daring initiative was not without its perils. Deploying thousands of vehicles for public use was a gamble, as user dissatisfaction could tarnish the brand's image.

Additionally, managing the logistics of the vehicles post-trial posed a challenge. The task of educating users and nurturing a market for an innovative product demanded considerable effort and resources. Embracing a user-focused strategy, SGMW opted to provide the cars for free use, with the goal of garnering comprehensive evaluations and engaging users directly in the refinement process.

From the latter half of 2016 through the early months of 2017, the Baojun E100 entered a pivotal phase of free trials, garnering an extraordinary response from the residents of Liuzhou. Tens of thousands of trial requests inundated the company, prompting organized events to allocate trial slots. These events attracted over 10,000 participants, including civil servants, healthcare professionals, educators, and corporate employees—reflecting a highly desirable demographic of potential buyers. The trials, typically scheduled for one to two weeks, offered participants a comprehensive experience, with some individuals enjoying extended periods of up to a month. Although Liuzhou was the primary location for these trials, additional sessions were also conducted in the Nanning region.

The feedback gathered from this extensive trial period proved invaluable, sparking innovative thinking among the designers and progressively honing the vehicle's development trajectory. This hands-on approach provided critical insights into product positioning and user experience, serving as a potent catalyst for refinement.

Electric vehicles signify a burgeoning transition that goes beyond their conventional role as mere modes of transport, intricately woven into the fabric of urban landscapes. In China, gasoline vehicles have matured into a well-established ecosystem since 1990, to the point where the origins of this infrastructure have faded from collective memory. Electric vehicles, however, are akin to newcomers in the urban environment, introducing a set of challenges that are as significant as they are novel.

The question arises: How should a city adapt to accommodate these new vehicles?

In the year the Baojun E100 underwent trials, the Liuzhou Municipal Government had already initiated efforts to create additional parking spaces and establish charging stations, laying the groundwork for the impending electric vehicle boom. New energy vehicles held the potential to redefine urban landscapes with bold strokes, imprinting fresh trajectories in the city's development blueprint. The logistical challenges of installing charging stations and allocating parking spaces for electric vehicles demanded meticulous coordination across various sectors, encompassing investment, transportation, public safety, environmental protection, urban management, housing, urban-rural development, quality supervision, pricing, and electricity provision. Adapting urban infrastructure to embrace electric vehicles often means revising existing regulations or bridging regulatory gaps, presenting a multifaceted challenge that serves as a litmus test for a city's governance capacity and its openness to champion innovative solutions.

To tackle these challenges head-on, the Liuzhou Municipal Government launched the tri-level government-enterprise coordination project, spearheaded by a leadership team dedicated to the promotion of new energy vehicles and in partnership with major local players such as SGMW and Dongfeng Liuzhou Automobile. This pioneering initiative aimed to forge a cohesive model for integrating new energy vehicle promotion with industrial growth, featuring structured collaboration among leadership, coordination, and implementation teams, with the latter drawing expertise from over 20 government sectors and enterprise technical specialists. Within a remarkably short span of six months, Liuzhou introduced 10,000 new parking spots and 20,000 charging points. Furthermore, the city implemented attractive road rights incentives for electric vehicle owners, granting privileges including the use of bus lanes and exemptions from driving restrictions. Additional measures, such as charging subsidies and free parking periods, alongside a noteworthy subsidy of RMB 0.1 per kilometer, capped at RMB 1,000 annually for three years, significantly reduced user costs and promoted sustainable transport.

Years into the future, when electric vehicles seamlessly integrate into the streetscape and effortless charging becomes a given, the pioneering endeavors undertaken by Liuzhou during this transformative period will be hailed as a seminal chapter in urban and industrial innovation. It establishes a replicable and insightful precedent for policymakers aspiring to nurture emerging industries within their jurisdictions.

Fostering new elements within urban landscapes is comparable to enriching the soil for growth, and once these elements take root, they often flourish independently. By July 2017, the Baojun E100 made its debut, offered at an affordable price of RMB 35,800 after accounting for both manufacturer and government subsidies. Its affordability, coupled with its convenience and user-friendly design, persuaded a significant number of trial participants to make a purchase, achieving an impressive conversion rate of over 60% from long-term trial users to owners.

Liuzhou's approach to advancing new energy vehicles involved a deepened synergy between the government and businesses, setting a groundbreaking precedent for integrating the promotion and application of such vehicles across the spectrum of production, sales, operation, parking, and charging. This integrated strategy, initially spearheaded in Guangxi, elevated the Liuzhou model to a broader Guangxi model[①]. Despite its success, the replication of this model in other cities encountered gradual uptake. Establishing a comprehensive and intelligent ecosystem for new energy vehicles is a long-term undertaking, necessitating dedicated collaboration from local authorities and a shift in perspective on the symbiotic relationship between cities and vehicles. The launch of the Baojun E100 was, in many respects, pioneering, arriving at a time when both the market and infrastructural readiness were still evolving.

8.4 Sizing Down: The Big Challenge

Following the initial success, the trajectory for advancement became increasingly evident. Building on the foundational accomplishments of the Baojun E100, the design team set its sights on refinement and innovation, culminating in the introduction of the Baojun E200. This new model not only enhanced the perception of quality but also retained its commitment to catering to urban commutes through its compact two-seater configuration. In Liuzhou, a city boasting a substantial urban population and an average daily commute of less than 20 kilometers, the practicality of charging the vehicle merely once or twice a week markedly mitigated concerns regarding its range. The Baojun E200 appeared well-suited not just for Liuzhou but for many other small- and medium-sized cities across China. Yet, the question remained: How could the Baojun E200 make inroads beyond Liuzhou?

The strategy pivoted toward the north, centering on Shandong and Henan—provinces renowned for their populous landscapes and expansive plains, traditionally serving as bastions for low-speed electric vehicles. Dubbed "leisure vehicles" due to their maximum speed cap of 70 kilometers per hour, these basic models offered affordability and convenience but lacked compliance with safety standards. Despite

---

① Mao Yuxian and Zou Zhenyuan. The Liuzhou Model for New Energy Vehicles: A Documentary on How New Energy and New Ecology Inject New Vitality into the Established Industrial City of Guangxi[J]. *Guangxi Electric Power*, 2021.

their widespread popularity, surpassing one million units in annual sales nationwide, these vehicles operated within a regulatory gray area—exempt from registration, driver's licenses, insurance, or periodic inspections—thus presenting significant challenges in terms of road rights, safety, and traffic management for authorities. Nonetheless, the era of lenient regulation was drawing to a close, as policies aimed at tightening controls and fortifying regulatory frameworks gradually took effect.

In recent years, the development of low-speed electric vehicles has become a focal point for economic innovation in various local counties and cities. In September 2016, 10 cities in Henan province, including Kaifeng, Luoyang, and Zhumadian, joined forces to establish the Henan Low-Speed Electric Vehicle Cooperative Demonstration Area, aiming to accelerate the growth of the electric vehicle market. At the time, Henan boasted over 50 manufacturers of low-speed electric vehicles, though most were small in scale.

Among these cities, Zhumadian showed a particular interest in SGMW's electric vehicles, with the hope of attracting a production base from the company. After conducting more than 20 field investigations, SGMW set out to design a specialized electric vehicle tailored to replace prevalent low-speed electric vehicles in Shandong, Henan, and other regions. The outlined criteria were unequivocal: the vehicle had to be the most cost-effective, compact, and safest option available on the market. The battery's cost emerged as a critical factor, necessitating adherence to the minimum national regulatory standards for energy efficiency. Given the widespread use of leisure vehicles for school runs and the recognition that a two-seater would not suffice for many families, the new design required four seats, irrespective of its compact size, posing a significant challenge in terms of innovative spatial design.

Despite a year of intensive negotiations, the envisioned cooperative project did not come to fruition. Nevertheless, this period was not without its achievements; it saw the birth of the E50, a new generation four-seater electric compact car designed to potentially succeed the conventional leisure vehicle. The E50, meticulously crafted, established a set of design principles for its appearance, reflecting a profound comprehension of the automotive design's overarching significance.

The art of car design is of paramount importance in the realm of automobile manufacturing, as it demands a harmonious blend of exterior aesthetics and interior functionality. Each line and curve is purposefully conceived to enhance the car's visual appeal while simultaneously addressing functional needs. In the nascent stages of automobile development, what we now know as the design department was initially dubbed the Art and Color Department[1]. This innovative concept was pioneered by GM, which, in a move that was anything but arbitrary, appointed a gifted designer to head this new department. GM underscored the profound impact of appearance on sales within its 1921 product planning project, but it was not until 1926, with the increasing prevalence of sedans in the market, that the practical implications of a car's exterior design started to be taken seriously, recognizing a notable disconnect between sedan aesthetics and consumer preferences. Over time, GM came to realize that a vehicle's luxury, appealing aesthetics, color schemes, and distinctiveness from competitors were crucial factors in attracting buyers—elements the company's future hinged on[2]. In 1927, the same year GM established its Art and Color Department, the Ford Model T ceased production, symbolizing a transition from one automotive era to another, underscoring the growing significance of exterior design in the industry. Car designers, much like Parisian couturiers attuned to the latest fashion trends, began to play a crucial role, transforming steel with the finesse that tailors apply to fabric.

Post-World War II, Alfred P. Sloan, then president of GM, foresaw that the allure of automobiles would hinge primarily on their design, automatic transmissions, and high-compression engines—in that specific order, which was subsequently affirmed by market trends. In 1954, Harley Jarvis Earl, GM's head designer, proclaimed the supremacy of the rectangle in automotive design. He dedicated 28 years to refining the car silhouette to be longer and lower, as the visual appeal of proportions favored the rectangle over the square.

The quest to reduce a vehicle's height introduced a plethora of engineering and design challenges. The principles of art and color honed in on two central themes: the evolution of form and the seamless integration of protruding elements into the car's body. Lowering the car's profile required innovative solutions for drivetrain placement, while extending its length often resulted in increased weight. In 1948, the introduction of tail fins, inspired by fighter aircraft, became a defining feature. These elements, purely aesthetic at their inception, resonated with the public's post-war sensibilities.

Hence, defining the space within a car became an indispensable facet of automotive design.

---

[1] Wu Renyan. Harley Jarvis Earl's Top Ten Designs[J]. *Car and Fan*, 2018.

[2] Alfred P. Sloan. *My Years with General Motors*[M]. trans. Liu Xin. Huaxia Publishing House, 2017, 255+257.

The E50 electric vehicle, succeeding the Baojun E100, exemplifies a core design philosophy focused on spatial efficiency. At the heart of this approach lies the "MM" space design concept, which seeks to push the boundaries of interior space maximization for occupants while minimizing the vehicle's mechanical footprint to the essential[①]. The E50's development was thus poised as an endeavor to master this challenging spatial paradigm.

In pursuit of maximizing space within a compact frame measuring less than three meters in length—occupying just half the parking space of a standard sedan—the technical team engaged in exhaustive ideation sessions. The vehicle adopts a minimalist rear-wheel-drive configuration, featuring four seats designed for versatility to enhance the utility of the interior space, 12 strategically placed storage compartments.

Integration emerged as another cornerstone of the E50's design strategy. Electric vehicles, by virtue of their engineering, afford the opportunity to consolidate multiple components into singular units, a departure from their traditional gasoline-driven counterparts. The team took on the task of reengineering essential parts with an eye toward spatial economy, culminating in the amalgamation of the onboard charger, converter, and high-voltage distribution box into an integrated three-in-one charging and distribution system. This consolidation not only reduced the component count from three to one, shedding 3.54 kilograms in weight, but also streamlined the assembly process by eliminating the need for eight bolts and two sets of connectors, saving 100 seconds per vehicle in assembly time. Through meticulous comparisons and adjustments, the engineers' dedication to precision and efficiency is evident in every calculation and time measurement, reflecting their commitment to innovation in electric vehicle design.

The minimalist design philosophy maximizes spatial efficiency, elevating space as the ultimate asset, which necessitates a critical reassessment of component dimensions and their interconnections. The concept of integration underpins the electric vehicle industry's approach, streamlining the architecture to seamlessly harmonize form and function.

Through iterative design and engineering, unforeseen advancements emerged. Initially projected to achieve a range of 100 to 150 kilometers, optimizations in

---

① China Association of Automobile Manufacturers, China Automotive Industry Advisory Committee. *History of China Automotive Industry, 1991–2010*[M]. China Machine Press, 2014, 185.

weight, aerodynamics, drive efficiency, motor performance, overall vehicle control, and advancements in battery energy density collectively extended the final test range to 120 to 170 kilometers.

This endeavor culminated in the birth of the Wuling Hongguang MINI EV, poised for its pre-launch trials—a pivotal moment for validation. Fresh from the experience gained in mask production during the pandemic, the Wuling team approached this milestone with a blend of anticipation and determination, eager to witness the impact of their latest innovation in urban mobility.

8.5 Pivot to Demand: Creating What the People Need

The spotlight on SGMW, fueled by its foray into mask production and the eager anticipation surrounding the E50 model, is converging both temporally and spatially.

As the COVID-19 pandemic gradually recedes, a notable societal shift is underway, marked by the widespread adoption of remote work, virtual meetings, and online education. Concurrently, this era is witnessing the emergence of an economy increasingly driven by e-commerce and live streaming. Platforms like Douyin and Kuaishou are transforming into stages for diverse content creators, while social media buzzes with lively interactions. In this era dominated by influencers, every concept effortlessly finds its audience, and niche opinion leaders wield considerable sway.

Against this dynamic backdrop, SGMW maneuvers through a torrent of public attention. The company's agile pivot to mask production, the debut of the innovative "street stall car" catering to mobile vendors, and the launch of the Wuling-branded luosifen have all captivated and engaged the public. This automotive firm, headquartered in a southern Chinese city, has become a focal point of keen public interest. Its marketing team, constantly immersed in a barrage of comments and queries, finds itself momentarily swamped by the deluge of engagement.

The fortuitous discovery of a video featuring two young women born after 1995 playfully filming themselves with the Wuling Hongguang MINI EV at a Wuling dealership has sparked significant interest. Their light-hearted comment, "This little car is so adorable, you guys should hurry up and buy it before it grows up and starts hauling cargo", raises questions about whether it was a moment of self-deprecation or carried an underlying inspirational message.

Was it a mere flash in the pan, or did it hint at something deeper?

The occurrence sparked a spirited debate within the marketing team, largely comprising individuals from the post-'95 generation. The deliberations culminated in a resounding consensus: this car genuinely appeals to the younger demographic.

This revelation swiftly made its way to the leadership of SGMW. Shen Yang and Yao Zuoping, surprised by the swift reorientation of the car's appeal, deliberated on the nature of this unexpected popularity. Shen Yang, notably absent from Douyin, wrestled with the question of whether this was a transient trend or a significant indicator. However, one notion emerged as increasingly plausible: the minimalist ethos of the Hongguang MINI EV strikes a chord with the younger audience. It becomes evident that the preferences and mindset of this new generation cannot always be decoded using traditional reasoning.

The decisive verdict on the Hongguang MINI EV's fate rested squarely with the younger generation. As a result, the marketing team's innovative ideas crystallized into a bold new direction: a strategic repositioning of the car to align with youthful aspirations. This pivot demanded a complete overhaul of the original sales strategy in favor of a fresh, uncharted approach.

Quickly mobilizing, the marketing team infused the product's branding with themes of youthfulness and personalized expression. They ventured beyond the bounds of traditional automotive marketing, tapping into digital platforms frequented by their target audience, such as Douyin, Xiaohongshu, and Bilibili. Their strategy extended to aligning with contemporary cultural phenomena, partnering with events like the West Lake Music Festival and Shanghai Fashion Week to cultivate a chic image. Even the decision to collaborate with HEYTEA, a trendy beverage brand, left Shen Yang, distant from the pulse of youth culture, in a state of bemusement.

This strategic realignment heralded the MINI EV as the embodiment of the young generation's spirit and their preferred mode of transportation.

In parallel with the online engagement efforts, over 2,000 dealerships were enlisted to create an appeal that resonated with young consumers, fostering a blend of excitement and tangible experiences. This harmonious blend of online presence and offline experiences created a surge in market interest, showcasing the potency of aligning product positioning with the evolving preferences of a new generation.

The boundless creativity of consumers, particularly within the younger demographic, quickly became evident as they embraced the ample blank spaces offered by the Hongguang MINI EV for personal customization. The car's minimalist design, far from being a limitation, proved to be its greatest asset, empowering owners to express their individuality by personalizing their vehicles, turning its simplicity into a canvas for creativity. The result was a vibrant tapestry of stories and legends woven by the public around this vehicle.

In its pricing strategy, SGMW strategically targeted the youthful market by encapsulating the essence of a "miracle car"—one that embodies simplicity, affordability, and enjoyment, demonstrating that with public experience, cost challenges could be effectively addressed through mass production and ecosystem strategies. Shen Yang's strategic foresight into revenue balancing hinged on an innovative aspect: as car sales increased, profits from carbon credits under the new energy vehicle policy would ensure profitability, even with an introductory price below RMB 30,000.

Launched in July 2020 with a price range of RMB 28,800 to 38,800, the Wuling Hongguang MINI EV instantly became a viral sensation, with orders swiftly nearing 30,000 units. This compact electric vehicle, measuring less than three meters in length and equipped with 27 horsepower, captivated the market upon its debut. The impressive sales figures it generated underscored its substantial market appeal, marking a joyous milestone for SGMW.

8.6 Epic Journey: The Grand Relocation

The summer of 2020 brought a mix of excitement and trepidation to the management team at SGMW. Initially launched to disrupt the market dominated by low-speed electric vehicles, particularly in Shandong with its significant market share, the production responsibility for the Hongguang MINI EV fell upon the Qingdao base. Initial sales forecasts at the year's start had pegged the expected monthly sales volume to range between 5,000 and 10,000 units, leading to a set maximum monthly production capacity of 20,000 units at the Qingdao base.

In August, the first full sales month for the Hongguang MINI EV, sales astonishingly reached 15,000 units. This surge not only vaulted it ahead of competitors like Tesla and BYD but also secured its position as the leader in the monthly sales rankings for pure electric vehicles. The market's swift embrace and high regard for the vehicle, coupled with its unexpectedly robust sales performance, surpassed all expectations.

Orders began pouring in.

As orders accumulated at a rapid pace, the production machinery began to overheat, and material shortages turned acute. The "miracle car" effect resulted in an unexpected stockpile in Qingdao, making the ramp-up of Hongguang MINI EV production SGMW's utmost priority. Faced with these challenges, the Qingdao production base was compelled to intensify its efforts, transitioning from one to two shifts daily. However, given the production demands of other models, the local output of the Hongguang MINI EV was capped at a maximum of 15,000 units per month.

The new generation of vehicles outpaced all expectations, pushing the Qingdao production base to its limits and presenting SGMW with an unprecedented supply challenge.

To meet the surging demand, a significant reshuffle of resources and reconfiguration of production capacities became imperative. The management swiftly concurred on a strategic move: to relocate production to alternate sites. A highly empowered, specialized action team was promptly formed to spearhead this initiative.

The mandate for the specialized action team was unequivocal: elevate the Liuzhou plant's production of the Hongguang MINI EV from zero to 30,000 units per month in record time. However, this formidable challenge of relocating production was tantamount to building from the ground up. The Hexi and Liudong Baojun bases in Liuzhou, initially ill-equipped for manufacturing this particular model, found themselves grappling with a scenario best described as facing a "triple-void"— lacking essential components, production molds, and the preparedness of production lines. Effecting this transition demanded a meticulous transportation of components covering a vast distance of over 2,000 kilometers, stretching from Qingdao in Shandong to Liuzhou in Guangxi, located deep in South China while ensuring no damage en route. Following the successful execution of this logistical feat, groundwork for assembly and production could finally begin at the Hexi and Liudong Baojun sites, representing a pivotal stride toward meeting the soaring demand.

In September, a monumental endeavor unfolded as the most extensive inter-regional production transfer in the annals of China's automotive history began.

This massive operation saw collaboration among over 100 entities to establish cohesive links in the industry chain, with Liuzhou's two primary production bases swiftly gearing up for machine calibration and production, eagerly anticipating the arrival of raw materials and components. Concurrently, the Qingdao base, now operating in continuous shifts, tightened the reins on the upstream supply chain, necessitating suppliers to significantly amplify their production output within a tight timeline to fulfill the distant supply demands.

Responding to the urgency, an emergency transportation corridor stretching from Qingdao to Liuzhou was promptly established.

The journey of components unfolded across both road and rail networks, with meticulous packaging of smaller parts directly at the factory, dispatched promptly to Liuzhou. Executing this intricate process, the specialized action team orchestrated partnerships with leading domestic logistics firms such as SF Express, JD.com, Cainiao, Anji Logistics, and Putian Logistics, deploying up to 82 logistics vehicles daily, a scale so extensive that it became widely known in the Shandong logistics sector that "Wuling has cargo moving from Qingdao to Liuzhou".

In a bid to streamline the process, SGMW initiated direct transportation of packaging materials to the premises of major component suppliers for immediate packaging. These packaged components were then sent directly to the Huangdao warehouse of China Railway Special Cargo Logistics in Qingdao, strategically positioned at the railway hub. This facilitated the operation of six dedicated trains each day, ferrying components to Luorong Railway Station, in close proximity to the Liuzhou Baojun base. Each train bore a load capacity of 960 tonnes, necessitating a substantial number of standard containers. Amidst the global container shortage during the COVID-19 pandemic, making the procurement of containers exceptionally arduous, SGMW harnessed virtually every accessible container resource within Shandong Province, to the extent of utilizing containers from the China Railway Express for shipments to Liuzhou, reaching a point where idle containers were scarce across Shandong. The wooden crates, designed to withstand the rigors of long-haul transport, including considerable jolts, stacking, and multiple loadings and unloadings, demanded stringent specifications for the wood's knots and thickness. The sudden spike in demand for these crates, driven by the Hongguang MINI EV's production, nearly depleted Shandong's supply of packaging wood, prompting a surge in local prices due to the ensuing scarcity.

Day after day, tens of thousands of components made their journey from China's eastern coast to the southern territory.

Upon reaching Liuzhou, the sheer volume of components prompted SGMW to requisition a local site spanning 18,000 square meters, where over 70 employees were tasked with daily unpacking duties. The continuous influx of parts from Qingdao quickly outpaced the available warehouse capacity in Liuzhou, resulting in a queue of trucks stretching over 100 meters from the factory gate to the roadside, all awaiting their turn for unloading. This forced the company to acquire additional warehousing space to enhance storage capabilities and mitigate the strain on existing facilities.

The escalated production demand mobilized over 110 suppliers, compelling departments such as SGMW's procurement center and production manufacturing to fully engage once again. The end of the year saw a resurgence of the bustling activity, reminiscent of the early pandemic period's mask production efforts. By December, the demand for the Hongguang MINI EV had surged beyond 50,000 units, prompting the two Liuzhou bases to accelerate production to its maximum, pushing output to an impressive 30,000 units.

This remarkable shift in production serves as a compelling testament that extraordinary achievements are underpinned by equally remarkable efforts.

This year, the electric vehicle sector rightfully claimed the automotive industry's spotlight, with Tesla at the forefront, catalyzing the electric vehicle revolution across major global markets with its influential prowess. The operational commencement of Tesla's Shanghai factory at the previous year's close markedly enhanced its production capabilities, and the Model 3, setting an industry standard, saw nearly 140,000 units delivered in 2020.

However, in the competitive landscape of pure electric vehicle sales since August, the Model 3 found its rival—the Hongguang MINI EV. Debuting with 15,000 units in its initial month, the latter experienced a remarkable surge, culminating in a staggering 35,000 units sold by December, solidifying its status as a phenomenal product.

Despite its limited range, the Hongguang MINI EV has successfully carved its unique niche in the market, with its notable price disparity from Tesla underscoring the diverse avenues of innovation within the electric vehicle domain. Rather than solely aiming to dethrone gasoline-powered cars, electric vehicles often serve the fundamental purpose of meeting commuter needs, and the Hongguang MINI EV exemplifies how aligning with national conditions and providing an affordable transportation solution can chart a distinctive trajectory in the electric vehicle market.

Echoing the mantra "Wuling builds what people need", Wuling adeptly addressed a diverse array of consumer demands in 2020, ranging from masks and luosifen to night market vending vehicles and electric vehicles.

The introduction of the assembly line by Ford in 1914, while not immediately recognized for its revolutionary impact, gained widespread acknowledgment in the 1940s as numerous automakers adopted this innovative approach. In the dance of innovation, pioneers tread the path unseen, their steps echoing into the future, uncelebrated yet audacious. Their impact, like whispers on the wind, only coalesces as the crowd follows, turning faint trails into highways of progress. This journey of advancement often cloaks itself in the garb of the mundane, weaving through the fabric of daily life, invisible yet omnipresent, silently sculpting the contours of our world. The year 2020 marked a pivotal moment for electric vehicles, with the success of the Hongguang MINI EV serving as a testament to how effectively these vehicles can fulfill people's transportation needs, making it a year destined to linger in our memory.

8.7 Banyan Roots: Sourcing Vitality and Mastery from the Depths

In Liuzhou, the banyan trees cast a pervasive spell of greenery, their evergreen canopies and aerial roots, capable of absorbing oxygen from the air, creating refreshing, dense shades. Some roots, like curious explorers, reach down and sprawl, hinting at the inception of a forest born from a solitary tree. Amidst the sweltering climate, where ground-level oxygen is scarce, these roots ingeniously draw life from the air above, showcasing a striking testament to resilience.

In Wuling, the supply chain is deeply rooted in local collaboration, particularly for components such as sheet metal and injection-molded parts, predominantly sourced from Liuzhou's vicinity. With around 160 key suppliers based in Liuzhou, a ripple effect ensues, bolstering 600 to 700 affiliated enterprises within the automotive sector.

Liuzhou's suppliers have honed the art of cost-efficiency. Initially, profits were not made directly from the parts themselves but rather from the sale of materials. Pressed and welded parts, often priced by weight, mirrored raw material costs, targeting mass production and scalability. SGMW nurtured these suppliers toward broader profit horizons through innovation, research, and the implementation of lean manufacturing practices, weaving a symbiotic relationship between the city and its automotive achievements. Here, Liuzhou's supply chain stands out, seamlessly integrating low cost with high quality, a testament to the city's contribution to the automotive world.

Navigating the intricate web of supplier quality presents a formidable challenge for automakers, especially for a company entwined with over 600 primary suppliers. Ensuring product quality across such an extensive network necessitates a rigorous, often painstaking process, underpinned by a cohesive system and standardized benchmarks. Consider GM, which exemplifies this approach by enforcing consistent stamping standards across its global manufacturing bases. Illustrated within a comprehensive manual, an impressive tome spanning over 200 pages, the company meticulously outlines procedures from steel smelting to mold adjustment. This rigorous standardization enables factories worldwide to essentially start from the ground up, ensuring indistinguishable molds are produced. However, adherence to standards alone does not automatically translate to cost reduction. SGMW, upon adopting these benchmarks, also ventured into localized innovation and spearheaded initiatives with suppliers to eliminate unnecessary expenses throughout the supply chain.

The year 2010 signified a pivotal shift for SGMW as it ventured into passenger car production, setting a high bar that naturally weeded out many potential suppliers. This new era subjected Liuzhou's suppliers to stringent quality metrics, marking a bold leap toward excellence.

The dynamic transformations within urban industrial landscapes demand a parallel evolution and recalibration of prevailing supply chains. For major automotive players like SGMW, this entails adopting a nuanced approach to support their suppliers. In the preceding year, the company's procurement and supply chain management department underwent a transformation, rebranded as the procurement and supply chain management center. This move centralized responsibilities for purchasing, supplier quality management, and logistics management under one umbrella, seamlessly integrating procurement and quality control functions. Negotiations with suppliers and quality audits now undergo rigorous scrutiny, ensuring a consistent standard of examination. Reflecting on the inception of the SGMW joint venture, it is evident how the enterprise, propelled by the momentum of its state-owned enterprise origin, skillfully married the "Three Comparisons" procurement method, integrated management, and the "overflow payment method" with GM's global procurement strategies. This amalgamation gave rise to a procurement system that not only upheld the principles of "low-cost, high-quality" but also resonated with the local essence of Liuzhou. By incorporating GM's global supplier quality 16-step process, SGMW crafted a structured network comprising platform suppliers, key suppliers, and strategic suppliers, which not only established rigorous criteria for the induction of new suppliers but also extended the advantages of economies of scale to them.

In lieu of sourcing passenger car suppliers externally, SGMW primarily leaned on its key tier-one suppliers, a decision driven largely by cost considerations. External suppliers, faced with the imperative of slashing per-product costs and maintaining profitability, might struggle to adapt. However, for Liuzhou's commercial vehicle suppliers, transitioning to passenger cars represented an opportunity to enhance product precision and command higher purchase prices, a change that was met with enthusiasm and a collective readiness to evolve and embrace change. The embodiment of the ethos "Perseverance with Self-Strengthening" subtly extended beyond the confines of Wuling's factory gate, permeating the ethos of its supplier network.

Historically, the quality of parts sourced from suppliers was marred by inconsistency. Workshops reliant on manual adjustments experienced significant variances in tolerance; even welding, performed with unwieldy pliers, was prone to inaccuracies, epitomizing a "heavy plier culture" that pervaded many factories. Another "screwdriver factory" syndrome, where quality hinged on an operator's proficiency with a basic tool, further exemplified the challenges in maintaining consistent quality standards. In response to these challenges, SGMW's manufacturing director took proactive measures, conducting weekly visits to the inspection room. During these visits, the director meticulously refined each process, introducing solutions such as stable tooling fixtures and digital display electric wrenches, all while encouraging suppliers to commit to equipment upgrades and engage directly in process improvements.

Improving quality among upstream suppliers continues to be a pressing challenge for SGMW's quality department, resulting in the gradual phase-out of some suppliers unable to keep pace. Their exit was not due to being outcompeted but rather outpaced by the evolving standards within the industry—a testament to the industry's self-regulatory mechanism.

While certain prominent domestic and international suppliers boasting advanced quality systems serve as benchmarks for SGMW, challenges concerning lower-value components persist, often magnifying quality concerns, a common issue across diverse sectors. Despite the clear distinctions established between OEMs and tier-one suppliers in China's evolving automotive industry, varying levels of quality among upstream parts suppliers expose a weakness in the country's industrial foundation. Particularly, small enterprises specializing in basic machining, stamping, and welding processes struggle to match the rapid advancements in the automotive sector.

The guardianship of these smaller component suppliers falls into a realm beyond governmental purview. Despite governmental incentives aimed at bolstering small and medium enterprises, the market imposes rigorous selection criteria, leaving those unable to adapt trailing behind. Nevertheless, the imperative for guidance, a beacon to illuminate the path forward, persists. In this context, the city's leading manufacturers shine as lighthouses for local small and medium enterprises, guiding them through the treacherous waters of market demands and quality standards. For suppliers willing to embark on this journey, the enhancement of component quality becomes a pivotal duty shouldered by these leading manufacturers. They spearhead initiatives, sending waves of supply chain quality teams directly to the suppliers' doorsteps. Stationed on the front lines, these teams play a vital role in uplifting suppliers' equipment standards, technological prowess, product quality, supply capabilities, and responsiveness to market demands.

While annual metrics provide insights in charting a company's progress, ecological shifts within a region unfold over a span of five to ten years. After establishing a foundation of standardized operations, SGMW set its sights on optimizing its extensive supply chains. In 2016, the introduction of the "Supplier Quality Q+" management system marked a pivotal turn toward employing systematic methods and tools aimed at bolstering the supplier ecosystem's overall capabilities. Wuling's innovative approach included deploying quality managers directly within supplier firms, accountable to their general managers. This strategy achieved a dual objective: facilitating on-site quality control to ensure operational capacity, and establishing standardized requirements while offering practical tools and strategies, crystallizing into actionable insights for operational excellence. To further refine its management approach, the supplier quality team adopted a model akin to that of sales teams, embracing territorial management. Each region was assigned an improvement officer tasked with compiling an annual report and fostering cross-interaction. One transformative impact was seen in a sheet metal factory, where the variety of material frames was streamlined from over 40 types to a mere 11. This adjustment negated the need for advance production scheduling for safety stock, resulting in a reduction in storage space from 6000 square meters to just 1500 square meters. This reclaimed space, in turn, facilitated the installation of new, large-scale stamping equipment. A supplier, boasting a turnover of less than RMB 200 million, ambitiously aimed to optimize not only per capita output but also factory floor productivity, echoing Toyota's "halving principle"—achieving equivalent production volume within half the factory space. It is evident that SGMW has instigated a profound transformation in the mindset of Liuzhou's local suppliers.

Through diligent and, at times, painstaking efforts, SGMW has incrementally propelled the Liuzhou industrial chain toward cost-effectiveness. The joint venture's shareholders, acknowledging the company's exceptional cost leadership, organized a delegation of over 20 individuals to study the operations in Liuzhou. While understanding the fundamentals of SGMW's system was achievable, attempting to replicate it proved to be a different challenge altogether. The cost system at SGMW is intricately interwoven into the fabric of Liuzhou's surrounding supplier network, deeply entrenched in the local ecosystem. For example, the practice of pricing certain body components based on steel weight finds ready acceptance among suppliers, who ingeniously repurpose scrap materials for secondary processing, catering to lighter manufacturers. This bespoke model, tailored to the specificities of the local context, poses significant challenges for emulation in different settings.

Beneath the surface of SGMW's corporate cost structure lies a network intricately woven with the assimilation of a region and the symbiotic relationships within a community, reminiscent of the expansive root system of a towering tree deeply entrenched in the earth. For SGMW, each stride in its developmental journey is anchored in the resilience cultivated through collective learning, charting a path of growth akin to a rigorous ascent where self-reliance plays a pivotal role. Much like the unique karst topography of the red soil shaping the dense jungles and towering limestone pillars that characterize the region, with solitary peaks rising distinctly against the skyline, SGMW's journey is likewise sculpted by the local terrain. In Liuzhou, the dearth of passenger car expertise, compounded by the absence of industry benchmarks in nearby cities, necessitates the adoption of a self-sustaining approach to talent development. Without the influx of high-level external expertise, the company's evolution follows a spiral trajectory, leveraging past experiences as the foundation for self-propelled growth. The advancement of each vehicle model—spanning design, manufacturing, and supply chain management—while occasionally benefiting from external insights, inherently demands that SGMW cultivate its capabilities from the karst-like foundation of Liuzhou, incrementally extracting and learning.

SGMW's growth not only injects vitality into the dynamic local small and medium enterprises landscape but also draws in substantial investments from major international firms. A notable example is United Automotive Electronic Systems, a joint venture specializing in automotive powertrain and body control systems solutions, which has closely monitored the burgeoning development in Liuzhou. Inspired by SGMW's trajectory of growth, it initiated its factory in Liuzhou in 2011, which was positioned a mere six kilometers away from Wuling's passenger car facility, the Liudong Baojun base. The frequent shuttle of trucks between these points weaves a vibrant tapestry within Liuzhou's automotive city. In tandem with SGMW's diversification in portfolio from mini-vehicles to passenger vehicles and electric models, the Liuzhou production base of United Automotive Electronic Systems has similarly broadened its business scope. By 2018, the completion of the base's second phase marked an expansion into engine control, body electronics, and transmission control products, mirroring the evolution of SGMW's product line. This pattern of growth and diversification is also reflected in the strategies of other international players such as Yanfeng and France's Faurecia, both of which have established their presence in Liuzhou, further contributing to the richness of the local automotive industry ecosystem.

Each excavation in Liuzhou, every layer of soil turned, cements the robust foundation of its automotive industry, with the "locomotive" of SGMW propelling continuous forward momentum. The absence of a trailblazing flagship company could cast a shadow over the future of any regional automotive sector. In 1992, the introduction of the Subaru REX model for manufacturing the Yunque mini-vehicle marked a significant step[1], facilitated by a technology transfer from the Guizhou Aircraft Industry Corporation. Before the inception of the SGMW joint venture in 1998, Fuji Heavy Industries and Guizhou Aircraft Industry Corporation jointly invested RMB 450 million in a joint venture to rebrand Yungque-Subaru[2], a golden era for Chinese automotive collaborations, with Yungque-Subaru at the helm of

---

① An Fang, Yan Mingwei, Sun Ying, et al. Disappearing and Emerging Brands: Are They Trustworthy?[J]. *Auto Life*, 2016.

② Geng Huili, He Beishi. Yungque-Subaru's Uncertain Journey Continues[J]. *China Automotive News*, 2005-07-11 (A06).

national support as a mini-vehicle hub, basking in widespread acclaim. However, the passage of time, as recorded in the annals of history, separates the steadfast from the transient. By 2021, Guizhou's automotive output had dwindled to about 80,000 units, placing it among the lowest in China, while Guangxi soared to 1.9 million units, securing the sixth national rank, trailing only behind powerhouses such as Guangdong, Shanghai, Jilin, Hubei, and Chongqing. Within this landscape, the Sino-foreign joint venture model exemplified by SGMW, embodying a philosophy of "Less the possession, more the value of the company in the society", reaffirmed its enduring vitality. This avant-garde approach not only enriches the local automotive heritage but also intricately intertwines with the essence of Liuzhou, cultivating a legacy that transcends mere shareholder disputes. The sustained growth of a company, mirroring the relentless spirit of a solitary banyan tree flourishing into a forest, stands as the ultimate testament to enduring success.

Chapter 9 Valor Across Borders 2021

9.1 At the Intersection of Progress and Regression

In 2021, SGMW reached a historic pinnacle in its global outreach, with its exports of complete vehicles and parts soaring to 145,550 units—a staggering 88% increase from the previous year[①]. This expansion extended its footprint across 40 countries, enveloping regions such as Latin America, Africa, the Middle East, and Southeast Asia. A pivotal force behind this success was PT SGMW Motor Indonesia, which recorded an annual sales volume of 25,650 units, propelling its market share from 1.6% to 2.9% and establishing it as the fastest-growing brand in the Indonesian automotive sector. Remarkably, even amid the widespread disruptions caused by the pandemic, Wuling's revenues in Indonesia outpaced the growth of Japanese car brands for the same period.

The essence of perseverance—akin to the relentless force of water shaping stone—is vital for the fruition of international endeavors, demanding an unwavering resolve to outlast the passage of time.

The seeds of this international ambition were sown back in 2004 when GM enlisted SGMW's expertise for the development of a GM facility in Indonesia, prompting Shen Yang to lead an exploratory team to Indonesia. A return visit in 2007, sparked by the ubiquity of the Japanese Toyota Avanza, inspired the development of the compact MPV Wuling Hongguang. These sequential milestones, akin to brushstrokes on an evolving canvas, gradually coalesce over time, enriching the tapestry of SGMW's international narrative.

The trials faced by GM, Ford, and Chrysler in 2009 underscored the American auto industry's global vulnerabilities. Following its bankruptcy declaration, GM underwent a transformation, emerging revitalized and reaffirming its status as a titan in the automotive realm. Nonetheless, as the sands of time shift, there arises a need

---

① Li Chongsen. Seven Strategic Pillars Propelling Wuling's New Energy Endeavors[J]. *Auto Review*, 2022.

for fresh paradigms in the global marketplace.

By 2013, discussions between SAIC Motor and GM pivoted toward their future in burgeoning markets, laying the groundwork for a global strategic division of labor. SGMW, renowned for its cost leadership and unique market differentiation, positioned itself as a pivotal player in these emerging territories.

A decisive moment ensued.

In 2013, China unveiled the Belt and Road Initiative in Indonesia, steering SGMW to capitalize on this strategic directive and extend its operations beyond domestic boundaries to international waters. In sync with China's Going Global strategy, and with manufacturing at the forefront, SGMW elevated its international business to one of its three strategic pillars and evolved from a singular focus on vehicle exports to exploring diverse international manufacturing models, charting a course for global expansion.

Southeast Asia, with Indonesia at its epicenter, emerges as a promising market, wherein Wuling distinguishes itself through its low-cost, high-value offerings suitable for both commercial and passenger use, positioning itself as a vanguard for market penetration.

Indonesia was chosen as the primary target for expansion.

Being geographically close to the Chinese mainland and a familiar terrain for the company, Indonesia played a pivotal role in the creative genesis of the Wuling Hongguang model during initial explorations.

The period between 2013 and 2014 was marked by a surge of enthusiasm within SGMW, spurred by the triumphs of their flagship models. This newfound vigor bolstered the team's morale, instilling them with a fervent determination to contend in the domestic SUV market while concurrently echoing a robust strategy for international expansion under the Going Global strategy. In June 2015, this ambition materialized with the establishment of PT SGMW Motor Indonesia, signifying the most substantial Chinese automotive manufacturing venture in Indonesia. The autonomy granted to SGMW by its board of directors to oversee and develop the Indonesian subsidiary underscored a commitment to agile and direct governance.

This milestone heralded a bold step forward for the Liuzhou automotive entity, symbolizing its confident entry onto the global stage with full sovereignty.

The Indonesian market, with its considerable appeal, presents itself as fertile ground for automobile ventures. As the fourth most populous nation globally, boasting a population of 260 million and the largest geographical footprint in

Southeast Asia, Indonesia's economic landscape holds great promise. By 2010, the country's GDP per capita had climbed over USD 3,000—a figure that stood out particularly when juxtaposed with China's automobile market, which saw its boom when GDP per capita reached around USD 1,700 in 2005[①].

In this context, SGMW's enthusiasm stands in stark contrast to GM, an entity with a legacy of international acclaim yet displaying a lackluster spirit in Indonesia. American car manufacturers, despite their formidable global presence, have often found their ambitions thwarted in this terrain, marked more by setbacks than by triumphs.

GM first entered Indonesia in 1995, setting up a facility near Jakarta with a workforce of 500[②]. However, by 2005, amidst mounting challenges, operations were suspended. In an effort to stage a comeback, May 2013 saw GM reintroduce itself with a new small MPV from Brazil. The Jakarta factory was revived to produce and market the Chevrolet Spin, targeting Southeast Asian markets with the expectation that its competitive pricing and cost-efficiency would secure a favorable position.

GM's Chevrolet Spin, designed to rival the acclaimed Toyota Avanza in Indonesia, faced significant challenges. Hindered by the necessity to import most of its parts and priced at approximately USD 12,000, the Spin struggled to assert its competitiveness. This seven-seater vehicle, on which GM had placed high expectations for the Indonesian market, fell short of achieving the sales figures required to sustain factory operations. In 2014, the Chevrolet Spin's production barely reached 10,000 units, with only 8,412 units sold locally in Indonesia. GM, renowned for its adeptness in global market strategies, seemed to have faltered. In February 2015, the company delivered the grim news of the permanent shutdown of its Indonesian car factory, resulting in the disbandment of the 500-strong workforce. The factory's equipment and production lines were dismantled and shipped to India, where they remained inactive, and materials intended for production were eventually discarded as scrap.

Concurrently, two GM Daewoo brands manufactured in Thailand, the Trailblazer and the Captiva, experienced similar downturns. With declining sales in the market, the fate of the manufacturing plants in Thailand—whether closure or sale—appeared inevitable.

---

① Mu Jia. Per Capita GDP Hits USD 1,703[J]. *China Business Times*, 2006-01-26 (001).

② The General Motors Bekasi facility.

The dilemma was evident: GM's head of international operations had grown disillusioned with the company's continual adjustments to its Southeast Asian production bases. The inability of these bases to align with market demands and adapt to cost fluctuations marked a significant setback in its globalization efforts, prompting a decision to "stop the bleeding". The company was also facing the imminent shutdown of its automotive production in Australia. The year 2015 marked a pivotal moment of global retreat for GM, with ramifications that would unfold over the next three to four years. The company appeared to shift its focus away from Southeast Asia, redirecting its strategic priorities toward the Chinese and American markets, all while grappling with the burgeoning fields of electrification and autonomous driving.

Even attempts with economy cars from Republic of Korea and Brazil failed to establish GM's foothold in Indonesia; the prestige of being a global brand within the GM portfolio failed to resonate.

Amidst this landscape, a tenacious competitor had long been solidifying its position, presenting a formidable challenge.

9.2 The Supply Chain Stranglehold

GM found itself forced to exit the Indonesian market, overshadowed by the entrenched dominance of Japanese vehicles. Decades of meticulous investment and development in the Southeast Asian region have enabled Japanese cars to establish a near-monopolistic hold in Indonesia.

The question then arises: how did Japanese companies achieve such a stronghold in the Southeast Asian automotive market?

Their strategy resembles the methodical constriction of a python. This constriction is deliberate, akin to the python encircling its prey with precision, regardless of its length. It is proficient at sensing the heartbeat of its prey, focusing its coiling strength around the heart. With no superfluous movements or indiscriminate attacks, its strategy is straightforward—suffocating the prey by impeding blood flow to the heart, resulting in an inevitable demise. This calculated approach ensures a fatal certainty.

In the competitive arena of Southeast Asia, Japanese car manufacturers exerted a stranglehold on the supply chain, akin to the lethal embrace of a python, effectively squeezing out European and American automotive giants from the fray. In Indonesia, powerhouses such as Toyota, Daihatsu, Suzuki, Honda, and Mitsubishi have virtually monopolized the automotive market, commanding over 90% of market share. This dominance compelled other international players like Ford, GM, and Volkswagen to retreat from the Indonesian landscape. Even Chinese brands, attempting to carve out a niche through direct exports or small-scale CKD assembly ventures, found only marginal success.

Despite GM's persistent optimism about Indonesia's market potential, its endeavors to introduce models from Republic of Korea, Brazil, and the United States encountered a decade-long struggle, ultimately failing to gain traction. The company's Indonesian operations saw the construction and subsequent closure of its factory not once, but twice, failing to lay down a stable manufacturing footprint. Eventually, GM had no recourse but to dismantle its equipment and relocate it to a facility in India.

This scenario underscores a broader competition concerning national supply chains.

The dominance of Japanese automakers in the Indonesian automotive market stems from their holistic approach to exporting their supply chain as an integrated package. This strategic transfer of industry is comparable to nurturing an entire forest rather than merely transplanting a single tree. Japanese car manufacturers have not ventured into the fray solo; they have implemented a full-scale strategy aimed at transferring an entire industrial ecosystem, rather than merely setting up a production facility for one brand. This comprehensive approach encompasses the supply chain, logistics, intelligence gathering, and financial services, presenting a formidable challenge that often overpowers competitors. The battle begins with an inherent imbalance when a national supply chain contends against a solitary company.

Japanese trading houses, known for their strategic acumen, excel in intelligence gathering while offering a diverse array of services in finance, logistics, and trade. A prime exemplar is Itochu Corporation, renowned for its exceptional knack for acquiring local market intelligence. It aids new Japanese entrants by furnishing them with potential customer lists and strategic recommendations from the outset. Itochu Corporation's considerable scale, evidenced by its 183rd rank on the Fortune 500 in 2014 with revenues of USD 55.2 billion[1], underscores its influence. Meanwhile,

---

① In 2018, Itochu Corporation experienced a significant revenue decline, halving its earnings. However, by 2020, it bounced back with a revenue of USD 100.5 billion, securing the 71st spot in the Fortune Global 500 ranking.

Mitsubishi Corporation, Japan's leading trading company, boasts even larger revenues of USD 75 billion.

This symbiotic relationship between intelligence, industry, and finance, a hallmark of Japanese market penetration strategies, lacks a direct equivalent in China. This discrepancy suggests that the global expansion of Chinese manufacturing has yet to reach its full potential. In Indonesia, entities like Itochu Corporation empower Japanese manufacturers to strike with precision, embodying a tactical advantage grounded in comprehensive market knowledge.

This scenario manifests as a strategic constriction through supply chain tactics. Japanese component suppliers, honed over years of development, are positioned to cater to international manufacturers, albeit at prices that can be more than triple those offered to domestic enterprises. Furthermore, the banking sector, under the sway of Japanese conglomerates, often imposes financing conditions on foreign companies that are approximately 50% more stringent than those for local businesses. Given Indonesia's archipelagic nature, which presents logistical challenges, reliance on Japan's advanced logistics and transportation networks becomes inevitable. However, this reliance comes with discriminatory hikes in shipping costs, adding another layer of complexity for international entrants navigating the Indonesian market.

The Japanese influence on the Indonesian automotive market extends to more subtle forms of market manipulation. Through strategic leadership in the drafting of regulations, standards, and policies, Japan has erected significant barriers to entry, effectively sidelining European and American automotive products in Indonesia. In 2013, the Indonesian government endorsed the Low Cost Green Car (LCGC) program, introducing various incentives to encourage the production of small cars. Preceding this initiative, Japan had actively engaged with the Indonesian government, leveraging its ambition to foster the development of lightweight and eco-friendly vehicles to shape the regulatory landscape in favor of such vehicles. Japan's historical expertise in manufacturing compact cars has led to the establishment of stringent industry norms, posing considerable challenges to foreign automakers. For example, the stipulation that cars must have a turning radius of less than 4.5 meters necessitates modifications to the wheelbase for many manufacturers, requiring significant redesigns of their vehicles. Additionally, the engine displacement limit of 1.5 liters imposes further constraints on numerous global brands. Tax incentives, pivotal in making vehicles financially appealing, are exclusively reserved for those meeting specific fuel consumption and pricing benchmarks, underscoring a meticulously orchestrated strategy to favor Japanese automotive dominance while constricting international competitors.

Japanese manufacturers have deftly ensnared their international competitors using a "soft rope", effectively nudging them out of contention in the Indonesian market. This strategic imposition of barriers has prevented automotive companies from other countries from penetrating the Indonesian market, essentially curtailing their growth opportunities while Japanese automakers continue to reign supreme.

The influence of Japanese standards extends even into the banking sector in Indonesia. Qualification exams for employees at Indonesian banks and financial institutions are established by Japan, with a historical precedent that even necessitated taking these exams in Japan. This control over professional standards illustrates a significant level of discourse power, indicative of the python supply chain strategy.

As countries progress through various stages of economic development, they may employ economic entanglement as a tactical approach, funneling extensive resources into developing countries for broad-spectrum investment collaboration. In Indonesia, property development giants like Sinar Mas have collaborated with Japanese consortia, often entities such as Mitsubishi Corporation and Toyota Tsusho Corporation, to co-manage industrial real estate ventures. The Indonesian banking landscape also features numerous joint ventures, underscoring the substantial support provided by Japanese banking institutions to industries like automotive, among others.

Within the automotive sector, Japanese brands have proliferated across Indonesia, establishing a comprehensive network of sales companies and accompanying manufacturing enterprises, thereby creating a full-fledged industry chain. This expansion has facilitated the entry of components from Republic of Korea and Taiwan of China into the Indonesian market, predominantly supporting the Japanese vehicle supply chain, albeit ultimately reinforcing Japanese automotive dominance—a strategy echoed in Thailand.

In his memoir *My Years with Renault*, Louis Schweitzer, former CEO of Renault, muses on the patient market cultivation and tolerance for initial financial setbacks characteristic of Japanese car manufacturers. This long-term strategy saw Japan operating at a loss in African and Southeast Asian markets for the first 15 to 20 years. By 2005, these regions, alongside the Middle East, had largely succumbed to Japanese vehicular dominance[1].

---

① Louis Schweitzer. *My Years with Renault*, trans. Yang Wenqian[M]. Qingdao Publishing House, 2009, 146.

Toyota's foray into the Chinese market followed a similarly cautious trajectory. In 2000, Toyota formed a joint venture with Tianjin Automobile Industry Group, establishing Tianjin FAW Toyota Motor Co., Ltd. Yet, Toyota's groundwork began well before official approvals, with the introduction of nearly 30 parts suppliers to China in anticipation. Since 1995, Toyota had been laying the groundwork with the establishment of the Toyota China Domestic Production Technical Support Center, underscoring a deliberate and methodical approach to market entry[1].

Toyota's patient approach to entering the Chinese market was far from passive; it was a strategic maneuver spearheaded by Toyota Tsusho[2], beginning in August 1993 with the construction of China's inaugural plant for aluminum wheel rims in Kunshan, Jiangsu. Subsequently, the establishment of 25 auto component factories followed suit, all laying the groundwork for Toyota's forthcoming automotive launch in China. Interestingly, many of these supporting businesses operated below their production capacity, prompting questions about the financial rationale behind such investments. However, Toyota Tsusho's strategic foresight is indicative of a deeper, more calculated plan. It was meticulously preparing the terrain for Toyota's successful market entry, emblematic of the Japanese approach to international expansion. Japan's commitment to exhaustive preparatory research is unparalleled globally, with a significant portion of investment in the analysis of the Chinese market originating from Japan.

Toyota's entry into the Chinese automotive market resembled a strategic chess game rather than a straightforward battle. Initially, Toyota engaged through joint ventures for small passenger cars with Tianjin (culminating in the Xiali in 1998) and large passenger vehicles in Sichuan (culminating in the Coaster in 2000), demonstrating strategic patience. With an astute eye on the evolving Chinese sedan market, Toyota, in 2002, encouraged its partner, FAW Group, to amalgamate these ventures, thereby optimizing its resources. This strategic consolidation set the stage for the formation of GAC Toyota with the GAC Group in 2004, aligning with the regulatory limit that restricted foreign automakers to establishing only two joint ventures within China. Concurrently, the groundbreaking of the GAC Toyota engine

---

① China Association of Automobile Manufacturers. *30 Years of Reform and Opening-up in China's Automobile Industry (1978–2008): A Retrospective and Outlook*[M]. China Logistics Publishing House, 2009, 124.

② Bai Yimin. *The Mitsui Empire in Action: Unveiling the Japanese Consortium's Strategic Layout in China*[M]. China Economic Publishing House, 2008, 174.

plant in the same year underscored the multifaceted strategy employed by Toyota—characteristic of seasoned strategists who plan several moves ahead rather than proceeding sequentially. By leveraging indirect tactics and maintaining agile mobilization, Toyota has strategically positioned itself as a frontrunner in the market, despite seemingly entering later than some competitors.

The misconception surrounding Toyota's belated entry into the Chinese market primarily stems from the timing of its flagship product launches, which might suggest trailing behind competitors. However, Toyota's strategy has been one of meticulous preparation and intelligence gathering, aimed at a profound comprehension of the dynamics of the Chinese market. Drawing on its extensive experience in global operations, Toyota subscribes to the philosophy that global expansion is akin to a marathon rather than a sprint, emphasizing the importance of a long-term, strategic approach over immediate, bold actions.

Competition exists not only globally but also among Japanese brands themselves. In Indonesia, for instance, Toyota's Daihatsu is in fierce contention with Suzuki, while Honda and Mitsubishi actively vie for market dominance. A core group of Toyota's suppliers shares technology, resources, and mutual stockholdings, creating a cohesive unit. Behind this network lie trading companies and banks, often interlinked with shared stakeholders, illustrating a complex tapestry of rivalry and collaboration that effectively excludes foreign competitors.

Stability in the upstream supply chain, essential for achieving cost reduction, is only attainable through a collective concentration of manufacturers. This scenario transcends mere corporate competition, embodying a deep-rooted collective effort toward internationalization within a country's supply chain.

9.3 Lost and Found Amidst Cultural Ambiguity

Indonesia's automotive market, though fiercely competitive, is not without its Achilles' heel. Japanese vehicles in Indonesia are often iterations of older, second-generation models, a strategy move by Japanese automakers to extend the lifecycle of existing technologies and maximize profit margins. In contrast, SGMW's lineup boasts the integration of cutting-edge automotive electronics, underpinned by robust confidence in cost management, hinting at the potential to fundamentally revolutionize the market.

The broader dynamics of the Indonesian market closely mirror those of Chinese cities, characterized by a pronounced demand for vehicles offering high cost-performance ratios, particularly targeting the more affordable segments of the market—a domain where SGMW excels. Over the past decade, Indonesia has witnessed a significant increase in its middle-class proportion, reaching 56.5% by 2010[①], reflecting a society with a penchant for group travel, thus favoring minivans. MPV models, which typically account for about 30% of vehicle sales in Indonesia[②], align well with this preference, catering to a demand for simple, multipurpose vans featuring three rows of seating for seven or eight passengers. Given this market landscape and SGMW's prowess in delivering low-cost, high-value vehicles with distinct features, the company is well-positioned to present a significant challenge to the entrenched dominance of Japanese automakers in Indonesia.

The seeds of curiosity sown by Shen Yang's exploratory journey to Indonesia 11 years prior have now bloomed in their due season. Amidst the tight-knit fabric of local Japanese automaker alliances and their entrenched market positions, SGMW courageously ventured into Indonesia, determined to carve out its niche. In the latter half of 2014, a pivotal step was taken as the independent overseas base project was initiated within the auxiliary building of SGMW's Hexi base in Liuzhou, laying the cornerstone for what would become the operational heart of the Indonesian subsidiary. Furthermore, in a demonstration of focused ambition, the "0062 Project Team" was established, deriving its name from Indonesia's international calling code. This determined, goal-driven ethos characterizes SGMW, underscoring a collective commitment to their aspirations and effectively articulating the company's mission to all stakeholders involved.

Embarking on the journey to establish operations in Indonesia, the 0062 Project Team from SGMW navigated through a sea of uncertainties. Their first and arguably most pivotal hurdle was selecting the right factory location in a country as vast as Indonesia. The automotive industry's heart beats strongly within a 50-kilometer radius east of Jakarta, nestled in the industrial corridor, where virtually all major automakers converge. This concentration presents a distinct challenge, as all

---

① Ji Liya. SGMW: From Egypt to Indonesia[J]. *Automotive Observer*, 2017.

② Zheng Wenqing, Hu Duojun, Peng Huibo. Analysis of Current Situation and Development Trend of Indonesian Passenger Car Market[J]. *Auto Time*, 2022.

industrial real estate within the region is privately owned, guiding the team through a labyrinth of decision-making process fraught with Indonesian-specific land issues. These included warrant traps, traffic dilemmas, passive land acquisition, energy shortages, private dominance, and discrepancies between central and local government directives, each adding layers of complexity to their mission. Following exhaustive investigation and deliberation, SGMW opted for a location within the Cikarang industrial zone in Bekasi, West Java. The chosen plot, situated in a depression and filled to ground level, intriguingly lay just below the elevation of the neighboring factory across the street, which was none other than a Suzuki factory. This positioning sets the stage for SGMW to directly confront a seasoned competitor at their doorstep—a bold move signaling their preparedness to compete.

Directly opposite the nascent SGMW venture, Suzuki's expansive new automotive facility sprawls across an impressive 1.3 million square meters. Launched in 2013 with a substantial investment of JPY 60 billion (approximately USD 611 million), it began operations in 2015, marking the relocation of Suzuki Ertiga MPV production from the Tambun Plant to this modern facility, which augmented Suzuki's Indonesian production capabilities to a robust annual output of nearly 250,000 vehicles across its two factories. In a similar vein, Mitsubishi Motors, another Japanese powerhouse, unveiled plans to establish a factory southwest of Suzuki's, with an investment matching Suzuki's JPY 60 billion, which was projected to have an annual production capacity of 160,000 vehicles. Furthermore, an expansive plot exceeding one million square meters, initially earmarked for GM, lay in wait. However, in a twist reminiscent of the narrative *Waiting for Godot*, GM—the anticipated "Godot"—never materialized, creating an opportunity for a Chinese manufacturer to enter the scene. Amidst this competitive landscape, largely dominated by Japanese manufacturers, August 2015 saw the groundbreaking of the SGMW Indonesia factory. With an ambitious investment plan totaling USD 700 million and spanning 600,000 square meters—equally divided between the main plant and a supplier park—the facility was envisioned to achieve a production capacity of 120,000 complete vehicles annually, encompassing the full spectrum of the four major manufacturing processes.

The venture of setting up manufacturing facilities abroad is more than just a business expansion; it is an immersive cultural experience. The selection of the site for SGMW's factory, following thorough deliberation and dialogue, presented its own set of cultural challenges. Originally owned by villagers and later acquired by a developer for industrial purposes, the land's transition lacked effective communication with the local community, who continued their traditional use of the space for grazing and agriculture. The commencement of construction caught the villagers off guard, prompting them to express their discontent by placing wooden stakes adorned with red cloth on the site—an emblematic gesture to halt the advancement of construction machinery. In navigating these intricacies, the project team turned to local insights for resolution. Through respectful gestures and offerings, they engaged with the Muslim village elders, paving the way for the progression of construction. Recognizing the importance of integrating into the local community, SGMW extended acts of goodwill on various occasions, including donating a cow for Eid celebrations, distributing backpacks to children, providing employment opportunities to local residents, and contributing to village welfare. In the realm of manufacturing, where the establishment is inherently long-term, the ability to adapt to local traditions, foster goodwill, and maintain harmonious relations with the community is paramount.

The establishment of SGMW's factory in Indonesia was a formidable international relocation endeavor, with 80% of the necessary components for the build, including crucial equipment such as large workshop fans, sourced from China. Remarkably, this massive undertaking consumed only 80% of the allocated budget, owing in part to the strategic procurement of materials during a period of favorable global steel prices. Capitalizing on this opportune moment, the project team sourced materials globally, with the exception of cement, which was locally procured. Key construction elements, such as steel structures, doors, windows, and glass, were imported from China, underscoring the factory's strong ties to its Chinese origins. The construction itself was executed by reputable Chinese firms, including the Jinan Second Machine Tool Group Co., Ltd. and the Fourth Design and Research Institute of Machinery Industry Co., Ltd., ensuring that all mechanical and electrical equipment was brought over from China.

This monumental effort painted the Indonesian skies with a symphony of Made-in-China excellence, with SGMW orchestrating the entire operation. Initially met with skepticism, the project quickly transformed into a showcase of Chinese efficiency and quality, earning widespread admiration from the Indonesian populace. This venture not only cemented SGMW's reputation for speed and quality but also elevated its standing at the governmental level in Indonesia, significantly enhancing its influence within the region.

SGMW's best operating practices (BOP) and business operations environment (BOE), honed through repeated applications across various regions in China—spanning from the Hexi base in Liuzhou to the Qingdao branch, and onward to the Liudong Baojun base launched in 2012, followed by the Chongqing branch operational by 2014—had reached a zenith of refinement by the initiation of the Indonesian factory. This extensive track record ensured that quality control and operational procedures were well-established, facilitating a seamless transition to the new facility.

On its inaugural day, strategically positioned directly opposite the Japanese Suzuki factory, SGMW's Indonesian factory unveiled itself with a grand ceremony, a bold proclamation of its competitive stance. The event garnered attention not only from Suzuki but also from representatives and audiences of nearby Honda and Mitsubishi plants, underscoring the significance of the occasion.

As the ceremony unfolded, marking the commencement of operations, it heralded the dawn of a new era in the automotive rivalry.

9.4 Blazing Trails Across Barriers

PT SGMW Motor Indonesia embraced GM's global manufacturing system while introducing significant adaptations tailored to the enterprise's developmental stage and unique characteristics. The adoption of SGMW's hallmark "low cost, high value" lean production philosophy notably slashed construction expenses, particularly in the paint shop, to less than half of what would typically be incurred by GM. This astute cost management strategy allowed for the creation of a factory designed for an annual output of 250,000 vehicles with a budget of under USD 500 million in Southeast Asia. Yet, SGMW's innovative approach in Indonesia brought this figure down to a mere USD 150 million. This efficient and cost-effective model of factory construction has since become a global standard within GM, particularly in developing markets such as India, South America, and Southeast Asia.

Automation in manufacturing processes at SGMW is nuanced by labor costs and operational scale, beginning with an evaluation of human potential before determining the appropriate level of automation. This approach is rooted in the conviction that human effort should underpin all endeavors. From an empty plot, they constructed a comprehensive vehicle manufacturing facility, integrating four critical manufacturing processes alongside a quality inspection system. However, establishing the factory was only the initial step; developing a robust supply chain is equally vital.

The inception of a complete vehicle factory in Indonesia necessitated the forging of alliances with both upstream and downstream partners within the industrial chain. In March 2016, Guangxi Automobile Group, a long-standing supplier to SGMW, expanded its horizons by setting up a passenger car component production base in Indonesia, marking its entry into international markets for mutual growth. By July of the same year, this endeavor reached fruition with the inauguration of PT. LZWL Motors Indonesia in Jakarta, signifying the formal completion and commencement of production operations. This venture represented Guangxi Automobile Group's inaugural overseas manufacturing base, supported by an investment of RMB 210 million, which enabled the establishment of six primary production lines, including stamping, welding, and assembly, thereby cultivating core competencies in the fabrication of passenger vehicle components like chassis and welded parts.

The collaborative ethos extended beyond borders as a cohort of prominent domestic and international suppliers, including industry giants such as China Baowu Steel Group, Nexteer Automotive, and Mann+Hummel, committed to investments in Indonesia. This collective endeavor saw 16 domestic suppliers establish their presence within the supply chain park, embracing the challenge of conducting international business operations in Indonesia. Concurrently with the commencement of complete vehicle production by PT SGMW Motor Indonesia, the component factories of these suppliers were erected and operationalized.

Integrating the supply chain into such overseas ventures was not merely strategic but imperative. In compliance with the stipulations of the Southeast Asian Free Trade Area, SGMW recognized the importance of fostering partnerships with local Indonesian suppliers. However, a significant challenge arose: the predominant alignment of local suppliers with Japanese automotive brands, leaving little room for newcomers.

How could SGMW effectively engage with Indonesian suppliers to integrate them into Wuling's manufacturing ecosystem?

The introduction of even the fundamental workflow procedures, commonplace in China, required detailed explanations and training sessions for Indonesian suppliers. This encompassed everything from standard process quotations and filling out forms for entry into the supply chain system to understanding general terms of purchase.

SGMW essentially had to train local suppliers from the ground up.

After evaluating close to 100 Indonesian enterprises, SGMW selected 23 to become official component suppliers, many of which had previously received training from Japanese automotive firms, leading to a strong inclination toward Japanese operational methodologies. Initially balked at SGMW's manufacturing guidelines, the local suppliers required multiple technical discussions for their implementation. This iterative process evolved into a reciprocal learning experience, with Indonesian suppliers also offering valuable insights to SGMW. A case in point involved the roof liner's production to mitigate vibration and wind noise. While Wuling typically opted for thicker materials to meet noise reduction standards, Indonesian suppliers suggested a technique favored by Daihatsu, involving thinner materials and a simpler installation process, augmented by just two additional clips. Despite the less polished appearance of these clips, they resonated well with Indonesian consumers, highlighting regional aesthetic preferences. Swiftly adapting, SGMW embraced this feedback, acknowledging the variability of aesthetic preferences and practical solutions across markets, emphasizing the absence of a universal standard in automotive manufacturing.

Venturing overseas entails not only the establishment of production facilities but also the development of an efficient market distribution network, a task laden with challenges, particularly in a country like Indonesia. Being the world's largest archipelago, with around 17,500 islands sprawled between the Pacific and Indian Oceans, Indonesia demands precise strategizing to focus distribution efforts in densely populated regions such as Java, Sumatra, and Bali. Identifying the most appropriate sales locations across these diverse islands, all while contending with the entrenched dominance of Japanese automobiles, poses a formidable challenge.

Exploring foreign customs reveals intriguing differences. In China, it is customary to see new car displays in malls as spectacles for passersby to admire and photograph, though actual purchases within these shopping complexes remain uncommon. Conversely, in Indonesia, the presence of cars showcased in large malls and supermarkets is more than a mere exhibition; these venues become hubs of active sales activity. The Indonesian penchant for leisurely walks in the cool comfort of air-conditioned malls translates into both a casual and deliberate car browsing experience. Encouraged by lively promotional events replete with music and dance, spontaneous purchasing decisions are not uncommon. Adjacent to the display areas, rows of tables facilitate one-on-one consultations, often resulting in on-the-spot orders during these mall-based events.

Beyond manufacturing and supply chain integration, the imperative to establish a robust sales and service infrastructure in Indonesia was palpable. Wuling faced initial reluctance from Indonesian automobile dealers and local component suppliers, who often benchmarked their operations against those of Japanese automakers. The Indonesian automotive market is distinguished by its heavy reliance on financial credit for vehicle purchases, presenting a unique challenge for Wuling, which initially lacked its own finance company. Consequently, engaging with the existing Japanese financial infrastructure would mean adhering to their stringent terms. For example, while the down payment for vehicles from Japanese brands stood at 10%, Wuling vehicles faced a minimum down payment requirement of 25%, imposing a greater financial strain on prospective Wuling car buyers. The robust trade in used cars in Indonesia further underscored the importance of a sophisticated financial system.

Credit serves as a lifeline for the automotive sector, and with Japanese firms holding sway over this crucial aspect, the barriers to entry for Chinese independent brands in the Indonesian market were significantly heightened. Faced with the financing disparities perpetuated by Japanese firms, the resolution lay in confronting the challenge head-on. In a landmark development in September 2018, China's first overseas automotive finance entity, PT. SGMW Multifinance Indonesia, was inaugurated in Jakarta. This strategic establishment empowered Indonesian customers to purchase Wuling vehicles with the same ease as Japanese brands, lowering the down payment ratio to just 10%.

To effectively challenge the prevailing dominance of Japanese automobiles in the market, these strategic approaches are indispensable. Every facet, from land allocation to regulatory frameworks, demands meticulous attention to facilitate the gradual establishment and deepening of Chinese manufacturing presence. In 2018, Dongfeng Motor Corporation capitalized on this imperative by introducing an SUV model under its DFSK brand in Indonesia. Notably, the entry-level version of this SUV was priced at just half of what Toyota's CHR was retailing for in Indonesia at that time. The convergence of strategies between SGMW and Dongfeng Motor Corporation hinged on their concerted efforts to scale up production capacity within Indonesia while leveraging competitive pricing as a key tactic to disrupt the entrenched dominance of Japanese vehicles. The burgeoning trend of Chinese manufacturers going global heralds a promising transformation, signaling a growing presence in the international arena.

9.5 Mastery of Localization

The SGMW facility in Indonesia has adopted the CKD assembly method for production. Despite the Wuling Hongguang's established success in China, its introduction to the Indonesian market encountered notable challenges necessitating adaptation. In July 2017, Wuling's Indonesian division celebrated a significant milestone with the debut of the Wuling Confero S, its inaugural product. The name "Confero," encapsulating the essence of "gathering" or "coming together", marked the model's entrance into Indonesia, drawing upon the legacy of the Wuling Hongguang from China.

Ahead of the product launch, extensive advertising initiatives were launched, and a multitude of vehicles were distributed to dealerships for test drives. However, these test drives brought to light an unexpected issue—transmission failures, a problem unprecedented in the model's history within the Chinese market, where millions of units had been sold without such an incident. Responding to this unforeseen challenge, the Indonesian branch of Wuling promptly activated an emergency response; key personnel were deployed to various dealerships to directly assess the issue and conduct thorough investigations.

The root cause of the issue was swiftly pinpointed to the vehicle's performance at high speeds. In Indonesia, where road surveillance cameras are scarce and speed regulations less stringent, it is common for drivers to exceed speeds of 150 kilometers per hour—a stark contrast to China's highway speed limits, typically capped at 120 kilometers per hour or lower. Dealers, often driving home after dark, would push the vehicles to such high speeds for prolonged periods, subjecting the transmission to stress levels beyond its design parameters. At speeds of 150 kilometers per hour, particularly when sustained for an extended duration, transmission components were susceptible to slipping out due to centrifugal force, subsequently becoming trapped in the reverse gear fork and leading to malfunctions.

Confronted with an impending product launch and pressed for time, Wuling's Indonesian division acted decisively. The company expedited the import of six lifting machines to the factory, where several hundred vehicles were elevated and their transmission assemblies dismantled for overnight modifications. Additionally, temporary production lines were set up, and personnel were promptly mobilized from the Liuzhou headquarters to Indonesia to rectify thousands of components. Over two weeks of intense and focused efforts, the team managed to resolve the faults, ensuring the product launch proceeded as planned.

The discovery of such malfunctions highlights a crucial aspect of global expansion: standard test drives may not reveal the myriad ways a vehicle could be used in foreign landscapes. These distinct usage patterns, while uncommon in the manufacturer's home country, can evolve into commonplace practices in overseas markets, underscoring a common oversight in the process of globalization. Relying solely on established norms without accounting for local intricacies can lead to unexpected setbacks.

For SGMW, making inroads into the Indonesian automotive sector rests heavily on its capacity to differentiate itself from established Japanese competitors. Mere exportation of popular models from the domestic portfolio proves insufficient. The inaugural product, adapted from the Wuling Hongguang, underwent substantial alterations tailored to the Indonesian market, including conversion to right-hand drive and adjustments to accommodate local road conditions, such as chassis recalibration. Given Indonesia's less developed infrastructure, characterized by sparse highways and subpar road conditions, coupled with the prevalent use of speed bumps to regulate traffic speed, these adaptations extended to broader modifications, such as the redesign of shock absorbers and springs. This scenario elucidates a vital lesson in global expansion: transplanting domestically successful products abroad without customization seldom meets the nuanced demands of diverse regional markets.

The 2019 agreement between GM and SGMW, whereby 2,500 vehicles customized for the Chevrolet brand were ordered from SGMW's Indonesian factory for export to Thailand, initially stood as a testament to Indonesia's industrial success, lauded by the Indonesian Minister of Industry. However, the narrative took an unexpected turn upon the vehicles' arrival in Thailand, coinciding with GM's decision to withdraw from the Thai market.

This abrupt change in strategy blindsided all parties involved. A fundamental element of SGMW's global expansion strategy hinged on leveraging the global networks of its shareholders. GM possessed an established distribution network in Thailand but lacked products, while SGMW possessed the necessary products but lacked a distribution network—a seemingly synergistic and ideal partnership. GM's departure from Thailand, however, left SGMW grappling with a complex dilemma.

With time being of the essence, entering the Thai market anew under the Wuling brand presented significant challenges. The establishment of new channels, the introduction of fresh products, and the cultivation of brand recognition and negotiating power would not only demand significant resources but would also squander a critical two- to three-year period that could have been pivotal for growth. This setback also impacted SGMW's broader strategy of utilizing its Indonesian manufacturing hub as a springboard for expansion across Southeast Asia.

The endeavor of globalizing a business is laden with unforeseen challenges. Stumbling into these obstacles may leave one mired in difficulties, but the path forward requires resilience—to rise above adversity, dusting oneself off and steadfastly navigating through barriers. The pursuit of globalization, though often viewed as prestigious, is fundamentally characterized by unwavering resolve and the perseverance required to confront the arduous trials encountered along the journey.

9.6 The Best Diplomatic Engagement

Localized manufacturing often serves as the cornerstone for fostering successful international relations. When the SGMW delegation first met with Saleh Husin, then Minister of Industry of Indonesia, in 2015, the proposition of concurrently establishing a primary plant and a supplier park appeared almost fantastical to him. Saleh Husin's skepticism was not unwarranted; no Chinese manufacturing company had ever proposed such an ambitious project in Indonesia. For the Indonesian government, SGMW's venture represented not only a significant investment but also the first full-scale automotive factory investment by a non-Japanese entity. The lingering question persisted: What drove SGMW to undertake such a daring investment, and was their motive solely to secure an audience with the minister?

The team's subsequent visit six months later turned skepticism into astonishment. They presented a signed contract for 600,000 square meters of land, accompanied by detailed plans to establish an automotive industrial park within just two years. Against all odds, a vision that initially seemed like a distant dream was on the verge of becoming a reality, marking the beginning of a miraculous journey in Indonesia's industrial landscape.

Following his initial meeting, Saleh Husin received an invitation to tour

SGMW's Qingdao base, an experience that profoundly impacted his perspective. The bustling activity within the workshops left a lasting impression on him, fueling a newfound enthusiasm for Wuling's products. Enthralled by the moment, Husin eagerly posed for photographs alongside the Wuling Hongguang and Baojun 730 models, exchanging his winter attire for a crisp white shirt to present the most favorable image for Wuling vehicles.

"I'm all in on backing Wuling."

"Make sure you get my pictures with these Wuling cars out to every big name in the Indonesian press."

"I'm happy to advertise for Wuling, free of charge."

This shift from skepticism to staunch advocacy highlighted a remarkable transformation. The Indonesian minister, now fully captivated by the prowess of Chinese manufacturing, became a fervent advocate for the Made-in-China narrative. He took every opportunity to share Wuling's story with his cabinet colleagues, local government officials, and potential investors, passionately endorsing a bold, innovative company striving to make its mark in an automotive market long dominated by Japanese brands. This advocacy, rooted in genuine admiration for Wuling's ambition and quality, stood as one of his tenure's most fulfilling accomplishments.

"I'll never stop sharing this story", vowed the former Minister of Industry, making it clear this was more than just lip service. At every car expo, Indonesian ministers of industry and commerce were consistently making a beeline for the Wuling display, snapping photos as their way of throwing support behind the brand. Even the president of Indonesia himself dropped by, genuinely impressed by SGMW's venture into Indonesia—a daring move from a foreign entity unfamiliar with the local language. In a setting where many factories shy away from hiring women, fearing they may not match the efficiency of their male counterparts, SGMW breaks the mold by championing gender equality on its assembly lines. Also acknowledging that many of their local workers are devout Muslims who observe prayer five times daily, even during work shifts, the company has integrated prayer rooms directly within the workshop area, reflecting its respect for local culture. Furthermore, recognizing the need for a larger gathering during Friday prayers, the decision to build a mosque right on the factory grounds speaks volumes. These thoughtful gestures deeply resonated with a visiting Indonesian minister, who perceived in these actions the hallmarks of a truly exemplary company—one that not only operates within the community but also enriches it.

The global recognition of the manufacturing sector's role in fostering local employment and pioneering innovation is increasingly evident, particularly in Southeast Asia, where governments prioritize the localization of manufacturing operations as a strategic imperative. Indonesia, endowed with world-leading nickel ore reserves estimated at about 1.3 billion tons of resources and 600 million tons of confirmed reserves, plays a pivotal role. Nickel holds significant importance for lithium-ion batteries, a cornerstone of the electric vehicle industry. In its quest to build a local manufacturing ecosystem, Indonesia has imposed restrictions on raw material exports, a challenge that Chinese manufacturers must navigate as part of their going global strategies.

The entrenched dominance of Japanese vehicles in Southeast Asia faces its challenges, particularly within the burgeoning electric vehicle sector, where substantial gaps in market coverage become apparent. SGMW's introduction of the global small electric vehicle (GSEV) platform is revolutionizing the small electric vehicle market by setting new benchmarks in spatial efficiency, safety, energy consumption, energy sourcing, and service offerings. Anchored in its Indonesian operations, SGMW proactively participates in shaping Indonesia's policies, technical standards, and infrastructure planning for new energy vehicles. In a landmark moment at the Indonesia International Motor Show (IIMS) in Jakarta in April 2021, the Indonesian Electric Vehicle Industry Association (Periklindo) was unveiled at Wuling's booth, with Wuling assuming a pivotal role as an important member. This occasion signifies a significant shift in the Indonesian automotive landscape, representing the first instance of an automotive association breaking free from the conventional influence of Japanese automakers.

The harmonization of Indonesia's electric vehicle standards with China's established benchmarks, including charging voltages (380-volt or 220-volt) and charging interface specifications, marks a pivotal juncture for the global expansion of Chinese electric vehicles. This alignment opens a door that could redefine competitive dynamics within Indonesia's automotive sector, particularly in the realm of electric vehicles. While the Japanese automotive industry once clinched dominance in Indonesia's small car sector through the LCGC initiative, the burgeoning electric vehicle market emerged as uncharted territory ripe for exploration.

Against the backdrop of the Belt and Road Initiative, Chinese manufacturing stands poised to assert a leadership position. Despite China's considerable experience in cross-border e-commerce and international trade, extending the global reach of its manufacturing bases introduces a unique set of challenges. SGMW is at the forefront of addressing these challenges, recognizing that successful integration into local markets and alignment with the trend toward localization can transform manufacturing into a potent instrument for diplomatic engagement at its best.

9.7 An Arduous Ascent

Globally, Japanese corporations not only replicate but often surpass their domestic successes in terms of earnings and scale. Data from 2021 reveal that Japan's international assets were over twice the size of its domestic GDP, illustrating the extensive global reach of its manufacturing capabilities. However, navigating the path to global prominence is rife with challenges, particularly in the automotive sector, where Chinese manufacturing is rapidly advancing, with its pioneers boldly stepping into the competition.

Bogotá, nestled in the highlands east of the Andes Mountains in northwestern South America, serves as the capital of Colombia and stands as the country's largest city[①], renowned worldwide for its rich coffee and exquisite emeralds. Nevertheless, when it comes to automotive traffic, Bogotá presents a distinctive tableau of congestion. In this city, the pace of vehicular movement is notably slow.

Nestled among the mountainous outskirts of Bogotá lies a road stretching nearly 80 kilometers, with a gentle average incline of 4%, reaching heights of 3,200 meters. This route is revered as a sanctuary for cyclists worldwide, offering a challenging yet picturesque journey. However, for drivers, the scenic landscape offers little respite as they often lament the slow-paced traffic that characterizes the area. The limited opportunities for passing on lengthy uphill stretches, particularly when stuck behind a lumbering bus in single-lane scenarios, can extend a journey over 20 or 30 kilometers to well over half an hour. These winding mountain roads are a common sight throughout Ecuador and Colombia, presenting a unique challenge for any automotive company vying for a foothold in these markets. The key lies in vehicles capable of handling the demanding ascents at high altitudes. Embracing this challenge, SGMW conducted rigorous test drives in the region to fine-tune transmission gear ratios from

---

① Bogotá is also the third-largest city in South America, boasting a population exceeding 10 million.

the design phase itself, ensuring their cars are well-suited for frequent uphill starts. The culmination of these meticulous efforts is the Wuling Hongguang V, initially manufactured for export by SGMW's Chongqing company and now proudly wearing the Chevrolet N400's golden bowtie, conquering the steep roads across Bogotá.

Mexico, with its vast population exceeding 100 million and an annual automotive market that sees the sale of around 1.3 million vehicles, has emerged as a pivotal destination for Chinese vehicle exports and a fiercely contested arena for Chinese automakers. The country's unique driving conditions, characterized by an average altitude of around 2,000 meters and the prevalence of cobblestone roads, present distinct challenges for vehicles, including persistent noise issues for drivers. Additionally, its rainy climate and susceptibility to flooding further complicate vehicle manufacturing and maintenance, particularly concerning paint durability. Furthermore, penetrating the Mexican market necessitates adherence to US emission standards, adding another layer of complexity for foreign manufacturers.

Acknowledging the unique demands and challenges of the Mexican automotive landscape, SGMW adopted a targeted approach with the development of the Baojun 530, rigorously optimizing the materials used for the vehicle's body components to enhance their resilience against the corrosive impacts of Mexico's frequent flooding. Recognizing the heightened demand for connectivity among Mexican users, particularly the necessity for smartphone mirroring capabilities, the Baojun 530 was engineered to support screen mirroring for both Apple and Android devices, ensuring a seamless user experience.

Throughout the project's developmental phase, the calibration testing of prototype vehicles in Mexico benefited from support provided by the GM technical team. To conduct high-altitude calibration tests, engineers found themselves coordinating with their counterparts in Mexico during the early hours, typically around 1:00 or 2:00 a.m., to bridge the significant time difference. This challenge of synchronizing across time zones paralleled the task of adapting to high-altitude conditions, effectively testing the collaborative synergy between the Chinese engineers and their Mexican colleagues.

In March 2021, the Chevrolet Captiva, rebranded from the Baojun 530, made a splash in the Mexican market, swiftly ascending to the top spot in the compact SUV category with an impressive 18% market share within a mere six months. This remarkable achievement placed it ahead of well-established competitors such as Honda and Toyota. By April 2022, it had risen to become the highest-volume Chinese export car model. Every manufacturer harboring global ambitions aspires to create a universal model that resonates across diverse markets, which not only prolongs the product's life cycle but also leaves a lasting imprint within a global strategy framework. Quietly ascending to this status, the Baojun 530 has emerged as a contender in various territories. Since early 2019, it has been rebranded into three international versions—the Chevrolet Captiva, Wuling Almaz, and MG Hector—marking its presence in markets spanning Indonesia, South America, Thailand, and India. It stands out as the first SUV to feature four distinct brand logos and has reached consumers in 19 countries, symbolizing a seamless fusion of multinational cooperation and strategy. The Baojun 530's journey exemplifies how globalization demands adaptability, showing that manufacturing, branding, and distribution can effectively connect across borders, propelling Chinese manufacturing to the forefront of the global stage.

This evolution signifies a new era wherein the patience and long-term vision of Chinese automakers are redefining their commitment to the global automotive landscape.

9.8 Reversing Fortunes: From Downturn to Triumph

Globalization strategies vary significantly among automotive companies worldwide, each characterized by unique approaches. Japanese automakers notably excel in adaptability, integrating deeply into local markets through extensive localization efforts. American companies, on the other hand, tend to adhere to universal standards while displaying flexibility in their global operations. Their approach to global sourcing, aimed at minimizing costs, can be likened to a "global nomadic strategy", moving across the globe in search of the most cost-effective solutions.

The path to internationalization for Chinese manufacturers is one of deep integration with local markets, tailoring their offerings to meet the specific demands and preferences of regional consumers. An exemplary illustration of this approach is SGMW's "Indonesia model", which emphasizes the development of self-built products, base, brand, supply system, and marketing networks. This strategy marks a departure from earlier phases centered on simple trade exports and price competition, ushering in a new era of globalization for Chinese manufacturing. The ability to deliver competitive products, operate with cost efficiency, and uphold a robust supply chain system has become the cornerstone of Chinese manufacturing's global strategy.

SGMW's developmental trajectory has not only fulfilled but far exceeded GM's most optimistic forecasts, seamlessly amalgamating global resources with the distinctive features of local industries and securing a prominent position in terms of Chinese cost-efficiency. This achievement underscores a unique contribution of Chinese manufacturing to the global arena, reflecting the distinctive characteristics of Chinese factory settings, where the ingenuity of hands-on engineers in the factory has forged innovative pathways that distinguish SGMW from its peers. Meanwhile, structural shifts have reshaped the manufacturing landscape in the United States, rendering the production of cars priced below RMB 200,000 increasingly unsustainable. German manufacturers, renowned for their quality, also face stiff competition, while Japan grapples with the formidable challenge posed by China's cost-effective manufacturing prowess.

The pace of mass production flourishes under the domain of high-speed machinery, achieving the remarkable feat of assembling two vehicles per minute. This necessitates the completion of assembly tasks at each station within a mere 60 seconds, allowing no margin for error. Such unparalleled efficiency stands as a testament to the adoption of GMS, originally inspired by Toyota's lean manufacturing principles from Japan, which have since been refined. The exponential growth in SGMW's annual production, scaling from several hundred thousand to more than two million units, is a direct result of this sophisticated manufacturing system.

While excelling in efficiency, the manufacturing system faces challenges in accommodating the need for flexible production, particularly when faced with rapidly changing orders. SGMW's production volume can fluctuate significantly, dropping to 50,000 to 60,000 vehicles per month during slower periods and swiftly escalating to 200,000 vehicles during peak seasons. This variability, stemming from diverse, small-batch, and flexible orders, puts pressure on the highly standardized manufacturing system. However, SGMW's commitment to integrating flexible production lines and maintaining low-cost manufacturing enhances its distinct manufacturing profile, showcasing an ability to adapt and thrive amidst fluctuating market demands.

GMS, a sophisticated ensemble of manufacturing system management tools, has been instrumental in enhancing operations at SGMW. Nonetheless, its effectiveness relies heavily on adaptability in application. A fundamental tenet of GMS dictates that the car body must not touch the ground to prevent unnecessary movements that could introduce waste and compromise quality. Ideally, from production onset to final assembly, the body remains elevated to ensure efficiency and maintain order, which is particularly crucial when dealing with high volumes, as placing the body down could disrupt storage timing and lead to operational disruptions. Yet, the supply chain disruptions in 2021, marked by critical shortages of chips and batteries, prompted a significant shift in approach. The procurement team worked fervently to secure any available chips amid the scarcity. Delivery schedules for chips and batteries fluctuated, often bunching up toward month-end, posing internal capacity challenges, notably in the painting section at the Baojun base. To optimize painting capacity and manage the end-of-month production surge, SGMW's manufacturing department made a bold decision to deviate from the GMS guideline; painted bodies were allowed to be temporarily placed on the ground, requiring an overhaul of the existing process but enabling continuous production of painted bodies. These bodies could then be stored until the bulk arrival of chips and batteries for final assembly. This strategic adjustment ensured that crucial components could swiftly bypass the painting bottleneck, meeting pressing demand from the sales department, which faced a backlog of orders awaiting fulfillment.

The ferocity of competition within the automotive sector has escalated to the point where triumphs and setbacks are measured in days, if not hours. The ability to expedite the delivery of finished vehicles to dealerships, even by a single day, can confer a significant advantage, highlighting the paramount importance of lean production principles such as "zero inventory". This approach, designed to minimize stock levels and thereby reduce capital tied up in inventory, has long been lauded for its operational efficiency. However, its viability is contingent upon stable market demand and a well-balanced supply chain, both of which have grown increasingly elusive. The meteoric rise of new energy vehicles, compounded by critical shortages of chips and batteries, has rendered the zero-inventory strategy nearly impracticable. Components, irrespective of their type—whether chips, batteries, or vehicle bodies— must now be stockpiled, awaiting the opportune moment when all elements align perfectly for production to surge in response to market demand. The GMS employed by GM embodies many such standards, which, due to their rigidity, may not always accommodate the dynamic shifts in production requirements. This scenario underscores a crucial lesson: the effectiveness of a manufacturing system lies not in its steadfast adherence to rigid, predefined protocols, but rather in its adaptability and resilience to changing circumstances.

Even in ordinary circumstances, manufacturing plants are hotbeds of innovation, where a profound understanding of processes plays a pivotal role. Consider, for example, the automotive paint production line, where achieving comprehensive coverage of vehicle bodies with electrophoretic paint (primer) is indispensable in preventing corrosion. GM employs a tumbling rotation immersion technique, which involves flipping the vehicle body 360° within an electrophoresis tank, necessitating a deep tank for the process. In contrast, SGMW's Liuzhou Baojun base employs a U-shaped pool method, which submerges the body in the electrophoresis pool in a motion that resembles a person diving and emerging from water, prompting inquiries about the adequacy of coating coverage. However, by engineering electrophoresis holes in alignment with the vehicle body's structure, part placement, and the body's electric field, effective coating of even the closed cavities on the body surface can be achieved. The strategic utilization of specialized materials also compensates for critical areas. This approach yields several advantages, including simplified painting equipment, streamlined coating processes, and enhanced production efficiency. Not only does it promise a rust-free condition for two decades, but it also significantly reduces the equipment investment required. This innovation caught the attention of process experts at GM in the United States, who were deeply impressed by its efficiency, prompting them to advocate for its adoption in other countries.

Merely replicating the equipment and blueprints from overseas factories in the construction of enterprise plants and workshops can drive investment costs to unsustainable heights. At SGMW, a culture of diligence prevails, underpinned by a management team predominantly comprising individuals with engineering backgrounds. It is this commitment to the "work clothes spirit" on the factory floor that fosters a profound understanding of machinery and processes, fostering the development of a manufacturing system that not only reflects the unique characteristics of the corporation but also secures a leading position in cost efficiency. Approaching the workshop with a mentality akin to confronting a battlefield, and diligently attending to the "three actuals"—the actual place, actual materials, and actual time (value stream)—is paramount for mastering the nuances of cost management.

Beyond refining the manufacturing system, how can one ensure the vehicle's low cost?

The inquiry into this matter has notably piqued the interest of the Japanese manufacturing sector, historically dominant in the mini-vehicle market. Japanese media, intrigued by the success of the Hongguang MINI EV and its cost-effective production, have diligently tracked and dissected this phenomenon, and they posit that SGMW's extensive expertise in developing ultra-compact vehicles has positioned it to target market segments that have previously eluded Japanese manufacturers, suggesting a shifting dynamic in the competitive arena of automotive production.

The Hongguang MINI EV revolutionizes the charging process by not solely relying on charging stations. Instead, it embraces a downward-compatible approach, allowing charging from a standard household 220-volt three-prong outlet, thereby enhancing user convenience without necessitating additional electrical infrastructure enhancements. In tandem with this, an innovative charging socket was devised, along with a compact, integrated high-efficiency charging gun designed for easy storage. SGMW advocates for a practical charging routine of driving in the daytime and charging overnight, with charging power under two kilowatts and full charge durations ranging between six and nine hours. This approach significantly simplifies the charging infrastructure requirements for users.

This user-centric design philosophy reflects a commitment to reassessing application details through the lens of real-world usage scenarios.

In prioritizing minimalist practicality, the Hongguang MINI EV's design philosophy consciously eschews elaborate systems deemed unnecessary for its intended purpose. For instance, its limited need for extended driving range negates the necessity for a regenerative braking system, commonly employed to recuperate kinetic energy during braking maneuvers. This decision also dispenses with the necessity for an inverter to convert alternating current to direct current, streamlining the vehicle's electrical system. Additionally, the motor's adoption of air cooling over water cooling further simplifies the vehicle's architecture by sidestepping the complexities associated with a circulating water-cooling system, thereby reducing reliance on numerous electronic components. Emphasizing ease of maintenance and repair, the Hongguang MINI EV uses standard, readily available components for critical parts like bearings, rather than relying on custom-made solutions. This approach extends to certain features, with the incorporation of consumer electronics, including USB ports and cameras, diverging from the conventional use of automotive-grade parts. Not only does this approach enhance accessibility for replacements and upgrades, but it also caters to individual preferences, allowing for personal customization. For those seeking enhanced functionalities, acquiring and installing higher-specification components is effortlessly achievable, enabling seamless integration of the vehicle's offerings with personal requirements.

The concept of platformization plays a pivotal role in cost reduction within the automotive industry. By employing a universal battery bracket module that accommodates the charging machine, battery, and air conditioning compressor, the Hongguang MINI EV optimizes component utilization across multiple models, such as the Baojun E100, E200, and E300, capitalizing on economies of scale.

The launch of the Wuling Hongguang MINI EV has introduced a compelling perspective: the recognition that diverse scenarios define cars. This perspective emphasizes the importance of precise product positioning and a thorough understanding of the target user demographic, involving an in-depth exploration into the specific contexts in which a vehicle is expected to operate. Through meticulous alignment of product positioning with these user scenarios, manufacturers can unlock opportunities to further refine cost structures, leveraging scenario validation and failure analysis to enhance product appeal and functionality.

Richard William Hamilton, celebrated as the "Father of Pop Art", articulated a provocative stance in the February 1960 edition of *Design*. He argued for a departure from the conventional principle of honesty in design—which champions authenticity in materials, functionality, and fulfilling basic human needs—in favor of closer alignment with market demands. He also posited that consumers should emerge from the "same drawing board" as the product, suggesting that influencing consumer demands might yield greater advantages than simply accommodating them. Echoing this sentiment, Arthur Justin Drexler, a prominent figure in automotive design, advocated for designers to receive psychoanalytic training to better understand and respond to consumer desires more effectively[1].

This realization underscores the imperative for companies to not only refine their marketing strategies but also swiftly adapt their product designs to reflect the unearthed preferences of younger consumers. The marketing team at SGMW discovered that 80% of Hongguang MINI EV users personalize their vehicles with accessories such as unique decals and seat covers, indicating a strong inclination toward customization. Notably, 60% of these owners are women, drawn to the Hongguang MINI EV for its user-friendly operation, absence of complex mechanical elements, and unparalleled convenience for parking.

In a bid to better align with the needs and tastes of female consumers, SGMW

---

[1] Bevis Hillier et al.. *The Style of the Century*[M]. trans. Lin He. Hebei Education Publishing House, 2002, 160.

identified vehicle color as a crucial element in catering to their diverse preferences. The fastest way to address this was through changing the vehicle's color palette. Therefore, SGMW took proactive measures by collaborating with Pantone to introduce a collection of macaron-inspired colors for their cars, including lemon yellow, avocado green, and peach pink, sparking a new trend in automotive aesthetics. This groundbreaking partnership marked the first of its kind between the automotive industry and the Pantone Color Institute. By March 2021, pre-orders for these macaron colors became available for the Hongguang MINI EV, reigniting public interest in car colors. While emphasis in car manufacturing had predominantly shifted toward form and performance in recent decades, SGMW's initiative represented a vibrant resurgence in the significance of color, reaffirming its pivotal role in the automotive landscape.

The resurgence of color as a decisive factor in consumer preference underscores its paramount significance within the automotive industry. Recent research highlights the remarkable speed at which the human brain processes color, with studies from MIT proposing that this recognition can occur in as quick as 0.013 seconds. This swift cognitive response aligns with the seven-second color theory in marketing, which posits that an object, such as automobiles, can establish a strong initial impression based on its color within the first seven seconds of observation.

This prompts a pertinent question: How has the automotive industry possibly overlooked the profound impact of color? Two-tone paint schemes for cars—such as red bodies with black roofs or green bodies with white roofs—have garnered widespread consumer favor. The adoption of two-tone painting, entailing the application of two or more distinct colors to a vehicle, has evolved into a sought-after aesthetic. However, transitioning to a two-tone body requires substantial modifications to the conventional painting process. Typically, two-tone painting is laborious and time-consuming, starting with the application of the primary color onto the vehicle's bare body, followed by a drying period. Next, areas not designated for the secondary color are masked off before the vehicle returns to the spray line for the secondary color's application. Each additional step of drying and painting can significantly slow down the production line, potentially halving its efficiency and emerging as a bottleneck in the manufacturing process.

Investing in brand-new paint equipment designed to accommodate both dual and single-color vehicles within a production line would incur prohibitive costs and is nearly inconceivable given practical constraints. In a bid to optimize the versatility of existing machinery, the technical department at SGMW embarked on an in-depth examination of the painting process, an endeavor culminated in the development of a revolutionary material formula that allows for rapid flash drying. This breakthrough effectively tackles the complexities associated with diverse wet-on-wet paint applications and the necessity for in-line body masking. The novel approach enables the application of a secondary color utilizing a swift flash drying technique before the initial spray process concludes. Furthermore, the process was restructured to incorporate manual auxiliary operations, making it possible to apply two colors in a single pass.

While this method may appear to deviate from the prevailing trend toward full automation—increasing the number of steps and manual labor involved—it introduced a streamlined single-pass base coat two-tone painting technique. At the Baojun base's production lines, about 70% of the models now undergo two-tone painting, translating to the production of tens of thousands of dual-color vehicles each month. This pivotal shift in the two-tone painting process not only reduces the energy consumption associated with the procedure but also substantially boosts production capacity.

Recognizing the essence of user needs is the key to crafting products that ignite widespread demand in the marketplace. The narratives of successful viral products are often underpinned by an efficient and robust manufacturing system, laying the groundwork for the rise of Chinese manufacturing onto the global stage. Bolstered by manufacturing prowess, a steadfast technical infrastructure within its factories, and a keen alignment with user preferences, Chinese manufacturing is poised for strategic competition against international automotive titans experiencing structural declines, thereby positioning itself to secure a larger slice of the global market.

In select regions, the opportunity for bold innovations and paradigm shifts is particularly conspicuous. The global automotive landscape has historically been shaped and dominated by powerhouses such as the United States, Japan, Germany, and France, each setting benchmarks and defining industry norms in their own sphere. The United States has long held a leading position in the global automotive landscape, driven by its capacity for innovation and expansive consumer market, essentially dictating the pace and trajectory of international automotive trends. Japan has solidified its status through a robust and efficient manufacturing system, while Germany has spearheaded the development of mid-to-high-end vehicles, underlined by an unyielding dedication to quality and perfection.

In the evolving landscape of electric vehicles, established global automakers, traditionally versed in internal combustion engine technology, find themselves at a significant crossroads, reevaluating their strategic trajectory toward future developments. Since China pledged its allegiance to the electric vehicle sector in 2009, significant progress has been achieved across the critical trifecta of electric components: batteries, electric drive systems, and electronic control technologies, along with strides in autonomous driving capabilities. The road ahead is fraught with uncertainties, necessitating the bold vision and resolve of trailblazers to navigate through uncharted territories. Chinese frontrunners have adeptly forged an early advantage in this expedition into the unexplored realms of electric mobility.

The shift toward new energy vehicles heralds a transformative juncture in the automotive sector, traditionally dominated by industry stalwarts from Europe, the United States, and Japan. In this new era, where standards for new energy vehicles are still in flux, Chinese energy vehicle manufacturers, notably SGMW, find themselves at a strategic vantage point. Bolstered by early achievements in electric mini-vehicle technology, they stand on the brink of reshaping and potentially establishing new global benchmarks for small electric vehicle architecture. This moment represents not merely a technological watershed but also an occasion to anchor the internationalization of these emerging standards. The leadership of the Association of Indonesia Automotive Industries (Gaikindo), traditionally dominated by veterans of Japanese automotive giants, underscores the longstanding influence of Japanese automakers. However, the recent emergence of Periklindo, spearheaded by SGMW, marks a significant departure. It heralds a direct challenge to the longstanding dominance of Japanese automakers in the Indonesian market for the first time, opening avenues for Chinese electric vehicles to gain significant international traction. With the landscape expanding, Chinese automakers possess distinct advantages in navigating the future of electric mobility, leveraging their competitive edge in cost-effectiveness and expertise in small electric vehicles. This places China at the forefront, poised to influence the norms and standards of the forthcoming generation of electric vehicles.

For Chinese manufacturing to ascend in the global value chain, it must extend its reach beyond domestic borders. Echoing the bold moves of multinational corporations that previously ventured into China, Chinese firms are now encouraged to pursue opportunities in international markets, identifying opportunities to enhance the global stature of "Made in China". With boundless horizons beckoning and global opportunities abounding, the time has come to journey into the vast, uncharted waters and imprint China's mark on the global stage.

Chapter 10 The Road Ahead 2022

10.1 Dawn of Electrification

The year 2021 marked a defining moment in the automotive industry, setting a new course for traditional car manufacturers amidst the surge of electrification and smart technology. This transformative wave has irrevocably altered the landscape of automotive manufacturing, with companies treading cautiously in the realm of autonomous driving while vigorously competing in the arena of powertrain innovations. A myriad of technological avenues—ranging from gasoline, pure electric, plug-in hybrid, to hybrid power systems—vie for dominance, each pursuing its own objectives. Hydrogen fuel cells have also begun to carve their niche, eagerly seeking their place in the market.

New entrants in the automotive arena, originating from diverse sectors and leapfrogging decades of industry evolution, now make their presence felt more assertively than ever before. Emphasizing features like large central displays, floating roofs, concealed door handles, and intelligent user interfaces, these newcomers inject fresh energy into the automotive landscape, electrifying the consumer experience in a way distinct from traditional paradigms. This "electrification" of the automotive experience, diverging significantly from historical norms, heralds a new era in consumer preferences, pointing toward a future where innovation and intelligence define the essence of vehicle design.

While initially lagging behind, in the past two years, traditional car manufacturers have experienced a remarkable resurgence, akin to ancient trees blossoming with renewed vigor. The pivotal challenge now lies in these established giants' ability to innovate swiftly and effectively to hold their ground amidst longstanding adversaries and the emergence of new contenders in this dynamic arena. This is shaping up to be an electrifying showdown of innovation.

The ascent of SGMW into the realm of new energy vehicles gained momentum in 2017, highlighted by the Wuling Hongguang MINI EV, which swiftly emerged as a beacon within its portfolio. However, this journey is far from solitary. The introduction of vehicles such as the KiWi EV, featuring a contemporary design imbued with futuristic elements, and the limited edition Wuling Nano EV, inspired by Disney's Zootopia, signifies the brand's expansion within the small electric vehicle market. Embracing a strategy centered on a collection of standout products, SGMW has crafted the global small electric vehicle architecture, now manifesting on a grand scale. This developmental approach prioritizes a minimalist physical framework, an open hardware platform, an integrated software ecosystem, and a smart cloud platform, all geared toward catalyzing a global revolution within the small electric vehicle domain.

The relentless wave of electrification continues its march forward. With the unveiling of the flexible drive-mode electric vehicle architecture, SGMW boldly articulates its strategic vision across pure electric, hybrid, and plug-in hybrid platforms. A significant milestone was achieved in November 2021 when the 25 millionth vehicle ceremoniously rolled off the assembly line, establishing SGMW as the trailblazer among Chinese national brand car manufacturers to breach the 25 million production and sales threshold. This milestone not only heralds a new era for hybrid platforms but also represents a monumental leap toward future electrification initiatives. The transition from gasoline to electric vehicles is characterized by a dynamic interplay of adoption and adaptation, necessitating traditional car manufacturers to closely monitor the evolving market landscape and embrace emerging technologies. While gasoline vehicles retain relevance in certain contexts, the trajectory toward electrification is unequivocal, encompassing all product lines toward a unified connection to power sources. This paradigm shift mandates a strategic extension of automakers' supply chains upstream. In a significant development in March 2022, SAIC Motor, a key stakeholder in SGMW, joined forces with Tsingshan Holding Group, the world's leading stainless steel producer, to establish a pioneering production base for battery cells and systems in Liuzhou. This venture not only aims to accelerate advancements in battery electrolyte fine chemicals and novel materials but also marks Liuzhou's foray into previously unexplored industrial sectors. As the manufacturing value chain evolves—transitioning from steel to chemicals, and from mechanical to electronic—the electrification process of the industry in Liuzhou gains momentum. The electrification of vehicles mirrors the broader electrification of the city itself, propelling Liuzhou toward a future imbued with technological advancement and electric mobility, reshaping its urban identity.

10.2 The 2C Revolution

Strengthening ties with upstream suppliers while recalibrating proximity to downstream users has become paramount. The fluctuating demands of consumers call for a more nuanced and adaptable approach from automakers. In 2022, SGMW wholeheartedly embraced the "2C" (To Customer) strategy, demonstrating a commitment to rapidly adjusting and responding to user needs. This strategic pivot was prompted by a period of reflection following a tepid response to the sales of connected smart vehicles in previous years.

SGMW's ethos, "Wuling builds what people need", embodies profound insight and foresight. The phrase "what people need" alludes to anticipatory needs, hinting at future rather than present demands. These needs may go unnoticed, embodying latent desires waiting to be discovered. Only those equipped with the acuity to discern subtle shifts in societal trends and the agility to act promptly can truly fulfill this aspiration, crafting solutions that not only react to but also anticipate and shape the evolving preferences of society.

As the populace's needs solidify, a marketplace buoyed by China's expansive manufacturing prowess is destined to morph into a hotbed of intense competition. It is those endowed with keen insight and the ability to forecast the future who can discern these emerging signals amidst the noise. While retrospection may render trend analysis appear straightforward, the real challenge lies in identifying these trends as they unfold. The capacity to anticipate and influence the trajectory of emerging trends is essential for tapping into unmet needs, putting entrepreneurs' strategic acumen to the test.

Translating subtle shifts in consumer psychology into tangible, appealing, and reliable automotive attributes poses a significant challenge. In this era, the conventional information network, primarily reliant on dealerships and characterized by layered communication, is woefully inadequate, as it fails to keep pace with rapidly changing tastes and trends. Thus, the 2C strategy emerges as the antidote to the complacency, oversight, and indifference that often plague traditional demand sensing methods. Looking further upstream, it is imperative for the entire supply chain to be attuned to consumer demands, ensuring alignment at every tier. Concerns about potential conflicts between 2C and 2B (To Business) are unfounded. Prioritizing and maximizing consumer interactions render the 2B model obsolete; all entities must evolve in response to the shifting demands of the end-user. Direct consumer engagement not only accelerates the pace at which companies can respond to these needs but also sets a new standard for immediacy and relevance in addressing consumer preferences.

Achieving the necessary agility to directly meet consumer demands presents a formidable challenge, necessitating a departure from the isolated information silos prevalent within organizations. It is essential for every member of a company to be attuned to the customer's voice, which means breaking away from traditional modes of thought. Despite its simplicity, the motto 2C resonates deeply, serving as a powerful call to action. It streamlines thought processes and aligns the entire organization and its supply chain toward a unified objective.

This ethos is emblematic of the culture at SGMW. Throughout its history, the company has embraced "vivid goals and simplified language" as fundamental pillars of its corporate identity. "2C!" stands as perhaps the most potent and succinct rallying cry in any global organization, encapsulating a directive in its purest form.

Direct engagement with customers, an acute understanding of socio-psychological trends, and the pursuit of distinctive market positioning form the core of SGMW's strategy, driving its relentless quest for innovation and market leadership.

10.3 Shifting from Funnel to Hourglass

The Hongguang MINI EV has boldly stepped into new territory by adopting macaroon colors as its hallmark, artfully merging the automotive realm with that of fashion and marking a pioneering movement spearheaded by Chinese manufacturing. This innovative approach is supported by comprehensive big data analytics, with intelligent products fostering deeper connection with consumers by prompting a reevaluation of user scenarios to creatively tailor product features.

In this era, the focus of products has transitioned from mere attention-grabbing to enriching experiences, underscoring the primacy of usability. The advent of Internet of Things technology has facilitated a more nuanced understanding of such scenarios. In the case of electric vehicles, this translates to the capability to monitor and predict battery data in real-time, even while the car is not in use, providing owners with advance warnings in case of potential battery discharge due to prolonged inactivity.

The year 2017 marked a significant turning point for SGMW as it ventured into offering smart customer services, uncovering a wealth of opportunities within the automotive aftermarket. The automotive industry, with its intricate service chain, demands a sophisticated network of call centers involving dealerships, rescue services, suppliers, and other third-party stakeholders, underscoring the critical importance of comprehensive offline services.

Shen Yang's vision heralds a transformative shift in the automotive industry's traditional dealership model, moving away from a funnel-shaped sales paradigm to an hourglass-shaped emphasis on service. The conventional sales approach resembles a funnel: a broad spectrum of potential customers narrows through various stages of engagement until a sale is concluded, with a diminishing number of prospects at each stage. However, once a vehicle is sold, the connection between the manufacturer and the car owner often diminishes significantly. Looking ahead, the focus is set to transition to an hourglass model, where the point of sale merely serves as the midpoint—the narrowest section of the hourglass—beyond which the expansive realm of after-sales service unfolds, marking the beginning of a more substantial journey. After the sale, the emphasis shifts toward accommodating the user's specific and evolving needs, offering swift responses to feedback, which, in turn, fosters enhanced engagement with the product, or "usage stickiness". This approach not only cultivates deeper loyalty but also reveals opportunities for generating additional revenue streams, transcending traditional notions of brand value.

The advent of manufacturer direct stores exemplifies this innovative hourglass strategy. Vehicles, particularly those priced under RMB 50,000, are now presented and marketed across a diverse spectrum of venues, including direct stores, exclusive brand outlets, large retail spaces, and even online platforms.

The inauguration of the Wuling experience center, LingHouse, situated along the bustling Nanjing Road in Shanghai, signifies SGMW's decisive pivot toward amalgamating lifestyle elements within experiential spaces. By integrating amenities such as milk tea, confectionery, floral, and coffee shops, LingHouse has transformed into a hub of daily recreation and interaction with trending merchandise, revolutionizing the paradigm of automotive retail spaces through the art of scenario-based marketing strategies. This pioneering approach illustrates that automotive retail need not be confined solely to the conventional parameters of 4S stores, but can flourish in spaces where consumers naturally gather. Despite potentially occupying a smaller physical footprint compared to traditional 4S stores, a manufacturer's direct outlet like LingHouse has the potential to generate sales volumes comparable to that of 10 conventional 4S stores, owing to an enhanced service experience that inherently encourages purchasing behavior. With a daily coffee consumption exceeding 1,000 cups, the experience center champions a lifestyle philosophy that deeply resonates with consumers.

Driven by a vision to extend its influence, SGMW is committed to developing more hourglass-shaped economic models beyond the flagship LingHouse experience centers. The company is actively pursuing the establishment of LingLab service stores, which will provide a spectrum of supplementary services, including beauty enhancements, vehicle modifications, and car wash facilities, among others. Designed with an accessible and proficient maintenance team, these spaces are designed to appeal to young car owners, fostering a welcoming and engaging ambiance that goes beyond conventional automotive service paradigms.

Against the backdrop of the burgeoning significance of new energy vehicles in urban logistics, SGMW's collaboration with the urban freight platform Lalamove serves as a prime exemplar of the hourglass economy. By acquiring a Wuling Hongguang brand vehicle and becoming members of the Driver's Home program, traditional Wuling 4S shops are reimagined as support centers, offering amenities such as battery swapping stations and rest areas for drivers, while Lalamove channels orders through its network.

This innovative partnership may evolve to encompass mobile mobility services, underscoring the hourglass economy's capacity to interlace vehicle sales with a broader tapestry of societal services.

The journey of discovery continues unabated. The dynamic between manufacturers' direct-operated experience centers and traditional dealerships remains an open question, yet both are united in their pursuit of delivering the ultimate user experience. The evolving landscape of manufacturer-initiated experience stores and the transformation of 4S shops signify one of the most eagerly anticipated developments in the automotive industry over the next decade. Within the crucible of this ongoing debate, the quest for the optimal solution unfolds.

The automotive industry, much like a century-old tree poised for rejuvenation, is on the brink of a new era of growth.

10.4 Nostalgia's Sweet Return

Time possesses a peculiar knack for diminishing our fascination with the past, often redirecting our focus toward the future's horizon. Yet, the weight of yesteryear does not press upon us any more heavily than the fading light of yesterday's sunset. As history relentlessly progresses, moments for introspection become increasingly scarce, leaving vast expanses of our collective memory barely skimmed, akin to pages in a book flipped too hastily. This hurried traversal through time obscures the myriad manifestations of courage and vulnerability, industriousness and idleness, might and fragility that have woven the tapestry of our shared human narrative. Paradoxically, however, the very insights we fervently seek about tomorrow often lie shrouded within the minutiae of yesterday, encrypted in the annals of bygone eras.

Established amidst a surge of ambition in 1958, the Liuzhou Power Machinery Factory ignited the first flame of industrial aspiration in Liuzhou. This embryonic venture reflects a broader, somewhat meandering, struggle for survival through the process of industrialization, mirroring the trajectory of many provinces and cities across China. While numerous initiatives have dissipated into the annals of history, like petals carried away by the wind, a handful of enterprises have weathered the relentless passage of time, destined to endure. This fortunate survivor, amidst the watershed of state-owned enterprise reform in 1999, rekindled the fires of ambition and adaptability within the local populace. Teetering on the brink of crisis, it reimagined its essence, and by 2002, as the dust settled from China's joint venture skirmishes within the automotive sector, it firmly staked its claim at the dawn of its modern corporate resurgence. China's accession to the WTO marked a pivotal moment, propelling Chinese manufacturing along divergent paths and urging each enterprise to carve out its unique route onto the global stage.

SGMW's strategy of keeping the original brand and independent R&D capability has emerged as a defining force since it reclaimed its dominance in the mini-vehicle market share in 2006. Amidst fierce competition within joint ventures, the company maintained a commitment to the ethos of in-house development. This triumph was not merely due to inherent design superiority but rather a result of astute judgment, unwavering dedication, and tangible outcomes in a seemingly uneven playing field. It was through sheer determination and resilience that the company managed to overturn its fortunes and secure a remarkable victory. By 2009, the Liuzhou-based enterprise had achieved a significant milestone—surpassing the production and sales of a million vehicles, vastly outdoing its initial joint venture goal of 300,000 vehicles by 2010. Decades of automotive ambitions and the dedication of multiple generations converged in Liuzhou's own fleet of a million vehicles. The same year also witnessed China's ascendancy to the summit of global automotive production and sales for the first time, a testament to the ascent of Chinese manufacturing prowess. This landmark achievement served as both a reward for the fortunate and a testament to the diligent.

In 2010, SGMW boldly ventured into the highly coveted and fiercely competitive passenger car sector, achieving what many in the automotive industry dreamt of. There is a popular saying within automotive circles: "One isn't considered a true hero until they've climbed the Great Wall, nor a genuine car enthusiast until they've crafted a sedan." While many people harbor expansive dreams in their youth, their aspirations often get tucked away with age, blending into the routine of everyday life like a mundane shopping list. Yet, for entrepreneurs, these dreams crystallize, becoming more focused, pure, and enduring. Eventually, at the opportune moment, they decide to share these dreams with the world.

Good fortune often favors those whose path is paved. In 2015, SGMW achieved the remarkable milestone of selling two million units and, in 2016, surpassed RMB 100 billion in sales, garnering widespread acclaim for its heroic spirit. Venturing into connected vehicles in 2018 marked a cautious return to the starting line for SGMW. Amidst the daunting challenges posed by the COVID-19 pandemic in 2020, the electric vehicle sector experienced a surge in growth. It was during this period, too, that SGMW's Hongguang MINI EV made significant inroads into the burgeoning young consumer market, marking the commencement of its foray into a new domain.

As 2021 unfolded, the automotive industry grappled with a severe semiconductor shortage, disrupting the supply chain and impeding factories from maintaining previous production levels. The availability of semiconductors became tantamount for securing sales, significantly straining domestic brands as the available supply of chips inadvertently favored international automotive powerhouses. Nevertheless, electric vehicles stood on the brink of a striking boom. By spring 2022, as the chip crisis persisted, SGMW adopted an innovative approach dubbed "long-arm innovation", collaborating closely with upstream suppliers to address the challenge of semiconductor localization.

The supply chain disruption persisted, characterized by intermittent shortages of controllers and chips, accompanied by a surge in the cost of power battery materials, suggesting a rising tide that lifted all boats.

The automotive sector is currently navigating through a sea of transformative disruptions. Historically, the fiercest battles for dominance within this realm were waged between American and Japanese car manufacturers, with Japanese vehicles ultimately securing a stronghold in the American market. The emergence of Korean automobiles added yet another dimension to this ongoing rivalry. For the past four decades, the global automotive landscape has remained largely stable and homogenous. However, the advent of electrification and intelligent technologies is fundamentally reshaping this terrain, dismantling the longstanding "iron plate" and paving the way for new contenders within the automotive brand hierarchy. Pioneers like American-based Tesla and Chinese marques such as Nio, Xpeng, and Li Auto are spearheading this transformative shift in this evolving scenario. Both established incumbents and emerging brands alike are now vying for a future foothold, including SGMW, ardently working to carve out its place on the global stage. In a significant stride toward this goal, SGMW is determined to showcase its international presence by providing 300 Wuling Air EVs as the official vehicles for the G20 summit that took place in Indonesia in November 2022, serving as transportation for delegates from across the globe and showcasing the prominence of Chinese electric vehicles on the world stage.

From tractors and mini-cars to MPVs, sedans, and SUVs, spanning the evolution from the Wuling brand to the Baojun brand and culminating in the Wuling global silver logo, SGMW has perennially adapted, flourishing through successive eras. As the guard changes, with veteran team members passing the baton to new faces, the company's momentum remains unabated. The brand's storied 35-year ascent as a domestic marque and its 20-year transformation as a joint venture encapsulate a profound odyssey through the ebbs and flows of consumer psychology. Staying ahead of the curve, anticipating shifts, and outpacing transitions are imperative for securing a leading position. The endurance of SGMW hinges not only on the legacy of Wuling's iconic vehicles—for even celestial bodies show signs of aging—but also on the enduring "Wuling mindset", a keen acumen for demographic and societal trends.

Deciphering the enigma of the era poses a formidable task. Only entrepreneurs adept at decoding societal dynamics stand as true navigators of the times, capable of taking preemptive actions that align with prevailing trends and secure strategic advantages. For SGMW, this challenge is especially significant. Situated in the central and northern regions of Guangxi, the region lacks inherent advantages in automotive manufacturing, whether in terms of natural resources, supply chains, or human capital, making it a territory of relative scarcity. This backdrop has instilled the core spirit of "Perseverance with Self-Strengthening" within SGMW. Thriving amidst a perpetual state of challenges necessitates that the company ensure its strategic initiatives are bullseyes. Should an initial effort fall short, swift and precise adjustments become imperative, akin to a bowler securing a strike on the second attempt. During a visit to Chongqing Chang'an in 2010, once a competitor in the mini-vehicle market, General Manager Shen Yang was surprised to learn that they boasted approximately 3,000 individuals in their R&D team, starkly contrasting with SGMW's team of about 1,000, prompting Shen Yang to realize that SGMW needed to channel its focus intensely, dedicating itself to the development of one product at a time. However, mere focus was not sufficient; excellence in execution was imperative. Each project undertaken had to not just succeed but surpass expectations, as achieving a comprehensive triumph with every endeavor could effectively counterbalance any resource deficiencies.

In this dynamic interplay, an enterprise and a city forge a symbiotic relationship. For many, a city represents a collective of living and working environments, emerging as the most significant human-crafted edifice in sight. It transcends generations, enduring upheavals through its inherent capacity for self-renewal. On the flip side, a business, serving as a vibrant hub of value generation, draws vitality from and enriches the city, contributing to its development narrative. The evolution of the automotive industry has bestowed a new layer of relevance upon Liuzhou, traditionally celebrated as a crossroads but now redefined by the concept of mobility. This adds to the city's enduring vibrancy, an homage from the ceaselessly meandering U-shaped Liujiang River to its inhabitants. For the greater part of the year, the air is as crisp as cream freshly spread on a cake, with boulevards adorned by clusters of pink Bauhinia blossoms and verdant bayan trees. The river, a streak of emerald silk, and the mountains, akin to jade hairpins, craft a poetic scenery of unique allure and sweetness, enchanting all who visit. However, such picturesque charm comes with its price, borne from the perseverance of those committed to their endeavor. For those who cross the Liujiang River twice or even fourfold daily, a fleeting moment of contemplation by its banks might lead to the epiphany that along these age-old, luminous waters, SGMW has chronicled a comprehensive saga of automobile manufacturing, simultaneously narrating the city's tale of evolution.

This tale is a testament to the enduring mantra, "Perseverance with Self-Strengthening". It is within this unyielding voyage of perseverance that the company navigates through the vast expanse of time, ensuring the everlasting flame of its legacy.